Artificial Intelligence in Cyberspace Security

Artificial Intelligence in Cyberspace Security

Guest Editors

Yuanzhang Li
Yu-an Tan
Chen Liang
Hongfei Zhu

MDPI

Basel • Beijing • Wuhan • Barcelona • Belgrade • Novi Sad • Cluj • Manchester

Guest Editors
Yuanzhang Li
School of Computer Science and Technology
Beijing Institute of Technology
Beijing
China

Yu-an Tan
School of Cyberspace Science and Technology
Beijing Institute of Technology
Beijing
China

Chen Liang
School of Information Management
Beijing Information Science and Technology University
Beijing
China

Hongfei Zhu
School of Computer Science and Technology
Chongqing University of Posts and Telecommunications
Chongqing
China

Editorial Office
MDPI AG
Grosspeteranlage 5
4052 Basel, Switzerland

This is a reprint of the Special Issue, published open access by the journal *Electronics* (ISSN 2079-9292), freely accessible at: https://www.mdpi.com/journal/electronics/special_issues/O29X2K53F4.

For citation purposes, cite each article independently as indicated on the article page online and as indicated below:

Lastname, A.A.; Lastname, B.B. Article Title. *Journal Name* **Year**, *Volume Number*, Page Range.

ISBN 978-3-7258-7943-4 (Hbk)
ISBN 978-3-7258-7944-1 (PDF)
https://doi.org/10.3390/books978-3-7258-7944-1

Contents

About the Editors

Yuanzhang Li

Yuanzhang Li received his BS degree, MS degree, and PhD degree in Computer Science and Technology in 2001, 2004, and 2015 from the Beijing Institute of Technology, respectively. He is a senior member of the China Computer Federation and has contributed to over 60 peer-reviewed journal and conference papers. He is currently an associate professor at the Beijing Institute of Technology, and his main research interests focus on AI security and information security.

Yu-an Tan

Yu-an Tan received his BEng degree in Computer Software in 1991 and his PhD in Computer Science in 2003. He has over 30 years of teaching and research experience and has been a professor at the Beijing Institute of Technology since 2010. He is a senior member of the China Computer Federation and has contributed to over 100 peer-reviewed journal and conference papers, including five papers in the top 1% of Essential Science Indicators. He has received over 20 research funds from the National Natural Science Foundation of China, the National Key Research and Development Program of China, and other sources. His research areas include artificial intelligence security, cybersecurity, and storage sub-systems.

Chen Liang

Chen Liang received his BS degree and PhD degree in Electrical Engineering, Computer Science, and Technology in 2014 and 2020 from the Beijing Institute of Technology, respectively. He has contributed to over 40 peer-reviewed journal and conference papers. Currently, he is an associate professor at the Beijing Information Science & Technology University, and his main research interests focus on ML security and data security.

Hongfei Zhu

Hongfei Zhu received his BS degree and PhD degree in Computer Science and Technology in 2009 and 2018, respectively. He has contributed to over 16 peer-reviewed journal and conference papers and is currently an assistant professor at the Chongqing University of Posts and Telecommunications. His main research interests focus on areas such as security and privacy, IoV, and intelligent security.

Preface

This Reprint presents a curated collection of research articles originally published in the Special Issue "Artificial Intelligence in Cyberspace Security". It focuses on advancing network intrusion detection through innovative algorithms and frameworks, including LLM-based secure storage, machine learning for Android malware detection, adversarial sample generation, and optimized feature selection with improved simulated annealing.

The scope of this Reprint encompasses cutting-edge approaches such as TPE-FL-LightGBM for fast intrusion detection, adversarial training for model robustness, and hybrid cloud data partitioning. The primary aim of this Reprint is to highlight how algorithmic innovations—ranging from cost-sensitive learning to ensemble and voting mechanisms—can address persistent challenges like data imbalance, feature redundancy, and computational efficiency in real-world security applications.

The motivation for compiling this Reprint arises from the growing complexity of cyber threats and the need for adaptive, high-performance detection systems. By bringing together diverse methodological advances within a unified framework, this Reprint offers readers a comprehensive perspective on current trends, challenges, and future directions in AI-driven cybersecurity.

This Reprint is intended for researchers, practitioners, and graduate students in network security, machine learning, and artificial intelligence, as well as professionals seeking deployable solutions for intrusion detection and threat mitigation. It serves both as a reference to recent developments and as a foundation for future innovation in the field.

Yuanzhang Li, Yu-an Tan, Chen Liang, and Hongfei Zhu
Guest Editors

electronics

MDPI

Editorial

Artificial Intelligence in Cyberspace Security

Hongfei Zhu [1], Yu-An Tan [2], Yuanzhang Li [3] and Chen Liang [4,*]

1 School of Computer Science and Technology (National Exemplary Software School), Chongqing University of Posts and Telecommunications, Chongqing 400065, China; zhuhf@cqupt.edu.cn
2 School of Cyberspace Science and Technology, Beijing Institute of Technology, Beijing 100081, China; tan2008@bit.edu.cn
3 School of Computer Science and Technology, Beijing Institute of Technology, Beijing 100081, China; popular@bit.edu.cn
4 College of Computer Science, Beijing Information Science and Technology University, Beijing 102206, China
* Correspondence: 20202441@bistu.edu.cn

1. Introduction

The rapid development of artificial intelligence (AI) has revolutionized numerous scientific and technological fields, including unmanned systems, pattern recognition, natural language processing, and expert systems. However, AI also poses critical security challenges to cyberspace security. With the explosion of data volume and the evolution of cyber threats, conventional security measures struggle to counter sophisticated attacks, necessitating innovative solutions. This Special Issue, titled "Artificial Intelligence in Cyberspace Security", aims to address these challenges by exploring cutting-edge research at the intersection of AI and cybersecurity. We invite scholars and experts in this field to submit original research contributions. By fostering interdisciplinary collaboration, this Special Issue seeks to advance trusted and scalable AI solutions for securing cyberspace.

2. The Present Issue

This Special Issue focuses on "Artificial Intelligence in Cyberspace Security", systematically exploring key topics such as AI-driven network security, AI-driven privacy protection, adversarial machine learning, cyberspace security, malware detection, secure communication, secure data sharing, security protocol, software security, vulnerability, etc. Through algorithmic innovation, system optimization, and interdisciplinary integration, 11 papers were selected through rigorous peer review. These papers demonstrate the multidimensional value of AI technologies in security protection systems, offering critical references for addressing emerging cyber threats. The research encompasses cutting-edge approaches, including hybrid cloud secure partitioned storage based on large models, high-precision malware classification, adversarial sample generation, intrusion detection framework optimization, IoT security authentication, chaotic communication education, edge-cloud data sharing, cross-project defect prediction, and firmware reverse engineering, highlighting the multifaceted applications of AI in security frameworks. This Special Issue aims to establish a platform for in-depth academic exchange among researchers, industry experts, and developers, promoting the synergistic evolution of AI and cybersecurity. The key findings of this Special Issue are summarized as follows:

Ran Zhou et al. propose the LLM-SPSS framework (Contribution 1), which integrates fine-tuned XLM-R base models, multi-dimensional data sharding, and MapReduce distributed processing technology. By employing adaptive prompt tuning to enhance context-aware classification capabilities, the framework achieves efficient large-scale dataset processing through MapReduce. It further constructs secure fine-grained storage isolation

 https://doi.org/10.3390/electronics15020365

in hybrid cloud environments via multidimensional cloud partition. This framework effectively balances high accuracy with computational efficiency, offering a reliable solution for hybrid cloud security and scalable storage.

Areej Alhogail et al. introduce a two-step machine learning framework combining feature engineering and efficient classifiers for Android malware detection and classification (Contribution 2). Initially, binary classification identifies malicious software, followed by dimensionality reduction using the Chi-squared test and model-based feature selection (Select-from-Model, SFM). Experiments demonstrate that the Random Forest (RF) model excels in detection accuracy and classification accuracy. By prioritizing relevant features, the framework achieves a balance between computational efficiency and high detection rates, providing a resource-efficient and scalable solution for practical deployment.

Jiankang Sun et al. propose a novel adversarial sample generation method based on model simulation (Contribution 3), enabling rapid adversarial sample creation and enhancing model robustness through adversarial training. Experimental results on the CICIDS-2017 dataset show that this method outperforms existing solutions, highlighting its potential to strengthen Intrusion Detection Systems' ability to address dynamic threats.

Yafei Luo et al. address the cybersecurity challenges driven by the rapid growth of the Internet, where traditional Intrusion Detection Systems (IDSs) face issues such as data imbalance, feature redundancy, and high computational complexity (Contribution 4). They propose a novel method integrating an Improved Binary Simulated Annealing algorithm (IBSA) with TPE-FL-LightGBM: Focal Loss mitigates class imbalance in LightGBM; IBSA optimizes feature selection through adaptive temperature adjustment, multi-neighborhood strategies, and S-shaped transfer functions; and TPE is employed to optimize the FL-LightGBM architecture. Experimental evaluations on the NSL-KDD and UNSWNB15 datasets, validated through visualization analysis, ablation studies, and comparative testing, demonstrate its effectiveness.

Junyi Mao et al. introduce a novel Intrusion Detection System (MFEI-IDS) combining Fully Convolutional Networks (FCNs) and Transformers (FCN-Transformer) (Contribution 5). FCN-Transformer captures local spatial patterns and global temporal dependencies in raw traffic, reducing reliance on manual feature engineering, while the inductive learning module enhances generalization for unknown attacks through dynamic routing. Evaluation on the ISCX 2012 and CIC-IDS 2017 datasets demonstrates that MFEI-IDS outperforms existing methods in accuracy, precision, and F1 scores, showcasing robust performance in small-sample scenarios, unknown attack detection, and cross-dataset validation.

Xiaoying Qiu et al. target the limitations of traditional Physical Layer Authentication (PLA), which relies on fixed thresholds and binary classification strategies, leading to poor reliability and insufficient access control in dynamic environments (Contribution 6). They propose a method integrating hierarchical security authentication with an attention-enhanced convolutional network (AECN), eliminating threshold dependence through attention mechanisms and confidence branches. This approach improves authentication accuracy and enables multi-level access control. Simulation results confirm its superiority over existing PLA schemes, validating effectiveness in dynamic heterogeneous wireless networks.

Sicheng Han et al. propose a deep learning-based method for VM-protected malware classification (Contribution 7), employing a deep convolutional neural network (CNN) with an enhanced spatial attention mechanism. To address the scarcity of ambiguous malware samples in real-world scenarios, they generate a dataset using VMProtect to ensure training on modern real-world threats. The spatial attention mechanism improves feature extraction efficiency by focusing on critical regions of obfuscated code, while deep convolutional

https://doi.org/10.3390/electronics15020365

operations reduce computational overhead. This work highlights the potential of attention-enhanced CNNs in addressing advanced malware obfuscation techniques.

Xuefang Zhou et al. introduce a chaos-based optical communication security teaching framework integrating Optisystem and Matlab (Contribution 8). They explain the Lang-Kobayashi (L-K) laser equations for generating electro-optical feedback chaos, analyze phase-intensity (P-I) feedback chaos via Matlab, and construct a chaos optical communication system in Optisystem. By optimizing parameters to simulate system performance, they emphasize abstract concepts such as chaos generation principles, system architecture, and performance metrics. Post-lesson exercises and questionnaires confirm the effectiveness of this approach in enhancing students' understanding of laser chaos communication and research capabilities.

Ye Li et al. propose a secure data sharing framework for edge-cloud collaborative scenarios (Contribution 9), targeting vulnerabilities in attribute-based keyword search (ABKS) protocols against keyword guessing attacks (KGAs). By combining attribute-based encryption (ABE) with group key agreement (GKA), the edge layer generates two encrypted session keys to re-encrypt keyword indices and traps, preventing cloud server exploitation. The framework, implemented using the JPBC library, demonstrates resistance to KGAs under the random oracle model while achieving fine-grained access control. Performance evaluations indicate its lightweight design, low storage consumption, and high computational efficiency, making it suitable for resource-constrained edge environments.

Tianwei Lei et al. introduce a cross-project software defect prediction framework (Contribution 10), SDP-MTF, to address challenges in feature information mining and cross-project feature discrepancies. By integrating code statistical features, deep semantic features, and multi-stage transfer learning, SDP-MTF improves prediction accuracy. Evaluations on six PROMISE projects demonstrate its superior performance in handling limited historical data and transfer learning gaps.

Siyi Chen et al. propose a protocol-centered static analysis method to reveal UEFI password policies via the HII (Human Interface Infrastructure) protocol (Contribution 11), addressing limitations of existing tools in firmware stripping. Through reverse engineering of the IFR (Internal Forms Representation), they identify sensitive data storage and explore hardware port configurations, using Secure Boot as a case study. This work represents the first systematic reverse analysis of UEFI via the HII protocol, uncovering firmware structure insights and enhancing security through improved policy detection and configuration understanding.

3. Future Directions

The future application of artificial intelligence in cyberspace security is expected to follow several key directions, as outlined in the research articles featured in this Special Issue. These directions are as follows:

- Multi-Level Feature Optimization for Intrusion Detection Systems: AI enhances real-time performance and accuracy through hierarchical feature extraction and network structure refinement. This direction can integrate adversarial sample generation to improve adaptability to emerging threats.
- Secure Data Sharing for Edge-Cloud Collaboration: Lightweight AI-driven models enable secure data collaboration in edge-cloud environments, meeting privacy and efficient transmission requirements. Future work could focus on dynamic trust assessment mechanisms to enhance cross-domain adaptability.
- Transferability Enhancement in Software Defect Prediction: AI models address defect prediction challenges in low-sample scenarios through cross-project feature transfer.

https://doi.org/10.3390/electronics15020365

Combining interpretability techniques can further refine developers' repair strategies and code quality.

- Automated Analysis and Detection for Firmware Security: AI-assisted tools enable automated firmware vulnerability detection and reverse engineering, reducing manual effort. Future exploration of behavioral pattern learning could improve identification of stealthy attacks like Rootkits.
- Lightweight Algorithm Optimization for Network Intrusion Detection: AI improves the efficiency and response speed of network intrusion detection by refining algorithms such as binary simulated annealing. Future research may explore real-time deployment on edge devices for resource-constrained environments.
- Deep Learning Applications in Cybersecurity Classification: AI leverages convolutional neural networks and attention mechanisms to enhance classification accuracy for obfuscated data. This direction can expand to multimodal data fusion, improving recognition of complex attacks.
- Lightweight Encryption and Secure Communication Mechanisms: AI optimizes encryption algorithm efficiency to support secure, high-performance communication in IoT scenarios. Future strategies may integrate dynamic resource allocation to further reduce edge device energy consumption.
- Transfer Learning Applications in Cross-Domain Security Models: AI addresses data distribution disparities in cross-project defect prediction and intrusion detection through transfer learning and feature fusion. Future work could explore multi-task joint training to enhance model generalization.

Author Contributions: Conceptualization and formal analysis, H.Z.; literature excerpts and arrangement, Y.-A.T.; writing-review and editing, Y.L.; supervision, C.L. All authors have read and agreed to the published version of the manuscript.

Funding: This work was partially supported by the Science and Technology Research Program of Chongqing Municipal Education Commission (No. KJQN202300617), and the research funding of Key Laboratory of Big Data Intelligent Computing (Grant No.BDIC-2023-B-006).

Data Availability Statement: Not applicable.

Acknowledgments: We would like to thank all the researchers who submitted their papers to this Special Issue for participating in the academic solicitation activities of the Special Issue. We congratulate the authors of the selected papers published in the Special Issue and thank them for presenting and sharing their excellent results through the platform. Our appreciation goes to the reviewers as well, who carefully, responsibly, and fairly selected excellent papers for this Special Issue with their professional knowledge and provided valuable review comments for the authors. We recognize the Editorial Board of *Electronics* for granting us the opportunity to guest edit this Special Issue. Lastly, we are grateful to the *Electronics* Editorial Office staff for their strict supervision and responsible management to ensure the timely publication of this Special Issue.

Conflicts of Interest: The authors declare no conflicts of interest.

List of Contributions

1. Zhou, R.; Che, B.; Yang, L. LLM-SPSS: An efficient llm-based secure partitioned storage scheme in distributed hybrid clouds. *Electronics* **2026**, *151*, 30.
2. Alhogail, A.; Alharbi, R.A. Effective ml-based android malware detection and categorization. *Electronics* **2025**, *14*, 1486.
3. Sun, J.; Yang, S. Adversarial sample generation based on model simulation analysis in intrusion detection systems. *Electronics* **2025**, *14*, 870.

4. Luo, Y.; Chen, R.; Li, C.; Yang, D.; Tang, K.; Su, J. An improved binary simulated annealing algorithm and tpe-fl-lightgbm for fast network intrusion detection. *Electronics* **2025**, *14*, 231.
5. Mao, J.; Yang, X.; Hu, B.; Lu, Y.; Yin, G. Intrusion detection system based on multi-level feature extraction and inductive network. *Electronics* **2025**, *14*, 189.
6. Qiu, X.; Zhao, G.; Yu, J.; Jiang, W.; Guo, Z.; Xu, M. Hierarchical security authentication with attention-enhanced convolutional network for internet of things. *Electronics* **2024**, *13*, 4699.
7. Han, S.; Yun, H.; Park, Y. Deep learning for cybersecurity classification: Utilizing depth-wise cnn and attention mechanism on vm-obfuscated data. *Electronics* **2024**, *13*, 3393.
8. Zhou, X.; Li, M.; Bi, M.; Yang, G.; Hu, M. Research on the teaching of laser chaotic communication based on optisystem and matlab software. *Electronics* **2024**, *13*, 3274.
9. Li, Y.; Xiong, M.; Yuan, J.; Zhang, Q.; Zhu, H. A secure data-sharing model resisting keyword guessing attacks in edge-cloud collaboration scenarios. *Electronics* **2024**, *13*, 3236.
10. Lei, T.; Xue, J.; Man, D.; Wang, Y.; Li, M.; Kong, Z. Sdp-mtf: A composite transfer learning and feature fusion for cross-project software defect prediction. *Electronics* **2024**, *13*, 2439.
11. Chen, S.; Tan, Y.-A.; Qiu, K.; Zhang, Z.; Li, Y.; Zhang, Q. Delving deep into reverse engineering of uefi firmwares via human interface infrastructure. *Electronics* **2023**, *12*, 4601.

https://doi.org/10.3390/electronics15020365

electronics

MDPI

Article

LLM-SPSS: An Efficient LLM-Based Secure Partitioned Storage Scheme in Distributed Hybrid Clouds

Ran Zhou, Bichen Che and Liangbin Yang *

School of Cyber Science and Engineering, University of International Relations, Beijing 100091, China; zhouran@uir.edu.cn (R.Z.); chebichen@uir.edu.cn (B.C.)
* Correspondence: ylb@uir.edu.cn

Abstract

With the growing adoption of hybrid cloud storage, the identification and protection of sensitive information within large-scale unstructured data has become increasingly challenging. Traditional rule-based and machine learning approaches have limitations in context-aware sensitive data classification and large-scale processing. In this work, a novel framework named LLM-SPSS, implementing a secure and confidential storage layout for distributed hybrid clouds through a fine-tuned XLM-R Base model and multi-dimensional data partitioning, is proposed. First, a fine-tuned XLM-R Base model with adaptive prompt tuning is employed to enable context-aware sensitive data classification and improve detection accuracy. In addition, MapReduce-based distributed processing allows the framework to scale efficiently to large datasets, thus enhancing computational efficiency. Furthermore, a multi-dimensional cloud partitioning scheme provides secure and fine-grained storage isolation within hybrid cloud environments. Experimental results demonstrate that LLM-SPSS achieves an F1-score of 99.66% and yields a 6.3× speed-up over the non-distributed baseline, outperforming traditional rule-based (F1 68.27%), conventional machine learning (SVM F1 98.32%, Random Forest F1 95.79%), and other LLM-based approaches (DePrompt F1 95.95%) and effectively balancing high accuracy with computational efficiency.

Keywords: hybrid cloud storage; large language model; MapReduce; sensitive data detection; context-aware classification; secure partitioned storage

1. Introduction

With the rapid expansion of cloud computing and storage, enterprises and personal data volumes continue to grow at an exponential rate [1]. To improve management efficiency and security, many organizations adopt hybrid cloud strategies that combine public and private clouds [2], assigning sensitive data to private clouds and non-sensitive data to public clouds. This approach ensures data security while leveraging the scalability and cost efficiency of public clouds. However, accurately and efficiently identifying sensitive data remains a significant challenge in hybrid cloud storage systems [3].

Traditional sensitive data detection relies heavily on regular expressions or rule-based matching, which perform well on structured data but struggle with semi-structured or unstructured text. For example, Bhatia et al. achieved high accuracy on database fields but reported a 15% false-positive rate on semi-structured and unstructured data [4], while OpenRaven showed limited coverage in unstructured documents despite good performance on fixed-format fields [5]. Mainetti et al. further emphasized that rule-based schemes lack semantic modeling capabilities [6].

Recent research has turned to machine learning techniques such as SVM, Random Forests, and deep learning to improve classification flexibility [7,8]. Mishra et al. proposed a hybrid rule-ML framework which reported an F1-score of approximately 91% for financial PII detection, despite limited contextual understanding [9]. Separately, Rama et al. [10] integrated SVM and Random Forest classifiers with a suite of cryptographic techniques, achieving a 5–10% encryption speed-up for cloud storage. Recent work by Addula et al. further advanced this direction by proposing an Autoencoder-GRU hybrid model optimized with the Honey Badger Algorithm for cyber-threat detection in IoT networks [11]. While such hybrid models enhance feature extraction for structured or temporal data, their reliance on fixed-length inputs and handcrafted feature hierarchies limits their effectiveness for large-scale, heterogeneous unstructured text classification—the core challenge addressed in this work. Despite these advances, computational bottlenecks persist in large-scale cloud environments. Li et al. achieved approximately 22% higher efficiency with parallel optimization [12], yet fundamental scalability barriers for ultra-large unstructured data remain. While hybrid deep learning models like CNN-LSTM/GRU are effective for structured anomaly detection, they often require fixed-length inputs and struggle with the variable-length, semantically rich nature of general unstructured text, limiting their direct applicability for context-aware sensitive data classification at scale. Crucially, many of these methods lack the deep contextual understanding required to accurately interpret nuanced semantics in unstructured text, a capability where large language models (LLMs) excel.

Large language models (LLMs) have demonstrated exceptional capabilities in understanding and classifying unstructured text, surpassing traditional schemes by capturing nuanced semantics and context to improve labeling accuracy [13,14]. Specific implementations, such as Sun et al.'s DePrompt for PII recognition (95.95% accuracy) [9] and Boehnke et al.'s news classification (97% accuracy) [15], highlighted this potential. However, these approaches often deploy LLMs directly, neglecting the inference efficiency required for high-frequency, large-scale processing [16]—a bottleneck Zhou et al. attribute to model size, attention complexity, and decoding overhead [17]. The MapReduce framework offers a proven solution for such distributed processing challenges [18].

On the storage front, research has focused on optimizing hybrid clouds via data partitioning. Representative works include Levitin et al., who separated sensitive data across distinct virtual machines [19], and Tang et al., who implemented a multi-layer model with dual-stage partitioning and load balancing [20]. While these strategies enhance resource utilization and storage throughput, they generally lack integrated capabilities for automated sensitive data labeling and parallel text processing, which limits their applicability for modern workloads dominated by unstructured data.

To address these challenges, a novel framework, termed an Efficient LLM-Based Secure Partitioned Storage Scheme in Distributed Hybrid Clouds (LLM-SPSS), is proposed. It ensures high labeling accuracy and enhances processing efficiency and storage security through the synergistic combination of its constituent fine-tuned model (XLM-R) and MapReduce parallel processing, alongside a three-dimensional partitioning scheme.

The main contributions of this work include the following:

(1) A Sensitive Data Annotation Scheme based on XLM-R: Fine-tuned LLMs comprehend semantic and contextual information, excelling in unstructured data sensitivity recognition. Parameter-efficient and prompt-guided fine-tuning enhances context-aware sensitive data classification, yielding an F1-score increase from 94.57% to 99.66% for binary sensitive classification. This outperforms traditional regular expression schemes (F1 68.27%), conventional machine learning models (SVM F1 98.32%, Random Forest F1 95.79%), and other LLM-based approaches like DePrompt (F1 95.95%).

https://doi.org/10.3390/electronics15010030

(2) A Distributed Data Partitioning Scheme based on MapReduce: Data is partitioned based on text length, type, and node load to achieve a three-dimensional balance. Integration with distributed computation frameworks enables efficient large-scale processing. Experimental results show that average processing time per partition reduced by 18.3%, and MapReduce-based parallel inference compresses runtime from approximately 510 s to 81 s, achieving 6.3× acceleration.

(3) A Hybrid Cloud Partitioning Management Method based on Sensitivity Levels: Sensitive and non-sensitive data are stored in private and public cloud databases, respectively. AES-256 encryption secures sensitive data in private clouds. The scheme alleviates private cloud storage pressure and enables partitioned management based on sensitivity levels, thus ensuring data security and operational efficiency.

The remainder of the document is organized as follows: Section 2 reviews related technologies, including LLMs, parameter-efficient fine-tuning, prompt tuning, MapReduce distributed computing, and hybrid cloud partitioning. Section 3 details the proposed sensitive data labeling scheme combining LLM fine-tuning with MapReduce. Section 4 presents experimental design and validation, including model performance, processing efficiency, and hybrid cloud partitioning effectiveness. Section 5 concludes and discusses future research directions.

2. Related Technologies

Accurate classification, efficient processing, and secure storage of privacy-sensitive data constitute core requirements in data governance for hybrid cloud environments, relying on the coordination of multiple key technologies.

2.1. Large Language Models

Large language models (LLMs), built upon the Transformer architecture, are pre-trained on large-scale corpora via self-supervised learning to capture long-range dependencies and complex semantics [21], making them highly suitable for text classification [22]. Downstream tasks are typically adapted by adding a classification head and minimizing the cross-entropy loss. To reduce fine-tuning cost, parameter-efficient fine-tuning (PEFT) and prompt tuning are widely used [23,24]. PEFT updates only a small set of adapter parameters, while prompt tuning learns continuous prompt vectors prepended to the input, both enabling effective adaptation without full model retraining. Pre-trained models learn universal linguistic features from large corpora and demonstrate strong performance in classification, tagging, and generation tasks. The T5 model further verified the high generalization capability of transfer learning in natural language processing [25], providing the foundational support for the fine-tuning-based sensitive data identification approach adopted.

Beyond LLMs, advanced hybrid deep learning architectures such as CNN-BiGRU and Autoencoder-GRU (AE-GRU) enhanced by metaheuristic algorithms have shown strong performance in security and anomaly detection tasks for IoT and cloud systems [11]. These models excel at capturing temporal patterns and feature hierarchies. However, for the core task of context-aware sensitive data classification in large-scale, heterogeneous unstructured text—where understanding nuanced semantics and long-range dependencies is paramount—LLMs like XLM-R offer a distinct advantage. Therefore, for the core task of this work—context-aware classification of heterogeneous unstructured text—we adopt an LLM-based approach.

We select XLM-R (cross-lingual RoBERTa) as our backbone model. Pre-trained on over 100 languages with a masked language modeling objective [26], XLM-R captures deep cross-lingual contextual representations and outperforms monolingual models like BERT in multi-

https://doi.org/10.3390/electronics15010030

lingual understanding tasks [26,27]. This capability is crucial for hybrid cloud environments with diverse data sources [28]. When combined with PEFT or prompt tuning, XLM-R can be efficiently adapted for high-precision, low-overhead sensitive data classification [23,24].

2.2. MapReduce Distributed Computing Framework

MapReduce is a distributed computing framework that simplifies large-scale data processing through a divide-and-conquer scheme, decomposing tasks into Map and Reduce phases [18]. Its core concept is divide-and-conquer, decomposing complex processing tasks into two phases: Map and Reduce. In the Map phase, input data is split into multiple data blocks, each processed independently by different nodes to generate intermediate key–value pairs (k, v):

$$\text{Map} : (k_1, v_1) \rightarrow [(k_2, v_2), \ldots] \tag{1}$$

where (k_1, v_1) denotes the raw input and (k_2, v_2) denotes the intermediate output. The Reduce phase aggregates all intermediate results with identical keys and applies reduce functions f to generate the final output:

$$\text{Reduce} : (k_2, [v_2, \ldots]) \rightarrow (k_3, v_3) \tag{2}$$

Through parallel task scheduling and data partitioning, MapReduce can significantly improve processing efficiency for massive datasets [29]. It features built-in load balancing and fault tolerance, which optimizes resource utilization and ensures computation stability by retrying failed tasks [30].

In privacy-sensitive data processing scenarios, MapReduce can be combined with sensitive data labeling schemes to achieve large-scale parallel inference on unstructured text. This approach overcomes limitations in single-machine computation and storage and facilitates distributed data management and classification in hybrid cloud environments, supporting high-throughput and low-latency processing demands [17,19].

2.3. Cloud Storage Partitioning Technologies

Cloud storage partitioning optimizes resource allocation and security by storing data in different clouds based on sensitivity—typically private clouds for sensitive data and public clouds for non-sensitive data [31,32]. Recent research has further optimized this. As Agyekum et al. [33] and Yolchuyev et al. [34], dynamic partitioning and migration strategies based on data sensitivity and access patterns improve cost-efficiency and resource utilization while maintaining security.

3. LLM-SPSS: An Efficient LLM-Based Secure Partitioned Storage Scheme in Distributed Hybrid Clouds

To address the challenges of sensitive information identification in large-scale unstructured text within hybrid cloud environments, LLM-SPSS addresses sensitive data identification in hybrid clouds by integrating fine-tuned LLMs with MapReduce processing. The approach combines prompt-guided inference and supervised fine-tuning to enhance context-aware sensitive data classification, with prompts optimized for text length and sensitivity. A three-dimensional sharding scheme balances text size, data type, and node workload to ensure efficient distributed computation. Combined with dynamic partitioning mechanisms, this enables secure hybrid cloud storage, completing the workflow from data ingestion to storage governance.

https://doi.org/10.3390/electronics15010030

3.1. System Architecture

The system is organized into three core layers: the Data Processing Layer, the Distributed Processing Layer, and the Hybrid Cloud Partitioned Storage Layer. The overall architecture is illustrated in Figure 1.

Within the Data Processing Layer, a large language model-based labeling approach is applied to unstructured text. Data entering the hybrid cloud platform—spanning documents, system logs, emails, user comments, and other forms of unstructured content—is first subjected to format normalization and text denoising, preparing standardized inputs for subsequent classification by the model.

Within the Distributed Processing Layer, a sharding scheme based on the MapReduce framework is adopted. The dataset is partitioned along three dimensions—load balance, text length, and data type—and Map tasks are executed in parallel across nodes in both private and public clouds. Each shard is processed using a fine-tuned XLM-R model for local sensitivity prediction, with batch sizes dynamically adjusted according to node resources. After the Map stage, the Reduce stage performs deduplication and aggregation using unique text identifiers (e.g., hash values).

Within the Hybrid Cloud Partitioned Storage Layer, a hybrid storage scheme is implemented. Sensitive data are stored in private-cloud dedicated databases, while non-sensitive data are encrypted using AES-256 and stored in public-cloud databases, balancing security and operational efficiency. Sensitivity labels and metadata for each data item are preserved in full to support compliance audits, thereby forming a complete closed-loop workflow from data ingestion to storage management.

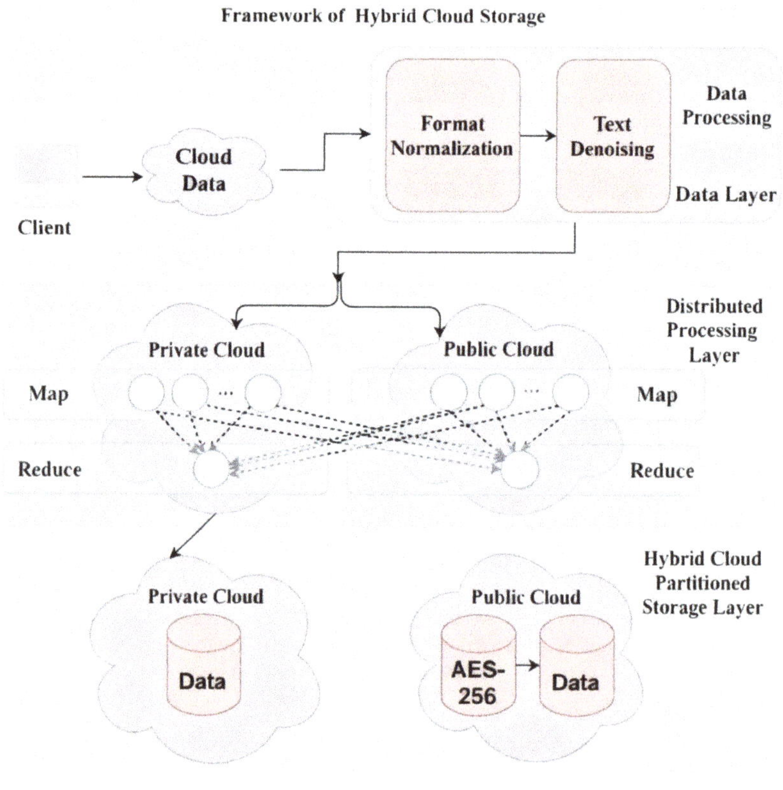

Figure 1. Framework of LLM-SPSS.

https://doi.org/10.3390/electronics1501003(

3.2. *Sensitive Data Labeling Model and Fine-Tuning Design*

3.2.1. Problem Definition

Sensitive data labeling is formulated as a binary classification task. Given a text $T = \{t_1, t_2, \ldots, t_n\}$, where t_i is represented as tokens, the goal is to predict its sensitivity label $y_i \in \{0, 1\}$ (0 for non-sensitive, 1 for sensitive). Text may contain multiple sensitive categories, such as health information, political beliefs, judicial data, sexual orientation, religious beliefs, and racial information. This challenge lies in the diverse expressions and contextual dependencies of unstructured text, requiring context-aware sensitive data classification.

3.2.2. Model Selection

For sensitive information detection in hybrid cloud environments, XLM-RoBERTa (XLM-R) is selected as the backbone model to achieve deep alignment between task requirements and model characteristics. Hybrid cloud data originates from diverse sources, including multiple languages and formats (e.g., cross-lingual documents and multi-system logs). XLM-R, pre-trained on over 100 languages, provides robust cross-lingual semantic alignment, outperforming monolingual models like BERT and reducing cross-language understanding bias [13].

Sensitive information recognition heavily relies on contextual understanding; certain expressions require surrounding text to be accurately interpreted. XLM-R Base, with a 12-layer Transformer architecture and multi-head attention, captures long-range dependencies and deep semantic features, overcoming shallow-feature limitations of traditional models such as SVM and Random Forest [14].

In practical hybrid cloud scenarios, labeled sensitive data is scarce. XLM-R supports few-shot fine-tuning, enabling rapid adaptation to domain-specific sensitive information detection with minimal labeled data, offering advantages over CNN or RNN models [18]. With approximately 110 M parameters, XLM-R Base balances context-aware sensitive data classification with resource efficiency, facilitating deployment across heterogeneous cloud nodes (CPU/GPU) and supporting parallel processing under the MapReduce framework [13]. Its [CLS] token provides a high-quality global semantic feature representation, suitable for binary sensitive classification tasks [13].

3.2.3. Large Language Model Fine-Tuning

The system adopts XLM-RoBERTa as the base encoder and performs supervised fine-tuning for the sensitive data labeling task. Text inputs are concatenated with prompt tokens P to form the model input $x_i = [P; t_i]$. The encoded [CLS] representation ($\mathbf{h}_{CLS} \in \mathbb{R}^d$, with a hidden size $d = 768$ for the XLM-R Base variant) is passed through a fully connected layer to generate the classification probability:

$$p(y = 1|X) = \sigma(W \cdot \mathbf{h}_{CLS} + b) \tag{3}$$

where $W \in \mathbb{R}^{d \times 1}$ is the weight matrix, $b \in \mathbb{R}$ is the bias term, and σ is the sigmoid activation function.

The optimization process adopts binary cross-entropy as the loss function to suit the binary classification objective:

$$\mathcal{L} = -\frac{1}{N} \sum_{i=1}^{N} [y_i \log p_i + (1 - y_i) \log(1 - p_i)] \tag{4}$$

where N is the batch size, y_i is the true label, and p_i is the predicted sensitivity probability.

https://doi.org/10.3390/electronics15010030

3.2.4. Sensitive Label Generation Process

During the inference phase, as illustrated in Algorithm 1, the system performs preprocessing steps to handle excessive text length, empty inputs, and semantically meaningless content. Texts exceeding a predefined length threshold or containing no meaningful information are processed using specific rules. A confidence threshold is applied, and samples with low confidence scores are flagged for manual inspection.

Algorithm 1 Sensitive- Data Labeling Workflow

Require: Text sample set $T = \{t_1, t_2, \ldots, t_N\}$, prompt P, fine-tuned large language model M
Ensure: Sensitive-label set $Y_{hat} = \{y_{hat,1}, y_{hat,2}, \ldots, y_{hat,N}\}$
for $t_i \in T$ **do**
  Concatenate prompt P with text t_i to generate model input x_i
  Input x_i into model M to obtain semantic representation $\mathbf{h}_i$
  Map $\mathbf{h}_i$ to prediction probability $p(y|x_i)$ through the classification layer
  Assign label $y_{hat,i}$ based on maximum probability
  Save predicted label $y_{hat,i}$
end forreturn Y_{hat}

The text is first concatenated with an adaptive prompt to construct the model input. The fine-tuned large language model then generates contextual semantic representations, which are subsequently passed through a fully connected layer to produce prediction probabilities.

This design incorporates abnormal-text handling mechanisms, adaptive prompt selection, and confidence-based validation, providing three layers of safeguards that enhance the accuracy and robustness of sensitive-information detection in large-scale unstructured text.

It integrates prompt-based guidance with supervised fine-tuning, enabling efficient identification of sensitive information within unstructured text while supporting rapid adaptation with minimal annotated data.

To systematically investigate the role of instructional guidance, we designed and compared three distinct prompting strategies, as defined in Table 1.

Table 1. Prompt designs for sensitive information classification.

Type	Description	Example/Template
None	No instruction is prepended. The raw text is fed directly into the model.	[Text]
Simple	A concise, direct instruction listing the sensitive categories.	"Determine whether the following text contains sensitive information (health, political, judicial, religious, sexual orientation, racial): [Text]"
Complex	A structured, multi-line instruction providing definitions for each sensitive category.	(Full template provided in Appendix A for reproducibility)

3.3. *Data Partitioning and MapReduce Parallel Processing*

To accommodate large-scale text processing and the substantial computational requirements of large language models, the system applies a three-dimensional balanced partitioning scheme based on dataset size, text length, and node load. The dataset D is partitioned into K independent shards S_i based on a three-dimensional balanced scheme considering text length, data type, and node load. The load balance dimension is estimated using a lightweight monitor that tracks each node's current CPU/memory utilization and

https://doi.org/10.3390/electronics15010030

pending task queue length prior to shard assignment. Shards are then distributed to strive for a balanced workload across nodes, ensuring no single node becomes a bottleneck.

$$D = \{S_1, S_2, \ldots, S_K\}, \quad |S_i| = \frac{N}{K} \tag{5}$$

Each shard is processed independently on a separate computation node during the Map phase. The Map phase task is formalized as

$$y_i = \arg\max_{y \in \{0,1\}} p(y|x_i), \quad \forall t_i \in S_k \tag{6}$$

The Map phase process is shown in Algorithm 2.

Algorithm 2 Map Phase: Local Sensitive Data Labeling

Require: Data-shard set $S = \{S_1, S_2, \ldots, S_K\}$, fine-tuned model M, prompt P
Ensure: Local sensitive-label results $R = \{R_1, R_2, \ldots, R_K\}$
for $S_k \in S$ **do** ▷ Executed in parallel
  for $t_i \in S_k$ **do**
    Concatenate prompt P with text t_i to generate model input x_i
    Feed x_i into model M to obtain semantic representation $\mathbf{h}_i$
    Compute sensitivity probability $p(y|x_i)$ through the classification layer
    Determine sensitive label $y_{hat,i}$ based on maximum probability
    Append result $(t_i, y_{hat,i})$ to shard-level result R_k
  end for
end forreturn Local result set R

This design ensures computation is fully isolated across nodes, avoiding communication bottlenecks and mitigating the feature-statistics distortion problem that traditional approaches (e.g., SVM) encounter after data partitioning. By leveraging parallel GPU/CPU resources, the system achieves high-throughput processing and significantly improves inference efficiency for large language models.

3.4. Reduce Phase: Result Aggregation and Global Label Generation

During the Reduce phase shown in Algorithm 3, the system aggregates outputs from all Map nodes. Duplicate texts across shards are identified using unique text identifiers. In cases of label conflict, the decision is made based on confidence-score priority, while samples with marginal confidence differences are marked for manual verification. Random sampling may be applied to validate the overall aggregation quality.

Algorithm 3 Reduce Phase: Result Aggregation

Require: Local result set $R = \{R_1, R_2, \ldots, R_K\}$ from all Map nodes
Ensure: Global sensitive-label set $Y_{hat} = \{y_{hat,1}, y_{hat,2}, \ldots, y_{hat,N}\}$
Initialize global result set $Y_{hat} = \emptyset$
for $R_k \in R$ **do**
  for $(t_i, y_{hat,i}) \in R_k$ **do**
    Add $y_{hat,i}$ to global result set Y_{hat}
  end for
end forreturn Y_{hat}

This component incorporates text deduplication, conflict resolution, and verification procedures, ensuring global label consistency and reliability. The final labels provide a high-precision decision basis for hybrid cloud storage partitioning and ensure the completeness and coherence of data-management workflows.

https://doi.org/10.3390/electronics15010030

3.5. Hybrid Cloud Data Partitioned Storage

In a hybrid cloud environment, data is categorized into sensitive and non-sensitive classes based on the inferred sensitivity labels. Storage management is then performed accordingly. Sensitive data is stored within the private cloud to ensure core security protection, while non-sensitive data is stored in the public cloud to reduce operational and storage costs. Sensitive data stored in the private cloud is further protected through encryption and access-control mechanisms to ensure security throughout its life cycle.

The framework centers on automating the classification of sensitive data and the subsequent storage-partitioning decisions. Once classified, data designated as sensitive can be routed to private cloud storage with encryption applied, while non-sensitive data is directed to cost-effective public cloud storage. This workflow ensures that standard data protection mechanisms (e.g., encryption and access control) are applied contextually based on the initial sensitivity label, fitting seamlessly into established hybrid cloud security operations.

4. Experimental Design and Implementation

4.1. Dataset and Preprocessing

The Sensitive Data Detection Dataset, generated by the OpenLLaMA model and released under the Apache 2.0 open-source license [35], is employed. The dataset contains diverse text types, including emails, news reports, personal resumes, and psychiatric reports, with sensitive category labels such as health information, political orientation, and sexual orientation, satisfying the requirements for multi-type sensitive information detection research.

Utilizing a high-quality synthetic dataset allows for a controlled and reproducible evaluation of the proposed framework's core capabilities, a common methodology in early-stage research on privacy-sensitive tasks where real-world data is often unavailable for sharing [9,35]. Taylor et al. demonstrated that carefully generated synthetic clinical records can preserve key statistical patterns of real patient data while enabling safe model evaluation in sensitive domains [36]. In addition, broader surveys on synthetic data generation also confirm that high-quality synthetic datasets can support reliable assessment of model performance before applying the methods to real-world sensitive datasets [37].

Since the core task is binary sensitive information detection, the raw dataset was standardized and preprocessed. In the data cleaning stage, HTML escape characters, redundant spaces, and special symbols were removed while retaining letters, numbers, and common punctuation. In the label conversion stage, original multi-class labels were mapped into binary sensitive/non-sensitive labels. Any sample containing at least one sensitive category was labeled as 1 (sensitive), otherwise as 0 (non-sensitive). The processed dataset was saved in a standardized JSON format for subsequent model training and inference. Stratified sampling was used to split the dataset into training, validation, and test sets in a 70%/20%/10% format ratio, ensuring a balanced representation of sensitive and non-sensitive samples and preventing data leakage. The final dataset contained 2051 samples, with 71.72% sensitive and 28.28% non-sensitive, providing a sufficient testbed for the initial validation and ablation studies conducted in this work. To further assess the practical robustness of the framework, we designed dedicated experiments involving artificial noise injection (Section 4.3.3) and variable training data scales (Section 4.3.4).

4.2. Experimental Environment and Configuration

Experiments were deployed on an Ubuntu 20.04 LTS 64-bit server with Intel(R) Xeon(R) Platinum 8358 CPU @ 2.60 GHz, NVIDIA RTX 3090 GPU (96 GB VRAM), and 128 GB RAM,

https://doi.org/10.3390/electronics1501003C

ensuring sufficient resources for model training and inference. Software was developed using Python 3.8.x with PyTorch 2.0.1+cu117 and Hugging Face Transformers libraries. A fixed random seed of 42 was used to maintain consistent experimental conditions for reproducibility. The detailed configuration is shown in Table 2.

Table 2. Experimental Environment.

Component	Specification
CPU	Intel(R) Xeon(R) Platinum 8358 CPU @ 2.60 GHz
GPU	NVIDIA GeForce RTX 3090
RAM	128 GiB
OS	Ubuntu 20.04 LTS (64-bit)

The experimental evaluation was designed to comprehensively validate LLM-SPSS from multiple perspectives. The key variables and configurations across all experiments are summarized in Table 3.

Table 3. Model configuration and experimental settings.

Experimental Aspect	Configurations/Values
Comparison Baselines	Regex, SVM, Random Forest, DePrompt [9]
Our Model (XLM-R) Variants	No Prompt, Simple Prompt, Complex Prompt (see Table 1)
Training Strategy	Direct (single node), MapReduce (four-node simulation)
Noise Robustness	Noise levels: 0%, 10%, 20%, 30%
Data Scale Sensitivity	Training data proportions: 5%, 20%, 50%, 100%
Model Scale Comparison	XLM-R-base, XLM-R-large, InfoXLM-base

Implementation Details for Reproducibility: For the XLM-R fine-tuning, we used the AdamW optimizer with a learning rate of 5×10^{-5}, a batch size of 16, and trained for 4 epochs with early stopping (patience = 1). The maximum sequence length was 256 tokens. Cross-entropy loss with a weight decay of 0.01 was applied. In the MapReduce simulations, the dataset was partitioned into shards of approximately 50 samples each, processed on 4 simulated CPU nodes (batch size 8; gradient accumulation steps 2). Textual noise for robustness tests was generated by randomly applying character-level operations (deletion, insertion, swap) at the specified ratios.

4.3. Experimental Design and Results

To validate the effectiveness of the proposed sensitive data processing scheme, a series of experiments were conducted to evaluate the accuracy of large language models for sensitive information detection, the performance impact of MapReduce shard-based training on large-scale data, and the feasibility of hybrid cloud partitioned storage for managing different sensitivity levels. Experiments included comparisons with traditional schemes, training scheme optimization, noise robustness, training data size impact, and same-scale large language model comparisons. The accuracy, precision, recall, and F1-score were used as evaluation metrics. The full content of the simple and complex prompts is provided in Table 1 and Appendix A, respectively.

https://doi.org/10.3390/electronics15010030

4.3.1. Comparison with Traditional Schemes

This experiment evaluates the performance of the proposed scheme against several baselines, including traditional techniques and a contemporary LLM-based approach. The baselines comprised the following: a rule-based regular expression (Regex) scheme; two classical machine learning models, Support Vector Machine (SVM) and Random Forest, which employed TF-IDF feature vectors for classification, replicating the scheme from prior work [10]; and DePrompt [9], a representative prompt-guided large language model for sensitive information recognition. To further investigate the role of prompt engineering, we included two ablated versions of our model: one augmented with simple prompts and another with complex prompts.

As illustrated in Figure 2, the results reveal a distinct performance gradient. The Regex scheme yielded the lowest scores, with an F1-score of only 68.27%, due to its limited generalization capability. SVM and Random Forest demonstrated substantial improvement, achieving F1-scores of 98.32% and 95.79%, respectively, confirming the effectiveness of machine learning for this task. Critically, the proposed XLM-R scheme achieved superior performance across all evaluation metrics, attaining a near-perfect F1-score of 99.66% and 100% recall. This outcome signifies that our approach not only excels beyond conventional schemes but also surpasses the existing LLM-based solution, DePrompt, which achieved an F1-score of 95.95%.

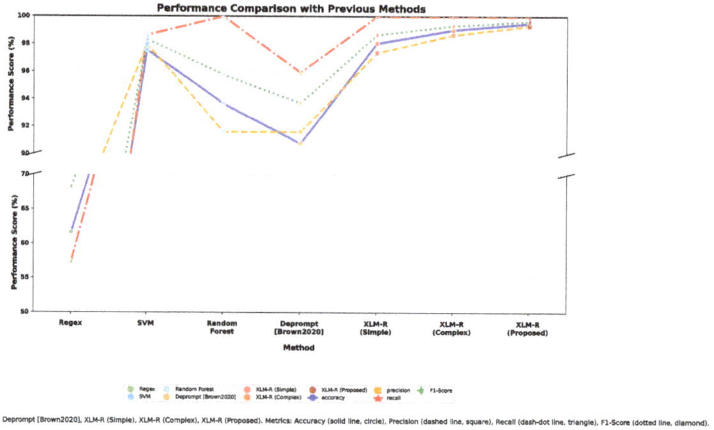

Figure 2. Performance Comparison with Traditional Schemes.

The ablation study on prompts offers valuable insights. Although the complex-prompt variant delivered strong performance with an F1-score of 99.33%, our primary scheme without prompts consistently achieved the highest accuracy, demonstrating that optimal performance does not necessitate explicit prompt guidance. Meanwhile, the simple-prompt variant attained an F1-score of 98.67%, still markedly outperforming all traditional baselines and DePrompt [14]. The exceptional capability of the fine-tuned XLM-R model stems from its deep context-aware sensitive data classification acquired during pre-training, allowing it to identify sensitive information contextually without handcrafted features or prompt dependencies.

4.3.2. Comparison of Training Strategies

To address the computational challenges of large-scale data processing, this study evaluates the efficacy of a MapReduce-based distributed scheme against a conventional direct training approach. The experiment encompassed a range of schemes, including Regex, SVM, Random Forest, zero-shot classification, DePrompt, and the XLM-R model with different prompting strategies (simple, complex, and the proposed no-prompt version). Under the MapReduce paradigm, the dataset was partitioned into fixed-size shards for independent parallel processing. The overall performance was averaged across shards, while the runtime was determined by the slowest node, simulating real-world large-scale processing constraints. Both classification metrics (e.g., accuracy and F1-score) and runtime efficiency were evaluated.

The results, summarized in Figure 3, reveal stark contrasts in the adaptability of each scheme to distributed computing. Schemes reliant on global feature statistics, namely SVM and Random Forest, suffered significant performance degradation under MapReduce, with their F1-scores dropping to approximately 84.0% and 85.3%, respectively. This decline is attributed to data sharding disrupting the integrity of their TF-IDF feature distributions. In contrast, rule-based Regex and the zero-shot approach remained largely unaffected but started from a lower performance baseline.

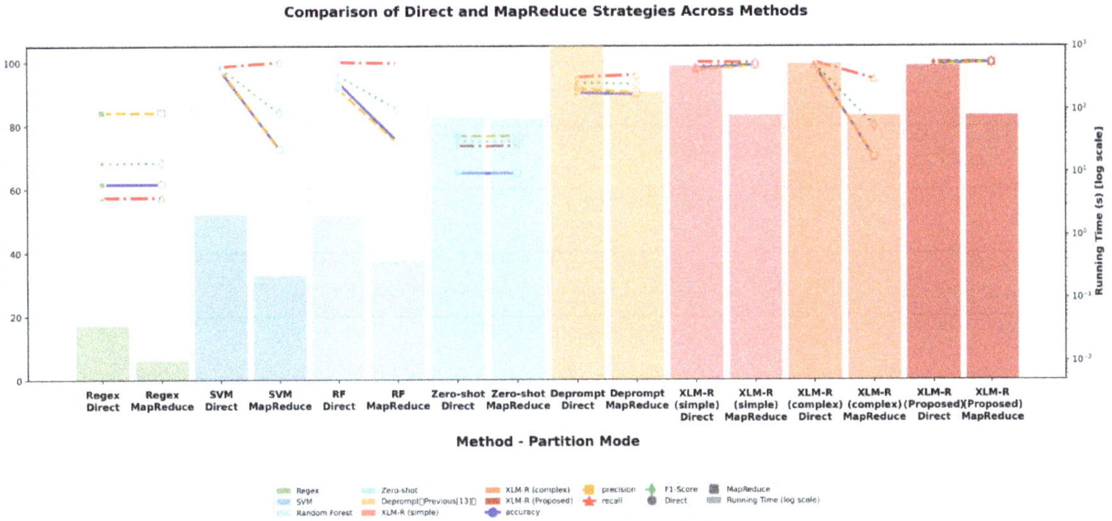

Figure 3. Comparison of Direct and MapReduce Strategies Across Schemes.

A key finding is the exceptional resilience of the proposed XLM-R scheme. It maintained a high F1-score above 99% and an accuracy of 99.8% even in the distributed setting, demonstrating minimal performance loss compared to the direct mode. The ablated XLM-R variants with simple and complex prompts also exhibited robust adaptability, preserving strong performance under MapReduce. More importantly, the MapReduce scheme conferred a substantial efficiency gain for the XLM-R models, reducing the inference time from nearly 510 s to approximately 81 seconds—a 6.3-fold speed-up. This result underscores that the proposed scheme uniquely fulfills the dual objectives of high accuracy and high efficiency in large-scale sensitive data detection, making it particularly suitable for distributed hybrid clouds.

4.3.3. Robustness Evaluation Under Noisy Conditions

To assess the practical viability of the proposed scheme, we evaluated its robustness against textual noise, a common issue in real-world data. The experiment introduced four levels of artificial noise (0%, 10%, 20%, 30%) into the test set. The proposed XLM-R scheme (without prompts) and its two ablated variants (with simple and complex prompts)

https://doi.org/10.3390/electronics15010030

were tested under both direct and MapReduce training modes, with accuracy serving as the primary robustness metric.

As depicted in Figure 4, the proposed scheme demonstrates commendable resilience to noise, particularly under the direct mode. In a noise-free environment, it achieved the highest accuracy of 99.51%. As noise levels increased, its performance experienced a predictable yet gradual decline, maintaining a significant advantage over the ablated variants. Notably, the complex-prompt variant exhibited severe performance degradation, with accuracy collapsing to 71.84% even without added noise, indicating that intricate instructions can fundamentally impair the model's core classification ability.

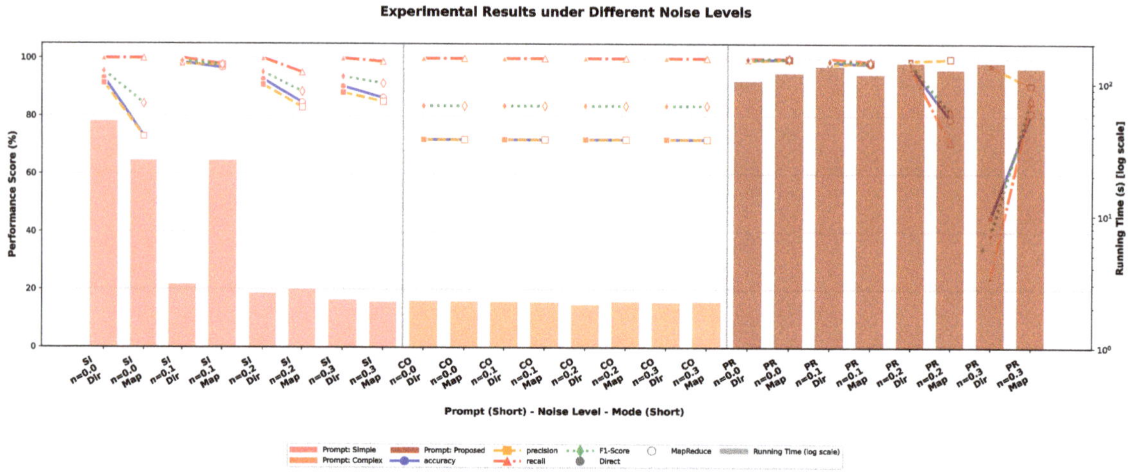

Figure 4. Experimental Results under Different Noise Levels.

Under the MapReduce mode, the robustness of all models was further challenged. While the proposed scheme retained strong performance at lower noise levels, its accuracy at 20% and 30% noise settled at 78.99% and 81.24%, respectively. This suggests that the combination of data sharding and high noise exacerbates feature distortion. Despite this, the proposed scheme consistently outperformed its prompted counterparts across almost all noise conditions in both operational modes. The results affirm that the proposed fine-tuning approach, devoid of prompt engineering, provides a more reliable and robust solution for sensitive data detection in noisy, real-world scenarios.

4.3.4. Impact of Training Data Scale on Model Performance

The scalability of a scheme with respect to training data volume is critical for its practical adoption. This experiment evaluates the performance of the proposed scheme and its ablated variants across a range of training data proportions (5% to 100%) under both direct and MapReduce modes.

As summarized in Figure 5, the proposed XLM-R scheme exhibits strong data efficiency and scalability. In the direct mode, our scheme achieves remarkable performance even with limited data, attaining an accuracy of 99.27% with only 20% of the training data. This performance is sustained as more data becomes available. The MapReduce mode showcases the scheme's efficiency advantage, drastically reducing runtime while maintaining competitive accuracy, particularly at data proportions of 20% and below. For instance, with 20% of the data, the proposed scheme in MapReduce mode delivers an accuracy of 98.74% in nearly half the time required by the direct mode.

The ablated variants exhibit contrasting behaviors. The model with simple prompts shows inconsistent performance in the direct mode and becomes highly unstable under MapReduce, with accuracy fluctuating significantly across different data scales. The variant with complex prompts reveals a critical limitation: its performance remains stagnant at a low baseline (71.71% accuracy) until a substantial amount of data (50%) is provided, indicating severe ineffectiveness in low-resource scenarios, which hinders practical application.

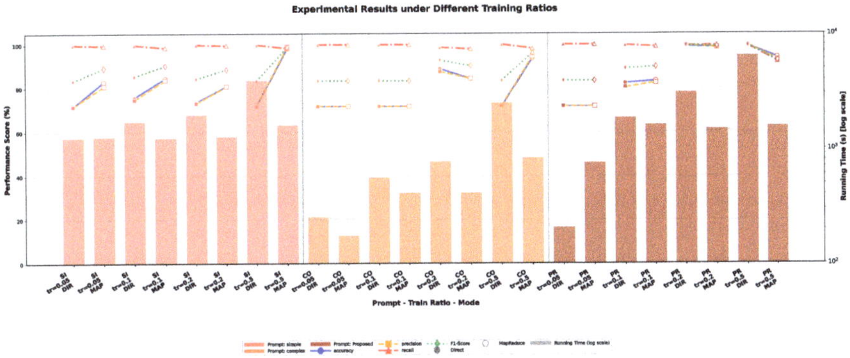

Figure 5. Experimental results under different training ratios.

4.3.5. Comparison of Large Language Models of Similar Scale

This comparative study validates our model selection scheme by evaluating four similarly scaled LLMs under identical conditions. As shown in Figure 6, our fine-tuned XLM-RoBERTa-base (proposed) achieves optimal performance with 100% accuracy and F1-score, confirming the effectiveness of our design approach.

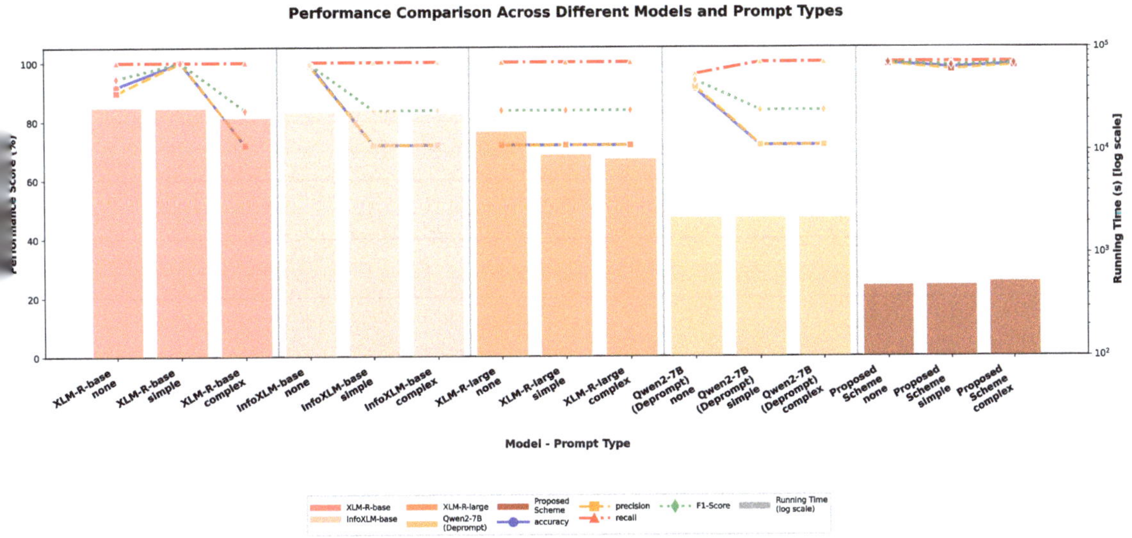

Figure 6. Performance comparison across different models and prompt types.

The results reveal critical architectural insights: While InfoXLM-base shows competitive native capability (99.03% accuracy) without prompts, it suffers severe performance degradation (to 71.84%) when prompts are introduced, demonstrating the instability of prompt-dependent approaches. Similarly, the larger XLM-RoBERTa-large fails to surpass its base variant, proving that model scale alone cannot ensure better performance.

XLM-RoBERTa-base demonstrates superior architectural suitability, maintaining robust performance across all prompt conditions. Through targeted fine-tuning, we transform the base model from a capable pre-trained encoder (91.75% zero-shot accuracy) into a precision tool for sensitive data detection (100% accuracy). This significant improvement, achieved without complex prompt engineering, validates our core schemeology: selecting an architecturally suitable foundation model and optimizing it through directed fine-tuning offers a more reliable solution than pursuing larger models or prompt-dependent strategies.

5. Conclusions

In conclusion, LLM-SPSS is an efficient LLM-based secure partitioned storage scheme designed for distributed hybrid clouds. By integrating a fine-tuned XLM-R Base model, MapReduce-based parallel inference, and a multi-dimensional sensitivity-aware storage layout, the framework effectively addresses sensitive data classification, large-scale unstructured data processing, and secure partitioned storage in hybrid cloud environments. Experimental results on a controlled dataset show that LLM-SPSS achieves an F1-score of 99.66% and a 6.3× speed-up compared with the non-distributed baseline, demonstrating a strong balance between detection accuracy and computational efficiency. The core competitive advantage stems from the fine-tuned XLM-R model's deep context-aware classification capability, which ensures robust and high accuracy without reliance on complex prompt engineering. Compared with traditional methods and existing LLM-based approaches, LLM-SPSS exhibits superior classification accuracy and processing efficiency, and its design is better suited to hybrid cloud environments with secure partitioned storage requirements, thus making it a practical and scalable solution for real-world deployment.

Building on the promising results achieved in this study, several directions for further enhancement and broader application can be envisioned. The model's generalization could be improved by training on more diverse, multi-modal datasets. While efficient, the distributed scheme currently employs a fixed sharding approach; a dynamic scheduler that adapts to node performance and data skew could further enhance efficiency. Furthermore, the hybrid cloud adaptation mechanisms can be matured by integrating with cloud-native security services (e.g., Key Management Services) and developing automated compliance auditing features based on the generated sensitivity labels. Addressing these aspects will be the focus of our subsequent studies. Finally, the promising results on the synthetic benchmark warrant future investigation into the framework's adaptability across a more diverse spectrum of data sources and formats encountered in practical deployments.

Author Contributions: Conceptualization, R.Z.; methodology and implementation, R.Z.; validation and analysis, R.Z.; writing—original draft, R.Z.; writing—review and editing, R.Z. and B.C.; supervision, B.C. and L.Y.; project administration and funding acquisition, L.Y. All authors have read and agreed to the published version of the manuscript.

Funding: This work was specially supported by Research Funds for NSD Construction, University of International Relations (2025GA04), and Student Academic Research Training Project of University of International Relations (No. 3262025SYJ08).

Data Availability Statement: Previously published articles were used to support this study, and these prior studies and datasets are cited at the relevant places within this article. The datasets and the code for this paper are publicly available at https://github.com/SimoDR/sensitive-data-detection (accessed on 28 November 2025).

https://doi.org/10.3390/electronics15010030

Conflicts of Interest: The authors declare no conflicts of interest. The funders had no role in the design of the study; in the collection, analyses, or interpretation of data; in the writing of the manuscript; or in the decision to publish the results.

Appendix A. Full Complex Prompt Template

The complete template for the complex prompt used in the ablation study is provided below.

```
Please judge whether the text contains sensitive information.
Sensitive information includes the following categories with detailed
definitions:
1. Physical or mental health information: Diagnoses, medical conditions,
   disabilities, treatment records, or health-related data.
2. Political beliefs: Party affiliation, political opinions, union
   membership, or participation in political activities.
3. Judicial information: Criminal records, charges, trial proceedings,
   court judgments, or legal disputes.
4. Religious or philosophical beliefs: Religious affiliation, spiritual
   practices, or philosophical viewpoints.
5. Sexual orientation and gender identity: Sexual preference, gender
   expression, or gender identity.
6. Racial or ethnic information: Racial background, ethnic origin, or
   tribal affiliation.
Please answer only "Yes" if the text contains any of the above sensitive
information; otherwise, answer "No".
```

eferences

Gantz, J.; Reinsel, D. *Extracting Value from Chaos;* IDC iView White Paper; IDC: Framingham, MA, USA, 2011. Available online: https://www.emc.com/digital_universe (accessed on 28 November 2025).

Gartner, Inc. *Gartner Forecasts Worldwide Public Cloud End-User Spending to Total $723 Billion in 2025;* Press Release; Gartner: Stamford, CT, USA, 19 November 2024. Available online: https://www.gartner.com/en/newsroom/press-releases/2024-11-19-gartner-forecasts-worldwide-public-cloud-end-user-spending-to-total-723-billion-dollars-in-2025 (accessed on 28 November 2025).

Sawle, P.; Baraskar, T. Survey on Data Classification and Data Encryption Techniques Used in Cloud Computing. *Int. J. Comput. Appl.* **2016**, *135*, 35–40. [CrossRef]

Salehi, M.A.; Mohammadi, M.; Hashemi, S. Regular Expression Search over Encrypted Data in the Cloud. In Proceedings of the 2014 IEEE International Conference on Cloud Computing Technology and Science (CloudCom), Singapore, 15–18 December 2014; pp. 453–458. [CrossRef]

OpenRaven. Introduction to Regex Based Data Classification for the Cloud. OpenRaven. 2022. Available online: https://www.openraven.com/articles/introduction-to-regex-based-data-classification-for-the-cloud-writing-and-developing-dataclasses-for-scale (accessed on 28 November 2025).

Mainetti, L.; Elia, A. Detecting Personally Identifiable Information Through Natural Language Processing: A Step Forward. *Appl. Syst. Innov.* **2025**, *8*, 55. [CrossRef]

Li, Q.; Peng, H.; Li, J.; Xia, C.; Yang, R.; Sun, L.; Yu, P.S.; He, L. A Survey on Text Classification: From Shallow to Deep Learning. *arXiv* **2020**, arXiv:2008.00364. Available online: https://arxiv.org/abs/2008.00364 (accessed on 28 November 2025).

Tang, W. Using Machine Learning to Help Detect Sensitive Information. *ISACA Now Blog*, 13 November 2023. Available online: https://www.isaca.org/resources/news-and-trends/isaca-now-blog/2023/using-machine-learning-to-help-detect-sensitive-information (accessed on 25 June 2024).

Sun, X.; Liu, G.; He, Z.; Li, H.; Li, X. DePrompt: Desensitization and Evaluation of Personal Identifiable Information in Large Language Model Prompts. *arXiv* **2024**, arXiv:2408.08930. Available online: https://arxiv.org/abs/2408.08930 (accessed on 25 June 2024).

10. Rama, B.K.; Thaiyalnayaki, S. A Novel Integration of Machine Learning-Based Data Classification with Optimized Cryptographic Techniques for Secure Cloud Storage. *J. Theor. Appl. Inf. Technol.* **2025**, *103*, 1808–1816. Available online: https://www.jatit.org/volumes/Vol103No5/14Vol103No5.pdf (accessed on 28 November 2025).
11. Addula, S.R.; Meesala, M.K.; Ravipati, P.; Sajja, G.S. A Hybrid Autoencoder and Gated Recurrent Unit Model Optimized by Honey Badger Algorithm for Enhanced Cyber Threat Detection in IoT Networks. *Secur. Priv.* **2025**, *8*, e70086. [CrossRef]
12. Rao, B.; Wang, L. A Survey of Semantics-Aware Performance Optimization for Data-Intensive Computing. *arXiv* **2021**, arXiv:2107.11540.
13. Devlin, J.; Chang, M.-W.; Lee, K.; Toutanova, K. BERT: Pre-Training of Deep Bidirectional Transformers for Language Understanding. In Proceedings of the 2019 Conference of the North American Chapter of the Association for Computational Linguistics: Human Language Technologies (NAACL-HLT 2019), Minneapolis, MN, USA, 2–7 June 2019; pp. 4171–4186.
14. Brown, T.; Mann, B.; Ryder, N.; Subbiah, M.; Kaplan, J.; Dhariwal, P.; Neelakantan, A.; Shyam, P.; Sastry, G.; Askell, A.; et al. Language Models Are Few-Shot Learners. In Proceedings of the Advances in Neural Information Processing Systems 33 (NeurIPS 2020), Vancouver, BC, Canada, 6–12 December 2020; pp. 1877–1901.
15. Boehnke, J.; Pontikes, E.; Bhargava, H.K. *Decoding Unstructured Text: Enhancing LLM Classification Accuracy with Redundancy and Confidence*; Technical Report; Graduate School of Management, University of California Davis: Davis, CA, USA, 7 June 2024. Available online: https://d30i16bbj53pdg.cloudfront.net/wp-content/uploads/2024/06/Decoding-Unstructured-Text-Enhancing-LLM-Classification.pdf (accessed on 28 November 2025).
16. Howard, J.; Ruder, S. Universal Language Model Fine-Tuning for Text Classification (ULMFiT). *arXiv* **2018**, arXiv:1801.06146. Available online: https://arxiv.org/abs/1801.06146 (accessed on 28 November 2025).
17. Zhou, Z.; Li, C.; Chen, X.; Wang, S.; Chao, Y.; Li, Z.; Wang, H.; Shi, Q.; Tan, Z.; Han, X.; et al. LLM × MapReduce: Simplified Long-Sequence Processing using Large Language Models. In Proceedings of the 63rd Annual Meeting of the Association for Computational Linguistics (Volume 1: Long Papers), Vienna, Austria, 27 July–1 August 2025; pp. 27664–27678. [CrossRef]
18. Dean, J.; Ghemawat, S. MapReduce: Simplified Data Processing on Large Clusters. *Commun. ACM* **2008**, *51*, 107–113. [CrossRef]
19. Levitin, G.; Xing, L.; Dai, Y. Optimal data partitioning in cloud computing system with random server assignment. *Future Gener. Comput. Syst.* **2017**, *70*, 17–25. [CrossRef]
20. Tang, T.; Li, M. Enhanced Secure Storage and Data Privacy Management System for Big Data Based on Multilayer Model. *Sci. Rep.* **2025**, *15*, 32285. [CrossRef] [PubMed]
21. Vaswani, A.; Shazeer, N.; Parmar, N.; Uszkoreit, J.; Jones, L.; Gomez, A.N.; Kaiser, Ł.; Polosukhin, I. Attention Is All You Need. In Proceedings of the Advances in Neural Information Processing Systems 30: Annual Conference on Neural Information Processing Systems 2017, Long Beach, CA, USA, 4–9 December 2017; pp. 5998–6008.
22. Wang, W.; Chen, W.; Luo, Y.; Long, Y.; Lin, Z.; Zhang, L.; Lin, B.; Cai, D.; He, X. Model Compression and Efficient Inference for Large Language Models: A Survey. *arXiv* **2024**, arXiv:2402.09748. Available online: https://arxiv.org/abs/2402.09748 (accessed on 28 November 2025).
23. Hu, Z.; Wang, L.; Lan, Y.; Xu, W.; Lim, E.-P.; Bing, L.; Xu, X.; Poria, S.; Lee, R.K.-W. LLM-Adapters: An Adapter Family for Parameter-Efficient Fine-Tuning of Large Language Models. In Proceedings of the 2023 Conference on Empirical Methods in Natural Language Processing (EMNLP 2023), Singapore, 6–10 December 2023; pp. 5254–5276. [CrossRef]
24. Qin, G.; Eisner, J. Learning How to Ask: Querying LMs with Mixtures of Soft Prompts. In Proceedings of the 2021 Conference of the North American Chapter of the Association for Computational Linguistics: Human Language Technologies (NAACL 2021), Online, 6–11 June 2021; pp. 5203–5212. [CrossRef]
25. Raffel, C.; Shazeer, N.; Roberts, A.; Lee, K.; Narang, S.; Matena, M.; Zhou, Y.; Li, W.; Liu, P.-J. Exploring the Limits of Transfer Learning with a Unified Text-to-Text Transformer. *J. Mach. Learn. Res.* **2020**, *21*, 5485–5551.
26. Conneau, A.; Khandelwal, K.; Goyal, N.; Chaudhary, V.; Wenzek, G.; Guzmán, F.; Grave, E.; Ott, M.; Zettlemoyer, L.; Stoyanov, V. Unsupervised Cross-lingual Representation Learning at Scale. In Proceedings of the 58th Annual Meeting of the Association for Computational Linguistics (ACL 2020), Online, 5–10 July 2020; pp. 8440–8451. [CrossRef]
27. Goyal, N.; Chaudhary, V.; Wenzek, G.; Guzmán, F.; Grave, E.; Ott, M.; Stoyanov, V.; Zettlemoyer, L. Larger-Scale Transformers for Multilingual Masked Language Modeling. *arXiv* **2021**, arXiv:2102.01373. Available online: https://arxiv.org/abs/2102.01373 (accessed on 28 November 2025).
28. Chai, Y.; Liang, Y.; Duan, N. Cross-Lingual Ability of Multilingual Masked Language Models: A Study of Language Structure. In Proceedings of the 60th Annual Meeting of the Association for Computational Linguistics (ACL 2022), Dublin, Ireland, 22–27 May 2022; pp. 3041–3054. [CrossRef]
29. White, T. *Hadoop: The Definitive Guide*, 3rd ed.; O'Reilly Media: Sebastopol, CA, USA, 2012.
30. Nghiem, P.P.; Figueira, S.M. Towards Efficient Resource Provisioning in MapReduce. *J. Parallel Distrib. Comput.* **2016**, *95*, 29–41. [CrossRef]
31. Zhang, Q.; Cheng, L.; Boutaba, R. Cloud Computing: State-of-the-Art and Research Challenges. *J. Internet Serv. Appl.* **2010**, *1*, 7–18. [CrossRef]

https://doi.org/10.3390/electronics15010030

2. Buyya, R.; Broberg, J.; Goscinski, A. *Cloud Computing: Principles and Paradigms*; Wiley: Hoboken, NJ, USA, 2011.
3. Agyekum, J.; Mazumdar, S.; Scheich, C. ADAPT: An effective data-aware multicloud data placement framework. *Cluster Comput.* **2025**, *28*, 825. [CrossRef]
4. Yolchuyev, A.; Levendovszky, J. Data Chunks Placement Optimization for Hybrid Cloud Storage Systems. *Future Internet* **2021**, *13*, 181. [CrossRef]
5. Simo, D.R.; Hernández-Cartagena, A.; Vázquez-Chávez, J.; Hernández, G.; Pulido, A. Sensitive-Data-Detection: Dataset and Code for Sensitive Data Detection. GitHub Repository. Available online: https://github.com/SimoDR/sensitive-data-detection (accessed on 28 November 2025).
6. Taylor, J.; Smith, A.; Johnson, R.; Brown, L.; Davis, M. Synthetic Data for Privacy-Preserving Clinical Risk Prediction. *Sci. Rep.* **2024**, *14*, 12345. [CrossRef] [PubMed]
7. Goyal, A.; Mahmoud, M. A Systematic Review of Synthetic Data Generation Techniques Using Generative AI. *Electronics* **2024**, *13*, 3509. [CrossRef]

https://doi.org/10.3390/electronics15010030

electronics

MDPI

Article

Effective ML-Based Android Malware Detection and Categorization

Areej Alhogail [1,]* and Rawan Abdulaziz Alharbi [2]

[1] STCs Artificial Intelligence Chair, Department of Information Systems, College of Computer and Information Sciences, King Saud University, Riyadh 11543, Saudi Arabia
[2] Department of Information Systems, College of Computer and Information Sciences, King Saud University, Riyadh 11543, Saudi Arabia; 445920622@student.ksu.edu.sa
* Correspondence: aalhogail@ksu.edu.sa

Abstract: The rapid proliferation of malware poses a significant challenge regarding digital security, necessitating the development of advanced techniques for malware detection and categorization. In this study, we investigate Android malware detection and categorization using a two-step machine learning (ML) framework combined with feature engineering. The proposed framework first performs binary categorization to detect malware and then applies multi-class categorization to categorize malware into types, such as adware, banking Trojans, SMS malware, and riskware. Feature selection techniques such as chi-squared testing and select-from-model (SFM) were employed to reduce dimensionality and enhance model performance. Various ML classifiers were evaluated, and the proposed model achieved outstanding accuracy, at 97.82% for malware detection and 96.09% for malware categorization. The proposed framework outperforms existing approaches, demonstrating the effectiveness of feature engineering and random forest (RF) models in addressing computational efficiency. This research contributes a robust and interpretable framework for Android malware detection that is resource-efficient and practical for use in real-world applications. It also offers a scalable approach via which practitioners can deploy efficient malware detection systems. Future work will focus on real-time implementation and adaptive methodologies to address evolving malware threats.

Keywords: malware detection; malware categorization; malware classification; cybersecurity; mobile application; mobile security; machine learning

1. Introduction

With the evolution of cybersecurity threats and the measures taken to address them, malware has remained one of the most alarmingly effective threats against digital systems globally. "Malware" is an umbrella term for malicious software, which refers to several harmful programs designed to gain access to, intercept, or harm the functionality of computer systems and networks. The growth in the number and complexity of malware attacks calls for effective and reliable techniques for malware detection and categorization. The crucial role of accurate malware categorization is beyond doubt. According to the Official Cybercrime Report [1], in 2023, the global economic losses from cybercrime due to malware abuse were believed to have reached $8 trillion. Malware attacks lead to expensive losses due to fraud and threats to personal, national, and infrastructural security.

In today's rapidly evolving digital landscape, malware is increasingly being crafted with sophisticated techniques that allow it to bypass traditional detection systems effectively and efficiently. While signature-based methods of malware detection remain prevalent, their limitations have become apparent over time. Attackers, including both commercial entities and freelance hackers, are leveraging advanced obfuscation and evasion techniques to create new, resilient strains of malware that can avoid conventional detection approaches. As these traditional methods reach their functional limits, there is a pressing need to explore more adaptive and robust alternatives. Machine learning (ML) has emerged as a powerful tool for malware detection and categorization, offering advantages over traditional approaches [2].

For example, unlike static methods, ML can incorporate dynamic behavior monitoring. It analyzes malware interactions within a system to enable precise malware categorization into families such as adware, ransomware, banking malware, and Trojans, facilitating targeted mitigation strategies [3]. ML algorithms process vast datasets in real time, identifying subtle anomalies and previously unseen threats, making them particularly effective against zero-day exploits and advanced, persistent threats. Additionally, they can adapt to evolving attack vectors, learning from historical data to improve detection accuracy with low computational overhead [4]. ML can prioritize critical features to enhance classification accuracy and interpretability [5]. Furthermore, ML's scalability allows it to handle increasing data complexity, reduce manual intervention, and enhance response efficiency, making it a vital asset in the ongoing fight against modern malware threats [6].

On the other hand, ML-based Android malware detection faces several challenges despite its advantages. Malware developers use polymorphism, metamorphism, and obfuscation to evade detection, dynamically altering malware's features to bypass traditional detection methods [3,7]. The high dimensionality of malware attributes, spanning file structures, behaviors, and network activities, increases computational complexity and, thus, the risk of overfitting and reducing generalizability regarding new threats [8]. Identifying meaningful features remains difficult, as encrypted and obfuscated malware can mask its malicious intent, limiting the effectiveness of structural and code-based analysis [9]. Additionally, resource constraints on mobile devices make real-time detection challenging, emphasizing the need for adaptive and efficient ML models.

Smartphones and mobile apps have led to an extraordinary increase in mobile malware, especially that targeting Android smartphones, due to their openness and broad use. As of 2023, Android smartphones accounted for approximately 70–72% of the global mobile operating system market, making them a major target for cyber threats and malware attacks [10]. Android malware has evolved dramatically, from harmless ads to dangerous banking Trojans and ransomware. Signature-based malware detection technologies are ineffective against quickly developing and polymorphic malware. Detecting such malware requires more powerful behavior-based detection algorithms. ML can potentially uncover malware patterns and traits that human analysts may miss. However, using ML for Android malware detection and categorization is difficult. Complications include high-dimensional feature spaces, real-time detection on resource-constrained mobile devices, and malware strategies that evolve to avoid detection. Malware detection and categorization are essential for targeted countermeasures and threat landscape comprehension [10].

While our study focuses on ML-based Android malware detection, it is important to acknowledge other security challenges, such as side-channel attacks, which exploit device behavior rather than executing malicious code [2]. One example is RF energy-harvesting attacks, in which adversaries passively analyze the signals emitted from mobile devices to infer user actions and extract sensitive data [11]. Unlike traditional malware, these attacks operate stealthily and without requiring direct code execution, making them difficult to detect and mitigate [12].

This study presents a comprehensive two-step ML-based framework for Android malware detection and categorization, addressing the key challenges in this domain. Our work is driven by the following objectives: (1) developing an efficient tool with which to differentiate between safe and malicious Android applications; (2) establishing a reliable approach to categorizing malware into distinct types, thereby enhancing threat comprehension; and (3) investigating the impact of feature selection and scaling on the performance of ML models regarding Android malware analysis. The proposed methodology operates in two stages: malware detection and categorization. During the malware detection stage, binary categorization is employed to identify potentially harmful applications instantly, providing rapid alerts about risky programs. During the malware categorization stage, multi-class categorization is utilized to determine the specific category of malware at work, offering deeper insights into the nature of the threat. This tiered approach is critical for real-world applications, as it balances speed and accuracy, making the system adaptable to various operational scenarios.

To implement the framework, we utilized four widely recognized classifiers, naïve Bayes (NB), K-nearest neighbors (KNN), decision tree (DT), and random forest (RF), for both malware detection and categorization. Feature selection techniques, including chi-squared testing and select-from-model, were applied along with feature scaling to optimize model performance. The proposed system achieves flexibility by separating the detection and categorization tasks into two stages. It can be deployed for rapid detection in high-traffic environments or detailed threat categorization when additional processing time is available.

The key contributions of this study are as follows:

- It presents a novel two-step ML framework for Android malware detection using binary classification, followed by malware categorization, addressing key challenges in mobile security;
- It provides optimized feature selection for improved performance through implementing chi-squared and SFM feature selection techniques to enhance classification accuracy and computational efficiency, which is critical for real-world applications;
- It performs comparative evaluation across features and scaling techniques for multiple ML classifiers, providing new insights into their effectiveness for Android malware detection. The analysis highlights the effects of preprocessing techniques;
- The study achieves 97.82% accuracy in malware detection and 96.09% in categorization, outperforming existing methods, including deep learning (DL) approaches;
- The framework offers a scalable and interpretable solution suitable for real-world applications, providing an efficient alternative for mobile security against evolving malware threats.

The remainder of this paper is organized as follows: Section 2 reviews related research on Android malware detection. Section 3 outlines the methodology, including dataset details, feature engineering techniques, and the ML classifiers used. Section 4 presents the results and compares them with those of existing studies, and Section 5 concludes the paper and provides suggestions for future research directions.

2. Literature Review

The rapid evolution of Android malware has driven extensive research into advanced detection and categorization methods. Various research projects have leveraged ML, DL, and innovative techniques to address challenges such as obfuscation, scalability, and computational complexity, thus effectively detecting Android malware. Ansori et al. [10] employed gain ratio feature selection and ensemble ML techniques, integrating RF, extra trees (ETs), K-nearest neighbors (KNN), Support Vector Machine (SVM), and naïve Bayes (NB) using the CICMalDroid2020 dataset [13]. Their ensemble classifiers (RF, ETs, and KNN) achieved 94.57% accuracy and a recall of 94.57%, demonstrating strong detection capabilities. However, the ensemble model's computational complexity increased training and inference time, making it less suitable for real-time applications.

Mohaisen et al. [14] introduced a behavior-based malware analysis system that leverages dynamic execution traces and ML for classification, achieving over 98% precision and recall in clustering tasks. This high-fidelity approach enhances resilience against evasion techniques, outperforming traditional static analysis. Similarly, Shen et al. [15] utilized complex information flows to detect malware, achieving 86.5% accuracy and improving resistance to obfuscation. Complementing these methods, Kang et al. [16] enhanced malware detection using static analysis with creator information, achieving 90% classification accuracy by analyzing permissions and behaviors.

Mohamed et al. [17] proposed an ML framework that compared static and dynamic API calls and permissions using KNN, naïve Bayes, SVM, and decision trees. Although SVM achieved 86% accuracy, the study did not categorize malware into different types, limiting its usefulness in threat intelligence. Additionally, challenges such as code obfuscation and the limitations of static and dynamic analysis were identified, emphasizing the need for novel methods that enhance adaptability to evolving malware.

Recent studies have explored DL techniques, such as convolutional neural networks (CNNs), long short-term memory (LSTM) networks, and transformer-based models, for Android malware detection using the CICMalDroid dataset. For example, Aboshady et al. [18] proposed a DL architecture that integrates static and dynamic analysis, utilizing base classifiers at each hidden layer to improve feature extraction. Their model achieved 92% precision and 91% recall, effectively addressing obfuscation, but it was constrained by binary classification, limiting its applicability to diverse malware families. Additionally, its reliance on large amounts of computational resources restricted real-time deployment.

Similarly, Wakhare et al. [19] applied LSTM-based models to analyze sequential patterns in API calls and developed a hybrid malware detection system that combined static and dynamic analyses. Their model demonstrates promising results, but at the cost of increased computational complexity and susceptibility to overfitting, reducing its scalability. Al-Fawa'reh et al. [20] introduced an innovative approach by converting binaries into grayscale images for classification using CNNs and transfer learning, achieving 95.9% accuracy on the CICMalDroid2020 dataset. Despite its success, this method was computationally expensive and limited to binary classification, requiring further enhancements to provide malware categorization.

A semi-supervised DL approach was introduced by Mahdavifar et al. [21], who employed pseudo-label deep neural networks (PLDNNs) to classify malware into five categories. Their study achieved an F1 score of 94%, demonstrating the potential of semi-supervised learning in cases involving limited labeled data. However, issues such as overfitting and the computational demands of neural networks restricted its real-world scalability. Moreover, Zhang [22] presents a CNN-BiGRU-based malware detection framework that leverages semantic API call sequences for improved accuracy. Using Skip-Gram embeddings and DL, the model achieves 98.28% accuracy. While effective, its static feature extraction and computational complexity may limit adaptability to evolving malware and real-time deployment.

Xu et al. [23] propose a graph convolutional network (GCN)-based approach to Android malware detection, leveraging API call graphs, sensitive permissions, and opcodes to capture complex malware behaviors. Their model integrates LSTM and attention mechanisms, achieving 98% accuracy. However, GCN models function as black boxes, with limited interpretability, and rely on complex graph-structured processing, making them computationally intensive and unsuitable for real-time deployment in resource-constrained environments. Moreover, the approach relies on static analysis, which may not fully capture dynamic malware behavior. Similarly, Liu et al. [24] introduce NT-GNN, a graph-based neural model that detects malware through network traffic flow analysis, achieving 97% accuracy. While effective, NT-GNN is resource intensive, relies solely on network traffic data, and is susceptible to malware evasion techniques that manipulate traffic patterns.

Giannakas et al. [25] evaluated 27 ML models and a deep neural network (DNN) regarding the usefulness in Android malware detection, using Optuna for hyperparameter tuning and SHAP for feature importance analysis. Their results show that a DNN outperforms shallow ML models, achieving 86% accuracy and an F1 score of 86.5%. However, their approach relies on computationally expensive DL models and binary classification, limiting real-world applicability.

Beyond traditional ML and DL techniques, some studies have explored hybrid approaches and proactive detection methods. Musikawan et al. [3] focused on malware detection during software design, that is, preventing threats before application deployment. They employed semantic query-based detection using reverse engineering, UML diagrams, and OWL ontologies on 600 Trojan-infected apps obtained from the CICMalDroid2020, achieving 92% precision and 91% recall. However, their approach faced scalability issues, as manual ontology construction was time consuming and required expert intervention.

While these methods show potential for robust malware detection, they often require substantial computational resources and large labeled datasets for effective training. Moreover, DL models tend to act as black boxes, limiting their interpretability in cybersecurity applications. Our study, in contrast, employs an ML-based model enhanced through effective feature selection techniques, which reduce the input dimensionality and overall feature set. This approach improves computational efficiency, maintains high detection accuracy, and leverages the inherent interpretability of ML models such as RF, making it more suitable for deployment in resource-constrained environments such as mobile devices.

The reviewed literature highlights significant advancements in ML and DL for Android malware detection. However, as summarized in Table 1, several challenges remain. Many studies focus on binary classification, limiting their ability to analyze diverse malware families. Others depend on computationally intensive deep learning models, making them less feasible for deployment on resource-constrained devices such as smartphones. Additionally, several models lack interpretability, which is critical in cybersecurity applications for trust and transparency in decision-making. Adaptability to evolving malware threats is also a recurring limitation. Studies that depend heavily on static analysis or predefined features often struggle to detect newly emerging variants. Furthermore, many approaches overlook feature selection and model scalability, both of which are essential for maintaining efficiency without compromising accuracy. These limitations are systematically compared in Table 1, which provides a concise overview of model types, classification capabilities, and technical constraints of representative studies.

Table 1. Comparative analysis of related studies.

Study	Classification Type	Model Type	Limitations
Ansori et al. [10]	Multi-class	Ensemble ML	High computational complexity; unsuitable for real-time use
Mohaisen et al. [14]	Clustering	ML (behavior-based)	Limited scalability; high overhead; complex data collection
Shen et al. [15]	Binary	ML (info flow)	Limited resistance to advanced obfuscation; limited adaptability
Kang et al. [16]	Binary	ML (static)	Limited adaptability to new threats
Mohamed et al. [17]	Binary	ML (API-based)	Limited adaptability to new threats
Aboshady et al. [18]	Binary	DL (CNN-based)	Resource-intensive
Wakhare et al. [19]	Binary	DL (LSTM-based)	Overfitting and scalability issues
Al-Fawa'reh et al. [20]	Binary	DL (image-based CNN)	High computational cost
Mahdavifar et al. [21]	Multi-class	DL (PLDNN—semi-supervised)	Overfitting; computational cost
Zhang [22]	Binary	DL (CNN-BiGRU)	Static-based; limited adaptability; computational cost; expensive inference
Xu et al. [23]	Binary	DL (GCN)	Black-box model; limited interpretability and real-time scalability; computational cost
Liu et al. [24]	Binary	DL (GNN—network traffic)	Susceptible to traffic manipulation and evasion-prone
Giannakas et al. [25]	Binary	ML + DL	High resource usage; interpretability limitations
Musikawan et al. [3]	Binary	Semantic + ontology-based	The manual process limits scalability

To address these gaps, our study introduces a two-step ML-based malware categorization framework that detects and classifies malware into distinct types. Our approach enhances efficiency, accuracy, and adaptability by incorporating optimized feature selection techniques, making it suitable for real-world cybersecurity applications.

3. Materials and Methods

The aim of this study is to employ ML to detect and classify Android malware effectively. This study proposed a two-stem Android malware categorization method that employs feature selection, feature scaling, and ML categorization. All these phases enhance malware detection and help to discover hazardous actions and categorize malware accurately. This approach improves model performance via feature selection and scaling and provides a robust basis for Android malware detection. Figure 1 shows a general schematic view of the malware detection and categorization techniques proposed in this research project. Feature selection, feature scaling, and malware detection and categorization are described in detail in the following subsections.

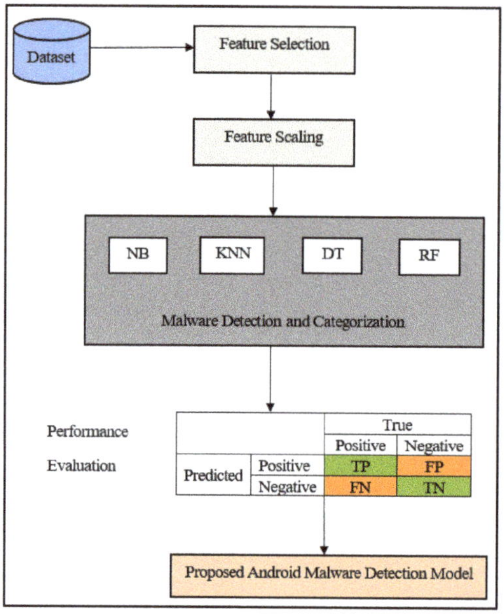

Figure 1. General schematic view of the study methodology.

Figure 2 shows a detailed schematic view of the proposed method, in which important features are first selected from an Android application sample. Then, these features are scaled. After that, an ML model is used to classify the Android application as either malware or benign. If the Android application is classified as malware, a second ML model classifies the malware as either adware, banking Trojan, SMS, or riskware.

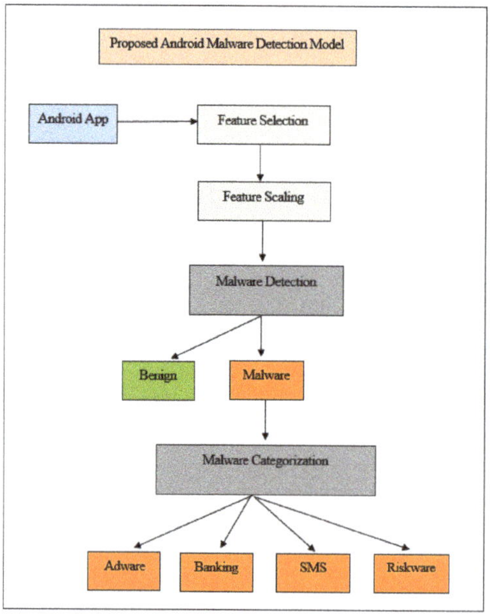

Figure 2. Detailed schematic view of the proposed framework.

3.1. Dataset Description

This study utilizes the CICMalDroid 2020 Android Malware dataset [13], which comprises 11,598 Android malware applications collected from diverse sources, including VirusTotal, Contagio Security Blog, AMD [26], MalDozer, and other academic and industrial cybersecurity datasets [27,28]. The dataset spans a broad spectrum of malware types, including adware, banking malware, SMS malware, riskware, and benign samples. Each malware category exhibits distinct behaviors and potential risks. Adware delivers intrusive advertisements through infected applications, frustrating users and potentially compromising their privacy. Banking malware impersonates legitimate banking applications to steal sensitive financial credentials. SMS malware manipulates or intercepts text messages, often defrauding users. Riskware, while initially legitimate software, can be exploited to cause harm or facilitate ransomware attacks. In contrast, benign samples consist of non-malicious applications that have been carefully verified to eliminate security concerns.

The dataset includes the following distribution across its five categories: 1253 adware samples; 2100 banking malware samples; 3904 SMS malware samples; 2546 riskware samples; and 1795 benign samples. This diversity ensures that the dataset is well suited for analyzing and detecting a wide range of Android malware threats. The main characteristics of the dataset are illustrated in Table 2.

Table 2. Dataset main characteristics.

Characteristic	Description
Total samples	11,598 Android applications
Class distribution	Benign: 1795 (15.5%) Adware: 1253 (10.8%) Banking malware: 2100 (18.1%) SMS malware: 3904 (33.6%) Riskware: 2546 (22.0%)
Malware ratio	84.5% malware, 15.5% benign
Malware examples	Adware (e.g., Airpush, Dowgin, Kemoge, Ewind) Banking malware (e.g., Bankbot, Anubis, Marche) SMS malware (e.g., FakeInst, Opfak, SmsSen) Riskware (e.g., Youmi, AdDown)
Feature categories	Static and dynamic features
Static features	Permissions, API calls, intents, activities, services, receivers, etc.
Dynamic features	Network traffic, system calls, CPU usage, memory usage, etc.
Features count	470 extracted features
Collection method	Real Android devices and emulators

3.2. Dataset Normalization

The dataset was normalized before training to increase malware classification accuracy and computational efficiency. We applied Z-score normalization and min–max normalization before training. These techniques ensure balanced feature scaling, reducing the risk of skewed learning and improving model generalization.

3.2.1. Z-Score Normalization

Z-score normalization standardizes feature values by transforming them to a mean of 0 and standard deviation of 1, preventing features with larger scales from dominating the learning process. It is based on the following formula: $Z = X - \mu/\sigma Z$. This method is particularly effective for high-dimensional datasets, such as Android malware classification, ensuring stable training across diverse feature distributions.

3.2.2. Min–Max Normalization

Min–max normalization scales feature values between 0 and 1, preserving relative feature relationships while preventing any single feature from dominating the model. This is particularly beneficial for distance-based models such as KNN, in which proportional scaling maintains data distribution with minimal distortion, enhancing classification accuracy. Both normalization methods were sequentially applied to the CICMalDroid2020 after feature selection but before training, as the dataset contained no missing values. Z-score normalization was used for RF, DT, and NB, while min–max normalization was applied for KNN. This step improves model generalization, reduces computational expense, and enhances detection accuracy. These steps proved essential in handling high-dimensional feature spaces, which is a key challenge in Android malware classification.

3.3. *Feature Selection*

We applied various feature selection techniques to rank features by importance and achieve dimensionality reduction [29]. This process offers several benefits, including reduced categorization time and model complexity, improved classifier accuracy, and minimal risk of overfitting [30]. The criteria for feature selection were based on statistical significance, feature importance, and redundancy reduction, allowing the model to focus on the most predictive features while minimizing noise. We utilized the chi-squared testing and select-from-model methods to optimize the performance of our ML models. These methods were selected to maximize classification accuracy, minimize computational burden, and improve model interpretation.

Chi-squared-based feature selection is used to identify key characteristics through statistical testing by analyzing the relationship between individual features and the target variable. The chi-squared values quantify the correlation between each attribute and the target, allowing the selection of the features with the highest scores [30]. Chi-squared testing was used to test the significance of each feature regarding malware classification. This method quantifies the dependence of the feature and target values, thus giving priority to the most informative ones. In addition, less informative attributes can be discarded. Dimensionality reduction also lowers the risk of overfitting, thus increasing model efficiency. The result is a high level of accuracy in the detection and categorization of malware. This filter-based approach is independent of specific classifiers and evaluates each feature as an isolated entity, making it a versatile method of initial feature evaluation. This technique identified the top 250 features of our method based on their statistical dependence on the target variable.

In contrast, SFM employs a model-centric approach to feature selection [31]. It uses a pre-defined relevance criterion to identify and eliminate uninformative features from the feature set. SFM uses the importance scores assigned to features by the classifier. This approach determines which features are most relevant to malware detection and classification and ensures that the model is trained on the attributes that will present the best predictive results. It then reduces the dataset by retaining only the features that are essential and discarding non-informative or repetitive attributes, thus enhancing computational efficiency without performance degradation. The combination of these attribute selection methods allows this approach to balance accuracy with computational efficiency within our framework. Such feature subsets grant optimized processing resources while enabling the effective detection and categorization of malware via ML models.

We tested malware detection and categorization models with varying numbers of reduced feature sets to compare the effectiveness of each set. By reducing the feature set, we observed improvements in both accuracy and efficiency. Removing less significant features allowed models to process data more effectively, leading to higher classification performance and reduced training time. This feature selection strategy ensures that our approach remains scalable and practical for real-world malware detection.

3.4. Feature Scaling

To enhance ML model performance in categorization, we tested two feature-scaling strategies: Z-score normalization [32] and min–max normalization [33]. Z-score normalization, also known as standardization, rescales data so that they have a mean of 0 and a standard deviation of 1. This approach is particularly effective for datasets with a normal distribution or when it is necessary to compare data points relative to the dataset's mean and range. By standardizing the data, this method ensures that features with different scales do not disproportionately influence the model. In contrast, min–max normalization rescales data to fit within a specified range, typically between 0 and 1. This method is advantageous for datasets with features on varying scales, as it uniformly adjusts all values to the same range. Min–max normalization is especially useful in algorithms like neural networks and K-nearest neighbors, where the size of data values can significantly impact performance. Both strategies play critical roles in preprocessing, ensuring that ML algorithms can effectively handle data with diverse distributions and scales. By applying these techniques, we aimed to increase the model's performance, accuracy, and reliability in terms of malware categorization [34].

3.5. Malware Detection and Categorization

After applying feature selection and scaling, we apply malware detection and categorization. During this phase, malware detection and categorization are designed as two distinct but interconnected stages. This approach is intended to systematically classify Android applications based on their behavior. The process begins with a broad categorization to determine whether an application is malware or benign, followed by a more detailed categorization to identify the specific type of malware at work, as outlined in the following subsections.

3.5.1. Malware Detection

This stage focuses on malware detection, in which programs in the dataset are classified as either benign or malware. This binary categorization assigns a label of "1" to malware and "2" to benign applications. During this stage, malware types, such as adware, banking malware, SMS malware, and riskware, are grouped into a single "malware" class. This simplification allows the detection process to focus solely on determining whether a program is malicious or safe. We evaluated four well-known ML classifiers (NB, KNN, DT, and RF) for malware detection, assessing their performance using various feature selection and scaling techniques on the CICMalDroid2020 dataset. In the following text, each selected classifier is described.

Naïve Bayes (NB): The NB classifier is simple, efficient, and based on probability theory. It assumes that features are conditionally independent, making it well suited for high-dimensional datasets, such as Android malware detection. However, its performance may be limited if the features are highly correlated, as the independence assumption is often violated in complex datasets [35].

K-nearest neighbors (KNN): KNN classifies malware by comparing unknown applications to the most similar samples in the dataset, making it useful for identifying anomalies. Its ability to detect outliers helps distinguish suspicious applications from benign ones.

However, KNN's performance relies on the choice of the optimal "K" parameter and requires feature scaling to ensure accurate distance computation. Despite its sensitivity to noise, KNN remains a practical choice for initial malware detection due to its simplicity and effectiveness in capturing local patterns [36].

Decision tree (DT): DT classifiers are known for their simplicity, interpretability, and ability to handle both numerical and categorical data without requiring feature scaling. By breaking down complex decision-making processes into simple, understandable rules, DT helps identify the key patterns distinguishing malware types. While it performs well in terms of identifying Android malware, DT is prone to overfitting, especially with noisy or unbalanced datasets, which can limit its accuracy as compared to ensemble methods [37].

Random forest (RF): RF is an ensemble method that builds multiple decision trees using random subsets of the dataset and combines their outputs to provide improved accuracy and robustness. This approach reduces overfitting and excels at capturing complex, non-linear relationships between features, making RF particularly effective for malware detection and categorization. Its stability across various feature engineering techniques and ability to process high-dimensional data make it a powerful and reliable tool for use in Android malware detection [38].

This initial detection stage is critical for real-world applications, in which the rapid identification of potentially harmful programs is essential. By streamlining the categorization process at this level, the system enhances the efficiency and accuracy of detection models. Malware-identified programs can then undergo further evaluation in the second stage, in which a more detailed categorization is performed. This layered approach provides an effective first line of defense, ensuring quick and reliable decisions about program safety.

3.5.2. Malware Categorization

Malware categorization follows the initial malware detection stage, categorizing malware into specific types, such as adware, banking malware, SMS malware, or riskware. This stage transforms malware analysis into a multi-class categorization problem, relying on each malware type's distinct behaviors and properties. For this stage, we used the NB, KNN, DT, and RF classifiers. Accurate categorization is essential in developing effective responses, as each category poses unique risks and operates differently than the others. By identifying the specific type of malware at work, cybersecurity systems can deploy targeted defenses and mitigation strategies to address the associated threats effectively.

3.6. Performance Evaluation

The proposed framework is evaluated for Android malware detection and categorization using the following key metrics: categorization accuracy, recall, precision, and F1 score [39]. Categorization accuracy measures the proportion of correct predictions across all instances. We also examined precision and recall, which evaluate the model's ability to correctly identify positive instances (malware) while minimizing false positives and false negatives. The F1 score is the harmonic mean of precision and recall. The F1 score emphasizes the importance of correctly identifying actual positives while reducing the impact of false positives and false negatives, making it particularly valuable in this context.

We split the dataset into 70% for training and 30% for testing to ensure robust evaluation and generalization. This split allowed the model to train on substantial data while testing its performance on unseen samples. This approach helps prevent overfitting and ensures that the model performs well on new Android malware samples, reflecting real-world evaluation criteria. This evaluation method provides a realistic and reliable comparison of the ML models' capabilities in detecting and categorizing Android malware.

In the next section, we present and analyze the experimental results obtained in our study. We thoroughly assess the effectiveness of the proposed methodology using performance metrics and conduct a comparative analysis to contrast our findings with those reported in previous research.

3.7. Experiment Environment

The experimental setup for this study utilized a dataset comprising Android applications categorized as either benign or malicious. All experiments were implemented using Python version: 3.11.5 with Anaconda version: 23.7.4, ensuring an efficient and reproducible experimental pipeline. An Acer personal computer with an Intel Core i7 12th Gen processor and 16 GB of RAM was used in the experiments. This study was conducted in November 2024, when the dataset was preprocessed and ML models were trained and evaluated.

4. Results

In this section, we evaluate the detection and categorization of Android malware with different ML classifiers: naïve Bayes (NB), K-nearest neighbors (KNN), decision tree (DT), and random forest (RF). We assess the models using various feature selection and scaling techniques applied to the CICMalDroid 2020 dataset, measuring accuracy, precision, recall, F1 score, and training time.

4.1. Malware Detection Results

To detect malware, we evaluated four classifiers: NB, KNN, DT, and RF. The results, presented in Tables 3–6, show the performance of these models across different feature selection and scaling methods. Chi-squared feature selection with 120 features and no feature scaling yielded the highest accuracy of 97.82% with RF (Table 3, Figure 3). This excellent performance remained consistent, with an accuracy of 97.79%, even when applying Z-score or min–max normalization. Random forest's ability to handle diverse data is attributed to its stability across different feature engineering techniques.

Table 3. Accuracy of ML models for malware detection.

Feature Selection Method	Feature Scaling Method											
	None				Z-Score Normalization				Min–Max Normalization			
	NB	KNN	DT	RF	NB	KNN	DT	RF	NB	KNN	DT	RF
All features	42.04	91.87	96.55	97.41	91.47	93.68	96.55	97.41	91.49	93.76	96.55	97.44
Chi-squared	86.72	91.75	96.44	97.82	92.64	94.45	96.49	97.79	92.50	94.34	96.47	97.79
SFM	85.03	91.90	96.12	97.61	92.56	95.11	96.18	97.59	92.56	95.29	96.12	97.61

Table 4. Precision of ML models for malware detection.

Feature Selection Method	Feature Scaling Method											
	None				Z-Score Normalization				Min–Max Normalization			
	NB	KNN	DT	RF	NB	KNN	DT	RF	NB	KNN	DT	RF
All features	86.05	91.49	96.60	97.39	91.11	93.43	96.60	97.39	91.02	93.60	96.60	97.42
Chi-squared	88.32	91.32	96.47	97.79	92.36	94.27	96.53	97.76	92.24	94.14	96.49	97.76
SFM	87.91	91.53	96.15	97.59	92.49	94.98	96.21	97.56	92.54	95.22	96.15	97.59

Table 5. Recall of ML models for malware detection.

Feature Selection Method	Feature Scaling Method											
	None				Z-Score Normalization				Min–Max Normalization			
	NB	KNN	DT	RF	NB	KNN	DT	RF	NB	KNN	DT	RF
All features	42.04	91.87	96.55	97.41	91.47	93.68	96.55	97.41	91.49	93.76	96.55	97.44
Chi-squared	86.72	91.75	96.44	97.82	92.64	94.45	96.49	97.79	92.50	94.34	96.47	97.79
SFM	85.03	91.90	96.12	97.61	92.56	95.11	96.18	97.59	92.56	95.29	96.12	97.61

Table 6. F1 score of ML models for malware detection.

Feature Selection Method	Feature Scaling Method											
	None				Z-Score Normalization				Min–Max Normalization			
	NB	KNN	DT	RF	NB	KNN	DT	RF	NB	KNN	DT	RF
All features	46.64	91.61	96.57	97.36	90.50	93.33	96.57	97.36	90.68	93.33	96.57	97.39
Chi-squared	87.35	91.43	96.45	97.79	92.45	94.19	96.51	97.76	92.34	94.08	96.48	97.76
SFM	86.07	91.64	96.13	97.58	92.52	94.92	96.19	97.55	92.55	95.05	96.13	97.58

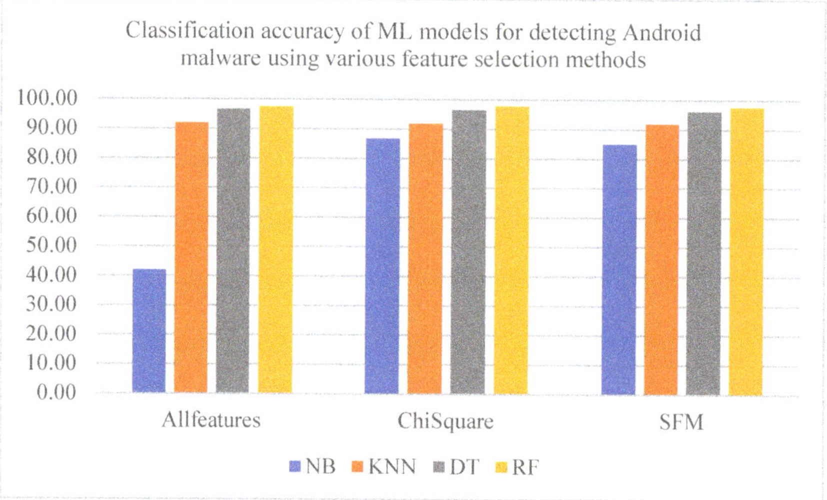

Figure 3. Categorization accuracy of ML models for detecting Android malware using various feature selection methods.

RF demonstrated outstanding accuracy, recall, and F1 scores, ranging from 97.39% to 97.79% (Tables 3–6). It performed consistently well across all metrics, with minimal false positives and false negatives when detecting malware and benign applications. This balanced performance highlights its reliability as a robust malware detection tool.

Feature engineering significantly improved the performance of KNN, which is sensitive to high-dimensional input. For instance, using chi-squared feature selection (Table 3), NB accuracy improved from 42.04% with all features to 86.72%. Similarly, feature scaling substantially impacted distance-based algorithms like KNN. Using SFM feature selection with min–max normalization, KNN accuracy increased to 95.29% (Table 3). These improvements underline the importance of normalizing features for distance-based methods of KNN.

In contrast, feature scaling had little effect on tree-based algorithms like DT and RF, as these models are inherently less sensitive to variations in feature scale. DT consistently achieved accuracy above 96% in all setups. However, RF outperformed it, demonstrating the advantages of ensemble methods.

These results confirm that our malware detection approach is highly effective. The RF model, in particular, excelled in accurately identifying both benign and malicious Android applications, showcasing its potential for real-world cybersecurity applications.

Moreover, we experimented with oversampling and undersampling techniques to assess the impact of class imbalance in the malware detection task. However, balancing led to a drop in detection accuracy from 97.8% to 95.08%, indicating that oversampling introduced noise rather than improving classification performance. Since the benign class constitutes around 15.5% of the dataset, the imbalance is moderate, and tree-based models like RF are inherently robust to such imbalances. Additionally, evaluation metrics such as precision, recall, and F1 score (97.7%, 97.82%, and 97.7%) confirmed that the model performs well across both classes. Therefore, balancing was unnecessary, and the original dataset was retained to ensure optimal performance.

Table 7 presents the training time results for different ML models used in malware detection with both 470 features and a reduced 120-feature set. These findings highlight how dimensionality reduction impacts training time across different learning algorithms, which is crucial for computational efficiency in real-world applications.

Table 7. Training time (in seconds) of ML models for malware detection using all features and reduced features.

Features Type	NB	KNN	DT	RF
All features (470 features)	0.066	0.001	0.800	2.108
Reduced reatures (120 features)	0.015	0.001	0.467	2.115

NB showed a 4.4× reduction in training time, decreasing from 0.066 s to 0.015 s, as it relies on conditional probability computations, making it highly sensitive to the number of input features. In contrast, KNN, a lazy learning algorithm, remained unchanged at 0.001 s, as it does not build an explicit model during training, and the reduction of features does not directly impact training time, emphasizing its insensitivity to feature dimensionality as a non-parametric model.

For DT, training time decreased from 0.800 s to 0.467 s, demonstrating how fewer features lead to fewer splits in tree-based methods, reducing computational overhead as it initially splits the feature space iteratively to build a hierarchical tree. Fewer splits mean fewer features, and a simple tree, so there is a reduced computational overhead. However, RF training time remained nearly unchanged, increasing slightly from 2.108 s to 2.115 s. This is due to RF's random feature selection mechanism, which inherently optimizes feature subsets, making explicit dimensionality reduction less impactful. Additionally, RF's complexity depends more on the number of trees rather than the number of features. Thus, it demonstrates less loss of RF's training time on feature reduction compared with DT.

Overall, the results of these demonstrate that the effect of dimensionality on different ML models varies. Probabilistic models like NB and decision-tree-based models like DT benefit substantially from feature reduction in terms of training time. On the other hand, KNN, which is a lazy learning model, is not affected and ensemble models such as RF are hardly influenced.

4.2. Malware Categorization Results

After detecting Android malware, we evaluated the models for multi-class categorization into banking malware, SMS malware, riskware, and adware, using the same ML models and feature engineering methods. The results presented in Tables 8–11 and Figure 4, show that RF consistently outperformed all models, achieving 96.09% accuracy with SFM feature selection (120 features) and Z-score normalization. Its strong performance across accuracy, recall, and F1 score (95.44–96.13%) highlights its ability to distinguish between malware types while handling high-dimensional data effectively and identifying important features without requiring explicit feature selection.

Table 8. Accuracy of ML models for malware categorization.

Feature Selection Method	Feature Scaling Method											
	None				Z-Score Normalization				Min–Max Normalization			
	NB	KNN	DT	RF	NB	KNN	DT	RF	NB	KNN	DT	RF
All features	55.49	88.34	93.47	95.65	65.11	90.72	93.40	95.65	66.51	90.96	93.57	95.72
Chi-squared	54.98	88.24	92.89	95.44	58.86	91.77	92.86	95.48	58.01	91.33	92.83	95.48
SFM	54.34	88.37	93.34	96.06	58.86	91.47	93.27	96.09	58.42	91.77	93.34	96.06

Table 9. Precision of ML models for malware categorization.

Feature Selection Method	Feature Scaling Method											
	None				Z-Score Normalization				Min–Max Normalization			
	NB	KNN	DT	RF	NB	KNN	DT	RF	NB	KNN	DT	RF
All features	60.43	88.27	93.44	95.70	69.66	90.68	93.37	95.70	72.47	90.99	93.54	95.76
Chi-squared	60.12	88.21	92.88	95.51	63.20	91.75	92.85	95.53	62.11	91.36	92.81	95.53
SFM	58.37	88.30	93.34	96.10	62.46	91.51	93.27	96.13	61.99	91.84	93.34	96.10

Table 10. Recall of ML models for malware categorization.

Feature Selection Method	Feature Scaling Method											
	None				Z-Score Normalization				Min–Max Normalization			
	NB	KNN	DT	RF	NB	KNN	DT	RF	NB	KNN	DT	RF
All features	55.49	88.34	93.47	95.65	65.11	90.72	93.40	95.65	66.51	90.96	93.57	95.72
Chi-squared	54.98	88.24	92.89	95.44	58.86	91.77	92.86	95.48	58.01	91.33	92.83	95.48
SFM	54.34	88.37	93.34	96.06	58.86	91.47	93.27	96.09	58.42	91.77	93.34	96.06

Table 11. F1 score of ML models for malware categorization.

Feature Selection Method	Feature Scaling Method											
	None				Z-Score Normalization				Min–Max Normalization			
	NB	KNN	DT	RF	NB	KNN	DT	RF	NB	KNN	DT	RF
All features	50.49	88.25	93.45	95.65	62.14	90.66	93.38	95.65	64.13	90.91	93.55	95.72
Chi-squared	49.66	88.16	92.88	95.45	54.85	91.73	92.85	95.48	53.85	91.31	92.81	95.48
SFM	48.99	88.29	93.33	96.06	55.03	91.45	93.27	96.09	54.62	91.76	93.34	96.06

RF maintained stable accuracy across both full and reduced feature sets, ranging from approximately 95.65% to 96.09%, demonstrating its robustness, whereas other models were more sensitive to feature selection and scaling. For instance, NB accuracy improved from 55.49% (no scaling) to 66.51% (min–max normalization), showing the importance of feature engineering for models dependent on feature distributions (Table 8). Similarly, KNN achieved its highest accuracy (91.77%) using chi-squared feature selection and min–max normalization, confirming the effectiveness of feature selection techniques. DT models consistently performed above 92% but were outperformed by RF, reinforcing the superiority of ensemble methods for complex categorization tasks.

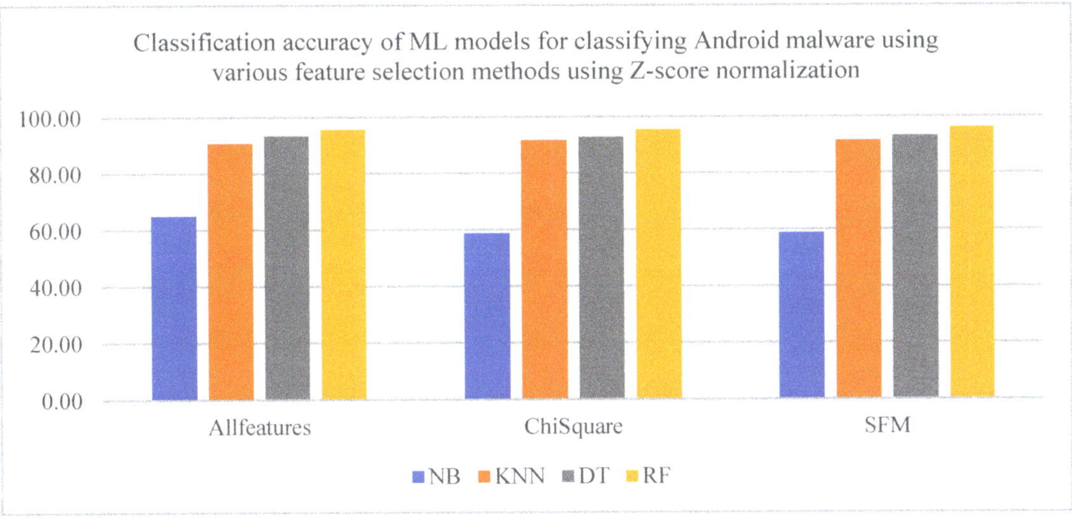

Figure 4. Categorization accuracy of ML models for classifying Android malware using various feature selection methods using Z-score normalization.

The performance gap between RF in binary detection (97.82%) and multi-class categorization (96.09%) was minimal. This small difference highlights the model's ability to both detect malware and accurately differentiate between various malware types. In conclusion, our malware categorization approach demonstrated high accuracy and resilience across all malware categories. The RF model, in particular, performed exceptionally well, reliably classifying Android malware with precision. This accurate categorization is crucial for identifying threats and enabling the development of targeted responses in real-world mobile security applications.

Table 12 presents training time results for malware categorization, providing insights into the computational efficiency of different ML classifiers when trained on 470 features versus a reduced set of 120 features. The results indicate that dimensionality reduction impacts training time differently across classifiers.

Table 12. Training time (in seconds) of ML models for malware categorization using all features and reduced features.

Features Type	NB	KNN	DT	RF
All features (470 features)	0.045	0.001	0.493	1.359
Reduced features (120 features)	0.014	0.001	0.218	1.518

For NB, reducing the feature set led to a significant decrease in training time from 0.045 s to 0.014 s, consistent with its probabilistic nature, where fewer features directly reduce computational overhead. Similar to malware detection, KNN's training time remained unchanged at 0.001 s, as it is a lazy learning algorithm that does not perform complex computations during training. Instead, KNN stores data and defers processing to the prediction stage, making training time independent of feature dimensionality.

The training time of the DT classifier decreases considerably when the feature set is reduced from 0.493 to 0.218 s, respectively. The reduction is significant and warrants the high dependency of computational complexity of DT on feature dimensionality. In addition, in malware categorization, rather than malware detection, the reduction in training time is even more significant (from 0.800 to 0.467 s). Thus, it seems that the distributions of feature importance and feature importance may vary slightly for these two tasks, so feature reduction can substantially influence training efficiency.

Interestingly, random forest (RF) increased training time from 1.359 s to 1.518 s when the feature set was reduced. Unlike in malware detection, where RF's training time remained stable, this result suggests that RF's random feature selection mechanism requires additional computation when fewer features are available. Since RF builds multiple decision trees by selecting a subset of features at each split, reducing the total feature set may increase processing overhead rather than decrease it.

Several key observations regarding the effect of feature reduction on the training time of different machine learning models are shown by the results. NB and DT benefit the most from feature reduction, significantly lowering training time. While KNN does not build a model during training, it is entirely unaffected by the number of features and remains unaffected. RF has a higher training time with a reduced feature set, which is a good indication that its internal random feature selection needs more work with fewer features and is not the case. Additionally, malware categorization generally requires less training time than malware detection, possibly due to differences in data distribution, feature relevance, or classification complexity. These findings highlight the importance of algorithm-specific evaluations of feature selection strategies, as dimensionality reduction does not always lead to improved training efficiency across all ML models.

5. Discussion

This study demonstrates that ML-based malware detection and categorization can achieve a good balance between accuracy, interpretability, and computational efficiency, making it suitable for deployment on resource-constrained devices such as mobile phones. Among the tested classifiers, RF consistently outperformed the others, achieving 97.82% accuracy in binary detection and 96.09% in multi-class categorization. Its ensemble learning capabilities and robustness to high-dimensional data contributed to its superior performance while avoiding the high computational overhead of deep learning models. Interpretability was maintained through the use of classical ML models like decision trees and RF, which offer transparent decision-making via feature importance—enhancing trust for security analysts. To further improve efficiency, feature selection techniques (chi-squared and select-from-model) were employed to reduce the feature set from 470 to 120, significantly shortening training times for models such as naïve Bayes and decision trees without sacrificing accuracy. Additionally, the use of a two-phase framework—beginning with binary malware detection followed by multi-class categorization—allowed for rapid initial filtering with the option for deeper analysis, supporting flexible, real-time deployment based on available system resources.

While DL models have demonstrated high accuracy in malware detection, they require substantial computational resources and often act as black-box models, limiting interpretability. In contrast, our study shows that well-optimized ML models can rival DL approaches while being more suitable for real-time applications in mobile security. A comprehensive comparison with previous research on Android malware detection and categorization emphasizes the effectiveness of our proposed approach. Table 13 summarizes this comparison, including various similar studies that proposed Android malware detection methods. Our proposed method outperforms several state-of-the-art ML and DL approaches.

Table 13. Comparative analysis between our proposed method and previous research for Android malware detection.

Year	Reference No.	Methods	Accuracy
2022	[6]	DNN	93.5
2022	[8]	Ontological semantic environment	92
2021	[7]	LSTM	94.22
2021	[9]	KNN, SVM, NB, DT	86
2020	[10]	CNN	95.9
2024	Proposed method	SFM, RF	97.82

Ansori et al. [10] employed an ensemble method combining RF, extra trees, and KNN classifiers, achieving an accuracy of 94.57% for multi-class categorization (five classes). Our RF strategy exceeded this by nearly three percentage points, demonstrating the effectiveness of our feature selection and model optimization techniques.

Recent studies have also explored DL methods. For instance, Aboshady et al. [18] employed a DNN for binary categorization in 2022, achieving 93.5% accuracy, while Al-Fawa'reh et al. [20] used a CNN in 2020, attaining 95.9% accuracy in binary categorization. Despite their potential, our methodology surpassed these DL approaches by 4.32 and 1.92 percentage points, respectively. This highlights the ability of well-optimized classical ML techniques to rival and even outperform DL models in certain contexts.

Mahdavifar et al. [21], in their 2020 study using the same dataset (CICMalDroid2020), achieved a multi-class categorization accuracy of 96.7% with a semi-supervised PLDNN. While our multi-class categorization accuracy of 96.09% is slightly lower, the RF model offers key advantages, including lower computational demands and greater interpretability, making it a more practical choice for resource-constrained environments. Wakhare et al. [19] applied LSTM networks combined with the synthetic minority over-sampling technique (SMOTE) in 2021, achieving a binary categorization accuracy of 94.22%. Similarly, in 2022, Musikawan et al. [3] achieved 92% binary categorization accuracy using the ontological semantic environment method. While these methods provide unique insights, our categorization accuracy remains notably higher.

Zhang et al. [22] proposed a malware detection framework that achieved 98.28% accuracy. However, its reliance on static features and predefined API sequences limits its adaptability to evolving malware. Its high computational cost also hinders real-time deployment. In contrast, our approach optimizes feature selection and leverages RF, ensuring high accuracy with low computational overhead, making it more efficient and scalable.

Our malware detection and categorization system is not only accurate but also balanced, achieving 97.82% accuracy in binary categorization and 96.09% accuracy in multi-class categorization. By employing chi-squared and SFM feature selection techniques, combined with feature scaling experiments, we enhanced the efficiency of our framework. This is particularly valuable for real-world applications, such as mobile devices, in which computational resources are often limited. In conclusion, our comparison with previous studies (summarized in Table 13) demonstrates that our methodology is a highly effective solution for Android malware detection and categorization. It delivers state-of-the-art accuracy while remaining efficient, interpretable, and versatile in both binary and multi-class settings. These qualities position our approach as a significant contribution to the field, with promising applications in mobile security.

The computational efficiency of the proposed framework is critical for real-time deployment, particularly on resource-constrained mobile devices. Our training time analysis demonstrates that NB and DT significantly benefit from feature reduction, reducing computational overhead and making them more suitable for real-time applications. KNN, while it maintains a constant training time, has a computationally expensive inference phase (O(n × k)), making it less ideal for mobile deployment. On the other hand, despite its high accuracy, RF experiences a slight increase in training time when features are reduced, likely due to its internal feature selection mechanism requiring additional processing.

To further assess real-time feasibility, we analyzed the time complexity of the RF model (O(t × n × log n)), and the complexity of RF inference is $O(t \times d)$O(t × d), where d is the number of features. While RF is more computationally demanding than other classifiers, it remains stable, highly accurate, and robust across feature selection methods, making it a strong candidate for mobile security applications. Optimizations such as model pruning, quantization, and federated learning can be explored to reduce computational overhead while maintaining detection accuracy to enhance real-time performance. Future research should focus on deploying RF on mobile devices, assessing its runtime efficiency, memory footprint, and energy consumption to ensure practical implementation in resource-constrained environments.

The practical implementation of our proposed malware detection and categorization framework can significantly enhance mobile security in various real-world applications. Due to its lightweight computational requirements, the system is well suited for integration into mobile security solutions, antivirus applications, and endpoint protection systems. Security firms can deploy the framework within mobile operating systems or cloud-based security platforms to detect and classify Android malware efficiently.

6. Conclusions

This study presents an ML-based framework for Android malware detection and categorization, achieving 97.82% accuracy in detection and 96.09% in multi-class categorization, surpassing similar studies. The approach effectively identifies and classifies malware by integrating feature selection, feature engineering, and a two-step categorization process. Tested on the CICMalDroid 2020 dataset with 11,598 samples, the framework demonstrates strong generalizability across malware variants.

Optimizing chi-squared and SFM feature selection reduced features from 470 to 120, improving computational efficiency, while feature scaling further refined performance. The two-step classification process enables rapid threat detection and detailed malware analysis, making it suitable for real-world security applications requiring speed and precision. The framework's robust performance across different feature selection and scaling methods, particularly with RF, highlights its adaptability across Android environments and effectiveness in addressing evolving malware threats. These findings establish our approach as a scalable, interpretable, and high-performing solution for Android malware detection.

7. Limitations and Future Work

While our model achieves strong performance on the CICMalDroid 2020 dataset, its ability to detect zero-day malware and evolving threats requires further validation. Future research should explore transfer learning with multiple datasets and adaptive learning techniques such as incremental model updates and real-time data augmentation to improve generalization. Additionally, cross-dataset evaluation could enhance robustness while reducing computational overhead. Additionally, the model may require fine-tuning when deployed in different environments, as variations in malware characteristics could impact classification performance.

To improve real-world applicability, future work should focus on real-time mobile implementation with optimized computational efficiency. Exploring the evolution of feature relevance as new malware types emerge could lead to more adaptable feature selection techniques, ensuring continued model effectiveness. Explainable AI (XAI) can further enhance interpretability, making malware detection more transparent and reliable. Integrating static and dynamic analysis could improve detection accuracy, particularly against sophisticated malware variants.

Our current study focuses on static analysis, which may have limitations against malware using code obfuscation or runtime evasive techniques. Integrating dynamic analysis could improve detection rates by analyzing malware behavior during execution. Moreover, evaluating real-time detection on live malware samples will further validate model robustness.

Moreover, while this study demonstrates that well-optimized machine learning models can achieve high accuracy in malware detection and categorization, we recognize the potential benefits of DL approaches. Future work could explore hybrid models that combine feature-based ML methods with DL architectures such as CNNs, LSTMs, or transformers to enhance malware detection capabilities further. Leveraging pretrained DL models and transfer learning techniques may help reduce computational overhead while improving generalization to new malware variants. Integrating DL models with real-time detection systems could enhance adaptability to evolving malware threats.

While the CICMalDroid 2020 dataset provides diverse Android malware samples, evolving threats require continuous dataset updates to maintain detection effectiveness. Future research should incorporate recent malware datasets or incremental learning techniques for adaptability. Evaluating real-time detection on live malware samples can further validate model robustness. Additionally, federated learning could enable models to learn dynamically from distributed mobile devices while preserving privacy. These advancements will help ensure the framework remains adaptive, scalable, and effective in addressing future malware threats.

Author Contributions: Conceptualization, A.A.; literature review, R.A.A.; methodology, A.A.; implementation, R.A.A.; validation, R.A.A.; formal analysis, R.A.A.; writing—original draft, R.A.A.; writing—review and editing, A.A.; visualization, R.A.A.; supervision, A.A.; project administration, A.A.; funding acquisition, A.A. All authors have read and agreed to the published version of the manuscript.

Funding: The authors are grateful to the Deanship of Scientific Research, King Saud University, for funding through the Vice Deanship of Scientific Research Chair.

Data Availability Statement: The original contributions presented in this study are included in the article. Further inquiries can be directed to the corresponding authors.

Acknowledgments: While preparing this work, the authors used OpenAI ChatGPT 4o to revise and enhance the language of this manuscript. The authors have reviewed and edited the content as needed and take full responsibility for the content of the published article.

Conflicts of Interest: The authors declare no conflicts of interest.

References

Cybersecurity Ventures. Cybercrime to Cost the World $8 Trillion Annually in 2023. *Cybercrime Magazine*. November 2022. Available online: https://cybersecurityventures.com/cybercrime-to-cost-the-world-8-trillion-annually-in-2023/ (accessed on 17 December 2024).

Goodfellow, I.; Bengio, Y.; Courville, A. *Deep Learning*; MIT Press: Cambridge, MA, USA, 2016.

Musikawan, P.; Kongsorot, Y.; You, I.; So-In, C. An Enhanced Deep Learning Neural Network for the Detection and Identification of Android Malware. *IEEE Internet Things J.* **2023**, *10*, 8560–8577. [CrossRef]

Baker del Aguila, R.; Contreras Pérez, C.D.; Silva-Trujillo, A.G.; Cuevas-Tello, J.C.; Nunez-Varela, J. Static Malware Analysis Using Low-Parameter Machine Learning Models. *Computers* **2024**, *13*, 59. [CrossRef]

5. Gupta, R.; Sharma, K.; Garg, R.K. Innovative Approach to Android Malware Detection: Prioritizing Critical Features Using Rough Set Theory. *Electronics* **2024**, *13*, 482. [CrossRef]
6. Panja, S.; Mondal, S.; Nag, A.; Singh, J.P.; Saikia, M.J.; Barman, A.K. An Efficient Malware Detection Approach Based on Machine Learning Feature Influence Techniques for Resource-Constrained Devices. *IEEE Access* **2025**, *1*, 12647–12665. [CrossRef]
7. Kazi, M.A. Detecting Malware C&C Communication Traffic Using Artificial Intelligence Techniques. *J. Cybersecur. Priv.* **2025**, *5*, 4 [CrossRef]
8. Akhtar, M.S.; Feng, T. Malware Analysis and Detection Using Machine Learning Algorithms. *Symmetry* **2022**, *14*, 2304. [CrossRef]
9. Lin, Y.; Liu, T.; Liu, W.; Wang, Z.; Li, L.; Xu, G.; Wang, H. Dataset Bias in Android Malware Detection. *arXiv* **2022**, arXiv:2205.15532 [CrossRef]
10. Ansori, D.B.; Slamet, J.; Ghufron, M.Z.; Putra, M.A.R.; Ahmad, T. Android Malware Classification Using Gain Ratio and Ensembled Machine Learning. *Int. J. Saf. Secur. Eng.* **2024**, *14*, 259–266. [CrossRef]
11. Muhammad, S.; Tiang, J.J.; Wong, S.K.; Rambe, A.H.; Adam, I.; Smida, A.; Waly, M.I.; Iqbal, A.; Abubakar, A.S.; Mohd Yasin, M.N Harvesting Systems for RF Energy: Trends, Challenges, Techniques, and Tradeoffs. *Electronics* **2022**, *11*, 959. [CrossRef]
12. Ni, T.; Lan, G.; Wang, J.; Zhao, Q.; Xu, W. Eavesdropping Mobile App Activity via Radio-Frequency Energy Harvesting In Proceedings of the 32nd USENIX Security Symposium (USENIX Security 23), Anaheim, CA, USA, 9–11 August 2023; pp. 3511–3528.
13. Mahdavifar, S.; Alhadidi, D.; Ghorbani, A.A. Effective and Efficient Hybrid Android Malware Classification Using Pseudo-Label Stacked Auto-Encoder. *J. Netw. Syst. Manag.* **2022**, *30*, 22. [CrossRef]
14. Mohaisen, A.; Alrawi, O.; Mohaisen, M. AMAL: High-Fidelity, Behavior-Based Automated Malware Analysis and Classification *Comput. Secur.* **2015**, *52*, 251–266. [CrossRef]
15. Shen, F.; Del Vecchio, J.; Mohaisen, A.; Ko, S.Y.; Ziarek, L. Android Malware Detection Using Complex-Flows. *IEEE Trans. Mob. Comput.* **2018**, *18*, 1231–1245. [CrossRef]
16. Kang, H.; Jang, J.W.; Mohaisen, A.; Kim, H.K. Detecting and Classifying Android Malware Using Static Analysis Along with Creator Information. *Int. J. Distrib. Sens. Netw.* **2015**, *11*, 479174. [CrossRef]
17. Mohamed, S.E.D.; Ashaf, M.; Ehab, A.; Shereef, O.; Metwaie, H.; Amer, E. Detecting Malicious Android Applications Based on API Calls and Permissions Using Machine Learning Algorithms. In Proceedings of the 2021 International Mobile, Intelligent, and Ubiquitous Computing Conference (MIUCC 2021), Cairo, Egypt, 26–27 May 2021; pp. 223–228. [CrossRef]
18. Aboshady, D.; Ghannam, N.; Elsayed, E.; Diab, L. The Malware Detection Approach in the Design of Mobile Applications *Symmetry* **2022**, *14*, 839. [CrossRef]
19. Wakhare, A.A. Malware Detection in Android Platform Using DNN. Master's Thesis, National College of Ireland, Dublin, Ireland, 2021
20. Al-Fawa'reh, M.; Saif, A.; Jafar, M.T.; Elhassan, A. Malware Detection by Eating a Whole APK. In Proceedings of the 2020 15th International Conference for Internet Technology and Secured Transactions (ICITST 2020), London, UK, 8–10 December 2020 [CrossRef]
21. Mahdavifar, S.; Kadir, A.F.A.; Fatemi, R.; Alhadidi, D.; Ghorbani, A.A. Dynamic Android Malware Category Classification Using Semi-Supervised Deep Learning. In Proceedings of the 18th IEEE International Conference on Dependable, Autonomic, and Secure Computing (DASC), Calgary, AB, Canada, 17–22 August 2020; pp. 654–661. [CrossRef]
22. Zhang, Y.; Yang, S.; Xu, L.; Li, X.; Zhao, D. A Malware Detection Framework Based on Semantic Information of Behavioral Features. *Appl. Sci.* **2023**, *13*, 12528. [CrossRef]
23. Xu, Q.; Zhao, D.; Yang, S.; Xu, L.; Li, X. Android Malware Detection Based on Behavioral-Level Features with Graph Convolutional Networks. *Electronics* **2023**, *12*, 4817. [CrossRef]
24. Liu, T.; Li, Z.; Long, H.; Bilal, A. NT-GNN: Network Traffic Graph for 5G Mobile IoT Android Malware Detection. *Electronics* **2023**, *12*, 789. [CrossRef]
25. Giannakas, F.; Kouliaridis, V.; Kambourakis, G. A Closer Look at Machine Learning Effectiveness in Android Malware Detection *Information* **2022**, *14*, 2. [CrossRef]
26. Wei, F.; Li, Y.; Roy, S.; Ou, X.; Zhou, W. Deep Ground Truth Analysis of Current Android Malware. In *Detection of Intrusions and Malware, and Vulnerability Assessment*; Springer: Cham, Switzerland, 2017; Volume 10327, pp. 252–276. [CrossRef]
27. Karbab, E.M.B.; Debbabi, M.; Derhab, A.; Mouheb, D. MalDozer: Automatic Framework for Android Malware Detection Using Deep Learning. *Digit. Investig.* **2018**, *24*, S48–S59. [CrossRef]
28. Abdul Kadir, A.F.; Stakhanova, N.; Ghorbani, A.A. Android Botnets: What URLs Are Telling Us. In *Network and System Security*, Springer: Cham, Switzerland, 2015; Volume 9408, pp. 78–91. [CrossRef]
29. Sun, W.; Du, Q. Hyperspectral Band Selection: A Review. *IEEE Geosci. Remote Sens. Mag.* **2019**, *7*, 118–139. [CrossRef]
30. Verma, A.K.; Pal, S. Prediction of Skin Disease with Three Different Feature Selection Techniques Using Stacking Ensemble Method. *Appl. Biochem. Biotechnol.* **2020**, *191*, 637–656. [CrossRef] [PubMed]
31. Al-Awadhi, M.; Deshmukh, R. Enhancing Honey Adulteration Detection with Optimal Subspace Wavelength Reduction in Vis-NIR Reflection Spectroscopy. *IEEE Access* **2023**, *1*, 144226–144243. [CrossRef]

2. Singh, D.; Singh, B. Investigating the Impact of Data Normalization on Classification Performance. *Appl. Soft Comput.* **2020**, *97*, 105524. [CrossRef]
3. Shantal, M.; Othman, Z.; Bakar, A.A. A Novel Approach for Data Feature Weighting Using Correlation Coefficients and Min–Max Normalization. *Symmetry* **2023**, *15*, 2185. [CrossRef]
4. Sriyanto, S.B.S.; Faizal, A.M.; Suryana, N.; Suhendra, A. MiMaLo: Advanced Normalization Method for Mobile Malware Detection. *Int. J. Mod. Educ. Comput. Sci.* **2022**, *14*, 24–33. [CrossRef]
5. Rish, I. An Empirical Study of the Naïve Bayes Classifier. In Proceedings of the IJCAI 2001 Workshop on Empirical Methods in Artificial Intelligence, Seattle, WA, USA, 4–10 August 2001; pp. 41–46.
6. Laaksonen, J.; Oja, E. Classification with Learning k-Nearest Neighbors. In Proceedings of the International Conference on Neural Networks (ICNN'96), Washington, DC, USA, 3–6 June 1996; pp. 1480–1483. [CrossRef]
7. de Ville, B. Decision Trees. Wiley Interdiscip. *Rev. Comput. Stat.* **2013**, *5*, 448–455. [CrossRef]
8. Breiman, L. Random forests. *Mach. Learn.* **2001**, *45*, 5–32. [CrossRef]
9. Grandini, M.; Bagli, E.; Visani, G. Metrics for Multi-Class Classification: An Overview. *arXiv* **2020**, arXiv:2008.05756. [CrossRef]

electronics

MDPI

Article

Adversarial Sample Generation Based on Model Simulation Analysis in Intrusion Detection Systems

Jiankang Sun [1,2] and Shujie Yang [1,2,*]

1 School of Computer Science, Beijing University of Posts and Telecommunications, Beijing 100876, China; sjk2022110737@bupt.edu.cn
2 State Key Laboratory of Network and Switching Technology, Beijing 100876, China
* Correspondence: sjyang@bupt.edu.cn

Abstract: The explosive development of artificial intelligence technology is profoundly affecting the strategic landscape of cyberspace security, demonstrating enormous potential in the field of intrusion detection. Recent research has found that machine learning models have serious vulnerabilities, and adversarial samples derived from this vulnerability can significantly reduce the accuracy of model detection by adding slight perturbations to the original samples. In our article, we propose a novel method called adversarial sample generation based on model simulation that quickly generates adversarial samples in a short period of time and improves the model's generalization and robustness after adversarial training. Extensive experiments on the CICIDS-2017 dataset demonstrated that the method consistently outperforms other current research methods.

Keywords: adversarial attack; intrusion detection system; machine learning

1. Introduction

With the continuous escalation of hacker attacks and the large-scale growth of network traffic data, machine learning-based malicious traffic detection methods are becoming the mainstream solution for intrusion detection systems (IDSs). Among them, shallow machine learning algorithms such as random forest, support vector machine, and artificial neural network are widely used in malicious traffic detection by researchers due to their fast computing power and natural advantages in handling classification problems. The robustness and generalization of network intrusion detection models are particularly important in the face of increasingly complex network threats. The current network intrusion detection models are susceptible to adversarial attacks that bypass detection systems through carefully designed malicious samples, leading to security incidents and thus reducing the effectiveness of network intrusion detection models. As a remarkably effective method of traffic intrusion detection, an adversarial attack plays a vital role in traffic intrusion detection to improve the robustness and accuracy of network traffic identification models.

Considering these ideologies, this research work aimed to develop an intrusion detection system based on a deep learning technique. In this paper, we propose a method for generating malicious encrypted traffic samples based on simulation model extraction. It can extract features from the original data samples and implement learning on its data from the training samples to obtain new samples. It aims to address the efficiency of malicious sample mutation generation in adversarial learning processes, and enhance the robustness and generalization of intrusion detection models through mutated samples so as to achieve accurate classification.

In a nutshell, our main contributions include the following:

We designed and simulated a comprehensive intrusion detection system method and testing its classification and detection models. Our approach focused on the targeted and rapid generation of adversarial samples, which closely resembled those seen in white-box attacks. This allowed for a more accurate representation of potential threats and vulnerabilities, ensuring that the system is robust under various attack scenarios.

We conducted an in-depth and systematic investigation into the adversarial robustness of intrusion detection systems. Our research aimed to understand the underlying vulnerabilities of these systems when exposed to adversarial samples, and based on this analysis, we proposed a novel and effective methodology to enhance their generalization and resilience. In leveraging adversarially generated samples, we present a robust approach that significantly improves the performance and reliability of intrusion detection systems in the face of evolving, sophisticated attack techniques.

2. Related Works

Intrusion Detection Systems. IDSs can be primarily categorized into three types. The first type is feature-based IDSs, which have mature technology and high detection accuracy. It can quickly and accurately identify known attacks. However, it has limitations when facing evolving and novel attack methods and requires regular updates to its signature database. The second type is anomaly-based IDSs, which are capable of detecting unknown attacks, their greatest advantage. However, challenges such as high false positive rates and issues with robustness during adversarial attacks remain persistent. The third type is hybrid-based IDSs, which combine the advantages of both feature-based and anomaly-based detection. They can accurately identify known attacks while also detecting some unknown attacks, thereby reducing false positives and missed detections [1]. In Virtual Reality(VR) virtual world research, there is the issue of intrusion detection systems being attacked, leading to data leakage. Xiao H [2] proposed a method that transfers computational tasks from centralized cloud servers to edge nodes closer to user devices to optimize computational capabilities. However, the security and privacy of the data were lacking. Xiao H [3] pointed out that in bandwidth-limited or network-congested environments, edge computing-based transcoding technology can be used to enhance the transmission quality and user experience of VR videos. However, there are significant issues related to malicious attacks. Xiao H [4] utilized a cloud–edge–terminal collaborative model to address dynamic network changes and optimize video caching and transmission strategies, but it may lead to the leakage of personal privacy data. Khraisat A [5] concluded that an IDS suffers from false negatives when facing unknown attacks and variants of known attacks. There is a need to explore more effective adversarial evasion techniques to enhance the robustness of IDSs under adversarial attacks. Zhao X [6] pointed out in generating attack samples of specific categories based on attack type labels, the data volume of rare attack categories is increased, alleviating data imbalance. This approach enhanced the generalization ability of the trained detection model. Nema A [7] adopted a method that enhances model robustness, and strategies such as adversarial training and retraining with added noise data were proposed. These approaches encourage the model to learn more generalized features, reduce the likelihood of being affected by attacks, and ensure the reliability and stability of the detection system. Spiekermann D [8] incorporated the preprocessing of virtual network traffic data in traffic encryption within virtual networks and improved overall detection performance by combining multiple deep learning models through an ensemble learning strategy.

In addition, researchers have also used machine learning models in IDSs. Bandyopadhyay S [9] proposed a decision tree(DT)-based intrusion detection system that constructs a tree structure to classify data incrementally based on the features of the input data.

Waskle S [10] pointed out that Principal Component Analysis(PCA) effectively reduces the dimensionality of features to lower the computational burden, while random forest(RF) enhances classification accuracy and robustness by integrating multiple decision trees. Balyan A K [11] combined Enhanced Graphics Adapter(EGA) and Particle Swarm Optimization(PSO) to select the most representative feature subsets, while classification is performed using multiple decision trees. However, when the feature dimensionality is high or the dataset is large, the computational time of the algorithm may increase significantly. Ajdani M [12] proposed that the PSO-RF hybrid model can effectively select features, but its optimization process may lead to a significant increase in computational time when the feature dimensionality is high, while also lacking sufficient transparency and interpretability. Laghrissi F E [13] proposed that the Long Short-Term Memory(LSTM) model, by converting network traffic data into time series, can better understand and predict changes in network traffic. However, it lacks resilience against adversarial sample attacks. Hnamte V [14] proposed the Dynamic Convolutional Neural Network(DCNN)-BiLSTM model, which demonstrates significant performance improvement in handling large-scale datasets and adapting to diverse attack patterns. However, it lacks the ability to detect adversarial samples in adversarial environments.

Adversarial sample generation and training. Goodfellow I J [15] first proposed a gradient descent optimization-based method to generate adversarial examples and introduced the Fast Gradient Sign Method (FGSM). This method generates perturbations by calculating the gradient of the model's loss function with respect to the input data. The magnitude of the perturbation can be controlled using a scaling factor, causing the model's classification result to be incorrect. Kurakin A [16] proposed that in large-scale adversarial machine learning research, attackers have knowledge of the target model's architecture, parameters, and training algorithms. With the advantage of complete information, attackers can precisely calculate gradients and use methods such as the Iterative FGSM and Projected Gradient Descent(PG) to carefully adjust input samples, minimizing perturbations while maximizing the misguiding effect. Chen J [17] pointed out that adding generated adversarial samples to the training set enables the intrusion detection model to learn to distinguish between normal and adversarial data, thereby strengthening its robustness. However, this approach may potentially reduce the model's original detection performance, highlighting the need to continuously update the samples to counter evolving attacks from adversaries. Alhajjar E [18] pointed out that incorporating generated adversarial samples into the training set allows the IDS model to learn to distinguish between normal and adversarial data, thereby enhancing its robustness. However, this strategy may sacrifice some of the original detection performance and requires the continuous updating of adversarial samples, posing a disadvantage in keeping pace with the evolving tactics of attackers.

Additionally, researchers have also enhanced the method through adversarial training in different environments. VR security systems are vulnerable to being bypassed by adversarial samples. Xiao H [19] improved task execution efficiency and resource utilization through a task-driven crowd-sourcing collaboration model, but data transmission between robots is prone to theft. Xiao H [20] proposed that the VAAC-IM model enhanced dynamic bitrate control and resolution adjustment. However, it was vulnerable to network traffic intrusion in low-latency scenarios. Schneider M [21] proposed that in the network intrusion detection scenario, perturbations of adversarial samples are often added to the feature values of network traffic data packets, such as key features like IP header fields, port numbers, packet sizes, and others. Shaham U [22] proposed that in adversarial training, uncertainty arises from the potential adversarial perturbations, with the goal of minimizing the model's loss in the worst-case scenario rather than the conventional expected loss. This approach integrates the generation of adversarial samples into the model's training process. In each iteration, the model parameters are updated not only based on the original samples but also by generating corresponding adversarial samples, with both being used to compute the loss and adjust the weights. Yuan X [23] pointed out a data augmentation method that diversifies the data and a model regularization technique. By combining adversarial training with data augmentation, the strategy effectively enhances the model's robustness. Roshan M K [24] proposed a disturbance correction method to mitigate potential adversarial perturbations when facing untargeted white-box optimization attacks. This method smooths the model parameters to reduce the impact of adversarial disturbances and enhances the model's robustness against attacks by incorporating adversarial examples into the training process. Haroon M S [25]pointed out that adversarial training incurs a high computational cost, especially when applied to large-scale datasets or deep learning models, as generating adversarial samples and incorporating them into the training set requires significant computational resources. Additionally, the model may still encounter generalization issues when facing unknown attacks or new attack methods. Wang M [26] proposed that continuous model updates and training can help the model adapt to new data distributions and improve its adaptability in real-world environments, particularly in the context of distribution shift. However, the paper did not fully analyze the comprehensive defense strategies.

In summary, addressing the issues identified in the existing research, we performed simulation analyses of the intrusion detection model to extract relevant features. Subsequently, we generated adversarial samples in a targeted manner and enhanced the model's robustness by merging the adversarial samples with the training data for model retraining.

3. Materials and Methods

In this study, our method consists of four main phases: traffic preprocessing, model extraction simulation, adversarial sample generation, and adversarial learning training. The main process of the method flow design is shown in Figure 1.

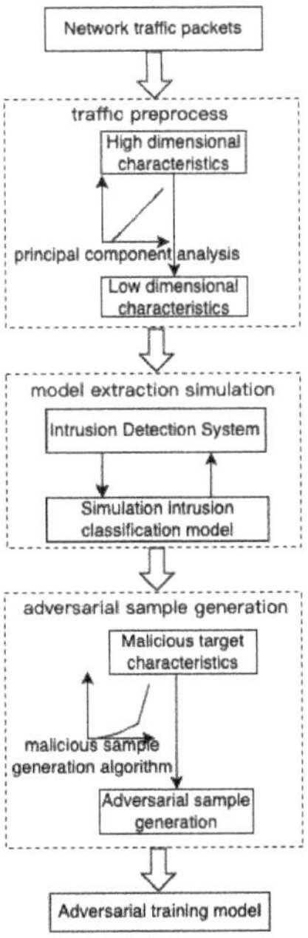

Figure 1. Overall framework of the model.

3.1. Traffic Preprocess

With regard to training attack detection systems on available public datasets (DARPA1998, KDD1999, ISCX2012, ADFA2013, etc.), the KDD 1999 dataset is relatively outdated and no longer represents current network attack scenarios. Similarly, the DARPA 1998 and ISCX 2012 datasets primarily focus on classic attacks such as Denial of Service (DoS) and SYN Flood, which are simple attack techniques. The ADFA 2013 dataset mainly focuses on attack behavior data from Linux and Windows systems, with a relatively small scale. In contrast, the CICIDS-2017 dataset is derived from a real-world experimental environment and provides a variety of traffic features, including traffic size, connection protocol types, and data transmission patterns. Each network traffic record in the dataset includes detailed annotations, making it highly suitable for training and validating various intrusion detection algorithms. The annotation information includes attack type, traffic source, timestamps, protocol type, and more. It is more representative of real-world network traffic distributions and attack methodologies. In summary, we chose the CICIDS-2017 dataset as the dataset for feature processing and subsequent model adversarial training.

The classifier in intrusion detection systems cannot directly process traffic packets, so it is necessary to extract features from the original network traffic, count traffic related parameters, and convert the traffic into multi-bit features for subsequent model training. In our research, we merged and filtered the data in the pcap file of the CICIDS-2017 data. Data preprocessing was the first step to transform the dataset into a suitable format for the following process. In the initial stage, we combined five CSV files in the traffic folder in the CICIDS-2017 dataset, totaling 2,830,540 instances.

The next phase was the encoding process to convert the categorical data on the Proto, Byte, and Flag attributes into numerical data and replace the non-numeric eigenvalues of "flow bytes/s" and "flow packets/s" with -1. We transformed categorical labels into numeric form with simple label encoding: "1" for samples with attacks and "0" for benign samples. To address the issue of imbalanced benign and attack samples, we adopted undersampling, which refers to the deletion of randomly selected non-attack class instances. The number of targets accounts for 70/30% of instances in the "benign" and "attack" categories. We calculated the mutual information between each feature and the target variable to determine the contribution of each feature to the prediction of the target. After sorting the feature importance in descending order, we cumulatively calculated the importance until it reaches 90%, and selected the top-ranked 10 features. The selected features are shown in Table 1. To improve the method performance, standardization was needed in the form of the StandardScaler command to change the class label data so that the distribution has an average of 0 and a standard deviation of 1. Then, the dataset was divided into 80% training and 20% testing data.

3.2. Model Extraction Simulation

The IDS leveraged advanced algorithms to analyze and classify network traffic in order to identify potential attack behaviors. The core of these systems is typically a machine learning classifier that learns the normal patterns of network traffic and can detect abnormal behaviors that deviate from these patterns. In our study, we aimed to improve the performance of the IDS by training a new machine model based on the classification results from a real-world IDS classifier. This approach was designed to simulate a more robust and realistic classification model, enabling better feature selection and mutation during adversarial training.

Table 1. Selected features.

No	Features	Notes
1	Average Packet Size	The average size of the data packet
2	Flow Bytes/s	The flow byte rate
3	Max Packet Length	The maximum length of the flow
4	Fwd IAT Min	The minimum time between two flows
5	Fwd Packet Length Mean	The average length of the flow
6	Total Length of Fwd Packets	The total size of forward packets
7	Flow IAT Mean	The average time between two flows
8	Fwd IAT Std	Standard deviation between two flows
9	Fwd Packet Length Max	The maximum size of the package in the forward direction
10	Fwd Header Length	The total number of bytes used for the header in the forward direction

We utilized machine learning classifiers to recognize network traffic patterns and simulated an attacker's process of observing the model's inputs and outputs. This allowed us to "mimic" the behavior of a black-box model, gaining the ability to simulate how an adversary might craft malicious inputs. To do this, we fed network traffic into the black-box model and obtained corresponding prediction results. By interacting with the simulated black-box model and analyzing the generated predictions, we trained a "mimicking" model. This model was fine-tuned to replicate the behavior of the original black-box IDS, providing us with an effective simulated network intrusion detection model.

This process was twofold. First, we aimed to strengthen the model's ability to identify and counter adversarial attacks by providing it with adversarially perturbed inputs during training. Second, by mimicking the black-box model, we gained insights into how an attacker might exploit weaknesses in the IDS, enabling us to improve the robustness of the system. The interaction between the real IDS model and the mimicking model also served to enhance the training process, allowing the system to adapt to evolving attack strategies and increase its resilience to adversarial perturbations.

Furthermore, this approach allowed us to iteratively refine the detection model by continuously feeding adversarial samples back into the training loop. This dynamic process of adversarial training ensured that the IDS remains effective not only in recognizing normal and anomalous traffic but also in detecting and mitigating attacks that may attempt to bypass detection. Ultimately, this method improved the IDS's performance in real-world environments, making it more robust against a wide range of cyber threats and ensuring that it can maintain high detection accuracy even in the presence of sophisticated adversarial attacks.

3.3. Adversarial Sample Generation

Building upon the functionality of our proposed method, we developed and implemented a sophisticated attack avoidance mechanism, coupled with an iterative process for adversarial sample generation. Our approach focused on simulating system models to identify and modify saved input samples, in order to create adversarial examples specifically designed to evade detection by a given classifier. This feedback-driven refinement ensured that the adversarial strategy was dynamic and evolved as the classifier's ability to detect attacks changes.

The core of the method was structured around a feature matrix that contains the original feature values of the input samples. We made modifications to these feature values by manipulating them within a certain range—specifically within the range of [original value, original value + 1000]. These modifications were applied selectively to the feature values of samples that were correctly classified as attacks by the classifier. The purpose of these changes was to introduce subtle but effective perturbations that make it more challenging for the classifier to correctly identify the modified samples while still maintaining the overall integrity of the original data. This process is shown in Algorithm 1.

The process is iterative and adaptive, meaning that for each adversarial sample, we continually refine the perturbations until the classifier misclassifies the altered samples consistently. This iterative refinement continued until either the classifier no longer detected the attack or the perturbations reached a predefined threshold, beyond that further modifications were deemed unnecessary or ineffective. This approach ensures that the generated adversarial samples are not only capable of evading detection but also preserve as much of the original data's structure and information as possible, thereby minimizing any noticeable distortion in the input data.

Furthermore, we incorporated a feedback mechanism to continuously adjust the feature modification process based on the classifier's response to the perturbed samples. This feedback loop plays a crucial role in improving the adversarial sample generation. If the classifier is still able to detect and correctly classify the perturbed sample as an attack, the modification process is refined further to make the perturbations more subtle or targeted to different features. These targeted changes focus on the features that most influence the classifier's decision-making process. This feedback-driven refinement ensures that the adversarial strategy is dynamic and evolves as the classifier's ability to detect attacks changes.

Algorithm 1: Malicious Sample Iteration Algorithm

Input: Malicious samples with model recognition and classification errors: Sample_Attack
Output: Adversarial samples: Sample_Evasion

```
function SampleGeneration(Sample_Attack)
  for i in range(0, samples.shape[0]):
    if (labels[i] == 1) and (model.predict(samples[[i]]) == 1)://Malicious samples and model recognition as malicious samples
      evasion_sample = samples[[i]]
      for characteristics_i in range(j, j + 1000)://Iterative modification of malicious samples to generate new samples
        evasion_sample[0, i] = characteristics_i
        pred = mode.predict(evasion_sample)
        if pred[0] < 1:
          Add to adversarial sample set Sample_Evasion
        end if
      end for
    end if
  end for
end function
```

The continuous adaptation of the attack strategy allows for the generation of more robust adversarial examples that are capable of evading detection under a variety of conditions. As the classifier adjusts or improves over time, the adversarial samples also evolve to stay ahead of these improvements, ensuring that the generated samples remain effective. By maintaining this dynamic interaction between the classifier's behavior and the adversarial sample generation process, we can ensure that the generated adversarial samples are both effective in evading detection and highly adaptable to different scenarios.

3.4. Adversarial Training

To protect our model from evasion attacks, we identified adversarial examples across the entire dataset and incorporate them into adversarial training. We adopted an adversarial training method in which the generated adversarial feature samples are added to the original dataset for retraining the model. This approach aimed to minimize the model's loss on adversarial samples. During the training process, the model's parameters were updated based on the loss from both normal and adversarial samples. Through back-propagation, the model continuously adjusts its weights to maintain good performance even under adversarial perturbations.

This method improved the model's generalization ability, ensuring that it performs well on unseen data and enhances its robustness against potential attacks. In including adversarial samples during training, the model learned to recognize and defend against a wide range of adversarial strategies, making it more resilient to future attempts at evasion or manipulation. This proactive approach significantly strengthened the model's security, allowing it to better withstand adversarial perturbations in real-world scenarios.

4. Results

The experimental part of this study chose Google Colab, an online platform that provides a cloud environment for Jupyter Notebook 6.5.4, allowing users to start working without complex local configurations. Colab also provides free GPU resources, which is a huge advantage for training deep learning models. The hardware configuration used in the experiment included an Intel Xeon (R) processor with a clock speed of 2.30 GHz, equipped with 31 GB of RAM, and accelerated support provided by Nvidia Tesla K80 GPU, which was manufactured by Nvidia in Silicon Valley of the United States and had 12 GB of video memory. At the software level, we used the Keras 2.3.1 framework to build and optimize the neural network model, with Pytorch 2.0.1 as the backend responsible for parallelizing the computation. The programming environment for the entire experiment is based on Python version 3.11.4.

4.1. Datasets and Evaluation Metrics

We utilized the CICIDS-2017 dataset compiled by the Canadian Institute for Cybersecurity based on the analysis of network images in an isolated environment. This dataset simulates the behavior of 25 legitimate users and the malicious activities of intruders. It incorporates over 50 GB of raw PCAP data, including eight CSV preprocessed files that contain labeled sessions with prominent features observed on different days. The dataset consists of a total of 84 features, with 80 numerical features and 4 non-numerical features. A brief description of the file and the number of datasets are listed in the Table 2.

Our research resulted in four possible outcomes for each sample. Finally, four values were obtained by testing each classifier:

- True Positive (TP): number of positive samples correctly predicted as positive.
- False Positive (FP): number of positive samples incorrectly predicted as negative.
- True Negative (TN): number of negative samples correctly predicted as negative.
- False Negative (FN): number of negative samples incorrectly predicted as positive.

Based on these values, four metrics were employed to compare the performances of the classifiers. The corresponding formulas for calculating the performance metrics are as follows:

$$accuracy = \frac{TP + TN}{TP + TN + FP + FN} \tag{1}$$

$$precision = \frac{TP}{TP + FP} \tag{2}$$

$$recall = \frac{TP}{TP + FN} \tag{3}$$

$$f1 - score = \frac{precision \times recall}{precision + recall} \times 2 \tag{4}$$

Table 2. Description of CICIDS-2017 dataset.

No	File Name	Attack Type
1	Monday-WorkingHours.pcap_ISCX.csv	Benign
2	Tuesday-WorkingHours.pcap_ISCX.csv	Benign, FTP-Patator, SSH-Patator
3	Wednesday-WorkingHours.pcap_ISCX.csv	Benign, DoS GoldenEye, DoS Hulk, DoS Slowhttptest, DoS Slowloris, Heartbleed
4	Thursday-WorkingHours-Morning-WebAttacks.pcap_ISCX.csv	Benign, Web Attack-Brute Force, Web Attack-Sql Injection, Web Attack-XSS
5	Thursday-WorkingHours-Afternoon-Infilteration.pcap_ISCX.csv	Benign, Infiltration
6	Friday-WorkingHours-Morning.pcap_ISCX.csv	Benign, Bot
7	Friday-WorkingHours-Afternoon-PortScan.pcap_ISCX.csv	Benign, PortSacn
8	Friday-WorkingHours-Afternoon-DDos.pcap_ISCX.csv	Benign, DDoS

4.2. Experimental Results and Analysis

By evaluating the effectiveness of different, simulated machine learning classification models, we compared the responsiveness of the models on our constructed good-quality, balanced datasets. In evaluating the performance of the models created, we used the accuracy, precision, recall, and f1-score. We then assessed the time required for training adversarial models to validate the effectiveness of our approach. The specific parameters of the model and training adjustment are shown in Table 3.

Table 3. Descriptions of parameters.

Parameters	RF	DT	LSTM
Model parameter	max_depth: 5 n_estimators: 5 max_features: 3	max_depth: 3 min_samples_split: 3 min_samples_leaf: 2 max_features: 3	input_size: 10 hidden_size: 4 units: 3 num_layers: 3
Training parameter		optimizer: adam learning_rate: 0.001 loss: binary_crossentropy epoch: 500	

4.2.1. Base Classifiers Result

The DT, RF, and LSTM models demonstrated strong performance in intrusion classification, achieving an average accuracy of 98.20%. However, after introducing adversarial samples generated by our method, the model's average accuracy dropped to 97.90%. This degradation was due to the fact that adversarial samples mislead the model. Subsequently, by augmenting the original dataset with the adversarial samples and quickly retraining the model, the average accuracy improved to 99.10%. We concluded that the targeted simulation model and sample generation process enhanced the model's robustness against adversarial attacks. The experimental results of the method are shown in Figure 2.

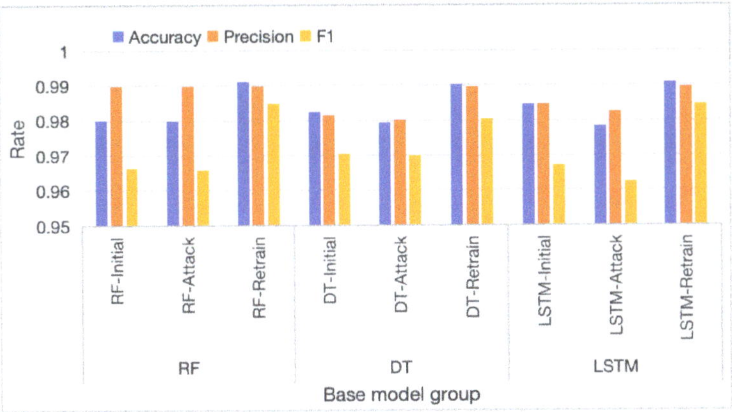

Figure 2. Results of base experiment.

4.2.2. Integrated Classifier Results

We conducted a comprehensive ensemble analysis of individual models utilizing both AdaBoost and Bagging methods to assess their performance in adversarial scenarios. These ensemble learning techniques were applied to a decision tree model, a widely used classifier, for a series of simulated classification tasks. The aim was to evaluate the effectiveness of adversarial attack methods in enhancing the robustness of ensemble based models. Through the application of AdaBoost and Bagging, we were able to observe the advantages of combining multiple weak learners to create a stronger, more resilient classifier. Specifically, we found that this ensemble approach allowed the decision tree model to generate targeted adversarial samples, which are samples crafted to intentionally deceive the model. By training on these adversarial samples, the ensemble method enabled the DT model to better adapt to these perturbations, thereby improving its robustness when adversarial attacks are a concern.

The experimental results of the method are shown in Figure 3. The ensemble model of DT's adaboost and bagging ensemble methods achieved an average accuracy of 99.30%. After adversarial sample attacks, the model accuracy decreased to 97.4%. Subsequently, after sample retraining, the model accuracy recovered to 99.50%. This suggests that integrating ensemble learning with adversarial training can significantly bolster the security and stability of machine learning models, making them more reliable in hostile environments.

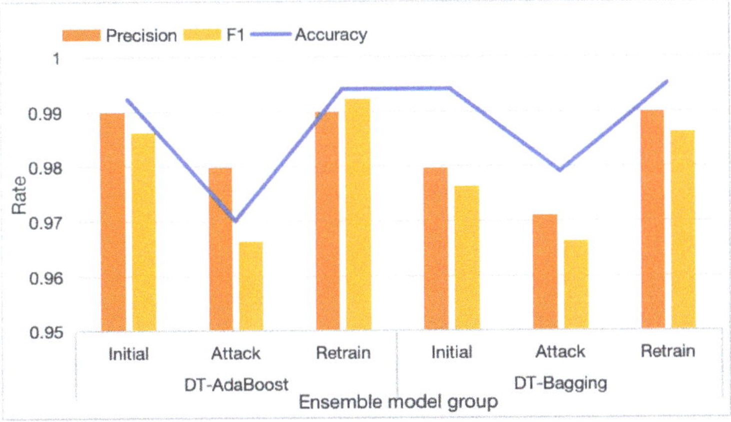

Figure 3. The results of the ensemble experiment.

4.2.3. Voting Classifier Results

Two mechanisms, hard voting and soft voting, were used to validate the effectiveness of adversarial samples in the simulation model. Based on the accuracy of the DT, RF, and LSTM models from Experiment 1, the soft voting mechanism allocated 30% to the DT model, 30% to the RF model, and 40% to the LSTM model. The results show that in the initial model phase, both hard voting and soft voting achieved an average accuracy of 99.57%. After performing an attack by rapidly generating adversarial samples, the average accuracy of the model dropped to 98.07%. Finally, following adversarial training with these samples, the defensive model achieved an average accuracy of 98.76%. This demonstrates that the adversarial samples were effectively able to generate malicious samples targeting the model's parameters, thereby enhancing the model's robustness. The experimental results are shown in Figure 4.

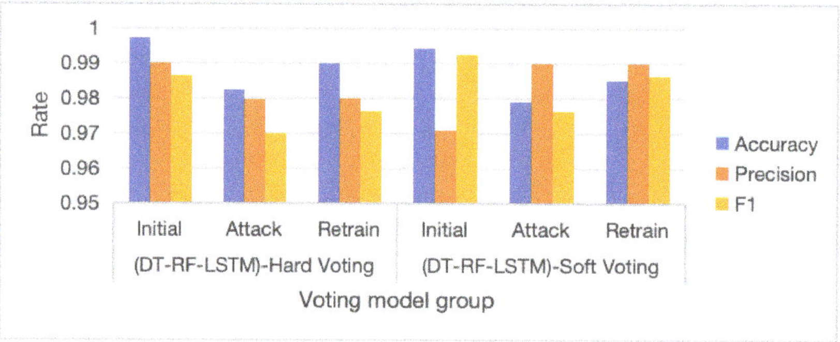

Figure 4. Results of voting experiment.

4.2.4. Sample Generation Time

Generating adversarial samples typically requires multiple iterations to fine-tune the features of the input traffic, ensuring that the modified traffic can effectively evade intrusion detection systems. This process leads to high computational resource consumption and long execution times. By simulating the model used in real-world environments and performing the batch selection of samples for iterative computation, we can reduce the computational overhead when applying adversarial samples in practical settings. Experimental results demonstrate that our method outperforms the FGSM algorithm in terms of the time required to generate adversarial samples, with an efficiency improvement of 0.78%. In addition, as the number of model parameters increases and the ensemble becomes more complex, the time required to generate adversarial samples also increases. The experimental results are shown in Table 4.

Table 4. Description of sample generation time.

Model	Our Method's Sample Generation Time (s)	FGSM's Sample Generation Time (s)
DT	94.215	94.545
RF	91.687	92.247
LSTM	98.412	98.624
DT-adaboost	103.324	104.449
DT-bagging	101.241	104.762
Hard Voting(DT-RF-LSTM)	120.325	124.523
Soft Voting(DT-RF-LSTM)	127.275	128.284

5. Conclusions and Discussion

With the continuous advancement of machine learning technology, patterns have been discovered, thereby achieving automatic recognition and responses to network attacks, which greatly improves the accuracy and efficiency of IDSs. However, attackers bypass IDS detection by generating targeted samples, resulting in a decrease in detection accuracy. We retrained the model after performing simulation-based analysis and achieved model convergence to improve the robustness of the model. Our method was highly effective in enhancing the robustness of deep learning-based intrusion detection models. This experiment was conducted using the CICIDS-2017 dataset, and the model was compared with a simulated intrusion detection model. Experimental results confirm that the sample generation speed for the targeted samples, after the simulation analysis, improved by 0.78%. In scenarios involving large-scale network traffic or high-frequency attacks, even a small time difference can reduce system latency and enhance the system's real-time response to attacks. For example, small improvements can enable the intrusion detection system to maintain low latency and high detection efficiency in cloud computing environments when faced with millions of network requests. Through comparative experiments involving base models, ensemble models, and voting models, the proposed method effectively enhanced the model's accuracy and robustness against adversarial attacks, improving its ability to detect attack samples.

In the future, we will be focused on generating adversarial samples that cover various attack vectors to enhance the robustness of the detection model. At the same time, since our models are trained offline and thus deviate from real-time detection systems, we plan to explore how to integrate dynamic sample selection into adversarial training to enhance the robustness of real-time detection systems. Future research aims to enable IDSs to respond to new emerging attack patterns in real time and improve their robustness.

Author Contributions: Conceptualization, J.S. and S.Y.; Methodology, J.S.; Validation, J.S.; Ormal analysis, J.S.; Investigation, J.S.; Resources, S.Y.; Data curation, J.S. and S.Y.; Writing—original draft preparation, J.S.; Writing—review and editing, J.S. and S.Y. All authors have read and agreed to the published version of the manuscript.

Funding: This work was supported by China Postdoctoral Science Foundation (grant No. 2024M750259).

Data Availability Statement: The data presented in the current study are available from the corresponding author upon request.

Conflicts of Interest: The authors declare no conflicts of interest.

eferences

Liu, H.; Lang, B. Machine learning and deep learning methods for intrusion detection systems: A survey. *Appl. Sci.* **2019**, *9*, 4396. [CrossRef]

Xiao, H.; Xu, C.; Ma, Y.; Yang, S.; Zhong, L.; Muntean, G.M. Edge Intelligence: A Computational Task Offloading Scheme for Dependent IoT Application.*IEEE Trans. Wirel. Commun.* **2022**, *21*, 7222–7237. [CrossRef]

Xiao, H.; Xu, C.; Feng, Z.; Ding, R.; Yang, S.; Zhong, L.; Liang, J.; Muntean, G.M. A Transcoding-Enabled 360° VR Video Caching and Delivery Framework for Edge-Enhanced Next-Generation Wireless Networks. *IEEE J. Sel. Areas Commun.* **2022**, *40*, 1615–1631. [CrossRef]

Xiao, H.; Zhuang, Y.; Xu, C.; Wang, W.; Zhang, H.; Ding, R.; Cao, T.; Zhong, L.; Muntean, G.M. Transcoding-Enabled Cloud–Edge–Terminal Collaborative Video Caching in Heterogeneous IoT Networks: An Online Learning Approach with Time-Varying Information. *IEEE Internet Things J.* **2024**, *11*, 296–310. [CrossRef]

Khraisat, A.; Gondal, I.; Vamplew, P.; Kamruzzaman, J. Survey of intrusion detection systems: Techniques, datasets and challenges. *Cybersecurity* **2019**, *2*, 20. [CrossRef]

Zhao, X.; Fok, K.; Thing, V. Enhancing Network Intrusion Detection Performance using Generative Adversarial Networks. *arXiv* **2024**, arXiv:2404.07464. [CrossRef]

7. Nema, A.; Tomar, R S.; Mani, A. Robust Anomaly Detection in Network Traffic using Deep Learning Models. In Proceedings of the 2023 IEEE International Conference on ICT in Business Industry & Government (ICTBIG), Indore, India, 8–9 December 2023; pp. 1–6.
8. Spiekermann, D.; Eggendorfer, T.; Keller, J. Deep Learning for Network Intrusion Detection in Virtual Networks. *Electronics* **2024**, *13*, 3617. [CrossRef]
9. Bandyopadhyay, S.; Chowdhury, R.; Banerjee, P.; Dey, S.D.; Saha, B. A Decision Tree Based Intrusion Detection System for Identification of Malicious Web Attack. 2020. Available online: https://www.preprints.org/manuscript/202007.0191/download/final_file (accessed on 14 November 2024).
10. Waskle, S.; Parashar, L.; Singh, U. Intrusion detection system using PCA with random forest approach. In Proceedings of the 2020 IEEE International Conference on Electronics and Sustainable Communication Systems (ICESC), Chennai, India, 19–21 March 2020; pp. 803–808.
11. Balyan, A.K.; Ahuja, S.; Lilhore, U.K.; Sharma, S.K.; Manoharan, P.; Algarni, A.D.; Elmannai, H.; Raahemifar, K. A hybrid intrusion detection model using ega-pso and improved random forest method. *Sensors* **2022**, *22*, 5986. [CrossRef] [PubMed]
12. Ajdani, M.; Ghaffary, H. Introduced a new method for enhancement of intrusion detection with random forest and PSO algorithm. *Secur. Priv.* **2021**, *4*, e147. [CrossRef]
13. Laghrissi, F.E.; Douzi, S.;Douzi, K.; Hssina, B. Intrusion detection systems using long short-term memory (LSTM). *J. Big Data* **2021**, *8*, 65. [CrossRef]
14. Hnamte, V.; Hussain, J. DCNNBiLSTM: An efficient hybrid deep learning-based intrusion detection system. *Telemat. Inform. Rep* **2023**, *10*, 100053. [CrossRef]
15. Goodfellow, I.J.; Shlens, J.; Szegedy, C. Explaining and harnessing adversarial examples. *arXiv* **2014**, arXiv:1412.6572.
16. Kurakin, A.; Goodfellow, I.; Bengio, S. Adversarial machine learning at scale. *arXiv* **2016**, arXiv:1611.01236.
17. Chen, J.; Gao, X.; Deng, R.; He, Y.; Fang, C.; Cheng, P. Generating adversarial examples against machine learning-based intrusion detector in industrial control systems. *IEEE Trans. Dependable Secur. Comput.* **2020**, *19*, 1810–1825. [CrossRef]
18. Alhajjar, E.; Maxwell, P.; Bastian, N. Adversarial machine learning in network intrusion detection systems. *Expert Syst. Appl.* **2021** *186*, 115782. [CrossRef]
19. Xiao, H.; Huang, Z.; Xu, Z.; Yang, S.; Wang, W.; Zhong, L.; Xu, C. Task-Driven Cooperative Internet of the Robotic Things Crowdsourcing: From the Perspective of Hierarchical Game-Theoretic. *IEEE Internet Things J.* **2024**, *35*, 2161–3915. [CrossRef]
20. Xiao, H.; Xu, C.; Fang, C.; Yang, S.; Zhong, L. VAAC-IM: Viewing Area Adaptive Control in Immersive Media Transmission. In Proceedings of the 2024 the 34th edition of the Workshop on Network and Operating System Support for Digital Audio and Video (NOSSDAV '24), Bari, Italy, 15–18 April 2024; pp. 8–14.
21. Schneider, M.; Aspinall, D.; Bastian, N.D. Evaluating model robustness to adversarial samples in network intrusion detection In Proceedings of the 2021 IEEE International Conference on Big Data (Big Data), Orlando, FL, USA, 15–18 December 2021 pp. 3343–3352.
22. Shaham, U.; Yamada, Y.; Negahban, S. Understanding adversarial training: Increasing local stability of supervised models through robust optimization. *Neurocomputing* **2018**, *307*, 195–204. [CrossRef]
23. Yuan, X.; Han, S.; Huang, W.; Ye, H.; Kong, X.; Zhang, F. A simple framework to enhance the adversarial robustness of deep learning-based intrusion detection system. *Comput. Secur.* **2024**, *137*, 103644. [CrossRef]
24. Roshan, M.K.; Zafar, A. Boosting robustness of network intrusion detection systems: A novel two phase defense strategy against untargeted white-box optimization adversarial attack. *Expert Syst. Appl.* **2024**, *249*, 123567. [CrossRef]
25. Haroon, M.S.; Ali, H.M. Adversarial Training Against Adversarial Attacks for Machine Learning-Based Intrusion Detection Systems. *Comput. Mater. Contin.* **2022**, *73*, 3513–3527.
26. Wang, M.; Yang, N.; Gunasinghe, D.H.; Weng, N. On the Robustness of ML-Based Network Intrusion Detection Systems: An Adversarial and Distribution Shift Perspective. *Computers* **2023**, *12*, 209. [CrossRef]

electronics

MDPI

Article

An Improved Binary Simulated Annealing Algorithm and TPE-FL-LightGBM for Fast Network Intrusion Detection

Yafei Luo [1,2], Ruihan Chen [3,4], Chuantao Li [3], Derong Yang [3], Kun Tang [3] and Jing Su [3,*]

1 College of Electronics and Information Engineering, Guangdong Ocean University, Zhanjiang 524088, China; luoyafei@gdou.edu.cn
2 Guangdong Provincial Key Laboratory of Intelligent Equipment for South China Sea Marine Ranching, Guangdong Ocean University, Zhanjiang 524088, China
3 School of Mathematics and Computer, Guangdong Ocean University, Zhanjiang 524088, China; ruihan_chen@stu.gdou.edu.cn (R.C.)
4 School of Microelectronics and Communication Engineering, Chongqing University, Chongqing 400030, China
* Correspondence: jingsu@gdou.edu.cn

Abstract: With the rapid proliferation of the Internet, network security issues that threaten users have become increasingly severe, despite the widespread benefits of Internet access. Most existing intrusion detection systems (IDS) suffer from suboptimal performance due to data imbalance and feature redundancy, while also facing high computational complexity in areas such as feature selection and optimization. To address these challenges, this study proposes a novel network intrusion detection method based on an improved binary simulated annealing algorithm (IBSA) and TPE-FL-LightGBM. First, by integrating Focal Loss into the loss function of the LightGBM classifier, we introduce cost-sensitive learning, which effectively mitigates the impact of class imbalance on model performance and enhances the model's ability to learn difficult-to-classify samples. Next, significant improvements are made to the simulated annealing algorithm, including adaptive adjustments of the initial temperature and Metropolis criterion, the incorporation of multi-neighborhood search strategies, and the integration of an S-shaped transfer function. These improvements enable the IBSA method to achieve efficient optimal feature selection with fewer iterations. Finally, the Tree-structured Parzen Estimator (TPE) algorithm is employed to optimize the structure of the FL-LightGBM classifier, further enhancing its performance. Through comprehensive visual analysis, ablation studies, and comparative experiments on the NSL-KDD and UNSW-NB15 datasets, the reliability of the proposed network intrusion detection method is validated.

Keywords: network intrusion detection; tree-structured Parzen estimator; FL-LightGBM; IBSA

1. Introduction

The rapid development of the Internet has deeply integrated into daily human life, becoming an indispensable component of modern society. However, while providing unprecedented convenience, it has also introduced increasingly severe cybersecurity threats. Enhancing the proactive defense capabilities and overall security of networks has become a pressing research focus, particularly in the rapid identification and detection of various network attacks. Intrusion Detection Systems (IDS) serve as a critical tool in cybersecurity, effectively safeguarding user privacy and data integrity by providing timely warnings against ongoing or potential malicious attacks [1–4].

Nevertheless, as network traffic continues to grow exponentially in complexity and scale, traditional intrusion detection methods struggle to cope with the dynamic nature of malicious attacks and emerging network threats [5,6]. Developing an efficient and robust Network Intrusion Detection System (NIDS) to protect sensitive information in online environments has therefore become a matter of urgency. NIDS operates by monitoring network traffic and issuing alerts upon detecting malicious or suspicious activities. Broadly, NIDS can be categorized into anomaly-based and signature-based systems.

Anomaly-based NIDS, which identifies deviations from normal behavioral patterns, is well-suited for detecting novel or previously unknown attacks, offering high flexibility. However, they typically suffer from high false positive rates, as certain benign anomalies can inadvertently trigger alerts [7]. Conversely, signature-based NIDS detects malicious activities by matching known attack patterns, thereby reducing false positives and finding widespread application in practice [8]. Despite this, signature-based systems face significant challenges, including overfitting and bias caused by irrelevant or redundant features, as well as imbalanced class distributions in network traffic data [9].

On one hand, traditional IDS datasets, such as UNSW-NB15 [10] and NSL-KDD [11], are often characterized by highly imbalanced class distributions. The predominance of majority class samples results in superior performance for detecting common attack types, but poor performance in identifying rare attacks due to insufficient minority class representation. Existing studies have primarily addressed this issue at the data level, employing techniques such as statistical adjustments, generative adversarial networks, and federated learning. However, these methods are often time-intensive, requiring substantial computational resources for training generative models or synthesizing data.

On the other hand, signature-based IDS rely on datasets containing multiple features, some of which may be irrelevant or redundant. High-dimensional data not only increase dataset size and computational cost but also exacerbate the risk of overfitting during model training, leading to elevated false positive rates in real-world scenarios [12]. To address these challenges, a variety of feature selection techniques have been proposed, categorized into embedded, filter, and wrapper methods. Embedded methods integrate feature selection within the model training process, often by incorporating penalty terms into the objective function to achieve a close coupling of feature selection and model performance optimization [13]. However, traditional embedded methods struggle to handle nonlinear feature interactions, limiting their capacity to capture complex data patterns [14]. Filter methods evaluate individual features based on statistical properties, enabling fast screening but failing to account for interactions among features [15]. In contrast, wrapper methods directly assess feature subsets using learning algorithm performance, producing optimal feature sets but at a high computational cost and with significant dependency on classifier performance.

To tackle these issues, this study proposes a novel NIDS based on an Improved Binary Simulated Annealing Algorithm (IBSA) and TPE-FL-LightGBM. Specifically, the focal loss from cost-sensitive learning is incorporated into the LightGBM classifier to balance attention across all classes, while IBSA is employed to select optimal feature subsets, and a Tree-structured Parzen Estimator (TPE) is used to optimize the classifier structure. This approach addresses imbalanced data distributions and varying sample difficulty, enabling efficient and accurate detection of network attacks. The main contributions of this study are as follows:

(1) Incorporation of cost-sensitive focal loss into the LightGBM classifier to improve the loss function, balancing the model's attention across all classes and enhancing its ability to learn from challenging samples, thereby boosting classification performance.

(2) Improvements to the simulated annealing algorithm, including adaptive initialization of temperature and Metropolis criteria, the introduction of multi-neighborhood search strategies, and integration of an S-shaped transfer function. The focal loss is further embedded in IBSA's base classifier to enhance its efficiency for NIDS feature selection tasks.
(3) Implementation of the LightGBM classifier for efficient network attack classification, with Tree-structured Parzen Estimator (TPE) employed to optimize classifier hyperparameters, significantly enhancing performance.
(4) Integration of these three techniques into a cohesive NIDS framework that achieves effective multi-class classification. Comprehensive visual analyses, ablation studies, and comparative experiments conducted on NSL-KDD and UNSW-NB15 benchmark datasets validate the adaptability and reliability of the proposed approach.

The remainder of this paper is organized as follows: Section 2 reviews the state-of-the-art methods in NIDS, highlighting research gaps and objectives; Section 3 elaborates on the proposed methodology; Section 4 presents experimental results and discussion to demonstrate its superiority; and Section 5 concludes with a summary of findings and prospects for future research directions.

2. Related Work

Traditional intrusion detection methods face increasing challenges in meeting the demands of the rapidly growing number of Internet users. To enhance the efficiency of network intrusion detection techniques and ensure cybersecurity, many researchers have integrated artificial intelligence algorithms with current methodologies to improve conventional intrusion detection systems.

2.1. Network Intrusion Detection Systems for Imbalanced Data

Data imbalance poses a significant challenge to the performance of network intrusion detection models. Liu et al. [16] combined the deep feature classification capabilities of Extreme Learning Machines (ELM) with the deep feature extraction capabilities of Convolutional Neural Networks (CNN), proposing a novel deep feature-based intrusion detection method. Liu et al. [17] further suggested an improved CNN algorithm for intrusion detection, optimizing the initial centroid selection compared to the original K-medoids algorithm, thereby enhancing detection accuracy. Lu et al. [18] integrated a neural network model with a whitelist rule database, employing neural networks for detection and updating results via whitelist comparisons to improve both detection accuracy and efficiency. However, these methods rely on existing labels and fail to address small-sample anomaly detection, leading to poor detection accuracy for minority classes.

Few studies in the literature focus on addressing data imbalance. Below, we analyze several key studies addressing this issue.

Yang et al. [19] proposed an anomaly detection method employing Synthetic Minority Over-sampling Technique (SMOTE) to balance the data, followed by classification using Gradient Boosting Decision Trees (GBDT). Fu et al. [20] utilized a combination of attention mechanisms and bidirectional Long Short-Term Memory (LSTM) to detect network anomalies, applying the Adaptive Synthetic Sampling (ADASYN) technique to collect additional data for minority classes, thus mitigating data imbalance. Although these oversampling techniques improve minority class detection, they increase computational complexity, particularly for large datasets, which limits their efficiency.

Tang et al. [21] introduced a federated learning-based intrusion detection approach to tackle data imbalance. This method reconstructs existing data into two dimensions and leverages federated learning and deep learning to enhance feature extraction. However, excessive feature simplification to achieve higher detection results led to performance degradation.

Liu et al. [22] employed Generative Adversarial Networks (GANs) to address data imbalance, training a separate GAN for each minority class to augment its data. Nonetheless, the insufficient sample size for minority classes raises questions about the method's efficacy in training adversarial networks.

Dlamini and Fahim [23] developed a deep generative model (DGM) based on conditional GANs, synthesizing samples for minority classes to improve detection in anomaly domains. Despite its promise, the approach suffers from critical limitations, including mode collapse and gradient vanishing in conditional GANs, resulting in synthetic samples that deviate from the real data distribution and may include noise or irrelevant features.

Most existing studies addressing data imbalance in network intrusion detection focus on data-level solutions, such as statistical methods, generative models, and federated learning. These methods often require extensive computation, such as model training or data synthesis, to resolve imbalance issues. Moreover, most related studies have not explored optimizations at the algorithmic level. For instance, although the LightGBM model is widely used in network intrusion detection, there is limited research incorporating cost-sensitive learning within this model to address data imbalance through modifications to the loss function. To overcome these challenges, this study introduces cost-sensitive learning with Focal Loss to improve the LightGBM classifier. By addressing imbalance at the algorithmic level, this approach enables balanced attention across all classes, emphasizing difficult-to-classify samples and improving predictive performance.

2.2. Intrusion Detection Systems Based on Feature Selection Techniques

Feature selection is a critical step in identifying the most relevant features for building robust models. By employing feature selection techniques, representative feature subsets can be extracted from the initial feature space, enabling the development of efficient and stable intrusion detection system (IDS) models.

Alsaleh et al. [24] proposed a discrete feature optimization method for network intrusion detection, employing different discretization and feature selection algorithms to generate diverse optimal feature subsets. The selected subsets were normalized and modeled using classification algorithms. However, this method is insufficiently sensitive to outliers, and irrelevant features in the dataset negatively impact predictive performance.

Akhone et al. [25] utilized a modified decision tree (MDT) and chi-square feature selection to distinguish benign and malicious events in SCADA systems. After normalizing the raw data using Z-scores, chi-square analysis identified the most statistically significant feature subsets, which were subsequently classified using MDT. Nevertheless, the inability to explore feature interactions limited the method's intrusion detection performance.

To enhance detection across diverse attack forms in large-scale data, Hagar and Gawali [26] proposed three models: Apache Spark, LSTM, and CNN. Random Forest was used to select 19 features from 84, minimizing dimensionality and identifying critical features for performance evaluation on the CSE-CIC-IDS2018 dataset. Although fast, the method's detection accuracy heavily depended on the training model's effectiveness, and its feature selection capabilities were suboptimal.

Alazzam et al. [27] introduced a wrapper-based feature selection method using the pigeon optimization algorithm, incorporating a cosine similarity-based heuristic for discrete problems. Comparative evaluations on three benchmark datasets demonstrated the method's superiority over six state-of-the-art algorithms. Bonab et al. [28] proposed a hybrid wrapper feature selection algorithm combining Fruit Fly Optimization (FFA) and Ant Lion Optimization (ALO), demonstrating effectiveness on the KDD CUP99, NSLKDD, and UNSW-NB15 datasets. However, these methods require manual parameter tuning and extensive iterations to identify optimal feature subsets, neglecting classifier loss function improvements during feature selection.

Simulated annealing (SA), an excellent algorithm adept at rapidly solving discretization and nonlinear optimization problems, has yet to be applied in the field of network intrusion detection. To fully exploit the advantages of SA and address the limitations of existing research, this study enhances the algorithm by adapting the initial temperature with the Metropolis criterion, incorporating multi-neighborhood search strategies, and integrating S-shaped transfer functions. Furthermore, cost-sensitive learning with Focal Loss is introduced into the benchmark classifier of the IBSA framework, enabling more effective feature selection for network intrusion detection tasks.

Table 1 presents a comprehensive summary of the related work, wherein FS denotes the feature selection method and DIP signifies the data imbalance processing technique.

Table 1. Summary of related work.

Authors	DIP	FS	Classifier	Dataset	Drawback
Liu et al. [16]	-	-	CNN	KDD-CUP 99 and NSL-KDD	The problems of sample imbalance and feature redundancy are not considered
Liu et al. [17]	-	-	CNN	NSL-KDD and UNSW-NB15	
Lu et al. [18]	-	-	LSTM	Self-built dataset	
Yang et al. [19]	SMOTE	-	GRU + GBDT	CICIDS2017	The computational efficiency of the statistics-based oversampling method is relatively low.
Fu et al. [20]	ADASYN	Stacked autoencoder	CNN + Bi-LSTM-Attention	NSL-KDD	
Tang et al. [21]	Two-dimensional data reconstruction	-	GRU	CICIDS2017	The characteristics of the data are degraded, resulting in performance degradation.
Liu et al. [22]	GAN	-	CNN	CCD-INID-V1 and CCD-IDSv1	The sample size of a few categories is not enough to support generating network training.
Dlamini and Fahim [23]	DGM (Based on CGAN)	-	-	NSL-KDD and UNSW-NB15	The generated sample has low authenticity.
Alsaleh et al. [24]	-	SSA	XGBoost	NSL-KDD and UNSW-NB15	The combined importance of features cannot be mined.
Akhone et al. [25]	-	Chi-square	DT	ICS-SCADA and WUSTL-IIOT-2018	
Hagar and Gawali [26]	Oversampling	RF	Apache Spark	CSE-CIC-IDS2018	Depends on the effectiveness of the training model.
Alazzam et al. [27]	-	PIO + cosine similarity	-	KDD Cup99, NSL-KDD and UNSW-NB15	Manual parameter tuning along with an extensive number of iterations is necessary, and the rationality of the loss function is not taken into consideration.
Bonab et al. [28]	-	FFA-ALO	-	KDD Cup99, NSL-KDD and UNSW-NB15	

3. Materials and Proposed Methodology

3.1. Data Description and Pre-Processing

The proposed framework begins with a detailed description of the datasets, followed by a discussion of the preprocessing techniques applied to prepare the data for analysis.

3.1.1. Dataset Description

This study utilizes two datasets: NSL-KDD and UNSW-NB15. Both are network intrusion detection datasets that cover a wide range of attack types, exhibit significant diversity, and have been extensively used in academic research. The datasets are described as follows:

NSL-KDD Dataset: An improved version of the KDDCup'99 dataset, the NSL-KDD dataset comprises 43 features, of which 42 describe network traffic, and one identifies the type of attack. The dataset includes 23 subcategories of attacks, of which 22 represent different attack types, while the remaining category corresponds to normal traffic. These attack subcategories are further grouped into four broader attack categories. The dataset is pre-divided into a training set (KDDTrain+) and a test set (KDDTest+). To mitigate potential discrepancies in data distribution between the pre-split training and test sets, this study combines them and performs a random split into new training and test sets in a 7:3 ratio.

UNSW-NB15 Dataset: Generated by researchers at the Australian Centre for Cyber Security (ACCS) using the IXIA tool, the UNSW-NB15 dataset was created from 100 GB of normal and modern attack traffic. The complete dataset comprises 2.5 million records, encompassing one normal category and nine attack categories: Analysis, Backdoor, DoS, Exploits, Fuzzers, Generic, Reconnaissance, Shellcode, and Worms. A smaller 10% subset of the dataset, containing 257,673 records and 43 features, is also available for easier processing. Of these, 42 features describe network traffic, while two features, attack_cat (multiclass labels) and label (binary labels), represent the classification targets. For the purposes of this study, which focuses on multiclass classification, the label feature is excluded, and the dataset is randomly split into training and test sets in a 7:3 ratio.

3.1.2. Data Preprocessing

Data preprocessing is a critical step to ensure that raw data are appropriately prepared for machine learning models. The following preprocessing techniques were applied:

(i) Handling Null Values: Missing and irrelevant data points were cleaned and removed to ensure a high-quality dataset.

(ii) Label Encoding: Categorical features, except for the target feature, were encoded into numerical values using label encoding. This transformation assigns integer values starting from 0 to make categorical data machine-readable.

(iii) Min–Max Scaling: After label encoding, the feature values were normalized to a range between [0, 1] using Min–Max scaling, as defined by Equation (1):

$$X_{new} = -\frac{X - X_{min}}{X_{max} - X_{min}}, \quad (1)$$

Here, X_{min} and X_{max} represent the minimum and maximum values of the feature vector, while X and X_{new} denote the original and normalized feature values, respectively.

(iv) Data Deduplication: Duplicate records in the datasets were removed to prevent overfitting, which can negatively affect the model's accuracy. This step minimizes potential errors in both model prediction and feature selection by ensuring a cleaner dataset for both the NSL-KDD and UNSW-NB15 datasets.

3.2. *An Improved Binary Simulated Annealing Algorithm (IBSA) for Feature Selection*

3.2.1. Theoretical Foundations of Simulated Annealing

The Simulated Annealing (SA) algorithm, first introduced by Metropolis et al. in 1953, derives its conceptual foundation from the annealing process observed in solid-state metallurgy. This algorithm was adapted for combinatorial optimization problems in 1983, where it gained widespread recognition for its unique efficacy in tackling discrete and nonlinear optimization challenges [29]. By mimicking the gradual cooling process of physical annealing, the algorithm systematically explores the solution space to approach the global optimum [30].

During the search process, SA probabilistically accepts solutions with increased energy to escape local optima, with the acceptance probability diminishing as the temperature decreases. The algorithm proceeds through the following steps:

Step 1—Initialization: Set initial parameters, including the starting temperature T_0, the number of outer iterations L_1, the number of inner iterations L_2, the minimum temperature T_{min}, and the cooling coefficient α. These parameters govern the search scope and convergence speed.

Step 2—Perturbation and Acceptance Criterion: Starting with an initial solution X_{old}, generate a perturbed solution X_{new}, compute their respective energy values, and decide acceptance probability P based on the Metropolis criterion:

$$P = \begin{cases} 1, & E(X_{new}) < E(X_{old}) \\ e^{-\frac{E(X_{new})-E(X_{old})}{T}} & E(X_{new}) > E(X_{old}) \end{cases}. \tag{2}$$

Step 3—Cooling Schedule: Common approaches include arithmetic and geometric cooling. This study employs a geometric cooling strategy, enabling extensive exploration in the early stages and refined local search later, as described by the equation:

$$T_{k+1} = \alpha \cdot T_k, \tag{3}$$

where $\alpha \in (0, 1)$ is the cooling coefficient.

Step 4—Termination Criterion: The algorithm concludes when the temperature falls below T_{min} or the outer iteration count reaches L_1. Otherwise, the perturbation and acceptance steps are repeated.

Simulated annealing's flexible and efficient design makes it particularly well-suited for solving large-scale discrete optimization problems. By leveraging the probabilistic acceptance of suboptimal solutions, SA circumvents the limitations of conventional methods prone to local optima. However, its performance is sensitive to the cooling schedule and parameter initialization, motivating the optimizations presented in this study.

3.2.2. Sigmoid Transfer Function

Given the binary nature of feature selection problems, conventional simulated annealing algorithms are not directly applicable. To address this, the Sigmoid transfer function, a well-established growth function in biological systems, is employed to map the continuous search space to a discrete one. The Sigmoid transfer function is defined as:

$$S\left(y^k{}_{i,j}(t)\right) = \frac{1}{1+e^{-y^k{}_{i,j}(t)}}, \tag{4}$$

where $y^k{}_{i,j}(t)$ denotes the position of the k-th dimension at iteration t. The corresponding binary update rule is given by:

$$y^k{}_{i,j}(t+1) = \begin{cases} 0 & if\ rand < S\left(y^k{}_{i,j}(t+1)\right) \\ 1 & if\ rand \geq S\left(y^k{}_{i,j}(t+1)\right) \end{cases}. \tag{5}$$

3.2.3. Enhancements to the Simulated Annealing Process

(a) Improved Initialization of Starting Temperature

Conventional simulated annealing algorithms typically set the initial temperature to a relatively high value in an attempt to achieve better search performance. However, excessively large initial temperatures, particularly when there is a significant magnitude difference, may not only lead to inefficient use of computational resources but also adversely affect the solution search process. To mitigate the magnitude disparity in the initial temperature and thus enhance the performance of the simulated annealing algorithm, this study sets the initial temperature based on the Metropolis criterion as follows:

$$T = -\frac{E(X_{max}) - E(X_{min})}{lnX_p}, \tag{6}$$

where $X_p = 0.9$ is a constant, and $E(X_{max})$, X_{min}, and $E(X_{average})$ represent the maximum, minimum, and average objective function values of N randomly sampled feasible solutions in the solution space ($N = 50$). These values are computed as:

$$E(X_{max}) = \overset{N}{\underset{i=1}{max}} S_i, \tag{7}$$

$$E(X_{average}) = \frac{1}{N}\sum_{i=1}^{N} S_i, \tag{8}$$

$$E(X_{min}) = \overset{N}{\underset{i=1}{min}} S_i. \tag{9}$$

(b) Refinement of the Metropolis Criterion

The Metropolis criterion is a crucial step that influences whether the perturbation results in the acceptance of a new solution, directly affecting both the algorithm's runtime and its optimization capabilities. For combinatorial optimization problems of varying scales, the difference in the values of $E(X_{new}) - E(X_{old})$ and the current temperature T may span several orders of magnitude, leading to excessively large (approaching 1) or small (approaching 0) probability values P, which in turn impacts the algorithm's performance in terms of both execution time and optimization effectiveness. In this project, the acceptance probability is defined as:

$$P = \begin{cases} 1, & if\ E(X_{new}) < E(X_{old}) \\ e^{-\frac{E(X_{new}) - E(X_{old})}{S_M \cdot T}} & otherwise \end{cases}, \tag{10}$$

where

$$S_M = e^{-\frac{E(X_{Average}) - E(X_{min})}{T_0}}. \tag{11}$$

By modulating the Metropolis acceptance criterion through S_M, it is possible to mitigate, to some extent, the potential disparity in the orders of magnitude between $E(X_{new}) - E(X_{old})$ and the current temperature T, thereby enhancing the sensitivity of the acceptance probability P.

(c) Multi-Neighborhood Solution Generation

Traditional SA generates neighboring solutions through minor perturbations, such as flipping a single feature. However, to enhance the algorithm's exploration capability of the current solution, this study proposes a multi-domain solution search mechanism to broaden the search space. Specifically, let the current solution be represented as $x_t = (x_1, x_2, \ldots, x_n)$, where $x_i \in \{0, 1\}$ indicates whether a feature is selected. The process of generating a neighboring solution is defined as follows:

$$x_{neighbor} = x_t \oplus d, \tag{12}$$

where $\oplus$ denotes the element-wise XOR operation, and d is a randomly generated feature flip vector, discretized via the Sigmoid function. C represents the number of features in the dataset. To enhance the algorithm's search capability without causing excessive changes to the current solution, the number of flipped features, k, is randomly chosen from the range $k \in [1, C/5]$. This design effectively prevents excessive jumps in the solution space during the search process, thereby balancing exploration and exploitation.

3.2.4. Pseudocode of the Proposed Algorithm

To clearly articulate the application process of the proposed improved binary simulated annealing algorithm (IBSA) for feature selection in network intrusion detection, Algorithm 1 presents the pseudocode of the algorithm. Specifically, Process 1 outlines the implementation of the algorithm initialization; Processes 2 through 12 represent the outer loop of the improved binary simulated annealing algorithm (IBSA); Processes 3 through 8 detail the inner loop of IBSA; Process 4 illustrates the computation principle of the loss function; Processes 5 and 6 provide a detailed explanation of the working mechanisms of the S-shaped propagation function and the multi-domain solution generation, respectively; and Process 7 defines the update mechanism for the feature selection state.

Algorithm 1 Pseudocode flow of the Improved Binary Simulated Annealing (IBSA)

1: Initialize the Simulated Annealing algorithm (SA).
    (a) Compute $E(X_{max})$, $E(X_{average})$, and $E(X_{min})$ using Equation (7) to Equation (9).
    (b) Calculate the initial temperature T using Equation (6).
    (c) Calculate the improved Metropolis criterion coefficient S_M using Equation (11).
    (d) Initialize the parameters α, L_1, L_2 and randomly initialize the feature set.
2: **while** (current iteration count $C_{Iter} < L_1$) or ($T < T_{min}$) **do**
3: **for** (i = 1 to L_2) **do**
4: Evaluate the loss of the objective function for the given feature subset:
    (a) Train the model using the current feature subset.
    (b) Calculate the loss of the objective function.
5: Randomly generate a feature flip vector using the Sigmoid function in Equation (4).
6: Generate a multi-neighbor solution using Equation (12).
7: Update the feature selection state using the improved Metropolis in Equation (10).
8: **end for**
9: Identify the current optimal feature subset (the best solution obtained so far).
10: Increment the current iteration count C_{Iter} by 1.
11: Temperature reduction using Equation (3)
12: **end while**
13: Return the optimal feature subset (x).

3.3. *Multi-Class Network Intrusion Detection Model: TPE-FL-LightGBM*

In this study, the optimal features selected through the IBSA method were compiled into a new feature set, which was subsequently utilized for final predictions using the LightGBM model. The introduction of the focal loss function was designed to enhance the LightGBM classifier's ability to address sample imbalance and handle hard-to-classify samples at the algorithmic level, thereby improving classification performance. Additionally, the study employed the Tree-structured Parzen Estimator (TPE) method to optimize the classifier's structure and hyperparameters, achieving optimal predictive performance.

3.3.1. Introduction to LightGBM

LightGBM is a fast, distributed, and high-performance gradient boosting framework based on decision tree algorithms, extensively applied to a variety of machine learning tasks, including regression, ranking, and classification [31]. As a Boosting algorithm, it constructs a strong learner by combining multiple weak learners. During training, the algorithm adjusts sample weights based on classification errors, ensuring that misclassified samples receive more focus in subsequent iterations [32]. Ultimately, the outputs of all weak learners are combined through weighted summation to form a strong model.

The core concept is expressed in the following Equation (13):

$$f(x) = \sum_{q=1}^{Q} \alpha_q T(x, \theta_q), \tag{13}$$

where $f(x)$ represents the target value corresponding to the training samples, Q is the number of base learners, α_q is the weight coefficient of the q-th base learner, x is the training sample, θ_q denotes the classification parameters of the learner, and $T(x, \theta_q)$ represents the output of the q-th base learner.

After defining the model's loss function and training data, the training process of the Boosting algorithm is formulated as an optimization problem aimed at minimizing the loss function. The objective function is expressed as:

$$argmin \sum_{h=1}^{H} L(y_h, f(x_h)), \tag{14}$$

where H is the number of samples, h is the sample index, y_h is the actual value of the data, $f(x_h)$ is the target value corresponding to the h-th sample, and $L(y_h, f(x_h))$ is the loss function value for the h-th sample.

In GBDT, this process results in a boosted tree model obtained via gradient descent. With each newly added sub-model, the gradient of the selected loss function decreases along the direction of the second-most informative variable, as shown in Equation (15):

$$L(F_j(x), Y) < L(F_{j-1}(x), Y), \tag{15}$$

where $L(F_j(x), Y)$ and $L(F_{j-1}(x), Y)$ denote the loss function values after the j-th and (j − 1)-th iterations, $F_j(x)$ and $F_{j-1}(x)$ represent the target values corresponding to the j-th and (j − 1)-th samples, and Y is the actual target value of the samples.

As a variant of GBDT, LightGBM effectively addresses the challenges faced by GBDT when processing large-scale data. The model incorporates two primary features:

Leaf-wise tree growth method: Adopting a leaf-wise growth strategy instead of level-wise growth, this method captures the data structure more efficiently and effectively avoids overfitting by controlling the minimum data per leaf and tree depth.

Histogram-based decision tree algorithm: LightGBM utilizes a histogram-based algorithm to select features, traversing only the discrete values of the histogram when searching for the optimal split point. This approach significantly reduces computational and storage costs, enhancing LightGBM's efficiency when handling large datasets.

3.3.2. Improvement of the Loss Function Based on Focal Loss

The loss function is pivotal to model optimization, directly influencing the efficiency of the training process and the model's ultimate performance [33]. This study addresses the issue of data imbalance from an algorithmic perspective by introducing a cost-sensitive learning approach. Cost-sensitive learning is an effective method for handling sample imbalance, primarily by adjusting the misclassification cost. By incorporating misclassification costs into the loss function, the model is encouraged to emphasize samples from the positive class, which often have higher misclassification costs.

For multi-class classification problems, the standard loss function is typically the multi-class cross-entropy loss, defined as:

$$CE(p, y) = -\sum_{i=1}^{C} y_i log(p_i), \tag{16}$$

where p_i represents the predicted probability for class i, and y_i is the true label.

The Focal Loss function builds upon the standard multi-class cross-entropy loss by introducing a dynamic scaling factor, which allows the model to focus on hard-to-classify samples during training, thereby enhancing its predictive capability across classes. The Focal Loss formula is expressed as:

$$FL(p_t) = -\sum_{i=1}^{C}(1 - p_i)^{\gamma} log(p_i), \tag{17}$$

Here, $(1 - p_i)^{\gamma}$ serves as a modulation factor to address the imbalance between easy and hard samples, where $\left(\gamma \geq 0\right)$ is a tunable parameter. Its mechanism operates as follows:

For misclassified samples, where $pt \to 0$, the modulation factor approaches 1, and the Focal Loss function is equivalent to the standard cross-entropy loss. For correctly classified samples, where $pt \to 1$, the modulation factor approaches 0, reducing the weight of easy-to-classify samples and their contribution to the total loss. As γ increases, the modulation factor amplifies the emphasis on misclassified samples, improving the model's ability to handle challenging instances.

To further address class imbalance, the cross-entropy loss coefficients are adjusted inversely proportional to the occurrence probabilities of each class. This is achieved by introducing a balanced cross-entropy function:

$$L(y, \hat{y}) = -\sum_{i=1}^{C} \alpha_i y_i log(p_i). \tag{18}$$

The improved Focal Loss function combines the balanced cross-entropy with the Focal Loss formulation:

$$FL(p_t) = -\sum_{i=1}^{C} \alpha_i (1 - p_i)^{\gamma} log(p_i)), \tag{19}$$

Here, α_i represents the inverse proportional weight, defined as:

$$a_i = \frac{N}{C \cdot N_i}, \tag{20}$$

where N is the total number of samples, C is the number of classes, and N_i is the number of samples in class i.

By incorporating the improved Focal Loss function as the loss function for the LightGBM model, this approach addresses the class imbalance issue in the dataset through inverse class-weighting, while also enabling the classifier to place greater emphasis on hard-to-classify samples, thereby enhancing the overall classification performance of the model.

3.3.3. Optimizing the Structure and Hyperparameters of Classification Models Using the Tree-Structured Parzen Estimator

In this study, the Tree-structured Parzen Estimator (TPE) optimization algorithm was employed to fine-tune the parameters of network intrusion detection classification models. The optimization process encompassed 300 iterations for each classification model, including comparative models, to achieve optimal performance. The underlying principles of the TPE optimization algorithm will be elaborated in the following sections.

The primary objective of parameter optimization is to maximize the model's performance or effectiveness [34]. This process can be formally expressed as follows, where the configuration space X encompasses all hyperparameters to be optimized. By iteratively adjusting these hyperparameters, an optimal configuration $x*$ is obtained:

$$x* = argmin\, f(x), \tag{21}$$

where X represents the configuration space, $f(x)$ is the objective function, and $x*$ is the set of hyperparameters within X that minimizes $f(x)$.

Bayesian optimization is an automated hyperparameter search method that optimizes the objective function by constructing a surrogate model based on prior evaluation results [35]. Unlike other search algorithms, Bayesian optimization reformulates the search problem as an optimization problem, leveraging prior observations and optimization outcomes at each iteration. Bergstra et al. [36] proposed a variant of Bayesian optimization, the TPE algorithm, specifically designed for hyperparameter optimization. This algorithm models $p(x|y)$ and $p(y)$ separately, rather than modeling $p(y|x)$ directly. Here, $p(y)$ represents the distribution of solutions, while $p(x|y)$ describes the distribution of parameter x given the solution. Additionally, the optimization criterion Expected Improvement (EI) is introduced to guide the search through the configuration space. The formulation for $p(x|y)$ is as follows:

$$p(x \mid y) = \begin{cases} l(x) & y < y' \\ g(x) & y \geq y' \end{cases}, \tag{22}$$

where y' is a predefined threshold, $l(x)$ denotes the density estimate of observations $x(i)$ with loss function values smaller than y', and $g(x)$ represents the density estimate of observations $x(i)$ with loss function values greater than or equal to y'.

To avoid local optima during the optimization process, it is essential to ensure comprehensive exploration of promising configuration regions. The EI criterion satisfies this requirement by quantifying the potential improvement of a solution relative to the threshold y'. The EI is defined as:

$$EI_{y'}(x) = \int_{-\infty}^{y'} (y' - y) p(y \mid x) dy. \tag{23}$$

By transforming $p(y \mid x)$ and constructing functions $\gamma = p(y' - y)$ and $p(x) = \int_R p(x \mid y)p(y)dy$, EI can be rewritten as:

$$EI_{y*}(x) \propto \left(y + \frac{g(x)}{l(x)}(1 - y)\right)^{-1}. \tag{24}$$

From this equation, it is evident that maximizing EI involves iteratively reducing $\frac{g(x)}{l(x)}$ to approach configurations where $l(x)$ is maximized, and $g(x)$ is minimized. This ensures convergence toward hyperparameter settings with the highest likelihood of improving model performance.

4. Experimental Results and Discussion

This section discusses the experimental setup, evaluation metrics, and the performance analysis of the proposed model.

4.1. Experimental Setup

The experiments were conducted using Python 3.9 within a conda environment, with the Sklearn library installed. The computational setup included a Windows 10 operating system, an Intel(R) Xeon(R) CPU E5-2670 @ 2.60 GHz, 64 GB RAM, an NVIDIA GeForce RTX 3090 GPU, and a 64-bit architecture with an x64-based processor.

4.2. Performance Metrics

A range of metrics was employed to evaluate the performance of the proposed data oversampling and optimization techniques across various classification models. These metrics, used for assessing multi-class classification effectiveness, are detailed below.

(i) Accuracy: Accuracy quantifies the proportion of correct predictions among all instances. It is computed as the ratio of correctly predicted instances for all classes to the total number of instances in the dataset, as shown in Equation (25):

$$Accuracy = \frac{\sum_{i-1}^{C} TP_i}{N}. \quad (25)$$

(ii) Precision: Precision measures the proportion of correctly predicted positive samples for a specific class iii. It is calculated using Equation (26):

$$Precision_i = \frac{TP_i}{TP_i + FP_i}. \quad (26)$$

(iii) Recall: Recall represents the proportion of actual positives correctly identified for a specific class iii. It is computed as shown in Equation (27):

$$Recall_i = \frac{TP_i}{TP_i + FN_i}. \quad (27)$$

(iv) F1-Score: The F1-score is the harmonic mean of precision and recall for a specific class iii. Its weighted form is calculated using Equation (28):

$$F1_i = \frac{2 \cdot Precision_i \cdot Recall_i}{Precision_i + Recall_i}. \quad (28)$$

(v) AUC-ROC: The Area Under the Receiver Operating Characteristic Curve (AUC-ROC) assesses the trade-off between the true positive rate and false positive rate.

$$AUC_{roc} = \int_0^1 \frac{TP}{TP + FN} d \frac{FP}{TN + FP}. \quad (29)$$

Here, True positives (TP) for each class i refer to the number of samples that genuinely belong to class i and are correctly predicted as such. True negatives (TN) for each class i denote the number of samples that do not belong to class i and are correctly identified as not belonging to it. False positives (FP) for each class i represent the number of samples that do not belong to class i but are incorrectly predicted as such. False negatives (FN) for each class i correspond to the number of samples that belong to class i but are mistakenly classified as not belonging to it. N represents the total number of samples in the dataset, and C denotes the total number of classes.

4.3. Performance Evaluation

4.3.1. Feature Selection Process Using the Improved Simulated Annealing Algorithm and Visualization-Based Evaluation

To enhance the global search capability of the algorithm while maintaining minimal computational overhead, and to ensure high exploratory behavior in the early stages while gradually narrowing the search space in the later stages to drive the solution toward optimality, this study sets the number of outer loop iterations L_1 to 300, the number of inner loop iterations L_2 to 1, and the cooling rate α to 0.95, without specifying a termination temperature. To visually analyze the feature selection process and performance of the IBSA algorithm, the best fitness values and corresponding feature counts for each epoch, along with global best values, were recorded and plotted as line graphs to illustrate the population iteration process.

The results in Figure 1 demonstrate that, during the early stages, the high temperature allows the algorithm to escape local optima, effectively identifying routes toward better solutions. As the temperature gradually decreases in later stages, the algorithm converges toward optimal feature combinations. After multiple iterations, the curve of the local best fitness aligns with that of the global best fitness, indicating successful convergence to a near-optimal solution with high search efficiency.

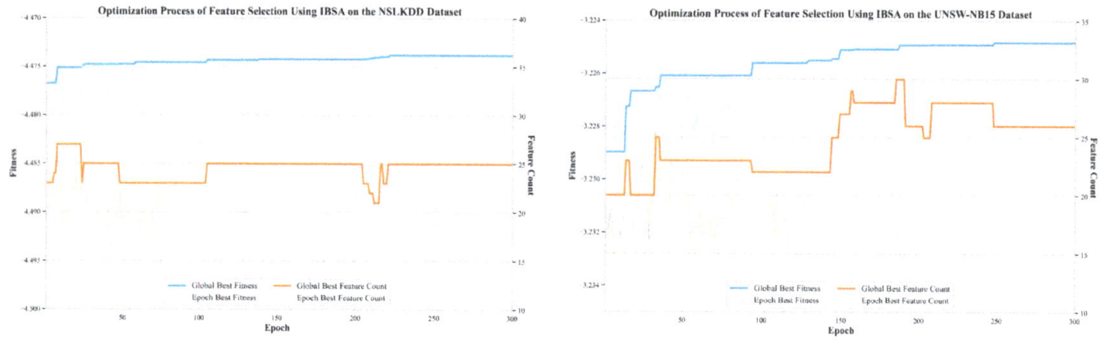

(**a**) (**b**)

Figure 1. Optimization process of feature selection using IBSA: (**a**) NSLKDD dataset; (**b**) UNSW-NB15 dataset.

For the NSLKDD dataset, the number of features was reduced from 42 to 25, while for the UNSW-NB15 dataset, the feature count was compressed from 44 to 26. The IBSA-based feature selection algorithm, employing a single particle population, demonstrated significantly faster search speeds compared to swarm intelligence optimization algorithms. In addition to reducing redundant features, the algorithm also effectively decreased the complexity of the network intrusion detection model. The experimental results of feature selection based on the improved Binary Simulated Annealing Algorithm on the NSL-KDD and UNSW-NB15 datasets are detailed in Table 2.

Table 2. Experimental results of feature selection using the improved binary simulated annealing algorithm on the NSL-KDD and UNSW-NB15 datasets.

NSL-KDD Dataset		UNSW-NB15 Dataset	
duration	service	dur	proto
src_bytes	dst_bytes	state	sbytes
num_failed_logins	logged_in	rate	sttl
num_root	num_file_creations	dloss	sjit
is_guest_login	count	smean	dmean
srv_serror_rate	rerror_rate	ct_srv_src	ct_state_ttl
diff_srv_rate	dst_host_same_srv_rate	ct_src_dport_ltm	ct_dst_sport_ltm
dst_host_same_src_port_rate	dst_host_srv_diff_host_rate	is_ftp_login	ct_ftp_cmd
dst_host_rerror_rate	flag	ct_srv_dst	is_sm_ips_ports
hot	num_compromised	service	response_body_len
num_outbound_cmds	srv_count	dbytes	ct_dst_ltm
same_srv_rate	dst_host_diff_srv_rate	sloss	ct_dst_src_ltm
dst_host_serror_rate		dtcpb	ct_src_ltm

4.3.2. Performance Evaluation of the Proposed Method

In this section, the performance of the proposed method is evaluated using intuitive performance metrics, confusion matrices, and ROC curves. A comparative analysis is conducted between the proposed method and the original LightGBM approach, which has not undergone IBSA feature selection, Focal Loss function enhancement, or Tree-structured Parzen Estimator (TPE) hyperparameter tuning.

(a) NSLKDD Dataset

To comprehensively assess the performance improvements for each class within the NSLKDD dataset, a comparison between the original method and the proposed method was conducted. Table 3 presents the key performance metrics of the two methods, including the weighted and absolute averages of Precision, Recall, F1 score, and Accuracy on the test set, as well as the accuracy obtained through five-fold cross-validation, denoted as CV Accuracy.

Table 3. Multiclass performance comparison before and after applying the proposed method to the NSLKDD dataset.

Class	Original Performance			Proposed Performance		
	Precision	Recall	F1-Score	Precision	Recall	F1-Score
Normal	96.46	99.51	97.96	99.65	99.71	99.68
Generic	99.35	98.93	99.14	99.84	99.93	99.88
Exploits	98.02	92.08	94.96	99.37	99.49	99.43
Fuzzers	97.55	68.89	80.75	97.70	95.67	96.67
Dos	100.00	6.49	12.20	97.10	87.01	91.78
Weighted	97.68	97.66	97.51	99.64	99.64	99.64
Macro	98.28	73.18	77.00	98.73	96.36	97.49
Accuracy	97.66			99.64		
CVAccuracy	97.65			99.66		

As shown in Table 3, the proposed method demonstrates superior generalization performance compared to the original method on the NSLKDD dataset. Notable improvements are observed in accuracy, weighted precision, recall, and F1-score, each increasing by approximately 2%. However, for the Dos class, precision decreased from 100% to 97.10%. This reduction can be attributed to the original method's limited focus on the Dos class, leading to high precision but a significantly low recall. The incorporation of a cost-sensitive focal loss function in the proposed method has addressed this imbalance by emphasizing underrepresented and hard-to-classify samples, which, while increasing the likelihood of misclassifications among other classes as Dos, resulted in a marked improvement in the Dos class F1-score, reaching 91.78%. Overall, these results highlight the enhanced detection capability of the proposed method.

To further assess the generalization ability of the proposed method, ROC curves and confusion matrices were generated for the NSLKDD dataset, as depicted in Figures 2 and 3.

The ROC curves in Figure 2a,b illustrate the performance of the baseline and proposed methods across various decision thresholds, with corresponding AUC values computed for each class. AUC values closer to 1 indicate superior classification performance. For the baseline method, classes such as Fuzzers and Dos exhibit significant fluctuations and unsmooth curves, indicating instability in prediction performance. Additionally, these classes cover considerably smaller areas under the curve compared to the majority classes. By contrast, the proposed method markedly improves the prediction stability across all classes, particularly for minority classes like Fuzzers and Dos, whose curves become smoother and encompass larger areas. These findings underscore the enhanced discriminatory power of the proposed method for minority classes. Moreover, AUC values exceeding 0.999 for all classes further corroborate the overall stability and effectiveness of the proposed approach.

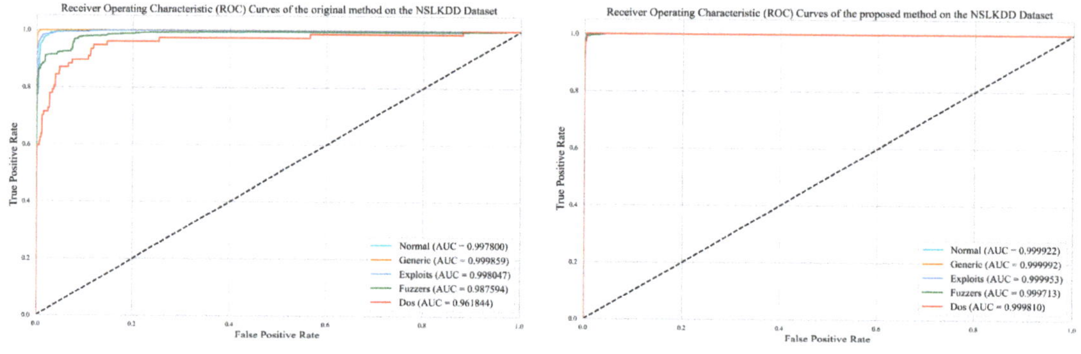

(a) (b)

Figure 2. ROC curves for the baseline and proposed methods on the NSLKDD dataset: (**a**) Original method; (**b**) Proposed method.

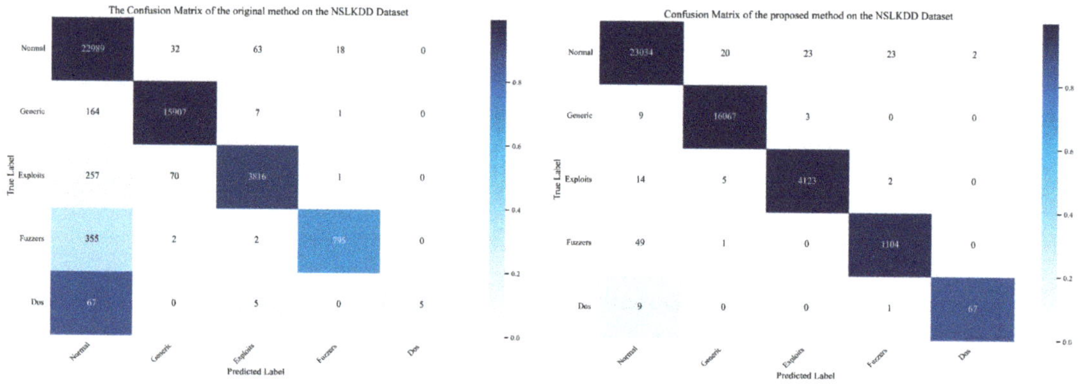

(a) (b)

Figure 3. Comparison of confusion matrices for predicting the test set on the NSLKDD dataset: (**a**) Original method; (**b**) Proposed method.

Figure 3 presents the classification outcomes for various attack types based on confusion matrices, with normalized color intensity to ensure equitable visualization of class importance. Despite occasional misclassifications, the proposed method accurately identifies both normal and attack types across the NSLKDD dataset. In contrast, while the original method performs well for the majority of classes, its performance for minority classes such as *Fuzzers* and *Dos* is significantly inferior. These results highlight the pronounced advantages of the proposed method in addressing classification challenges for the NSLKDD dataset.

(b) UNSW-NB15 Dataset

To comprehensively evaluate the performance improvements achieved for each class within the UNSW-NB15 dataset, the original method was compared against the proposed approach. Table 4 presents the primary performance metrics of the two methods, including the weighted and absolute averages of Precision, Recall, F1 score, and Accuracy on the test set, as well as the accuracy obtained through five-fold cross-validation, denoted as CV Accuracy.

Table 4. Multiclass performance comparison before and after applying the proposed method to the UNSW-NB15 dataset.

Class	Original Performance			Proposed Performance		
	Precision	Recall	F1-Score	Precision	Recall	F1-Score
Normal	95.79	95.38	95.59	96.94	96.52	96.73
Generic	99.68	98.39	99.03	99.76	98.71	99.23
Exploits	65.45	81.32	72.52	68.34	83.28	75.08
Fuzzers	75.91	75.24	75.57	80.49	78.98	79.73
Dos	37.39	29.59	33.04	43.24	35.59	39.04
Reconnaissance	91.28	76.33	83.14	93.34	78.36	85.19
Analysis	61.96	14.45	23.43	66.76	29.02	40.46
Backdoor	45.65	11.90	18.88	76.33	22.38	34.61
Shellcode	68.32	67.16	67.74	75.11	74.49	74.95
Worms	63.41	55.32	59.09	73.68	59.57	65.88
Macro	70.48	60.51	62.80	77.40	65.72	69.09
Weighted	84.55	84.70	84.17	86.78	86.66	86.32
Accuracy	84.70			86.66		
CV Accuracy	84.66			86.63		

As shown in Table 4, the proposed method demonstrated a significant improvement in generalization performance on the UNSW-NB15 dataset compared to the baseline method. Specifically, the accuracy increased by approximately 2%, while the weighted F1-score and macro-average F1-score improved by 2.15% and 6.29%, respectively. F1-scores for all classes outperformed those of the original method, with particularly notable gains for minority classes such as Analysis, Backdoor, Shellcode, and Worms, which saw improvements of 17.03%, 15.73%, 7.21%, and 6.79%, respectively.

Notably, the F1-scores for Analysis and Backdoor under the original method were both below 25%, indicating that the original method was nearly ineffective at detecting these classes. In contrast, the proposed method increased their F1-scores to 40.46% and 34.61%, respectively. The poor performance of the original method likely stems from the low representation of these classes, compounded by the inherent difficulty in detecting them. The proposed method's incorporation of the Focal Loss function enhanced the classifier's focus on minority and hard-to-detect classes. Additionally, the IBSA-based feature selection effectively removed redundant features, further improving prediction accuracy.

To further investigate the generalization ability of the proposed method, ROC curves and confusion matrices for both methods on the UNSW-NB15 dataset are presented in Figures 4 and 5, respectively.

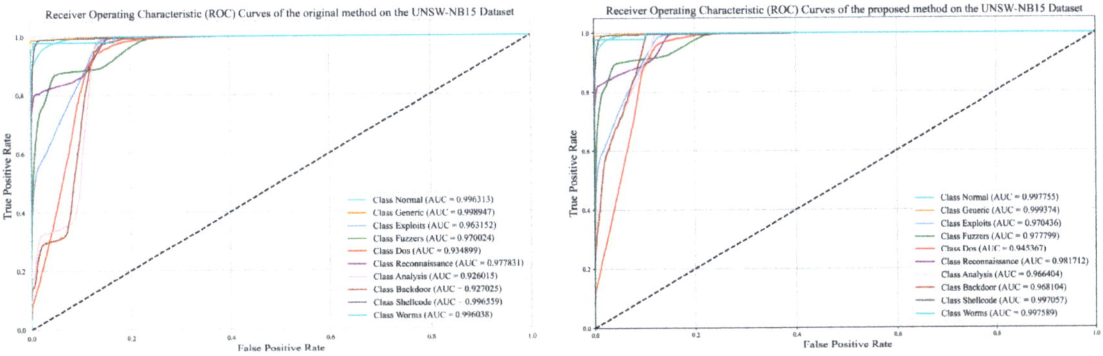

(a) **(b)**

Figure 4. ROC curves for the baseline and proposed methods on the UNSW-NB15 dataset: (**a**) Original method; (**b**) Proposed method.

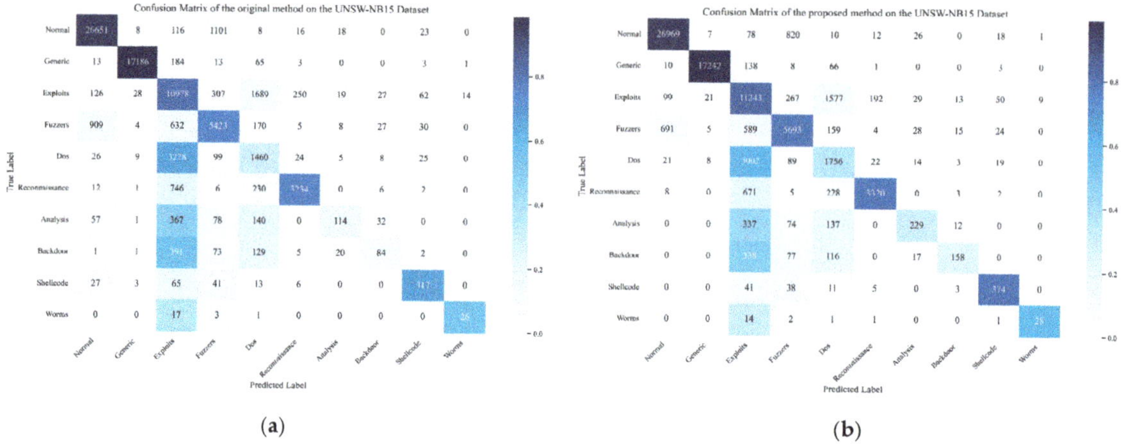

Figure 5. Comparison of confusion matrices for the test set on the UNSW-NB15 dataset: (**a**) Original method; (**b**) Proposed method.

Figure 4a,b depict the ROC curves for the baseline and proposed methods, respectively, alongside the calculated AUC values for each class. The original method yielded AUC values below 0.93 for minority classes such as Analysis and Backdoor, with noticeable curve fluctuations indicating instability in predictions. By contrast, the proposed method substantially improved prediction performance, yielding smoother curves and increasing AUC values to 0.966 and 0.968 for these classes. Furthermore, the proposed method enhanced detection performance across all classes, surpassing the original method in every instance. The near-unity AUC value for the Normal class further attests to the model's ability to distinguish normal traffic from attack traffic with high precision, demonstrating superior overall stability and effectiveness.

Figure 5 visualizes the classification outcomes across attack types based on confusion matrices. On the UNSW-NB15 dataset, the original method exhibited significant misclassification issues, particularly for minority classes such as Analysis, Backdoor, and Shellcode, which were often misidentified as normal traffic or other attack types. Misclassifications were also observed between Exploits, Fuzzers, and normal traffic. These inaccuracies were exacerbated by the similarity of traffic features, class imbalance, and redundant features in the input data.

While the proposed method still encountered some misclassifications, it substantially alleviated these issues. For instance, minority classes such as Analysis, Backdoor, and Shellcode were no longer misclassified as normal traffic, significantly reducing the likelihood of undetected attack traffic. As a result, the proposed method exhibited notable superiority in improving multi-class detection performance on the UNSW-NB15 dataset.

4.3.3. Results of Ablation Analysis

Tables 5 and 6 summarize the comprehensive results of the ablation analysis performed on the NSLKDD and UNSW-NB15 datasets, respectively, using the LightGBM classifier as the network intrusion detection model. The experiments were divided into four groups: no modifications applied, the inclusion of the cost-sensitive Focal loss, the application of IBSA for feature selection, and the combination of both methods.

Table 5. Results of ablation analysis on the NSLKDD dataset.

Number	Focal Loss	IBSA	Accuracy (%)	Precision (%)	Recall (%)	F1-Score (%)
1	—	—	97.66	97.72	97.66	97.51
2	√	—	99.11	99.10	99.11	99.10
3	—	√	98.92	98.88	98.92	98.74
4	√	√	99.64	99.64	99.64	99.64

Table 6. Results of ablation analysis on the UNSW-NB15 dataset.

Number	Focal Loss	IBSA	Accuracy (%)	Precision (%)	Recall (%)	F1-Score (%)
1	—	—	84.70	84.55	84.70	84.17
2	√	—	85.93	85.86	85.93	85.87
3	—	√	85.65	85.06	85.65	85.24
4	√	√	86.66	86.78	86.66	86.32

The results indicate that incorporating the cost-sensitive Focal loss significantly enhances all performance metrics of the model, particularly Precision and F1 score. This improvement can be attributed to the mitigation of class imbalance, enabling the intrusion detection model to better focus on hard-to-classify samples and minority classes. When IBSA feature selection was applied independently, the model demonstrated improved generalization performance; however, the F1 score remained notably lower than Accuracy, highlighting the persistent impact of class imbalance.

The ablation results demonstrate that the proposed network intrusion detection method achieves optimal performance when both techniques are employed in tandem, substantiating the remarkable effectiveness of the approach developed in this study.

4.3.4. Comparative Analysis

(a) Performance Evaluation Between Original and Proposed Methods

The performance of machine learning models under the original and proposed methodologies was evaluated. Tables 7 and 8 summarize the performance metrics of several mainstream classifiers on the NSL-KDD and UNSW-NB15 datasets, respectively. Across the NSL-KDD dataset, the proposed method demonstrated notable performance improvements across nearly all classifiers compared to the original approach. Notably, while LightGBM consistently outperformed most other models except XGBoost in terms of predictive accuracy, it surpassed XGBoost in training speed. For the UNSW-NB15 dataset, the proposed methodology enhanced the performance of all classifiers. LightGBM exhibited superior generalization capabilities in both datasets, solidifying its status as an effective classifier for network intrusion detection.

Table 7. Comparative analysis of multiple mainstream classifiers between the original and proposed methods on the NSLKDD dataset.

Model	Original Method				Proposed Method			
	Accuracy	Precision	Recall	F1-Score	Accuracy	Precision	Recall	F1-Score
KNN	96.89	96.96	96.89	96.75	98.09	98.11	98.09	98.07
SVM	95.22	95.28	95.22	95.07	97.12	97.12	97.12	97.12
DT	97.16	97.25	97.16	97.03	98.70	98.71	98.70	98.69
RF	97.42	97.49	97.42	97.27	99.11	99.11	99.11	99.11
MLP	97.01	97.08	97.01	96.87	98.97	98.97	98.97	98.97
XGB	97.66	97.72	97.66	97.51	99.64	99.64	99.64	99.64
LGBM	97.65	97.71	97.65	97.50	99.64	99.64	99.64	99.64

Table 8. Comparative analysis of multiple mainstream classifiers between the original and proposed methods in the UNSW-NB15 dataset.

Model	Original Method				Proposed Method			
	Accuracy	Precision	Recall	F1-Score	Accuracy	Precision	Recall	F1-Score
KNN	78.14	76.58	78.14	76.95	80.76	79.73	80.76	79.83
SVM	77.54	75.65	77.54	75.87	80.28	79.46	80.28	79.88
DT	82.57	82.34	82.57	82.01	85.26	85.27	85.26	84.82
RF	84.39	84.29	84.39	83.73	86.53	86.55	86.53	86.10
MLP	82.37	81.27	82.37	80.55	82.93	82.61	82.93	81.90
XGB	84.69	84.55	84.69	84.16	86.65	86.76	86.65	86.30
LGBM	84.70	84.55	84.70	84.17	86.66	86.78	86.66	86.32

(b) Comparative Analysis of Focal Loss and Multiple Imbalance Handling Methods

Focal loss, as a cost-sensitive learning approach, addresses data imbalance by increasing attention to hard-to-classify samples. To further investigate, we compared Focal loss with several data imbalance handling methods, including traditional statistical synthetic techniques such as SMOTE and ADASYN, as well as a generative model-based method using conditional GAN (CGAN) [22,37,38]. Tables 9 and 10 present the performance outcomes on the NSL-KDD and UNSW-NB15 datasets, respectively, using the LightGBM classifier. While SMOTE and ADASYN achieved stable performance gains, their lack of emphasis on hard-to-classify samples resulted in inferior performance compared to classifiers incorporating Focal loss. Conversely, CGAN demonstrated the lowest performance, likely due to poor-quality generated data caused by limitations in its loss function and insufficient training samples for minority classes, leading to mode collapse. The integration of Focal loss not only surpassed other methods in performance but also significantly reduced computational overhead associated with synthetic data generation. These findings validate the efficacy of the proposed cost-sensitive learning approach in addressing data imbalance at the algorithmic level.

Table 9. Comparative analysis of focal loss with multiple imbalance handling methods in the NSLKDD dataset.

Imbalance Handling Methods	Accuracy	Precision	Recall	F1-Score
Original Dataset	97.66	97.72	97.66	97.51
SMOTE [37]	98.51	98.50	98.51	98.50
ADASYN [38]	98.74	98.75	98.74	98.75
CGAN [22]	92.95	93.02	92.95	92.92
Proposed Focal loss	99.11	99.10	99.11	99.10

Table 10. Comparative analysis of focal loss with multiple imbalance handling methods in the UNSW-NB15 dataset.

Imbalance Handling Methods	Accuracy	Precision	Recall	F1-Score
Original Dataset	84.70	84.55	84.70	84.17
SMOTE [37]	84.87	84.83	84.87	84.76
ADASYN [38]	85.14	85.11	85.14	85.08
CGAN [22]	80.62	80.07	80.62	79.54
Proposed Focal loss	85.83	85.76	85.83	85.77

(c) Comparative Analysis of the IBSA Feature Selection Method and Other Feature Selection Techniques

This section examines the performance of the proposed model using five additional feature selection methods: XGBoost feature importance, IGRF-RFE [39], and three heuristic algorithms—Binary Grey Wolf Optimization (BGWO) [40], Genetic Algorithms (GA) [10], and Binary Pigeon Inspired Optimizer (BPIO) [27]. Focal loss was incorporated into the classifiers, followed by the application of each feature selection method. For XGBoost feature importance, the number of selected features was constrained to match that identified by the proposed method. The IGRF-RFE method used thresholds of 0.25 for information gain and 0.02 for random forest importance, as outlined in prior work, followed by RFE to eliminate redundancy. The three heuristic algorithms were iterated 300 times to identify optimal feature subsets. The datasets, processed with these feature selection methods, were then analyzed for their impact on classifier performance.

Table 11 compares the performance of these feature selection techniques with the proposed IBSA approach on the NSL-KDD and UNSW-NB15 datasets. Among the techniques, the improved binary simulated annealing algorithm (IBSA) demonstrated exceptional performance. While the XGBoost feature importance method excelled in identifying individual feature significance, it was less effective in capturing feature interdependencies. The IGRF-RFE method, characterized by its strong interpretability, maintained competitive performance even with fewer features but fell short of the proposed approach. Despite 300 iterations, heuristic methods such as BGWO, GA, and BPIO failed to outperform the feature subsets identified by IBSA. Furthermore, the IBSA-based feature selection algorithm, with a single particle group, exhibited significantly faster search speeds compared to other population-based optimization methods, particularly genetic algorithms. By reducing redundant features, IBSA effectively lowered model complexity while maintaining superior performance in network intrusion detection.

Table 11. Comparative analysis of the IBSA feature selection method and other feature selection techniques.

Method	NSLKDD Dataset				UNSW-NB15 Dataset			
	Num	Precision	Recall	F1-Score	Num	Precision	Recall	F1-Score
XGBoost	25	99.11	99.11	99.11	26	86.21	86.09	85.77
IGRF-RFE [39]	18	99.31	99.31	99.31	25	86.44	86.31	86.07
BGWO [40]	24	99.44	99.44	99.44	23	86.51	86.38	86.07
GA [10]	24	99.54	99.54	99.54	27	86.64	86.50	86.26
BPIO [27]	25	99.48	99.48	99.48	22	86.42	86.31	86.03
Proposed IBSA	25	99.64	99.64	99.64	26	86.78	86.66	86.32

5. Conclusions

With the widespread proliferation of the internet, individuals frequently leverage the opportunities and facilities it provides in their daily lives. However, the growing cybersecurity threats continue to jeopardize user interests. Consequently, establishing an effective system for monitoring malicious internet activities and issuing timely warnings upon detection has become crucial. In this context, network intrusion detection systems (NIDS) have emerged.

Most existing intrusion detection systems typically exhibit strong classification performance on majority class samples but perform poorly on minority class samples. On the other hand, feature redundancy remains a critical issue, as it leads to increased training costs and suboptimal model performance.

To address these challenges, this study introduces Focal loss-based cost-sensitive learning and an improved Binary Simulated Annealing Algorithm (IBSA) for network intrusion detection, with LightGBM employed as the classifier. Focal loss addresses data imbalance at the algorithmic level and enhances the classifier's sensitivity to difficult-to-classify samples, thereby improving overall performance. Moreover, the proposed IBSA utilizes an S-shaped propagation function to apply traditional simulated annealing for feature selection, while improvements to the initial temperature and Metropolis criterion mitigate the detrimental effects of large differences in algorithm parameters on search performance. Additionally, the multi-neighborhood solution generation mechanism expands the search space, alleviating the risk of the algorithm converging to local optima. Subsequently, the LightGBM classifier, further optimized by the Tree-structured Parzen Estimator (TPE) algorithm, achieves a more accurate and robust classification of intrusion traffic. The cross-validation experimental results demonstrate that, compared to the original method, the proposed approach achieves an accuracy improvement of 2.01% on the NSL-KDD dataset and 1.97% on the UNSW-NB15 dataset. Furthermore, through visual analysis, ablation studies, and comparative experiments, the adaptability and reliability of the proposed method in the field of network intrusion detection are further validated.

Although this study successfully enhances the distinction between normal and intrusion categories in multi-class scenarios, challenges remain in differentiating similar intrusion categories, with false positives being a notable issue for single classifiers. To further improve the detection success rate between different intrusion categories, we plan to develop a multi-stage, multi-classifier network intrusion detection system in future work. This system will conduct initial detection of specified intrusion categories, followed by misdetection identification using classifiers trained on those categories and their similar counterparts, ensuring a more precise classification of specific intrusion types. While this approach may increase computational resource consumption, it is expected to be a more effective detection method.

Author Contributions: Conceptualization, Y.L. and R.C.; Data curation, C.L.; Formal analysis, R.C.; Funding acquisition, Y.L. and J.S.; Investigation, R.C.; Methodology, R.C.; Project administration, Y.L. and J.S.; Resources, R.C.; Software, R.C.; Supervision, Y.L., D.Y., K.T. and J.S.; Validation, R.C.; Visualization, R.C.; Writing—original draft, R.C.; Writing—review & editing, Y.L. and R.C. All authors have read and agreed to the published version of the manuscript.

Funding: This research was supported by a special grant from the National Natural Science Foundation of China under Grant No. 42206187, the program for scientific research start-up funds of Guangdong Ocean University under Grant No. 060302102303 and R20010, Guangdong Provincial Science and Technology Innovation Strategy under Grant No. pdjh2023b0247, Undergraduate Innovation Team Project of Guangdong Ocean University under Grant No. CXTD2023014 and CXTD2025007, National College Students Innovation and Entrepreneurship Training Program under grant No. 202410566027.

Data Availability Statement: The datasets used and/or analyzed during the current study are available from the corresponding author upon reasonable request. The data used in this study can be found in the Canadian Institute for Cybersecurity (https://www.unb.ca/cic/datasets/index.html) (accessed on 1 October 2024).

Conflicts of Interest: The authors declare that the research was conducted in the absence of any commercial or financial relationships that could be construed as potential conflicts of interest.

References

1. Xia, L.M.; Li, Z.M. A new method of abnormal behavior detection using LSTM network with temporal attention mechanism *J. Supercomput.* **2021**, *77*, 773223–773241. [CrossRef]
2. Zhu, Y.K.; Gaba, G.S.; Almansour, F.M.; Alroobaea, R.; Masud, M. Application of data mining technology in detecting network intrusion and security maintenance. *J. Intell. Syst.* **2021**, *30*, 664–676. [CrossRef]
3. Lu, H.M.; Wang, T.; Xu, X.; Wang, T. Cognitive memory-guided autoencoder for effective intrusion detection in internet of things *IEEE Trans. Ind. Inform.* **2022**, *18*, 3358–3366. [CrossRef]
4. Ramalingam, G.P.; Annie, R.A.X.; Gopalakrishnan, S. Optimized fuzzy enabled semi-supervised intrusion detection system for attack prediction. *Intell. Autom. Soft Comput.* **2022**, *32*, 1479–1492. [CrossRef]
5. Ragab, M.; Alshammari, S.M.; Al-Ghamdi, A.S. Modified Metaheuristics with Weighted Majority Voting Ensemble Deep Learning Model for Intrusion Detection System. *Comput. Syst. Sci. Eng.* **2023**, *47*, 2497–2512. [CrossRef]
6. Sarkar, A.; Sharma, H.S.; Singh, M.M. A supervised machine learning-based solution for efficient network intrusion detection using ensemble learning based on hyperparameter optimization. *Int. J. Inf. Technol.* **2023**, *15*, 423–434. [CrossRef]
7. Ponmalar, A.; Dhanakoti, V. Hybrid Whale Tabu algorithm optimized convolutional neural network architecture for intrusion detection in big data. *Concurr. Comput. Pract. Exp.* **2022**, *34*, e7038. [CrossRef]
8. Gu, Q.; Li, Z.; Han, J. Generalized Fisher score for feature selection. *arXiv* **2012**, arXiv:1202.3725.

Zhang, Y.; Wang, Z. Feature Engineering and Model Optimization Based Classification Method for Network Intrusion Detection. *Appl. Sci.* **2023**, *13*, 9363. [CrossRef]

). Zorarpaci, E. A fast intrusion detection system based on swift wrapper feature selection and speedy ensemble classifier. *Eng. Appl. Artif. Intell.* **2024**, *133*, 108162. [CrossRef]

1. Srivastava, A.; Sinha, D.; Kumar, V. WCGAN-GP based synthetic attack data generation with GA based feature selection for IDS. *Comput. Secur.* **2023**, *134*, 103432. [CrossRef]

2. Nazir, A.; Khan, R. A novel combinatorial optimization-based feature selection method for network intrusion detection. *Comput. Secur.* **2021**, *102*, 102164. [CrossRef]

3. Ohanyan, H.; Portengen, L.; Huss, A.; Traini, E.; Beulens, J.W.J.; Hoek, G.; Lakerveld, J.; Vermeulen, R. Machine learning approaches to characterize the obesogenic urban exposome. *Environ. Int.* **2022**, *158*, 107015. [CrossRef] [PubMed]

4. Liu, Z.; Thapa, N.; Shaver, A.; Roy, K.; Siddula, M.; Yuan, X.; Yu, A. Using Embedded Feature Selection and CNN for Classification on CCD-INID-V1—A New IoT Dataset. *Sensors* **2021**, *21*, 4834. [CrossRef] [PubMed]

5. Zouhri, H.; Idri, A.; Ratnani, A. Evaluating the impact of filter-based feature selection in intrusion detection systems. *Int. J. Inf. Secur.* **2024**, *23*, 759–785. [CrossRef]

6. Liu, G.J.; Zhang, J.B. CNID: Research of network intrusion detection based on convolutional neural network. *Discret. Dyn. Nat. Soc.* **2020**, *2020*, 4705982. [CrossRef]

7. Liu, J.; Zhao, H.B. Application of convolution neural network in medical image processing. *Technol. Health Care* **2021**, *29*, 407–417. [CrossRef]

3. Lu, J.Z.; Liu, X.L.; Zhang, S.B.; Chang, Y. Research and analysis of electromagnetic Trojan detection based on deep learning. *Secur. Commun. Netw.* **2020**, *2020*, 6641844. [CrossRef]

). Yang, J.; Sheng, Y.Q.; Wang, J.L. A GBDT-paralleled quadratic ensemble learning for intrusion detection system. *IEEE Access* **2020**, *8*, 175467–175482. [CrossRef]

). Fu, Y.; Du, Y.; Cao, Z.; Li, Q.; Xiang, W. A Deep Learning Model for Network Intrusion Detection with Imbalanced Data. *Electronics* **2022**, *11*, 898. [CrossRef]

1. Tang, Z.Y.; Hu, H.Y.; Xu, C.H. A federated learning method for network intrusion detection. *Concurr. Comput.-Pract. Exp.* **2021**, *34*, e6812. [CrossRef]

2. Liu, Z.; Hu, J.; Liu, Y.; Roy, K.; Yuan, X.; Xu, J. Anomaly-Based Intrusion on IoT Networks Using AIGAN—A Generative Adversarial Network. *IEEE Access* **2023**, *11*, 91116–91132. [CrossRef]

3. Dlamini, G.; Fahim, M. DGM: A data generative model to improve minority class presence in anomaly detection domain. *Neural Comput. Appl.* **2021**, *33*, 13635–13646. [CrossRef]

4. Alsaleh, A.; Binsaeedan, W. The influence of salp swarm algorithm-based feature selection on network anomaly intrusion detection. *IEEE Access* **2021**, *9*, 112466–112477. [CrossRef]

5. Ahakonye, L.A.C.; Nwakanma, C.I.; Lee, J.-M.; Kim, D.S. SCADA intrusion detection scheme exploiting the fusion of modified decision tree and Chi-square feature selection. *Internet Things* **2023**, *21*, 100676. [CrossRef]

5. Hagar, A.A.; Gawali, B.W. Apache Spark and deep learning models for high-performance network intrusion detection using CSE-CIC-IDS2018. Comput. *Intell. Neurosci.* **2022**, *2022*, 3131153. [CrossRef]

7. Alazzam, H.; Sharieh, A.; Sabri, K.E. A feature selection algorithm for intrusion detection system based on pigeon inspired optimizer. *Expert Syst. Appl.* **2020**, *148*, 113249. [CrossRef]

3. Bonab, M.S.; Ghaffari, A.; Gharehchopogh, F.S.; Alemi, P. A wrapper-based feature selection for improving performance of intrusion detection systems. *Int. J. Commun. Syst.* **2020**, *33*, e4434. [CrossRef]

). Jiménez-Martín, A.; Mateos, A.; Hernández, J.Z. Aluminium Parts Casting Scheduling Based on Simulated Annealing. *Mathematics* **2021**, *9*, 741. [CrossRef]

). Kuznetsov, A.; Wieclaw, L.; Poluyanenko, N.; Hamera, L.; Kandiy, S.; Lohachova, Y. Optimization of a Simulated Annealing Algorithm for S-Boxes Generating. *Sensors* **2022**, *22*, 6073. [CrossRef] [PubMed]

1. Zhang, S.; Yuan, Y.; Yao, Z.; Yang, J.; Wang, X.; Tian, J. Coronary Artery Disease Detection Model Based on Class Balancing Methods and LightGBM Algorithm. *Electronics* **2022**, *11*, 1495. [CrossRef]

2. Xing, C.; Liu, M.; Peng, J.; Wang, Y.; Liu, Y.; Gao, S.; Zheng, Z.; Liao, J. Disturbance Frequency Trajectory Prediction in Power Systems Based on LightGBM Spearman. *Electronics* **2024**, *13*, 597. [CrossRef]

3. Xiang, W.; Wu, Y.; Peng, C.; Cai, K.; Ren, H.; Peng, Y. A Fault Diagnosis Method for Electric Check Valve Based on Res-Net-ELM with Adaptive Focal Loss. *Electronics* **2024**, *13*, 3426. [CrossRef]

4. Li, J.; Chen, Z.; Li, X.; Yi, X.; Zhao, Y.; He, X.; Huang, Z.; Hassaan, M.A.; Nemr, A.E.; Huang, M. Water quality soft-sensor prediction in anaerobic process using deep neural network optimized by tree-structured Parzen estimator. *Front. Environ. Sci. Eng.* **2022**, *17*, 67. [CrossRef]

35. Massaoudi, M.; Abu-Rub, H.; Refaat, S.S.; Trabelsi, M.; Chihi, I.; Oueslati, F.S. Enhanced deep belief network based on ensemble learning and tree-structured of Parzen estimators: An optimal photovoltaic power forecasting method. *IEEE Access* **2021**, *9* 150330–150344. [CrossRef]
36. Bergstra, J.; Bardenet, R.; Kégl, B.; Bengio, Y. Algorithms for Hyper-Parameter Optimization. In Proceedings of the Advances in Neural Information Processing Systems, Sierra Nevada, Spain, 16–17 December 2011. Available online: https://proceedings neurips.cc/paper_files/paper/2011/hash/86e8f7ab32cfd12577bc2619bc635690-Abstract.html (accessed on 7 November 2024).
37. Liu, J.; Gao, Y.; Hu, F. A fast network intrusion detection system using adaptive synthetic oversampling and LightGBM. *Comput. Secur.* **2021**, *106*, 102289. [CrossRef]
38. Talukder, M.A.; Hasan, K.F.; Islam, M.M.; Uddin, M.A.; Akhter, A.; Yousuf, M.A.; Moni, M.A. A dependable hybrid machine learning model for network intrusion detection. *J. Inf. Secur. Appl.* **2023**, *72*, 103405. [CrossRef]
39. Yin, Y.; Jang-Jaccard, J.; Xu, W.; Singh, A.; Zhu, J.; Sabrina, F.; Kwak, J. IGRF-RFE: A hybrid feature selection method for MLP-based network intrusion detection on UNSW-NB15 dataset. *J. Big Data* **2023**, *10*, 15. [CrossRef]
40. Hu, P.; Pan, J.; Chu, S. Improved binary grey wolf optimizer and its application for feature selection. *Knowl.-Based Syst.* **2020**, *195*, 105746. [CrossRef]

electronics MDPI

Article

Intrusion Detection System Based on Multi-Level Feature Extraction and Inductive Network

Junyi Mao [1,2,†], Xiaoyu Yang [1,†], Bo Hu [1], Yizhen Lu [3] and Guangqiang Yin [1,3,4,*]

1 School of Information and Software Engineering, University of Electronic Science and Technology of China, Chengdu 611730, China; jmao0023@student.monash.edu (J.M.); yangxy@std.uestc.edu.cn (X.Y.); hubo@std.uestc.edu.cn (B.H.)
2 Faculty of Information Technology, Monash University, Clayton, VIC 3800, Australia
3 Shenzhen Institute for Advanced Study, University of Electronic Science and Technology of China, Shenzhen 518110, China; 202152280911@std.uestc.edu.cn
4 Kashgar Regional Electronic Information Industry Technology Research Institute, Kashi 844000, China
* Correspondence: yingq@uestc.edu.cn
† These authors contributed equally to this work.

Abstract: With the rapid development of the internet, network security threats are becoming increasingly complex and diverse, making traditional intrusion detection systems (IDSs) inadequate for handling the growing variety of sophisticated attacks. In particular, traditional methods based on rule matching and manual feature extraction demonstrate significant limitations in dealing with small samples and unknown attacks. This paper proposes an intrusion detection system based on multi-level feature extraction and inductive learning (MFEI-IDS) to address these challenges. The model innovatively integrates Fully Convolutional Networks (FCNs) with the Transformer architecture (FCN–Transformer) for feature extraction and utilizes an inductive learning component for efficient classification. The FCN–Transformer Encoder extracts multi-level features from raw network traffic, capturing local spatial patterns and global temporal dependencies, significantly enhancing the representation of network traffic while reducing reliance on manual feature engineering. The inductive learning module employs a dynamic routing mechanism to map sample feature vectors into robust class vector representations, achieving superior generalization when detecting unseen attack types. Compared to existing FCN–Transformer models, MFEI-IDS incorporates inductive learning to handle data imbalance and small-sample scenarios. Experiments on ISCX 2012 and CIC-IDS 2017 datasets show that MFEI-IDS outperforms mainstream IDS methods in accuracy, precision, recall, and F1-score, excelling in cross-dataset validation and demonstrating strong generalization capabilities. These results validate the practical potential of MFEI-IDS in small-sample learning, unknown attack detection, and dynamic network environments.

Keywords: intrusion detection; inductive networks; small-sample learning; FCN–transformer; unknown attacks

1. Introduction

With the rapid development of information technology and the internet, the number of globally connected devices has increased significantly, highlighting the growing importance of cyberspace. However, this progress has also exacerbated the complexity and frequency of cyberattacks, threatening personal information, business data, and national security. Traditional intrusion detection systems (IDSs) have been widely deployed to safeguard network security, and are broadly categorized into rule-based, signature-based, misuse-based, and anomaly-based systems [1]. While these systems perform well against known attacks, their reliance on predefined rule sets or manually extracted features imposes critical limitations when identifying novel or evolving threats.

In recent years, with the rapid advancement of deep learning technologies, researchers have applied them to the field of cybersecurity, attempting to improve intrusion detection through automated feature learning. For instance, convolutional neural networks (CNNs) excel in recognizing spatial patterns in network flows, while Recurrent Neural Networks (RNNs) are adept at capturing temporal dependencies. Deep learning methods perform remarkably well in scenarios with abundant labeled data but often struggle to generalize in environments with limited labeled data. For example, in real-world network traffic, most data are normal, while labeled malicious traffic data are sparse and diverse, making it challenging for traditional deep learning models to effectively capture the characteristics of malicious traffic [2]. Furthermore, as attack patterns evolve, models trained on past data quickly lose their effectiveness in real-world settings. For instance, traditional models have demonstrated insufficient robustness against supply chain attacks and Advanced Persistent Threats (APTs) emerging after 2020 [3].

Few-shot learning has emerged as a promising solution to address these challenges. Techniques such as Matching Networks and Prototypical Networks have shown potential in leveraging limited samples to detect unknown attacks. However, existing few-shot learning methods exhibit limitations in high-dimensional and dynamic network traffic scenarios. This is primarily due to their reliance on simple similarity measures (e.g., Euclidean distance), which perform poorly in multi-dimensional network traffic data, such as traffic data with temporal sequence features. For instance, these methods struggle to capture device-specific traffic patterns when detecting attack traffic targeting specific IoT devices [1,4]. Inductive learning offers an alternative approach by extracting class vectors from known samples and inferring the categories of unseen samples. This approach enhances classification performance through similarity-based measures and effectively addresses few-shot scenarios. Compared to traditional deep learning methods, inductive learning better handles data imbalance issues and enhances the detection of unknown impactful attacks through similarity awareness [5,6]. However, integrating inductive learning with advanced feature extraction techniques to improve robustness against unknown attacks remains an unresolved research challenge.

Moreover, the introduction of Transformer models has opened new possibilities for cybersecurity. Recently excelling in natural language processing and computer vision, Transformer mechanisms improve multi-head self-attention, effectively capturing long-range dependencies and complex patterns [7]. Zhang et al. combined CNNs and Transformers to learn local and global network traffic features, thereby improving model detection accuracy [8]. While Transformer models exhibit potential in handling complex temporal patterns in network traffic—for instance, the FlowTransformer framework achieves multi-dimensional feature extraction through modular design [7]—their performance significantly degrades in cross-dataset generalization tasks. This is especially evident when detecting new attack types, such as when training a model on the CIC-IDS 2017 dataset and transferring it to the ISCX 2012 dataset [9].

To address these key issues, this paper proposes a novel intrusion detection framework, MFEI-IDS, which is designed to tackle critical challenges in modern cybersecurity. The MFEI-IDS framework combines FCN and Transformer architectures to enhance the detection of unknown attacks by generating robust class vectors. For instance, in real-world environments, it enables the rapid detection of previously unseen network attacks, such as malicious traffic exploiting zero-day vulnerabilities, using only a few labeled traffic samples. The main contributions of this study are as follows:

1. Multi-Level Feature Extraction: A multi-level network feature learning method (FCN–Transformer) is proposed to address network traffic feature extraction challenges. Fully Convolutional Networks (FCNs) are used as input Encoders for Transformers. FCNs effectively capture local spatial patterns in raw network traffic, minimizing reliance on manual feature engineering, while the self-attention mechanism of Transformers models long-range dependencies and complex temporal patterns. This hybrid architecture provides robust multi-scale feature representation, making it well-suited for high-dimensional and sequential network data.
2. Inductive Learning Module: An intrusion detection method based on inductive networks is proposed to tackle data imbalance and few-shot unknown attack detection issues. By introducing an inductive learning module equipped with a dynamic routing mechanism, robust class vectors are generated from limited samples, enabling effective classification of unknown attack types. Compared to traditional supervised learning methods, this module supports zero-shot and cross-dataset classification, significantly improving the applicability and generalization ability of the model in scenarios with insufficient labeled data.
3. Modular and Explainable Design: By utilizing the explainability of class vector representations and the modular structure of FCN–Transformer, MFEI-IDS provides insights into its decision-making process, addressing common criticisms regarding the lack of explainability in deep learning models.

Experiments on the ISCX 2012 and CIC-IDS 2017 datasets demonstrate that MFEI-IDS outperforms existing state-of-the-art methods in terms of accuracy, F1-score, and detection robustness. Notably, it exhibits stronger generalization in cross-dataset validation and zero-shot classification capabilities, enabling the detection of unknown attack types without retraining.

The remainder of this paper is organized as follows: Section 2 reviews related work. Section 3 elaborates on the system details. Relevant experiments are discussed in Section 4. Section 5 concludes the paper and outlines future research directions.

2. Related Work

In recent years, with the increasing frequency and complexity of cyberattacks, network intrusion detection systems have become a significant research focus in cybersecurity. Researchers have proposed various techniques to meet different intrusion detection needs, primarily including rule-based detection methods, machine learning and deep learning approaches, and few-shot learning techniques. This section primarily reviews the latest research achievements of deep learning and few-shot learning methods in IDS, highlighting the advantages, limitations, and gaps this study addresses.

2.1. Intrusion Detection System Based on Deep Learning

With the proliferation of the internet, network traffic has grown exponentially, and traffic data have become more complex. The challenge of designing a set of features that accurately represent traffic is a critical research issue for network anomaly detection methods due to the limitations of manual feature design. Deep learning, with its powerful feature extraction capabilities, has emerged as a promising solution to address these challenges. By automatically learning representative features directly from raw data, deep learning methods eliminate the reliance on manual feature engineering and provide robust solutions for anomaly detection.

Javaid et al. [5] proposed a self-learning intrusion detection technique that uses a sparse autoencoder to learn feature representations from large amounts of unlabeled data. Wang et al. [2] introduced a CNN-based malicious traffic classification method that transforms network traffic into grayscale images and uses CNNs to learn the intrinsic features of these images. Wei et al. [10] proposed a hierarchical spatiotemporal feature learning (HAST-NAD) method for network anomaly detection, utilizing CNNs to learn local spatial features and LSTMs to learn global temporal features from raw traffic. This approach effectively considers the spatio-temporal properties of network traffic, demonstrating superior classification accuracy and robustness, especially in high-dimensional data and dynamic scenarios. Deng et al. [11] proposed a method combining random forests and LSTMs for traffic anomaly detection. The random forest algorithm calculates feature importance scores to eliminate redundant features, while LSTMs identify abnormal traffic. The accuracy of detecting abnormal traffic in the CIC-IDS-2017 dataset reached 99%, although its generalization ability was limited by data diversity and scale. Alhaj et al. [12] introduced a deep learning-based traffic classification method with attention mechanisms, demonstrating that combining CNNs enhances feature extraction. However, this approach focuses primarily on performance optimization for labeled datasets, with limited exploration of few-shot learning and zero-shot generalization capabilities.

Many researchers introduced Transformers into network intrusion detection as Transformer models gained prominence in large language models and proved effective in capturing complex patterns and relationships in sequential data, including images, graphs, and speech [3,13]. For example, Vaswani et al. [7] first proposed the Transformer model, which excels in capturing global features and long-range dependencies. Luo et al. [13] and Chen et al. [14] explored the applications of Transformers in network traffic analysis, demonstrating their effectiveness in anomaly detection. However, these studies lack investigation into generalization capabilities in few-shot environments and do not leverage the local feature extraction capabilities of CNNs. Zhang et al. [8] introduced a dual-layer network structure combining CNNs and Transformers to learn local and global features, significantly improving detection accuracy and reducing training time. Manocchio et al. [4] proposed the FlowTransformer framework for Transformer-based intrusion detection systems. This framework allows flexible replacement of Transformer components for input encoding, classification, and feature learning, providing a modular approach for intrusion detection. However, most of these methods rely on supervised learning frameworks, failing to effectively address few-shot scenarios and cross-dataset generalization requirements. Additionally, the computational complexity of Transformer models for high-dimensional data remains unresolved.

2.2. Intrusion Detection System Based on Small-Sample Learning

Few-shot learning (FSL) is a technique that enables learning under conditions of limited samples. In recent years, it has garnered attention for its ability to generalize models with minimal data. FSL techniques utilize meta-learning, transfer learning, and other approaches to achieve generalization capabilities under limited data conditions. Typical FSL methods include Matching Networks and Prototypical Networks. In cybersecurity, few-shot learning has been applied to detect unknown attacks. Shu et al. [15] proposed an intrusion detection system based on Prototypical Networks, enabling the detection of unknown attacks by learning from a small number of known attacks. Zhao et al. [16] combined transfer learning and few-shot learning to achieve cross-domain attack detection. However, existing FSL methods face challenges in handling high-dimensional, temporally complex network traffic data. Vinyals et al. [17] introduced Matching Networks, optimizing the matching relationship between support and query samples through metric learning, thereby improving classification accuracy. However, these methods primarily rely on simple similarity measures (e.g., Euclidean distance or cosine similarity), limiting their effectiveness in handling high-dimensional complex features.

Inductive learning extracts class vectors from known samples, effectively detecting unknown attacks. Metric learning enhances the distinction between different category samples by learning similarity measures. Xu et al. [18] proposed an intrusion detection method combining inductive and metric learning, achieving efficient detection in complex network environments by learning intra-class features and inter-class differences. Li et al. [19] introduced a multi-head self-attention mechanism, improving detection accuracy and robustness. However, existing studies have not fully explored the potential synergy between advanced feature extraction architectures (e.g., FCN and Transformer) and inductive learning, limiting their performance in addressing high-dimensional data and dynamic network environments.

2.3. Summary and Gaps

Despite significant progress in intrusion detection through deep learning and few-shot learning, several limitations persist, creating gaps between existing methods and the requirements of modern network security. Current studies often separate feature extraction and classification, such as feature extraction methods based on CNNs or Transformers that are not deeply integrated with inductive learning. This disconnect limits the performance of models in handling few-shot scenarios and cross-dataset generalization. While deep learning methods excel in automatic feature extraction and classification, their reliance on large, labeled datasets hampers their practicality in real-world scenarios with limited labeled data, especially in dynamic and evolving network environments. Additionally, although Transformer models excel in capturing long-range dependencies and complex patterns, their application in intrusion detection is still in its infancy and predominantly limited to supervised learning paradigms.

Few-shot learning offers an alternative for handling limited data scenarios but faces challenges in dealing with high-dimensional and sequential network traffic. Existing techniques (e.g., Prototypical Networks and Matching Networks) rely on simple similarity measures, which are insufficient for modeling complex relationships in intricate network environments. These methods often fail to detect unknown attack types effectively, particularly when facing heterogeneous traffic data. Furthermore, the computational complexity of Transformer models constrains their applicability in resource-limited environments. While inductive learning demonstrates the potential for enhancing generalization capabilities, its integration with advanced feature extraction architectures like FCN and Transformers remains underexplored, limiting its performance in high-dimensional and dynamic network environments.

To address these challenges, this study proposes the MFEI-IDS framework, which combines FCN–Transformer architecture with an inductive learning module equipped with dynamic routing. Unlike existing methods, MFEI-IDS leverages FCNs to extract local spatial features and Transformers to model global temporal dependencies, providing multi-scale feature representation suitable for high-dimensional and sequential traffic data. The inductive module maps sample features to compact, robust class vectors, effectively generalizing unknown attack types. This approach enhances adaptability through dynamic routing mechanisms, addressing the limitations of existing few-shot learning techniques. MFEI-IDS aims to adapt to few-shot scenarios, heterogeneous data, and dynamic attack patterns without requiring extensive retraining. Its modular design ensures scalability, making it suitable for practical deployment.

3. Method

MFEI-IDS integrates Fully Convolutional Networks (FCN), Transformer architecture, and an inductive learning module to address the challenges of intrusion detection in dynamic and few-shot scenarios. Its design prioritizes efficient feature extraction, robust classification, and adaptability across datasets. This section provides a detailed methodology overview, including architecture, preprocessing, feature extraction, and classification workflows.

3.1. Model Architecture Design

The proposed intrusion detection model incorporates few-shot learning principles using an FCN–Transformer Encoder and inductive network to enhance detection capabilities. As illustrated in Figure 1, the whole architecture consists of three main components: the Encoder, inductive module, and relational module. C represents the number of classes in the dataset, K represents the number of supported samples for each classes, and d represents the dimension of the feature embedding. These components work collaboratively to process raw network traffic, generate robust class vectors, and effectively classify query samples. This section elaborates on the methodology, detailing how input data are processed and utilized throughout the workflow.

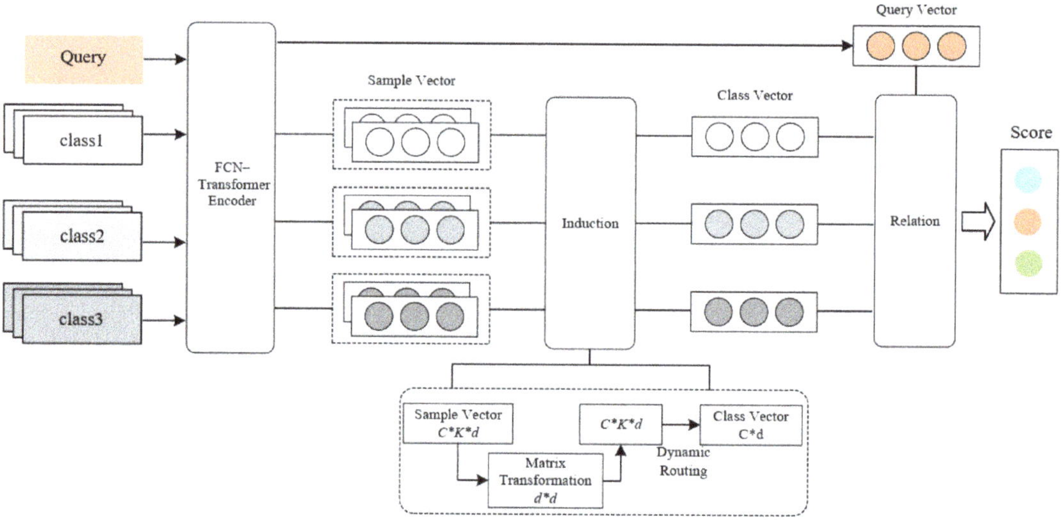

Figure 1. MFEI-IDS structure.

Encoder: The Encoder extracts features from raw network traffic data. This study employs a one-dimensional Fully Convolutional Network (1D FCN) combined with Transformer architecture, referred to as the FCN–Transformer model, to extract local spatial and global temporal features from traffic. The Encoder transforms raw network traffic into high-dimensional feature vectors, forming the basis for subsequent classification and detection.

Inductive Module: The inductive module learns from a small, labeled dataset (support set) to generate class vectors. These class vectors represent the feature space of specific attack types or normal traffic. The model infers the categories of unknown samples through these class vectors. This module utilizes the key principles of few-shot learning by learning features from a few labeled samples to infer new, unseen attack types.

Relational Module: This module, consisting of a simple neural tensor layer, calculates the relationship scores between query samples and class vectors. These scores reflect the similarity between query samples and different categories, determining their classification. Using a similarity-based classification method, this module enables precise traffic classification and detection without relying on many samples.

The model workflow consists of two primary stages:

Training Phase: The Encoder processes labeled session data to extract high-dimensional feature representations, which the inductive module then uses to generate compact class vectors.

Classification Phase: The Encoder processes unlabeled query samples, and the relational module classifies them based on their similarity to class vectors.

3.2. FCN–Transformer Encoder

The primary function of the Encoder is to extract multi-level spatial and temporal features from raw network traffic. This study employs a hybrid architecture combining FCN and Transformer. The Encoder architecture, as shown in Figure 2, consists of four main components: the data preprocessing module, the local spatial feature extraction module, the global temporal feature extraction module, and the output classification module.

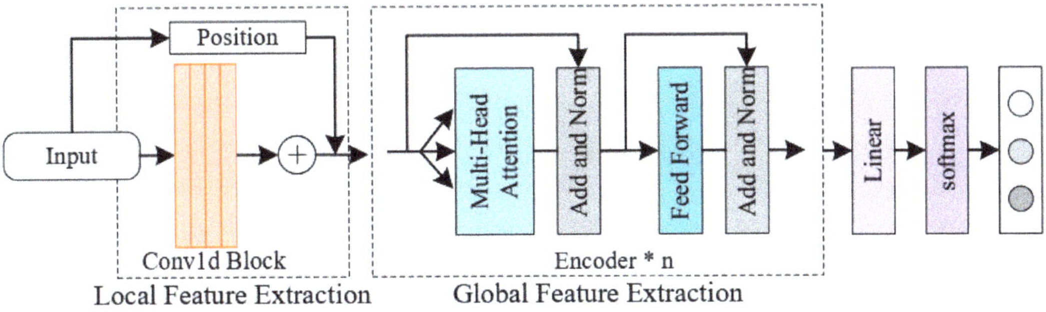

Figure 2. Encoder model architecture.

The data preprocessing module takes raw traffic data in PCAP format as input. Since the raw traffic contains redundant information and network security traffic datasets are typically captured in laboratory environments, this redundant information differs from that in real-world network environments. Therefore, it is necessary to clean this part of the data.

After inputting the data into the model, the model begins processing in the data encoding module, including input and positional encoding. The data encoding step transforms the input sequence into a representation that the model can process while preserving the sequence's information. Positional encoding employs a learnable approach to retain the sequence's positional information.

Next are the local spatial feature extraction module, the global temporal feature extraction module, and the classification module. These two modules form the core of the network. This study does not simply use FCN to extract the local spatial features of packets; instead, it uses a transformer to extract the temporal features of bidirectional traffic flows; as such, an approach processes data sequentially. The FCN network lacks parallel processing capabilities, which limits the parallelism of the Transformer. Instead, this study integrates the FCN network into the Transformer model, placing the FCN network after the input encoding stage. This approach mitigates the shortcomings of both FCN and Transformer and effectively leverages their respective strengths. It enables efficient learning of spatiotemporal features from network traffic while improving the model's speed and accuracy.

After training, the FCN–Transformer network can map raw traffic to a multi-level spatiotemporal feature vector space. Finally, the learned feature vectors are passed through a fully connected layer and input into the classifier. The classifier uses the softmax activation function to classify the traffic to produce the final intrusion detection results.

The data preprocessing, local spatial feature extraction, and global temporal feature extraction are described below.

3.2.1. Data Preprocessing

The raw traffic is stored in PCAP file format, which is huge in size, so when using it for deep learning model training, the continuous traffic needs to be sliced into multiple discrete units according to a certain granularity.

Currently, there are six commonly used network traffic-slicing methods in network intrusion detection [20,21]: packet, connection, flow, session, service, and host. Researchers need to choose the appropriate data-slicing method according to the research needs, and more data at packet, stream, and session levels are currently used in related research. A packet is the basic data unit transmitted between computer network nodes, including the packet header, load, and activity information. A flow is defined as all packets with the same quintet (source IP, source port, destination IP, destination port, transport layer protocol). A session (a bidirectional flow) is defined as all packets where the source and destination IPs and ports are interchangeable. Packets provide only spatial characteristics of the traffic and cannot identify attacks that rely on sequential information to be detected. In high-speed network environments, the amount of packet-level data is enormous, and computational complexity is high. Suppose the analysis is based only on individual packets. In that case, it may result in different parts of the same session being dispersed into multiple batches, leading to the loss of traffic context. Session-level slicing, on the other hand, can aggregate related data and reduce the risk of misclassification. Stream and session data not only contain spatial characteristics of the traffic but also reflect the temporal information of the traffic. In contrast, the session data eliminate the possible confusion problem of the stream data, so this paper uses the session data as the input sequence of the model.

In raw data processing, this paper draws on the discretization method in Parsaei et al. [22] to internalize continuous features to improve the compatibility and robustness of data representation. To further improve the model's performance, we carry out the data processing flow on the traffic data, as shown in Figure 3. Data preprocessing primarily involves traffic segmentation and cleaning, along with an optional data truncation and padding step.

Figure 3. Data pre-processing process.

Traffic Segmentation: Complete traffic data are segmented and aggregated into session data based on the five-tuple information. This process involves dividing the entire traffic data into packets and then aggregating the packets into flow data. Subsequent operations are performed in the form of session data. It is important to note that PCAP format data are inherently binary.

Traffic Cleaning: At the session level, meaningless empty flows and duplicate flows are removed, as they essentially represent noise. Alternatively, these flows can be introduced as noise during training. To ensure the model focuses more on attack traffic patterns rather than non-attacking IP addresses and to avoid overfitting caused by dataset-specific characteristics, randomly generated new data are used at the packet level to populate fields such as source IP, source port, destination IP, destination port, and MAC address.

Data Truncation and Padding: The proposed FCN–Transformer model can accept variable-length sequences of packets, making this step optional and primarily aimed at reducing training time. Data interception is used to limit the maximum length of packets and sessions, i.e., only the first m bytes of data are kept for each packet, and only the first n packets are kept for each session. At the same time, packets smaller than m bytes can also be padded with 0×00 and all 0×00 packets to bring the number of packets in the session up to n. To reduce the burden of model operations, the maximum length of the input sequence is limited to 200, and the packet length is reserved to 512 bytes.

3.2.2. Local Spatial Feature Extraction

Before learning the local features of the traffic data, the input data are first encoded and processed; this includes Position Embedding and Input Coding, as shown in Figure 4.

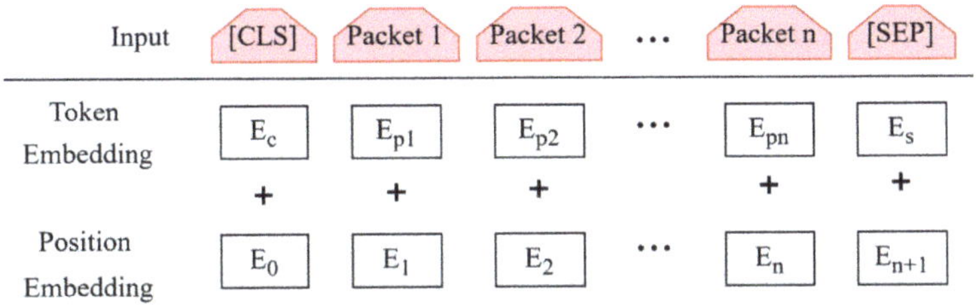

Figure 4. Input representation.

The multi-head self-attention mechanism in Transformer cannot capture the sequential relationships between positions within a text sequence. Compared to methods that process sequence inputs serially, this approach lacks order information for traffic sequences. Positional representation was introduced to address this issue. The original Transformer computes position encodings using a fixed formula, which is unsuitable for representing positions in traffic sessions. This is because packets are highly diverse and their positions are not fixed, as they are mainly related to network protocols and the connection, request, and response methods of application services.

Therefore, the FCN–Transformer model does not use a fixed transformation formula to calculate relative positional encodings. Instead, it adopts the positional encoding method of the BERT model [23], using a standard embedding approach to learn the position of each packet, resulting in position vectors.

The local features of network traffic represent the information carried by individual packets. Hence, local feature extraction networks can replace packet encoding. To extract local spatial features, an optimized one-dimensional fully convolutional neural network (1D-FCN) is used.

Different types of convolutional neural networks (CNNs) are suitable for processing data of different dimensions [24]. One-dimensional convolution kernels are well suited for handling sequential data and are widely used in the field of text processing. Similarly, traffic packets can be viewed as a special type of text. To handle variable-length packet data, this model employs a one-dimensional FCN network.

In CNNs, convolutional layers use multiple convolution kernels to extract features from the input. Each convolution kernel slides over the input using a small window, and the processing of the convolutional layers remains consistent regardless of the input size. Standard CNN networks typically require input sizes to be fixed because they include

Dense or fully connected (Dense) layers. These layers require a fixed input size because, after processing through convolutional and pooling layers, the flattened output must match the input size of the Dense layer. As a result, the input size ultimately determines the feature dimensions passed to the Dense layer. FCN, on the other hand, is a convolutional network without Dense layers, allowing it to handle inputs of varying sizes.

The 1D-FCN used in this study is an improved version of the standard FCN. Based on specific requirements, one-dimensional convolutional blocks (Conv1d Blocks) can be stacked, as illustrated in Figure 5.

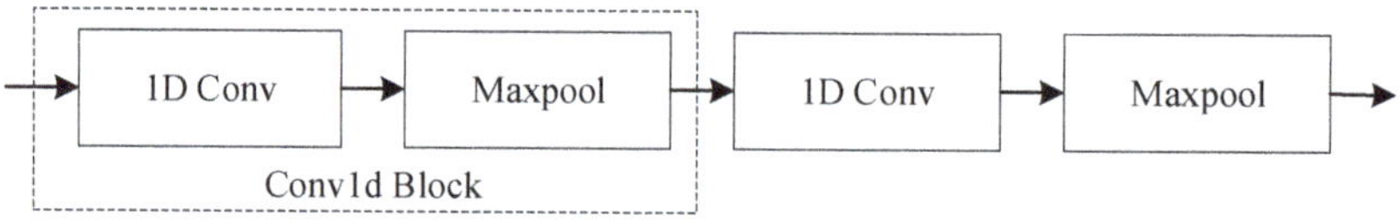

Figure 5. One-dimensional FCN structure diagram.

A convolution block consists of a convolutional layer and a max pooling layer. The computation of a one-dimensional convolution kernel is defined as shown in Equation (1).

$$y_j^l = \sum_{i \in X} y_j^{l-1} \times w_{ij}^l + b_i^l \tag{1}$$

From here, *f(x)* represents the activation function, X denotes the set of input feature vectors, and y_j^{l-1} is the i feature vector of the output from the $l-1$ convolutional layer and is also the input to the l convolutional neural network. w_{ij}^l is the weight of the convolutional kernel in the l layer, b_i^l is the bias of the l layer, and y_j^l represents the output of the l convolutional neural network after convolution with the j kernel.

After position encoding and the 1D FCN local feature extraction network, the embedding vector Y_{FCN} of the data packet and the position encoding P of the session are obtained, and then the embedding vector and position encoding are fused according to Equation (2).

$$Y_L = Y_{FCN} \oplus P \tag{2}$$

3.2.3. Global Temporal Feature Extraction

The global features of network traffic represent the sequential information carried by bidirectional data flows. This paper constructs the global feature extraction module by stacking multiple Transformer Encoders, as shown in Figure 6.

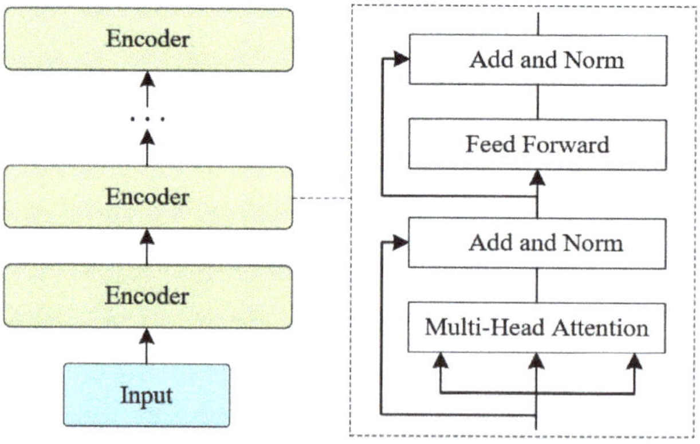

Figure 6. Global feature extraction module structure.

The Transformer Encoder adopts the multi-head self-attention mechanism to address the issue of long-term dependencies. By stacking multiple Encoders in series, it learns the dependencies within long sequences, enabling Transformers to have excellent capabilities in handling ultra-long sequences. This allows them to effectively detect complex network traffic patterns indicative of attacks. The vector Y_L, obtained from the fusion of the packet vector and session position encoding, is processed through the calculations in Equation (3), resulting in the self-attention output $MultiHead(Q, K, V)$.

$$Attention(Q, K, V) = softmax\left(\frac{QK^T}{\sqrt{d_k}}\right)V \quad (3)$$

The model then introduces a residual connection, adding the input before the multi-head self-attention mechanism to the output after it, which helps prevent the vanishing gradient problem in deep networks. Next, LayerNorm [25] is used as the normalization method, which can also speed up training convergence. The output representation obtained after residual joining and normalization is shown in Equation (4).

$$Y_{Norm} = LayerNorm(Y_L + MultiHead(Q, K, V)) \quad (4)$$

The feedforward layer consists of two linear fully connected layers connected by the activation function *ReLU*. The output of the feedforward layer is shown in Equation (5).

$$Y_{Forward} = Linear(ReLU(Linear(Y_{Norm}))) \quad (5)$$

Finally, the residual connection and LayerNorm described above are applied again, yielding the output of the first Transformer Encoder, as shown in Equation (6).

$$Y_{Encoder} = LayerNorm(Y_{Forward} + Y_{Norm}) \quad (6)$$

3.3. Inductive Model

In computer networks, due to different network protocols and environments, there are often different representations for the same category of network traffic. Simply summing or averaging the sample features to represent a category may accumulate interfering information that is not relevant to the classification, thus negatively affecting the final classification performance. The induction module simulates a nonlinear mapping process from sample vectors to category vectors to obtain an embedding vector that best represents the category. Therefore, the induction module is the core of the induction network. In this study, we draw on the insights of Hostiadi et al. [26] on efficient feature selection and utilize the induction model to extract the most representative features from a small number of samples, thus achieving the classification of unknown attack types [27,28]. The inductive module is described in detail below.

Let the sample vectors of the support set obtained after encoding through the Encoder be e^s and the query vectors obtained through encoding through the Encoder be e^q. The induction module exploits the dynamic routing concept of capsule networks to achieve a nonlinear mapping from low-level features to high-level features by iteratively optimizing the relational weights between the samples and the categories. In the induction model, this dynamic routing mechanism is redesigned to generalize the sample representation e_{ij}^S in each category to the representation c_i of the class vector, as shown in Equation (7).

$$\left\{e_{ij}^S \in R^{2u}\right\}_{i=1,\ldots,C;j=1,\ldots,K} \rightarrow \left\{C_i \in R^{2u}\right\}_{i=1}^{C} \quad (7)$$

In this process, the sample vectors in the support set are treated as input capsules. After a layer of dynamic routing transformation, the resulting output capsules are regarded as the feature representations of each class, as illustrated in Figure 7.

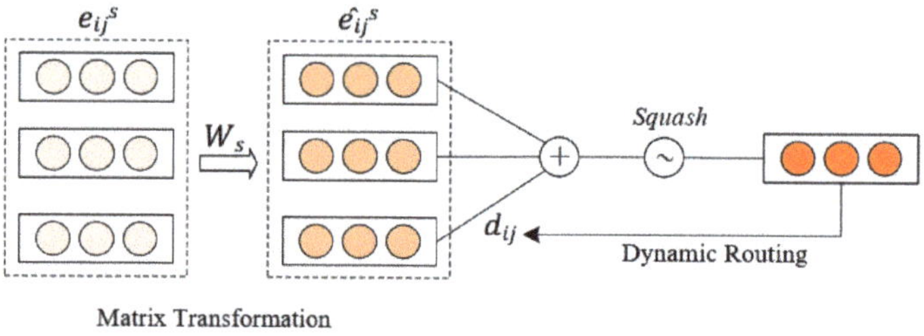

Figure 7. Dynamic routing algorithm of the inductive module.

The specific steps are as follows:

(1) Through matrix transformation, the initial features of all samples are converted from the sample-level semantic space to the category-level semantic space. In the original capsule network, different category sample representations use different transformation matrices, W. However, to support different sizes of C, the model uses the same transformation matrix W_s and bias b_s for all sample vectors in the support set, resulting in the predicted sample vector $\hat{e}_{ij}^{S}$, as shown in Equation (8). This allows the model to handle support sets of arbitrary sizes, meaning the model can adapt to any-way, any-shot scenarios.

$$\hat{e}_{ij}^{s} = squash\left(W_s e_{ij}^{s} + b_s\right) \tag{8}$$

The squash function is a nonlinear activation function used to normalize the magnitude of a vector, restricting its length within a specific range. This helps reduce noise and enhances the robustness of classification tasks, ensuring that features are represented consistently. Given an input vector xxx, the computation of the squash function is defined as shown in Equation (9).

$$squash(x) = \frac{||x||^2}{1 + ||x||^2} \frac{x}{||x||} \tag{9}$$

(2) Next, the irrelevant information is filtered through dynamic routing, and a weighted sum of the transformed sample representations is computed to obtain the initial class representation. In each iteration of dynamic routing, the connection coefficients di between the upper and lower layers are dynamically adjusted using the softmax operation, ensuring that they sum to 1, as shown in Equation (10).

$$d_i = softmax(b_i) \tag{10}$$

Here, b_i is the logit value of the connection coefficients, initialized to 0 before the first iteration begins. For a given predicted sample vector $\hat{e}_{ij}^{S}$, each candidate class vector $\hat{C}_j$ is the weighted sum of all predicted sample vectors within that candidate class, as shown in Equation (11).

$$\hat{c}_i = \sum_i d_i \hat{e}_{ij}^{s} \tag{11}$$

Then, the squash function is applied to ensure that the length of each class vector does not exceed 1, as shown in Equation (12).

$$c_i = squash(\hat{c}_i) \tag{12}$$

(3) Finally, the connection strength is adjusted using a routing protocol. The specific implementation is that when the dot product between the generated candidate class vector and a sample predicted vector is large, the connection strength between them is increased; conversely, it is decreased when the dot product is small, as shown in Equation (13).

$$b_{ij} = b_{ij} + \hat{e}_{ij}^{s} \cdot c_i \tag{13}$$

By modeling the nonlinear mapping process from sample vectors to category vectors through this dynamic routing mechanism, it effectively filters out interfering information and obtains category features. This method is referred to as dynamic routing induction, as outlined in Algorithm 1. The dynamic routing mechanism optimizes the generation process of category vectors, ensuring that they are highly representative of the features of each category within the support set.

Algorithm 1: Dynamic Routing Induction

Require:
  Support Set Sample Vectors: e_{ij}^{S}
  $b_{ij} = 0$
Ensure:
  Class Vector: C_i
1: **for** all samples $j = 1, \ldots, K$ in class i **do**
2: $\hat{e}_{ij}^{S} = squash\left(W_S e_{ij}^{S} + b_S\right)$
3: **for** *iter* iterations **do**
4: $d_i = softmax(b_i)$
5: $\hat{C}_i = \sum_j d_{ij} \hat{e}_{ij}^{S}$
6: $C_i = squash(\hat{C}_i)$
7: **for** all samples $j = 1, \ldots, K$ in class i **do**
8: $b_{ij} = b_{ij} + \hat{e}_{ij}^{S} C_i$
9: **end for**
10: **Return** C_i

3.4. Relationship Model

After constructing the data pairs between the query sample and each category in the support set, obtaining the class vectors c_i for each category in the support set, and encoding the query sample into the query vector e^q, the next step is to use the relationship module to assess the correlation between e^q and c_i. The relationship module is a neural tensor layer [29], which models the interaction between each class vector and the query vector pair using a three-dimensional tensor:

$$v(c_i, e^q) = f\left(c_i^T M^{[1:H]} e^q\right) \tag{14}$$

Here, $M^{[1:H]} \in R^{2u \times 2u}$ is a slice of the tensor parameters, and $f(\cdot)$ is the ReLU activation function. The next step is to calculate the relationship score (also referred to as the similarity score) between the class vector and the query vector.

$$\mathrm{r_{iq}} = \mathrm{sigmoid}(\mathrm{W_r c(c_i, e^q)} + \mathrm{b_r} \tag{15}$$

When evaluating the model, the relationship scores need to be regressed to the true labels, y_q. The induction network transforms the multi-classification problem into a 0–1 classification problem in the classification process. Specifically, it compares the relationship scores between each query and the class pairs, where the score for matching classes and queries approaches 1, while the scores for non-matching pairs approach 0. Thus, the query vector is classified into the class corresponding to the maximum relationship score. The model is trained using the mean squared loss, and for each episode, given the support set S and query set Q, the objective function is defined as shown in Equation (16).

$$L(S,Q) = \sum_{i=1}^{C} \sum_{q=1}^{n} \left(r_{iq} - 1\left(y_q == i\right)\right)^2 \tag{16}$$

After the training is completed, the model will not require fine-tuning when recognizing entirely new categories, as sufficient generalization capability has already been imparted to the model during the meta-training phase. Moreover, this capability will continue to accumulate with each iteration of the model.

4. Experiment

4.1. Dataset

We selected two datasets containing raw traffic in PCAP format, the ISCX 2012 dataset [30] and the CIC-IDS 2017 dataset [31], to conduct the experiments.

The ISCX 2012 dataset, released in 2012, contains traffic data representing seven days of network activity. The dataset includes normal traffic and four types of malicious traffic, totaling 1,520,158 session samples. Most of the data consist of normal traffic, with attack traffic accounting for less than 3%.

The CIC-IDS 2017 dataset, released in 2017, is an intrusion detection and prevention dataset comprising five days of captured data. It contains traffic data for normal behavior and 14 common attack types, with a total of 2,825,404 session samples, of which attack traffic constitutes 19.6%. Some attack types, such as Heartbleed, Infiltration, and SQL Injection, have only 11, 35, and 21 samples, respectively.

Both datasets were collected by the same laboratory using different methodologies and under varying hardware and software environments. The datasets, captured and published in different years, reflect the evolution of network environments to some extent. Over time, network traffic has become more complex, and attack types have grown more diverse, as evident from the differences in the composition of the ISCX 2012 and CIC-IDS 2017 datasets. Conducting experiments on these datasets helps evaluate the model's ability to handle both simple and complex data.

Both datasets were preprocessed using the steps described in Section 3.2.1, which include traffic sessionization, noise removal, and truncation. Session-level slicing was employed to preserve temporal and spatial dependencies, while data truncation ensured consistency and computational feasibility. These preprocessing steps were applied uniformly to all evaluated models, including baseline models such as LSTM, BiGRU, and standard Transformer architectures, to ensure a fair comparison.

To validate the proposed intrusion detection approach, a series of experiments were conducted. The experiments were run on a hardware platform equipped with an Intel processor, GTX 4060 GPU (8 GB VRAM), and Windows 10 operating system. The models were constructed using the PyTorch framework and Transformers library, with GPU acceleration employed for training. The experimental setup is detailed in Table 1.

We used evaluation metrics such as accuracy, precision, recall, and F1-score to evaluate the detection ability of the model. These metrics are calculated based on the confusion matrix, and the binary confusion matrix is shown in Table 2, where each row corresponds to the actual results and each column corresponds to the predicted results. True positives (TPs) are the number of samples correctly predicted as positive and are actually positive. False positives (FPs) are the number of samples incorrectly predicted to be positive or are actually negative. False negatives (FNs) are the number of samples that were incorrectly predicted to be negative and that were positive. True negative (TN) is the number of samples correctly predicted to be in the negative sample category that were also negative. These metrics provide a comprehensive evaluation of the model's classification performance across different aspects.

Table 1. Experimental environment.

Hardware and Software Experimental Environment	Detail
CPU	Intel(R) Core(TM) i5-12400
Video Card	NVIDIA GeForce GTX 4060 8G
CUDA	11.4.2
RAM	16 GB
Operating System	Windows 10
Programming Languages	Python 3.7
Software Framework	Pytorch = 1.13.1, Transformers = 4.30.2
IDE	PyCharm 2023.3.2

Table 2. Confusion matrix.

Real Sample	Sample Projections	
	Positive Sample	Negative Sample
Positive sample	TP	FN
Negative sample	FP	TN

Accuracy refers to the number of samples correctly predicted by the model as a proportion of the total number of samples. It is one of the most intuitive metrics to assess, but it is not meaningful when the categories are severely imbalanced.

$$\text{Accuracy} = \frac{\text{TP} + \text{TN}}{\text{TP} + \text{TN} + \text{FP} + \text{FN}} \quad (17)$$

Precision refers to the proportion of samples that are truly positive among those predicted as the positive class by the model. It measures the accuracy of the model in predicting the positive class. Mathematically, it is defined as follows:

$$\text{Precision} = \frac{\text{TP}}{\text{TP} + \text{FP}} \quad (18)$$

Recall refers to the proportion of samples in the true positive category that the model predicts to be in the positive category. It measures the model's ability to find positive category samples.

$$\text{Recall} = \frac{\text{TP}}{\text{TP} + \text{FN}} \quad (19)$$

The F1-score is the harmonic mean of precision and recall, providing a balanced measure that considers both false positives and false negatives. The F1-score ranges from 0 to 1, with higher values indicating better model performance. The formula for calculating the F1-score is as follows:

$$\text{F}_1 = \frac{2 \times \text{Precision} \times \text{Recall}}{\text{Precision} + \text{Recall}} \quad (20)$$

4.2. *FCN–Transformer Encoder Experiment*

4.2.1. Parameter Experiment of FCN Transformer Encoder

We conducted a binary classification experiment on the ISCX 2012 dataset to investigate the impact of the number of Conv1d Blocks, Transformer Encoder units, and self-attention heads on the model's performance. The objective was to determine the optimal parameter settings for subsequent experiments. During the experiment, all other model parameters were kept constant, except for those being tuned. The initial parameter settings were as follows: the 1D FCN network consisted of two stacked Conv1d Blocks, the number of Encoder units and self-attention heads was set to six, the batch size was 256, and the model was trained for a total of 60 epochs. The learning rate was set to 0.001, and the Adam optimizer was used. The results of the parameter tuning experiments are shown in Figure 8.

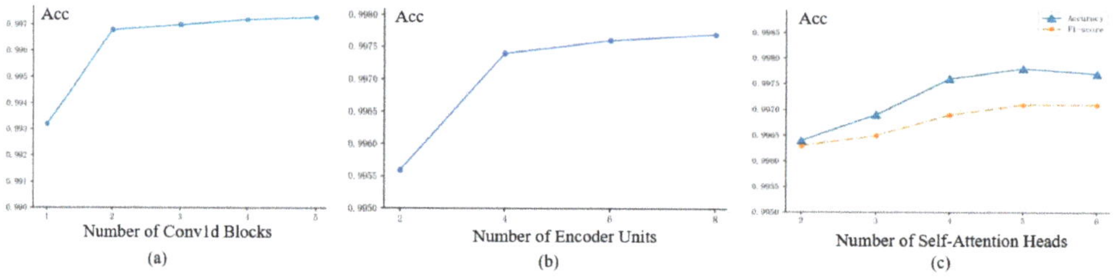

Figure 8. Impact of parameters on model performance: (**a**) number of Conv1d Blocks; (**b**) number of Transformer Encoder units; (**c**) number of self-attention heads.

When optimizing the model parameters, the experimental results reveal that increasing the number of Conv1d Blocks from one to two significantly improves the model's spatial feature learning capability and accuracy. However, further increases in the number of blocks yield limited accuracy improvements while significantly increasing model complexity.

Due to hardware constraints, the range of Encoder units in the experiments was limited to two to eight. The results show that as the number of units increases, the model's feature extraction capability improves, but the processing speed decreases.

For the multi-head self-attention mechanism, the experiments demonstrate that increasing the number of heads from two to six initially improves accuracy and steadily enhances the F1-score. However, beyond four heads, the improvement slows down, and accuracy even declines slightly at six heads.

In summary, blindly increasing the number of Conv1d Blocks or self-attention heads in pursuit of higher accuracy is not advisable, as this leads to higher computational complexity and slower model performance. Based on the experimental results, a set of optimal model parameters was determined to balance speed and accuracy, as shown in Table 3.

Table 3. FCN–Transformer model parameter settings.

Parameter	Value
Number of Conv1d Blocks	2
Number of Encoder Units	4
Number of Self-Attention Heads	4
Batch Size	128
Number of Training Iterations	60
Learning Rate	10^{-3}
Optimizer	Adam
Loss Function	CrossEntropy Loss

4.2.2. Comparison of FCN–Transformer with Other Models

To verify the effectiveness of the FCN–Transformer architecture in MFEI-IDS, we compared it with several baseline models widely used in intrusion detection. Based on the HAST-II model described in [10], we constructed the CNN-BiLSTM model and the CNN-BiGRU-Attn model. These, along with the LSTM, BiGRU, and Transformer models, formed the baseline comparison models.

All input data consisted of raw traffic data preprocessed in the same manner. The packet length was retained at 512 bytes, and the session length was set to 200, consistent with the configuration of the proposed model. The number of epochs for the training was set to 60 for all models. The parameters of each model are listed in Table 4, where the Attn suffix indicates the inclusion of an attention mechanism.

Table 4. Comparison of model parameter settings.

Model	Number of Hidden Layers and Units	Dropout	Learning Rate	Batch Size
LSTM	128	0.2	10^{-4}	128
BiGRU	128,128	0.2	10^{-4}	128
CNN-BiLSTM	CNN: 128@2*1, 256@2*1; 192@2*1, 320@2*1 GLobalMaxpool BiLSTM: 92, 92	0.1	10^{-3}	10
CNN-BiGRU-Attn	CNN: 128@2*1, 256@2*1; 192@2*1, 320@2*1 GLobalMaxpool BiGRU: 92, 92 Attention	0.1	10^{-3}	10
Transformer	Token Embedding Position Embedding Encoder: 6 Decoder: 6 Attention Head: 4	0.1	10^{-3}	128

We first conducted a binary classification experiment on the ISCX 2012 dataset, with the results presented in Table 5. From the results, it can be observed that the proposed FCN–Transformer architecture outperforms all other models across all evaluation metrics, demonstrating optimal performance.

Table 5. Binary classification comparison results on ISCX 2012 dataset.

Model	Accuracy	Precision	Recall	F1-Score
LSTM	94.19%	91.86%	95.98%	0.9837
BiGRU	95.06%	93.12%	97.04%	0.9504
CNN-BiLSTM	97.91%	95.16%	98.76%	0.9693
CNN-BiGRU-Attn	98.73%	96.27%	99.18%	0.9770
Transformer	97.47%	96.82%	98.86%	0.9783
FCN–Transformer	99.78%	98.79%	99.90%	0.9934

Among all the models, the two single-level models performed the worst, highlighting that single-level models are incapable of learning the complete multi-level spatiotemporal features of network traffic. In contrast, the dual-layer network models showed significant improvements in all aspects compared to single-level models. The CNN-BiGRU-Attn model outperformed the CNN-BiLSTM model in overall performance, indicating that the attention mechanism enhances model performance. The Transformer model's performance fell between the CNN-BiLSTM and CNN-BiGRU-Attn models. This demonstrates that while Transformers are powerful, incorporating mechanisms such as attention and dual-layer structures can further boost performance.

We conducted a binary classification experiment on the more complex CIC-IDS 2017 dataset, and the results are shown in Table 6. Compared to the binary classification experiment on the ISCX 2012 dataset, all models experienced a decline in performance due to the increased complexity of the dataset.

Table 6. Results of binary classification comparison experiments on the CIC-IDS 2017 dataset.

Model	Accuracy	Precision	Recall	F1-Score
LSTM	92.59%	90.14%	95.28%	0.9264
BiGRU	93.84%	92.32%	96.05%	0.9415
CNN-BiLSTM	97.05%	94.53%	98.53%	0.9649
CNN-BiGRU-Attn	98.34%	95.85%	99.07%	0.9743
Transformer	97.29%	95.87%	98.32%	0.9708
FCN–Transformer	99.47%	98.52%	99.81%	0.9916

Despite this, the proposed FCN–Transformer model achieved an impressive 99.47% accuracy and an F1-score of 0.9916, demonstrating the best overall performance. These results indicate that the proposed model is highly effective in adapting to the temporal variations in network traffic, showcasing its robustness and ability to handle complex datasets.

Finally, a multi-class classification experiment was conducted on the CIC-IDS 2017 dataset, and the results are shown in Table 7. The proposed FCN–Transformer model also demonstrated the best overall performance in this multi-class classification task, with all metrics exceeding 99%, outperforming the other comparison models. The proposed model achieved optimal results across all evaluation metrics, highlighting its capability to represent the multi-level features of complex traffic effectively. Furthermore, these results suggest that the model is equally applicable to other traffic datasets, exhibiting excellent robustness and adaptability to different network traffic scenarios.

Table 7. Comparison results of different models for multi-categorization on the CIC-IDS2017 dataset.

Model	Accuracy	Precision	Recall	F1-Score
LSTM	91.8%	90.13%	93.37%	0.9172
BiGRU	92.79%	90.26%	94.07%	0.9213
CNN-BiLSTM	95.92%	93.87%	96.94%	0.9538
CNN-BiGRU-Attn	98.55%	95.83%	98.76%	0.9727
Transformer	96.33%	94.57%	96.43%	0.9549
FCN–Transformer	99.32%	99.03%	99.16%	0.9909

To illustrate the performance of FCN–Transformer under complex data, the detection effectiveness of the model for each category was analyzed, as shown in Table 8. It can be observed that the model can achieve a recall of more than 92% and an F1-score value of more than 0.99 for certain attacks, such as DoS Hulk, PortScan, DDoS, and DoS GoldenEye, because these attacks have enough samples to provide the model with training. As for the categories that lack training samples, the model cannot learn the features of these categories, so the detection performance is poorer; for example, attacks such as SQL Injection, XSS, and Infiltration, all of which have less than 50 total sample data, and are even more sparse after being partitioned into training and testing sets, show poorer performance, which illustrates how the unbalanced dataset seriously affects the model's performance. From another perspective, the model's recall for Infiltration, SQL Injection, and Heartbleed is not zero, and its precision rates reach 100%. This indicates that the model can detect the data for these attacks. However, the lack of sufficient samples prevents the model from adequately updating its parameters to learn all the representative features of these attacks. This observation demonstrates the powerful feature extraction capability of the FCN–Transformer model, despite the challenges posed by data imbalance.

Table 8. Multi-classification experimental results of FCN–Transformer on the CIC-IDS2017 dataset.

Traffic Category	Precision	Recall	F1-Score
Benign	99.85%	99.54%	0.997
DoS Hulk	99.29%	99.91%	0.996
PortScan	99.93%	99.89%	0.9991
DDoS	99.86%	98.92%	0.9939
DoS GoldenEye	99.12%	99.41%	0.9926
FTP-Patator	99.93%	99.68%	0.995
SSH-Patator	99.83%	98.39%	0.991
DoS slowloris	99.82%	99.23%	0.9953
Dos Slowhttptest	99.27%	99.09%	0.9918
Bot	80.72%	92.9%	0.8638
Brute Force	65.89%	98.75%	0.7904
XSS	97.94%	55.88%	0.7116
Infiltration	100.0%	42.89%	0.6
SQL Injection	100.0%	40%	0.5714
Heartbleed	100.0%	33.33%	0.5

To validate the model's utilization of the Transformer multi-head self-attention mechanism for parallel computation on sequential data, we conducted a comparison experiment on training and testing times. Table 9 presents the training and testing time comparisons for binary classification on the ISCX 2012 dataset. The proposed model achieved a training time of 54 min and a testing time of 1.7 min on the entire ISCX 2012 dataset, achieving the best performance in both training and testing times. Even when compared to the structurally simpler CNN model, the results underscore the parallelism of the Transformer architecture and demonstrate the efficient processing capability of the model proposed in this chapter.

Table 9. ISCX2012 dataset binary classification training and testing time comparison.

Model	Training Time	Test Time
CNN	57 min	1.9 min
LSTM	76 min	2.7 min
BiGRU	71 min	2.6 min
CNN-BiLSTM	128 min	3.5 min
CNN-BiGRU-Attn	135 min	3.5 min
FCN–Transformer	54 min	1.7 min

Combining the above experimental results, the proposed FCN–Transformer architecture achieved excellent performance on both datasets. It demonstrated the ability to learn highly generalized deep spatiotemporal features of traffic data, outperforming both single models and traditional multi-level CNN-RNN models.

4.3. *Analysis of Experimental Results*

4.3.1. Comparison with Other Small-Sample Learning Models

To validate the efficiency of the MFEI-IDS model in few-shot learning and evaluate the impact of the number of support set categories and sample sizes on the training results, we conducted comparative experiments with FC-Net [32], Induction-Network-Attention (IN-Attention) [33], and the proposed few-shot learning method.

In these experiments, IN-Attention employed the same encoding module as our model, but its attention mechanism served as the induction module, whereas the proposed model uses a dynamic routing induction method to construct the induction module. The experiments primarily used the CIC-IDS 2017 dataset, which has a finer-grained division of attack categories, while extracting Infiltration attack data from the ISCX 2012 dataset to expand the test set for this attack type.

The CIC-IDS 2017 dataset consists of 15 data types. However, the Heartbleed and SQL Injection attack categories, with only 11 and 25 samples, respectively, were excluded from the comparison experiments due to insufficient sample size.

For the experiments, the number of support set categories C was set to 2, 3, 5, and 7, with a fixed sample size of 10. Additionally, for each selected class, 20 random samples were chosen as the query set, and the test set size was set to 500 samples. The results are shown in Figure 9. From the experimental results, it can be seen that all three models are a bit sensitive to the number of classes, C. The FC-Net model shows an accuracy trend that initially increases and then decreases as the number of categories increases, achieving its best performance when C = 5. Similarly, the proposed model and IN-Attention also achieve optimal performance at C = 5. However, the performance for the three-way configuration is slightly lower than for the two-way configuration. These findings suggest that the number of categories in the support set significantly impacts few-shot learning performance and that balancing the number of categories and samples is crucial for optimal model results.

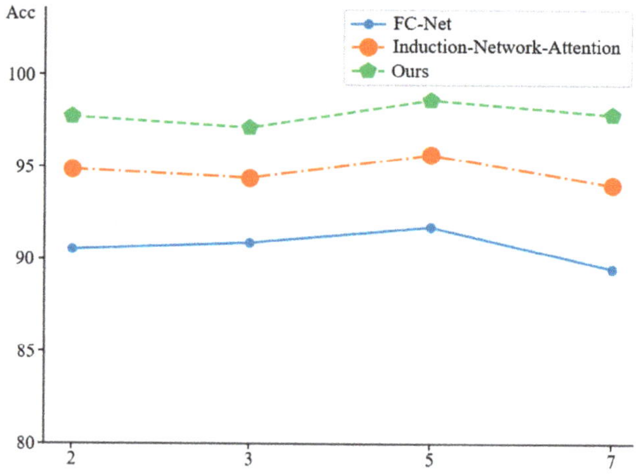

Figure 9. Accuracy–variation in the number of sample categories.

The number of experimental categories was set to five, and the support set sample size K was varied at 5, 10, 15, 20, and 25 to construct six groups for comparative experiments. During each iteration, 20 random samples from the selected classes were additionally chosen as the query set. The results are shown in Figure 10.

The accuracy of all three models improved as the number of samples increased. The improvement was most pronounced when K increased from 5 to 10, as both were in the few-shot learning scenario, but the sample size doubled, enabling the models to better learn the differences between categories.

From the accuracy trends across all models, it can be observed that few-shot learning differs from traditional supervised learning methods that require large sample sizes for training. Few-shot learning methods exhibit significantly less dependency on sample size, demonstrating their robustness and efficiency in scenarios with limited data.

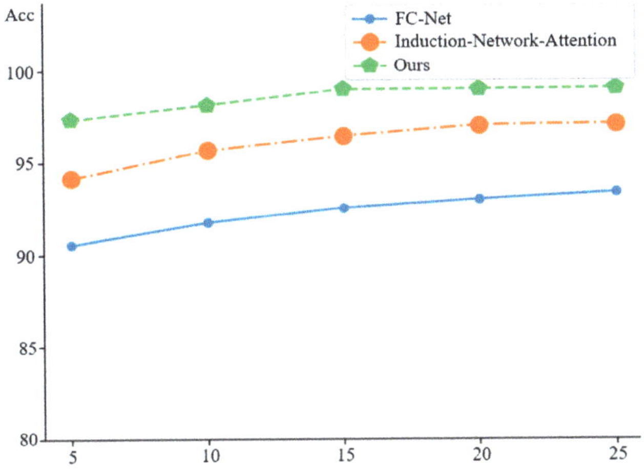

Figure 10. Accuracy–sample number variation.

From the above experiments, it can be observed that the proposed model achieves the best performance, while FC-Net performs the worst. This is because FC-Net uses a three-dimensional convolutional neural network (F-Net) for feature extraction and another CNN to measure sample similarity. While this approach captures differences between samples, it neglects the modeling of the mapping from sample representations to category representations. The IN-Attention model employs an attention mechanism as the induction module. However, since the FCN–Transformer used as the Encoder module has already extracted the temporal information of the traffic, IN-Attention fails to fully utilize its induction capability. Thus, in few-shot learning-based intrusion detection methods, MFEI-IDS demonstrates superior capability in mapping network traffic to attack types, resulting in better attack detection performance.

4.3.2. Comparison with Full Sample Learning

Based on the experimental parameters, the results of the MFEI-IDS model under the five-way 15-shot setting are presented in Table 10. These results are compared with the multi-class classification results on the CIC-IDS 2017 dataset (Table 8).

Table 10. Five-way 15-shot detection results for various attacks.

Traffic Category	Detection Rate	Recall Rate	F1-Score
Benign	93.52%	98.2%	0.958
DoS Hulk	99.39%	97.99%	0.9869
PortScan	97.98%	97.2%	0.9759
DDoS	96.84%	98%	0.9742
DoS GoldenEye	99.19%	97.6%	0.9838
FTP-Patator	99.8%	99.2%	0.995
SSH-Patator	99.2%	99%	0.991
DoS slowloris	98.79%	98.2%	0.985
Dos Slowhttptest	96.4%	96.4%	0.964
Bot	96.18%	95.8%	0.9599
Brute Force	96.63%	97.4%	0.9701
XSS	99.8%	98.4%	0.9909

In terms of precision, the full-sample method and the few-shot method each demonstrate advantages in different cases. When sufficient data are available, the full-sample supervised learning method generally achieves better recall. However, for categories with only a small number of samples, the MFEI-IDS method consistently achieves better detection performance. This comparison highlights the strength of the MFEI-IDS model in handling imbalanced or limited-sample scenarios, making it particularly effective for detecting rare or infrequently encountered attack types.

4.4. Experimental Results Across Datasets

The ISCX 2012 and CIC-IDS 2017 datasets can both be considered network traffic data generated under different hardware and software environments. While the attack types in these datasets share some similarities, they also exhibit significant differences. Compared to ISCX 2012, the CIC-IDS 2017 dataset contains more diverse traffic types, more complex attack techniques, and a larger volume of attack data, reflecting the evolution of network traffic over time.

Using these two datasets for cross-dataset experiments not only evaluates the proposed model's adaptability to different network environments but also assesses its potential to detect future network attacks. For convenience, the Infiltration, Heartbleed, and SQL Injection categories, which have the fewest samples in CIC-IDS 2017, were excluded from the experiments. For each task, the experimental setup included $C = 3$ (number of categories), $K = 15$ (support set size), and a test set containing 500 samples per class.

The first cross-dataset experiment involved training on the CIC-IDS 2017 dataset and testing on the ISCX 2012 dataset. The results are shown in Table 11.

Table 11. Training at CIC-IDS 2017, testing experimental results at ISCX 2012.

Type of Flow	Detection Rate	Recall Rate	F1-Score
Benign	93.18%	95.6%	0.9437
BFSSH	98.79%	98%	0.9839
Infiltration	96.39%	96.2%	0.963
HttpDos	94.5%	92.8%	0.9364
DDoS	94.81%	95%	0.9491

The results reveal that among all categories, the model achieved the lowest precision for normal traffic, at 93.18%, indicating that a considerable amount of attack traffic was misclassified as normal traffic. This suggests that some attack data were not detected. However, it also demonstrates the model's accuracy in detecting attacks.

The recall for all traffic types exceeded 92%, showing excellent detection capabilities across all attack categories. These results clearly demonstrate the model's strong generalization ability, achieving impressive performance even in cross-dataset scenarios.

Then, there was a cross-dataset training experiment on the ISCX 2012 dataset and a testing experiment on the CIC-IDS 2017 dataset, and the experimental results are shown in Table 12. Compared with the experimental results (Table 11), where both training and testing are performed on the CIC-IDS 2017 dataset, the model's detection performance for each class of attack is slightly degraded, mainly due to the fact that the ISCX 2012 data have fewer classes and the data are slightly simpler, and the model did not fully learn the subtle differences in the mapping of the sample data of the similar attacks to the class space when training on the ISCX 2012 dataset, which resulted in more misclassifications when tested on the more complex CIC-IDS 2017 dataset. Even so, the model still maintains a high detection and accuracy rate.

Table 12. Trained using ISCX 2012, tested using CIC-IDS 2017 experimental results.

Type of Flow	Detection Rate	Recall Rate	F1-Score
Benign	86.02%	97.2%	0.9127
DoS Hulk	97.11%	94.2%	0.9563
PortScan	97.11%	94.2%	0.9563
DDoS	96.41%	96.6%	0.965
DoS GoldenEye	97.74%	95.19%	0.9645
FTP-Patator	98.78%	97.4%	0.9809
SSH-Patator	98.38%	97.19%	0.9778
DoS slowloris	95.53%	98.2%	0.9684
Dos Slowhttptest	95.12%	93.6%	0.9435
Bot	94.02%	91.38%	0.9268
Brute Force	90.94%	96.4%	0.9359
XSS	99.78%	90.4%	0.9486

From the two experiments, it is evident that the MFEI-IDS model maintained high precision and recall rates in both cross-dataset experiments, indicating that cross-dataset training and testing are feasible. These two datasets were collected by the same laboratory under different hardware and software environments using different methodologies. The model's ability to achieve excellent cross-dataset results on these datasets demonstrates that the MFEI-IDS model can be deployed in new environments and future network scenarios without requiring fine-tuning.

This also highlights the model's strong adaptability. Even when encountering data types during testing that were not present during training, the model could still classify them effectively. This suggests that the MFEI-IDS model learns to inductively map sample representations to class representations during training, rather than merely memorizing the features of the training samples.

4.5. Results of Zero-Sample Unknown Intrusion Experiments

In order to test the detection capability of MFEI-IDS for unknown attack detection, the experiment also constructs the experimental dataset, as shown in Table 13. In this experiment, seven types of data were selected from the CIC-IDS2017 dataset, including normal data and six types of attack data, and the test set was expanded with the Infiltration data from the ISCX 2012 dataset. The seven types of data were classified into two categories, one of which was the known traffic set containing normal traffic and four types of attack data. The other is the unknown attack traffic set, consisting of Heartbleed and SQL Injection attack types, which were not used in the model training process. The number of known traffic samples in the training set was 35, where the number of samples in the support set was 15, the number of samples in the query set was 20, and the number of samples in the test set was 100. This setup allowed the model to be evaluated on its ability to detect both known and unknown attacks, emphasizing its potential for generalization to unseen traffic types.

Table 13. Unknown attack detection dataset description.

Data Definitions	Data Types	Training Volume	Test Volume	Code
Known flow	Benign	35	100	iA
	DDoS	35	100	iB
	PortScan	35	100	iC
	DoS Hulk	35	100	iD
	Infiltration	35	100	iE
Unknown attack	Heartbleed	0	10	iF
	SQL Injection	0	25	iG

Table 14 presents the detection results for unknown attacks in a zero-shot scenario. Precision and recall were used as evaluation metrics for unknown attack types because the small sample size of unknown attacks makes other metrics less effective in assessing the model's detection capabilities.

Table 14. Zero-sample unknown attack detection results.

Code	FC-Net		IN-Attention		MFEI-IDS	
	Detection Rate	Recall Rate	Detection Rate	Recall Rate	Detection Rate	Recall Rate
iA	88.99%	97%	91.67%	99%	95.24%	100%
iB	97.98%	97%	98.98%	97%	99%	99%
iC	90.62%	87%	92.93%	92%	96%	96%
iD	97%	97%	98%	98%	98.99%	98.99%
iE	90%	90%	93.94%	93%	97.94%	95%
iF&iG	93.55%	82.86%	100%	88.57%	100%	94.29%

For the CIC-IDS 2017 dataset, the MFEI-IDS model outperformed other models in detecting all types of attacks, achieving the best results. For the unknown attacks iFiFiF and iGiGiG, the detection rate reached 94.29%. However, the detection of unknown attack types is determined by a relation score threshold, meaning the model can identify unknown attacks but cannot further differentiate between specific unknown attack types.

The precision for unknown attacks reached 100%, indicating that any data predicted as unknown attacks genuinely belong to the unknown attack category. These experiments demonstrate that the proposed model has a high detection rate for unknown attacks and achieves exceptional accuracy in identifying them, highlighting its strong generalization capabilities for unseen attack scenarios.

To further demonstrate the superiority of the MFEI-IDS model, confusion matrices for the three models are presented in Figure 11. From the confusion matrices, it is evident that the MFEI-IDS model achieves a 100% recognition rate for normal traffic, with no instances of normal traffic being misclassified as attack traffic. This is of critical importance in practical applications, as it allows for detecting network attacks without disrupting normal operations.

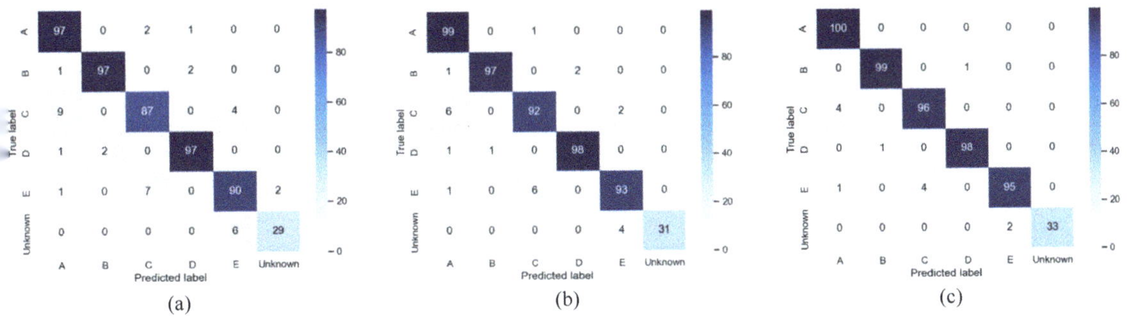

Figure 11. Confusion matrix: (**a**) FC-Net; (**b**) Induction-Network-Attention; (**c**) MFEI-IDS.

In contrast, The FC-Net and IN-Attention models tend to confuse PortScan with Infiltration and Infiltration with unknown attacks. This is because PortScan is part of the reconnaissance phase of an attack, and SQL Injection is inherently a form of web penetration, leading to misclassification between these categories. All three models occasionally misclassify PortScan data as normal traffic. This is because reconnaissance activities, such as slow scans, may not involve overtly malicious operations and closely resemble normal traffic patterns.

The MFEI-IDS model clearly stands out, achieving the highest detection rate for unknown attacks and having the fewest misclassifications overall. This further highlights the model's exceptional inductive capability in distinguishing between categories, making it the most robust and reliable model among the three.

The above experiments demonstrate the performance and advantages of few-shot learning in detecting unknown attacks. By combining the excellent feature extraction capabilities of the FCN model with the inductive network's ability to map samples to categories, the MFEI-IDS model achieves strong generalization and robustness.

The model surpasses the other two methods in terms of the detection rate and precision for unknown attacks. This enables the proposed model to identify entirely new categories without requiring fine-tuning, making it adaptable to various network environments and future challenges.

5. Conclusions

This paper proposes a Multi-level Feature Extraction and Inductive Network-based Intrusion Detection System (MFEI-IDS), which combines a one-dimensional fully convolutional neural network (1D FCN) and Transformer architecture to achieve efficient feature extraction. The system utilizes an inductive learning module to map sample vectors into robust class representations, enabling effective detection of unknown attacks. The experimental results demonstrate that MFEI-IDS outperforms other models on the ISCX 2012 and CIC-IDS 2017 datasets. For instance, the model achieved an accuracy of 98.5% on the ISCX 2012 dataset and an F1-score of 0.92 on the CIC-IDS 2017 dataset. Notably, the model exhibited outstanding robustness and generalization capability in cross-dataset validation, few-shot learning, and unknown attack scenarios, validating its applicability and potential in complex traffic environments.

Despite its strong performance, MFEI-IDS has some limitations and areas for improvement worth exploring:

(1) In terms of real-time inference and processing, the current design of MFEI-IDS is primarily tailored to batch processing. This approach requires the completion of data collection, slicing, cleaning, and preprocessing before performing intrusion detec-

tion. While effective for offline detection tasks, this batch analysis framework may face limitations in scenarios demanding real-time responses. For instance, existing session-level slicing methods efficiently aggregate contextual traffic information but rely on session completion prior to processing, which can introduce delays in dynamic and high-speed network environments. To overcome these limitations and meet the demands of real-time inference, several optimizations can be explored. One potential direction is the introduction of stream processing frameworks, utilizing sliding windows and stream-level slicing techniques to facilitate the real-time analysis of incomplete sessions, thereby reducing response time. Additionally, optimizing the data preprocessing module by simplifying data cleaning and filling processes can lower the complexity of preprocessing steps. Incorporating dynamic data truncation strategies may further reduce latency. Furthermore, enhancing the model architecture to support lightweight operation and incremental inference is essential. By refining the FCN and Transformer modules, the system can incrementally process incoming packets, achieving efficient real-time inference. In practical applications, the implementation of real-time inference requires a careful balance among model accuracy, response speed, and computational resources. While the current model is primarily designed for offline detection, optimizing it for real-time inference represents an important avenue for future research, particularly in scenarios that require rapid detection of zero-day attacks and high-frequency traffic anomalies.

(2) Further Optimization of the Feature Extraction Model: The experimental results demonstrate that bidirectional networks, such as BiGRU, outperform more complex models like LSTM in feature extraction, underscoring the importance of comprehensive feature extraction for model performance. This advantage likely arises from the ability of bidirectional networks to simultaneously capture both forward and backward sequence information, thereby providing a more complete representation of temporal dependencies and contextual features. To further optimize the feature extraction process, the introduction of the BERT model as the backbone for temporal feature extraction is a promising direction. BERT, a deep bidirectional model based on the Transformer architecture, is capable of capturing global dependencies in long sequences with high precision. Additionally, its pretraining and fine-tuning mechanisms enable the model to leverage extensive existing datasets, significantly enhancing generalization performance, particularly in few-shot scenarios.

For the extraction of local spatial features, an improved WordPiece tokenization method could be employed for traffic packet analysis. Traditional tokenization methods may lead to the loss of fine-grained features within traffic data, whereas an enhanced WordPiece method can more precisely extract local features, such as protocol fields or application-layer data details. By incorporating this method, finer-grained embedding vectors can be constructed, enabling the model to exhibit stronger analytical capabilities when handling complex traffic patterns. Combining the BERT model with an optimized tokenization approach would not only strengthen the extraction of temporal and local features but also fully exploit the multi-scale characteristics of network traffic. This integration would further enhance the model's detection accuracy and robustness. Such an optimization strategy offers a robust theoretical foundation and practical potential for the application of the model in complex traffic environments.

(3) Memory Mechanism in Few-Shot Learning: Current few-shot learning models face the challenge of catastrophic forgetting when switching between tasks in large-scale categorical datasets. Catastrophic forgetting reduces the ability of intrusion detection systems to generalize across tasks and retain prior knowledge, significantly

impacting overall performance. This issue leads to instability in key performance metrics, such as accuracy and recall, thereby undermining the reliability of the system. Moreover, the loss of prior knowledge weakens the system's capability to detect unknown attacks, as it struggles to identify anomalies based on previously acquired information. Additionally, catastrophic forgetting increases the need for retraining, which elevates computational costs and decreases adaptability to emerging threats. To address this challenge, memory-enhanced modules based on Transformer architectures could be introduced. While few-shot learning models can effectively detect unknown attacks, they currently lack the capability to further classify these attacks. Future research could explore fine-grained classification mechanisms to improve the model's classification performance and enhance its ability to handle unknown attacks.

(4) Intelligent Detection with Knowledge Graphs: The integration of knowledge graphs represents a critical future direction in network intrusion detection. By constructing semantic networks of attack paths, behavior patterns, and their interrelationships, knowledge graphs provide intuitive logical associations and contextual information for analyzing complex attack behaviors. This approach enables the integration of multi-source heterogeneous data, uncovering potential attack paths and anomalous patterns, thereby equipping detection systems with more comprehensive analytical capabilities. The application of knowledge graphs in intrusion detection is primarily reflected in three areas. First, they facilitate the integration of attacker behavior characteristics, target system vulnerabilities, and attack techniques, providing a comprehensive understanding of attacks. Second, when combined with inference engines, knowledge graphs enable the real-time evaluation of anomalous traffic and rapid response, allowing for the inference of potential attack types and their consequences. Third, they enhance system explainability by visually presenting the reasoning processes and related cases, thereby improving the credibility of detection results. Nevertheless, constructing and maintaining high-quality knowledge graphs poses significant challenges, such as addressing data sparsity, dynamic changes, and complex entity relationships. Future research could explore automated knowledge graph construction techniques, such as extracting entities and relationships from security reports and logs. Furthermore, the introduction of dynamic updating mechanisms would ensure that knowledge graphs remain consistent with the latest attack patterns. Integrating knowledge graphs into intrusion detection not only enhances detection accuracy and real-time response capabilities but also provides profound insights into complex attack behaviors, offering robust support for combating modern cybersecurity threats.

In summary, MFEI-IDS provides an efficient solution to modern network security challenges through its innovative architecture and feature extraction mechanism. Future research will focus on optimizing feature extraction capabilities, expanding few-shot learning performance, and exploring the application of knowledge graphs in intrusion detection to further advance the field of network security.

Author Contributions: Conceptualization, J.M. and G.Y.; Data curation, B.H.; Formal analysis, X.Y. and Y.L.; Methodology, J.M., X.Y., and G.Y.; Resources, B.H.; Software, J.M., Y.L., and G.Y.; Supervision, B.H.; Validation, X.Y. and G.Y.; Visualization, Y.L.; Writing—original draft, J.M.; Writing—review and editing, B.H., Y.L., and G.Y. All authors have read and agreed to the published version of the manuscript.

Funding: This paper was supported by Kashgar Science and Technology Plan: KS2023024.

Data Availability Statement: Data are contained within the article.

Conflicts of Interest: The authors declare no conflicts of interest.

References

1. Spadaccino, P.; Cuomo, F. Intrusion detection systems for IoT: Opportunities and challenges offered by edge computing. *ITU J. Future Evol. Technol.* **2022**, *3*, 408–420. [CrossRef]
2. Wang, Z. Deep Learning-Based Intrusion Detection with Adversaries. *IEEE Access* **2018**, *6*, 38367–38384. [CrossRef]
3. Ferrag, M.A.; Shu, L.; Yang, X.; Derhab, A.; Maglaras, L. Security for Intelligent Autonomous Networks: A Survey. *IEEE Commun. Surv. Tutor.* **2020**, *22*, 2282–2314. [CrossRef]
4. Manocchio, A.; Tinnirello, I. FlowTransformer: A Novel Approach for Intrusion Detection in IoT Environments Using Transformers. *IoT Secur. J.* **2021**, *9*, 141–158. [CrossRef]
5. Javaid, A.; Niyaz, Q.; Sun, W.; Alam, M. A Deep Learning Approach for Network Intrusion Detection System. In Proceedings of the 9th EAI International Conference on Bio-Inspired Information and Communications Technologies (Formerly BIONETICS), New York, NY, USA, 3–5 December 2015; pp. 21–26. [CrossRef]
6. Shu, J.; Zhang, Y.; Li, X. Few-shot Learning for Intrusion Detection: A Novel Prototype Network-based Approach. *IEEE Trans. Inf. Forensics Secur.* **2020**, *15*, 5036–5048. [CrossRef]
7. Vaswani, A.; Shazeer, N.; Parmar, N.; Uszkoreit, J.; Jones, L.; Gomez, A.N.; Kaiser, L.; Polosukhin, I. Attention is All You Need. *Adv. Neural Inf. Process. Syst.* **2017**, *30*, 5998–6008.
8. Zhang, W.; Lu, H.; Zhou, H.; Liu, X. FlowTransformer: A Hybrid CNN and Transformer Model for Network Traffic Analysis. *IEEE Access* **2021**, *9*, 88878–88890. [CrossRef]
9. Zhang, J.; Wang, H.; Sun, Y. FlowTransformer: A Transformer-based Framework for Network Intrusion Detection. *Appl. Intell.* **2023**, *56*, 2917–2970. [CrossRef]
10. Wei, G.; Wang, Z. Adoption and realization of deep learning in network traffic anomaly detection device design. *Soft Comput.* **2021**, *25*, 1147–1158. [CrossRef]
11. Deng, H.; Sun, W.; Luo, H.; Feng, D. Random Forest and LSTM-Based Network Anomaly Detection. *IEEE Access* **2022**, *10*, 22837–22847. [CrossRef]
12. Alhaj, T.; Al-Hadhrami, A.; Mohammad, R.; Al-Khanjari, Z. Deep Learning and Attention Mechanisms for Traffic Classification: Challenges and Future Directions. *J. Artif. Intell. Soft Comput. Res.* **2023**, *13*, 59–71. [CrossRef]
13. Luo, S.; Zhao, Z.; Hu, Q.; Liu, Y. A hierarchical CNN-transformer model for network intrusion detection. In Proceedings of the 2nd International Conference on Applied Mathematics, Modelling, and Intelligent Computing (CAMMIC 2022), Kunming, China, 25–27 March 2022. [CrossRef]
14. Chen, X.; Li, J.; Zhang, H. Transformer-Based Intrusion Detection System for Network Security. *J. Netw. Comput. Appl.* **2023**, *234*, 104527. [CrossRef]
15. Shu, Z.; Liu, Z.; Shen, C.; Wang, H. Few-shot learning for intrusion detection system. In Proceedings of the 2018 IEEE International Conference on Big Data (Big Data), Seattle, WA, USA, 10–13 December 2018; pp. 5473–5477.
16. Zhao, Y.; Chen, Y.; Wu, Y.; Zhang, X. Cross-domain few-shot learning for intrusion detection system. *IEEE Access* **2020**, *8*, 176872–176884.
17. Vinyals, O.; Blundell, C.; Lillicrap, T.; Kavukcuoglu, K.; Wierstra, D. Matching Networks for One Shot Learning. In Proceedings of the 30th Conference on Neural Information Processing Systems (NIPS), Barcelona, Spain, 5–10 December 2016; pp. 3630–3638.
18. Xu, Y.; Liu, G.; Hu, Z.; Li, X. Inductive learning and metric learning for network anomaly detection. *IEEE Trans. Inf. Forensics Secur.* **2019**, *14*, 2893–2906.
19. Li, H.; Zhang, T.; Wang, Y.; Gao, S. Attention-based metric learning for network intrusion detection. *IEEE Access* **2021**, *9*, 48965–48978.
20. Dainotti, A.; Pescape, A.; C1affy, K.C. Issues and future directions in traffic classification. *IEEE Netw.* **2012**, *26*, 35–40. [CrossRef]
21. Jing, X.; Yan, Z.; Pedrycz, W. Security data collection and data analytics in the Internet: A survey. *IEEE Commun. Surv. Tutor.* **2018**, *21*, 586–618. [CrossRef]
22. Parsaei, M.; Taheri, R.; Javidan, R. Perusing The Effect of Discretization of Data on Accuracy of Predicting Naïve Bayes Algorithm. *J. Curr. Res. Sci.* **2016**, *1*, 457–462.
23. Devlin, J.; Chang, M.-W.; Lee, K.; Toutanova, K. BERT: Pre-training of Deep Bidirectional Transformers for Language Understanding. In Proceedings of the 2019 Conference of the North American Chapter of the Association for Computational Linguistics: Human Language Technologies, Florence, Italy, 28 July–2 August 2019; Association for Computational Linguistics: Minneapolis, MN, USA, 2019; Volume 1 (Long and Short Papers), pp. 4171–4186.
24. Wang, W. Research on Network Traffic Classification and Anomaly Detection Methods Based on Deep Learning. Ph.D. Thesis, University of Science and Technology of China, Anhui, China, 2018.
25. Ba, J.L.; Kiros, J.R.; Hinton, G.E. Layer normalization. *arXiv* **2016**, arXiv:1607.06450.

6. Hostiadi, D.P.; Atmojo, Y.P.; Huizen, R.R.; Susila, I.M.D.; Pradipta, G.A.; Liandana, I.M. A New Approach Feature Selection for Intrusion Detection System Using Correlation Analysis. In Proceedings of the 2022 4th International Conference on Cybernetics and Intelligent System (ICORIS), Prapat, Indonesia, 8–9 October 2022; pp. 1–6. [CrossRef]
7. Bhuva, D.; Kumar, S. Securing Space Cognitive Communication with Blockchain. In Proceedings of the 2023 IEEE Cognitive Communications for Aerospace Applications Workshop (CCAAW), Cleveland, OH, USA, 20–22 June 2023; pp. 1–6. [CrossRef]
8. Bhuva, D.; Kumar, S. A novel continuous authentication method using biometrics for IoT devices. *Internet Things* **2023**, *24*, 100927. [CrossRef]
9. Socher, R.; Chen, D.; Manning, C.D.; Ng, A. Reasoning with neural tensor networks for knowledge base completion. In Proceedings of the Advances in Neural Information Processing Systems, Lake Tahoe, NV, USA, 5–8 December 2013; pp. 926–934.
0. Shiravi, A.; Shiravi, H.; Tavallaee, M.; Ghorbani, A.A. Toward developing a systematic approach to generate benchmark datasets for intrusion detection. *Comput. Secur.* **2012**, *31*, 357–374. [CrossRef]
1. Sharafaldin, I.; Lashkari, A.H.; Ghorbani, A.A. Toward generating a new intrusion detection dataset and intrusion traffic characterization. In Proceedings of the ICISSP, Funchal, Portugal, 22–24 January 2018; pp. 108–116.
2. Xu, C.; Shen, J.; Du, X. A method of few-shot network intrusion detection based on meta-learning framework. *IEEE Trans. Inf. Forensics Secur.* **2020**, *15*, 3540–3552. [CrossRef]
3. Geng, R.; Li, B.; Li, Y.; Zhu, X.; Jian, P.; Sun, J. Induction Networks for Few-Shot Text Classification. *arXiv* **2019**, arXiv:1902.10482. [CrossRef]

electronics

MDPI

Article

Hierarchical Security Authentication with Attention-Enhanced Convolutional Network for Internet of Things

Xiaoying Qiu [1,*], Guangxu Zhao [1], Jinwei Yu [2], Wenbao Jiang [1], Zhaozhong Guo [1] and Maozhi Xu [3]

1 College of Computer Science, Beijing Information Science and Technology University, Beijing 100192, China; 2023020981@bistu.edu.cn (G.Z.); 20051452@bistu.edu.cn (W.J.); guozhaozhong@bistu.edu.cn (Z.G.)
2 School of Information and Communication Engineering, Beijing University of Posts and Telecommunications, Beijing 100876, China; hahayuswag@bupt.cn
3 School of Mathematical Sciences, Peking University, Beijing 100871, China; mzxu@math.pku.edu.cn
* Correspondence: 20192329@bistu.edu.cn

Abstract: As security authentication issues continue to arise in future wireless communication networks, researchers are working hard to further improve authentication techniques. Recently, physical layer authentication (PLA) has received widespread attention for its lightweight nature compared to traditional encryption methods based on keys and blockchain. However, the existing PLA mechanisms based on a fixed decision threshold have low reliability in dynamic environments. Moreover, PLA solutions are typically based on binary authentication, and these binary-type schemes cannot provide different levels of access control. To address these challenges, this article introduces the concept of hierarchical security authentication, aiming to achieve multi-level secure authorization access. In order to further improve the accuracy of identity verification, we design an Attention-Enhanced Convolutional Network (AECN) model that integrates the attention mechanism. Specifically, by introducing a confidence score branch, the proposed AECN-based PLA scheme completes authentication without a threshold, thus avoiding the issues stemming from inappropriate threshold settings in conventional PLA schemes. The simulation results show that our proposed AECN framework outperforms existing algorithms at different levels of security authentication.

Keywords: artificial intelligence; blockchain security; physical layer security; privacy protection; machine learning

1. Introduction

The Internet of Things (IoT), as the core technology of the fourth industrial revolution [1], has become a significant driver of global scientific and technological advancement, as well as industrial modernization. It promotes technological advancements in fields such as smart healthcare [2], smart home [3] and wearable devices [4], resulting in significant improvements in work and lifestyle [5]. However, the large number of connected smart devices in IoT networks make them vulnerable to spoofing attacks, making it particularly important to prevent unauthorized access to resources [6]. The conventional authentication procedures predominantly rely on upper-layer protocols [7] and cryptographic algorithms [8]. Blockchain, a distributed ledger technology, is used in cryptographic algorithms for its secure, trustworthy and tamper-proof feature [9]. For example, in [10], blockchain is used to store key ciphertext. The deployment of key-based encryption technology for repeated authentication in latency-sensitive IoT environments may result in latency and computational overhead, posing a challenge to the processing capabilities of these smart IoT devices [11]. In addition, the rapid development of quantum computing has also posed challenges to system security, especially in brute force password cracking scenarios. In view of this, more efforts are needed to enhance the security authentication technology of IoT.

In recent years, physical layer authentication (PLA) [12] has become a novel security authentication scheme that utilizes the spatiotemporal uncorrelated characteristics of different channels to achieve identity recognition. As is supported by the well-known Jakes model, the received signals decorrelate over a distance of half a wavelength. It is difficult for an attacker to forge the channel between legitimate transceivers [13]. Upon receiving the signal, the receiver verifies its legitimacy by confirming whether it originates from a permitted or unauthorized device. This process not only ensures the validity of the signal but also traces its source, effectively identifying unauthorized users. Common physical layer attributes include radio frequency (RF) fingerprinting [14], channel information [15], and carrier frequency offset (CFO) [16], which are difficult for attackers to imitate. However, RF fingerprinting techniques face two different forms of replay attacks: signal replay and feature replay. Furthermore, RF features are susceptible to fluctuations caused by changes in the channel environment [17]. Therefore, channel state information (CSI) is employed for the secure authentication of devices accessing the IoT, and the reasons are outlined as follows: In wireless communication, CSI delineates the characteristics of signal propagation channels, encompassing signal attenuation, phase offset, multipath effect, and more. Distinct physical conditions between transmitters and receivers give rise to variances in CSI, endowing it with notable variability and distinctiveness, which renders CSI a potent identifier for authentication purposes. The resilience of CSI to alteration is a consequence of intrinsic dependence on physical environments. Consequently, malevolent entities encounter considerable challenges when attempting to falsify or imitate authentic CSI with the intention of subverting authentication systems.

Research in PLA has concentrated on two principal areas: firstly, statistical model-based PLA, which employs parameters or thresholds to distinguish between different users; and secondly, PLA using machine learning (ML) and deep learning (DL), whereby network models are trained to make autonomous decisions.

Statistical model-based PLA: Conventional PLA relies on hypothesis testing, which typically involves setting a threshold to complete the authentication process [12]. Xiao et al. [18] proposed a statistical distribution model that incorporates established or estimated parameters to characterize channel attribute. Subsequently, hypothesis testing was employed to define a precise threshold. The proposed approach leverages the inherent similarities and differences in channel characteristics as a means of discerning legitimate users from potential intruders. In [19], Lu considered the influence of general channel conditions in the system model, proposed a scheme to improve authentication performance by exploiting channel correlation coefficient information, and provided closed-form expressions for decision thresholds under binary hypothesis testing. Xie et al. [20] presented two PLA schemes and performed a theoretical analysis to derive the closure expressions. The results of the subsequent experimental investigation demonstrate an improvement in authentication performance. Due to the dynamic changes in channel conditions, traditional hypothesis testing methods that rely on thresholds are no longer applicable. Xiao et al. showed that, through reinforcement learning technology, even when the system parameters are unknown, the threshold can be dynamically adjusted to optimize the detection performance. However, despite the optimal adjustment of the threshold, limitations persist in the detection performance [21,22]. Blockchain is used to assist security authentication due to its decentralization and tamper-proof quality [23]. Fang et al. [24] proposed a blockchain-assisted handover authentication scheme for the Internet of Vehicles (IoV), utilizing the threshold for authentication and storing information on the blockchain.

ML and DL-based PLA: Classical classification algorithms, in particular support vector machine (SVM), are used in PLA. Pei et al. [25] employed SVM to construct classifiers that could effectively differentiate between channel feature vectors with high and low similarity. SVM technology is implemented for user authentication at the packet level, ensuring the ability to distinguish different users even in cases where their signal fingerprints exhibit similarity [26]. In [27], a multi-dimensional adaptive PLA scheme is presented, which employs fuzzy theory to model multiple physical layer attributes that are inherently imperfect and uncertain, thereby enabling the design of a compact authentication model. In [28], a collaborative PLA scheme based on horizontal federated learning is proposed, which distributes computational tasks among multiple edge nodes or cloud servers. Nevertheless, the preliminary authentication process does not occur at the physical layer. In order to address the challenge of determining testing thresholds in dynamic network environments, Wang et al. [29] used the multi-dimensional characteristics of wireless channels and training data generated from pseudo-spoofing models. In [30], a threshold-free PLA approach is proposed as an alternative to traditional threshold-based decision-making. In contrast, the channel matrix estimated from wireless nodes is employed as the authentication input, thereby facilitating more adaptive classification through the application of ML algorithms. Qiu et al. [31] proposed a PLA enhancement scheme based on a Gaussian mixture model (GMM), which conducted clustering analysis on channel information through a two-dimensional feature space to detect and distinguish legitimate users from potential spoofing attackers. A PLA scheme based on logistic regression is proposed [32]. The training of the model is expedited by reducing the training dataset [33] and optimizing the training process [34], while ensuring that the authentication performance remains uncompromised. In [33], Meng demonstrated that authentication performance can be optimized even with a limited training dataset by introducing Gaussian noise into the smooth potential space. By integrating a deep neural network (DNN), a multi-user PLA scheme with data augmentation is proposed, and three gradient descent methods are proposed as a means of accelerating the training of the network [34]. Nevertheless, the above scheme adopts binary authentication, which allows the receiver to either accept or reject. Consequently, a binary authentication scheme results in misdetections, leading to a waste of resources.

In short, it is difficult for the PLA to set appropriate thresholds when channel conditions dynamically change, as fixed thresholds not adapt to rapid changes, leading to misjudgments or missed detections. Moreover, existing binary authentication schemes are unable to provide multi-level access control for the system. Therefore, we propose a hierarchical security authenticator for PLA, which includes a confidence branch and an attention-enhanced convolutional network (AECN). The proposed AECN model, by introducing hierarchical security authenticator, enables multi-level secure authorized access, thereby better accommodating the needs of different devices and users in IoT environments. The specific contributions of this work are summarized below:

- To provide multi-levels access control, a hierarchical security authenticator is proposed. The receiver evaluates the trustworthiness of the smart devices based on the proposed PLA solution. In our proposed neural networks, we transform the hierarchical security issue into a multi-classification problem for security authentication.
- A confidence score branch is introduced, which is designed to evaluate the model's prediction probability and assign a corresponding confidence score. Furthermore, we propose an attention module that incorporates a bottleneck structure and depthwise separable convolution. The proposed AECN model integrates an attention module that processes the input feature map, generates attention weights, and allows the model to focus on key information, thereby enhancing the accuracy of identity verification.
- We conducted comparative experiments on our proposed AECN scheme and CNN-based PLA scheme. The simulation results show that our solution provides more reliable protection for IoT devices at different levels of security authentication.

The subsequent sections of this article are structured as follows: Section 2 offers a comprehensive overview of the system model. Section 3 introduces the proposed hierarchical security authentication scheme, hierarchical security authenticator, and attention module. Section 4 is the presentation of evaluation indicators and performance analysis. Section 5 is the discussion and future work. Section 6 is the conclusions. Abbreviations lists the abbreviations that appear in this paper and their spelled-out terms.

2. System Model

As shown in Figure 1, the classic Alice–Bob–Eve communication model is considered., in which IoT nodes (Alice_1, Alice_2, ..., Alice_N) carry out secure communication with the base station (BS) Bob. The communication between Alice_i and Bob requires secure and continuous signal transmission. Bob needs to verify the received message to ascertain whether it was sent by Alice_i. Eve is an illegitimate sending node, also known as a spoofer. Eve attempts to mimic the identity of a legitimate device Alice_i, conducting deception through an independent spoofing channel to gain unauthorized access to the system or introduce false data. Spoofing attacks lead to unauthorized access, privacy breaches, and erroneous decisions in IoT scenarios.

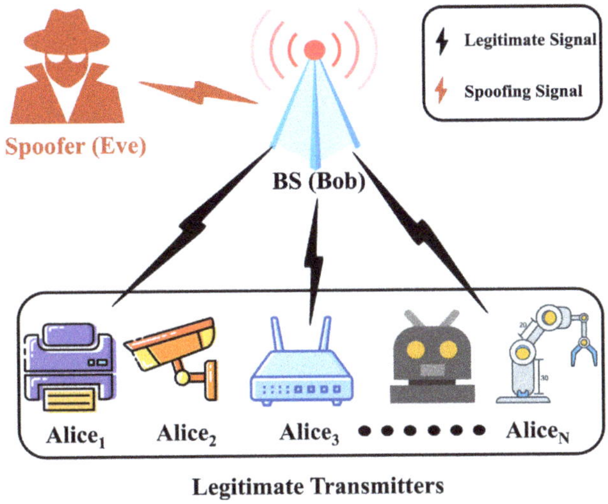

Figure 1. System model.

Assuming Bob is furnished with N_r antennas and Alice_i has N_t antennas, it is assumed that Orthogonal Frequency Division Multiplexing (OFDM) technology is used in the communication process, and N_s subcarriers are allocated for data transmission. Then, we have

$$\vec{P} = \mathbf{CSI} \cdot \vec{Q} + \vec{N} \tag{1}$$

where $\vec{P}$ and $\vec{Q}$ represent the received signal vectors and the transmitted signal vectors, $\vec{N}$ denotes the Gaussian noise, and **CSI** represents the channel state information matrix. The matrix $\mathbf{CSI}_{\mathrm{mn}}$ is a complex value. Defined as

$$\mathbf{CSI}_{\mathrm{mn}} = \mathrm{real}(\mathbf{CSI}_{\mathrm{mn}}) + \mathrm{img}(\mathbf{CSI}_{\mathrm{mn}}) \tag{2}$$

where the real value represents the m-th antenna and the imaginary value represents the n-th subcarrier.

Alice_i and Bob utilize the unique physical layer attribute as the basis for authentication and have established an initial authentication mechanism before the communication begins, which serves as a prerequisite for PLA. At initial authentication stage, the estimation value of Alice_i's CSI can be obtained, which is represented as

$$C_{A1}, C_{A2}, \ldots, C_{At} \tag{3}$$

where C_{At}, with $t \in \{1, 2, \ldots, T\}$, represents the information received from a legitimate device. The new CSI estimation C_{Ot} $(t = 1, 2, \ldots)$ clearly shows the examples of physical layer estimation. The new CSI estimation C_{Ot} may come from Alice$_i$ or Eve. The CSI at $t+1$ is represented as

$$\Delta C_{O1} = f(C_{A1}, C_{A2}, \ldots, C_{AT}, C_{O1}) \tag{4}$$

where f represents the discrepancy evaluation function between C_{A1}, C_{A2}, ..., C_{AI} and C_{O1}. Furthermore, a hierarchical security authentication model is introduced, comprising n categories, with each category assigned a corresponding authorization level based on the different resources.

3. Hierarchical Security Authentication Scheme and Attention Module

We propose a hierarchical security authenticator for PLA that includes a confidence score branch and an attention module. The confidence score branch is responsible for authenticating the receiver by assigning confidence score to the predicted probabilities, and the attention module generates attention weight.

3.1. Overall Framework of Hierarchical Security Authentication Scheme

Figure 2 shows the overall framework of Hierarchical Security Authentication scheme for multi-level access control of IoT devices. During the data collection phase, BS obtains the original CSI values from the IoT devices. In the stage of converting CSI data to images, the obtained CSI data are constructed as images as input to the authenticator. The CSI matrix is considered in the form of an image, where the first channel is a real value and the second channel is a imaginary value. Considering that there are 64 antennas and 52 subcarriers in the IoT scene, the CSI matrix can be viewed as a three-dimensional image with dimensions of $64 \times 52 \times 2$. Afterwards, the CSI image samples are input into the authenticator for training to obtain training weight. In the course of the online authentication phase, BS verifies the received data packets by making use of the trained authenticator and the recently obtained CSI image. The authenticator furnishes a prediction probability and security score, and the purpose is to ascertain the legitimacy of the data packet's source device.

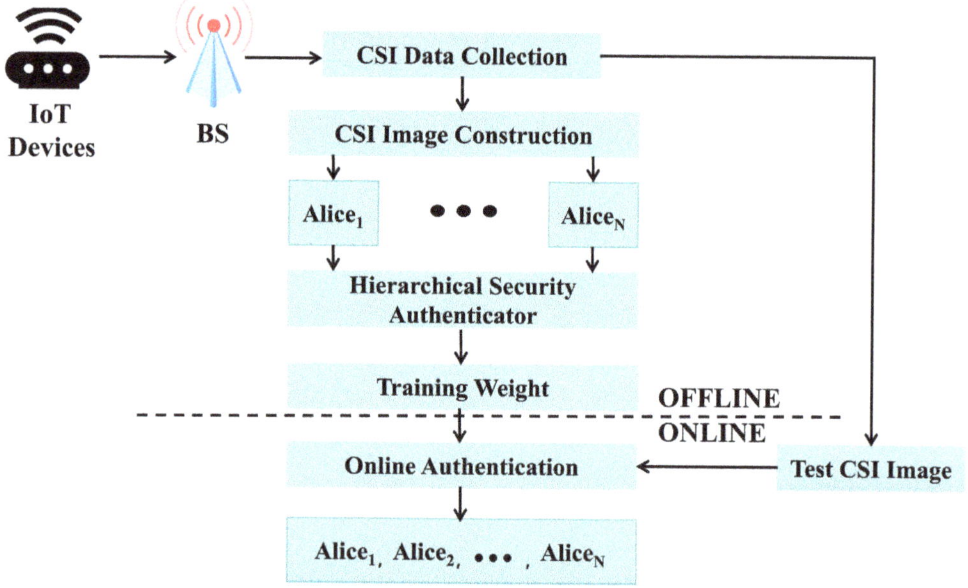

Figure 2. Overall framework of hierarchical security authentication scheme.

3.2. Hierarchical Security Authenticator

Figure 3 illustrates the comprehensive architectural framework of our proposed Hierarchical Security Authenticator, which integrates our proposed AECN and confidence score branch. During the data processing phase, the received signals are used to extract CSI attributes, which are then processed as a training dataset. Subsequently, the data dimensions are adjusted to a four-dimensional matrix of 64 × 52 × 2 × 40,000, where 40,000 is the number of CSI images, before being input to the AECN.

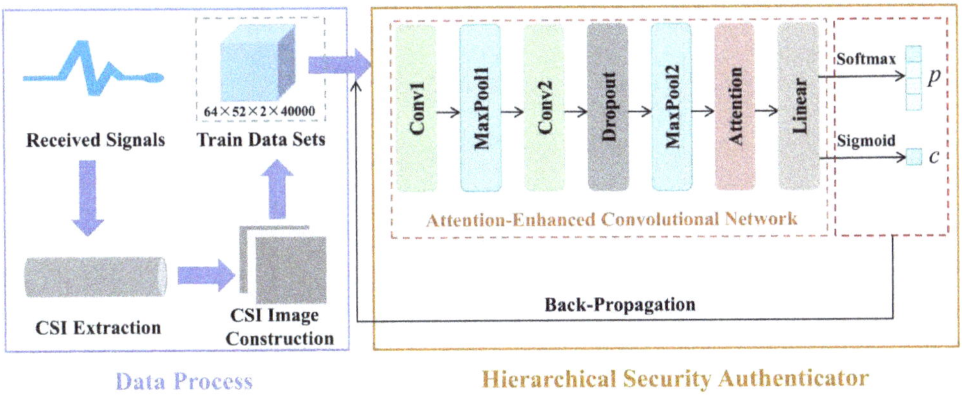

Figure 3. Architecture of Hierarchical Security Authenticator.

The AECN model comprises a series of layers that are designed to facilitate the extraction and classification of features. The network initially extracts preliminary features of the input CSI image through convolutional layer 1 (Conv1). Next, MaxPool1 is used to reduce the spatial dimension of the feature map and focus on preserving the most important features. Subsequently, the second convolutional layer (Conv2) serves to further refine the process of feature extraction. To prevent overfitting, a dropout layer is incorporated into the network. This is achieved by randomly discarding a portion of the activation values of neurons. MaxPool2 continues the process of dimensionality reduction, further abstracting the feature representations. The core of the network is the attention layer, which emphasizes the features in the input feature map through attention mechanisms, enhancing the recognition ability of the model. For a detailed description of this attention layer, please refer to Section 3.3. Subsequently, the linear layer transforms these features into a prediction space suitable for classification task.

We use AECN to automatically learn a representation of CSI feature maps. CSI images provide a structured form of data for the AECN model, facilitating the model to automatically learn complex spatial features through convolutional neural networks. This approach captures subtle changes in the CSI data and enhances the recognition ability of the model.

Both the branch tasked with calculating the confidence score and the one responsible for generating the Softmax predictions are linked to a same fully connected layer. The Softmax function is applied in order to obtain prediction probabilities p, while the sigmoid function is applied in order to obtain the confidence score c. The authenticator should output c close to 1 if it is confident that it can produce a correct prediction for the given input. Conversely, if the authenticator is not confident that it can produce the correct prediction, it should output c close to 0.

$$p, c = F(img, \theta), p_i, c \in [0, 1], \sum_{i=1}^{N} p_i = 1 \tag{5}$$

where *img* is the training data of the input convolutional network and θ denotes parameters of the AECN.

The softmax prediction probabilities are adjusted during training to provide authenticator with the hints they need. This is done by interpolating between the original predictions and the target probability distribution y, with the degree of interpolation indicated by the confidence.

$$p' = c \cdot p + (1 - c)y \tag{6}$$

A negative log-likelihood function is employed to calculate the task loss. However, to prevent the network from consistently selecting $c = 0$ to minimize the loss function, a logarithmic penalty mechanism is incorporated into the confidence loss. The revised loss function L combines the task loss L_{AECN} with the confidence loss L_c, weighted by the hyper-parameter λ, in order to achieve a balance between the task loss and the confidence loss.

$$L = L_{AECN} + \lambda L_c = -\sum_{i=1}^{N} \log(p_i')y_i + -\lambda \log(c) \tag{7}$$

3.3. Attention Module

The attention module is shown in Figure 4, which uses a bottleneck structure and depth-wise separable convolution to generate attention weights. The following presents the specific details:

The feature map is fed into a bottleneck structure, which aims to reduce the input dimensionality of the feature while preserving crucial information. The first component of the bottleneck structure is a convolutional layer with a kernel_size of 1, which independently processes the neighborhood of each pixel, thereby reducing the number of channels in the feature map. This is followed by a BatchNorm2d layer that accelerates the training process, and its output undergoes non-linear processing through a ReLU activation function. The feature map is processed by a depth-wise separable convolutional layer, which consists of a depth-wise convolutional layer and a pointwise convolutional layer. The depth-wise convolutional layer performs spatial convolution independently for each input channel, using a kernel_size of 3. Following this layer, there is another BatchNorm2d layer and a ReLU activation function. Then, the pointwise convolutional layer transforms the output of the depth-wise convolutional layer across channels. After the bottleneck structure, a second 1×1 convolutional layer is utilized to adjust the number of channels. Subsequently, the features undergo batch normalization for standardization and are activated by the ReLU function to introduce non-linearity. These processed features then pass through a Sigmoid activation function, which scales their values to the range of [0, 1], representing the attn_weights for each feature location. The computed attention weights attn_weights are utilized to enhance the feature representation of the input feature maps x. This is achieved by performing an element-wise multiplication between the attention weights and the original input feature maps:

$$\text{attended\_features} = x \odot \text{attn\_weights} \tag{8}$$

where $\odot$ represents the element-wise multiplication operation. By multiplying the input features with their corresponding attention weights, the model is able to focus more on important features and suppress less significant information. This process effectively enhances the discriminative power of the feature representation.

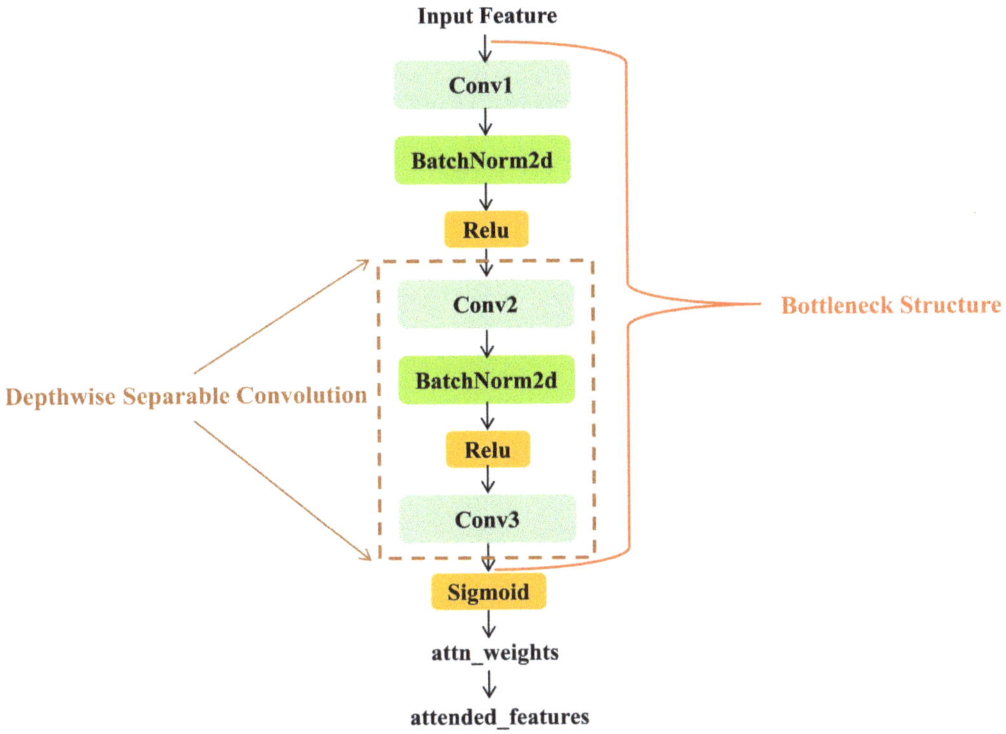

Figure 4. The proposed attention module.

4. Performance Evaluation

In this section, we compare the performance of the CNN with the AECN model, which integrates an attention mechanism. In this paper, we define two different security authentication levels, N = 5 and N = 10, to denote different levels of stringency in the authentication process to control the rights of a device to perform resource access (there are incremental security requirements between each level). The experimental environment is built on the PyTorch 2.1.0 framework, executed within a Python 3.10 environment, and hosted on Ubuntu 22.04 to ensure compatibility and stability. Furthermore, by leveraging CUDA 12.1 acceleration technology, we utilize a high-performance RTX 4090 GPU with 24 GB of memory to maximize training efficiency. The principal parameter values are presented in Table 1.

Table 1. Parameter values.

Parameter	Value
Batch size	180
Optimizer	Stochastic Gradient Descent (SGD)
Inital learning rate	1×10^{-2}
Weight decay	1×10^{-3}
Momentum	9×10^{-1}
Nesterov	True

4.1. Dataset and Implementation Trick

We utilized MATLAB R2020a simulation to compute the signals from both the direct and reflection paths at various locations. The signal at each position is obtained by subtracting the direct and reflection paths to simulate multipath effects in actual signal propagation. In the IoT scenario, consider a BS with 64 antennas, each collecting CSI data from 52 various subcarriers. The CSI matrix is considered in the form of an image, where the first channel is a real value and the second channel is a imaginary value. Considering that there are 64 antennas and 52 subcarriers in the IoT scene, the CSI matrix can be viewed as a three-dimensional image with dimensions of $64 \times 52 \times 2$. The training data consists of 40,000 CSI images, and the testing data consist of 10,000.

In the course of our experiments, learning rate is one of the most important hyperparameters. In order to optimize the model performance and avoid overfitting, a learning rate strategy with decreasing segments is employed. In particular, the learning rate is decreased at the 6th, 12th, 18th, 24th, and 30th epochs, reducing to 20% of the original value at each stage. A range of learning rates was explored, commencing at 0.01 and decreasing sequentially to 0.002, 0.0004, 0.00008, 0.000016, and 0.0000032. This exponentially decaying learning rate tuning strategy has been demonstrated to be effective in deep learning training.

4.2. Evaluation Indicator

Accuracy: Accuracy is the ratio of correct predictions to all legitimate samples. Accuracy indicates the performance of the authenticator in classifying legitimate users.

$$Accuracy = \frac{TP + TN}{TP + TN + FP + FN} \tag{9}$$

where positive samples that are correctly predicted as positive are designated as True Positives (*TP*), negative samples that are correctly predicted as negative are designated as True Negatives (*TN*), negative samples that are erroneously predicted as positive are classified as False Positives (*FP*), positive samples mistakenly classified as negative are labeled as False Negatives (*FN*).

Precision Rate: Precision rate is an indicator of the model's capacity to accurately predict the positive samples.

$$Precision = \frac{TP}{TP + FP} \tag{10}$$

Recall Rate: Recall rate measures the proportion of samples correctly identified by the model as positive classes (true classes) out of all actual positive class samples.

$$Recall = \frac{TP}{TP + FN} \tag{11}$$

4.3. Performance Analysis

Figure 5 illustrates the loss variation in the AECN and CNN across different epochs. In the initial 20 epochs, the loss of the AECN model decreases rapidly. As the number of epoch increases, the rate of loss reduction gradually slows down and ultimately trends towards 0, indicating the convergence of the AECN model. In contrast, the CNN model demonstrates a slower rate of convergence compared to the AECN model. Furthermore, within the initial 20 epochs, the CNN model exhibits larger fluctuations in loss compared to the AECN model, indicating that the AECN model exhibits superior generalization ability and is capable of demonstrating excellent performance on new data.

Figure 6 illustrates the authentication accuracy of the CNN and AECN with a authentication levels fixed at 5 and 10, respectively. At the authentication level of 5, the authentication accuracy of the CNN is 95.2%, while that of the AECN is 99.7%, representing a 4.5% increase in accuracy compared to the CNN. Upon raising the authentication level to 10, the authentication accuracy of the AECN remains at 98.3%, although this is lower than at the authentication levels of 5. In contrast, the authentication accuracy of the CNN is 91.6%. This demonstrates that our proposed attention mechanism module is capable of maintaining excellent authentication accuracy when the security authentication level increases.

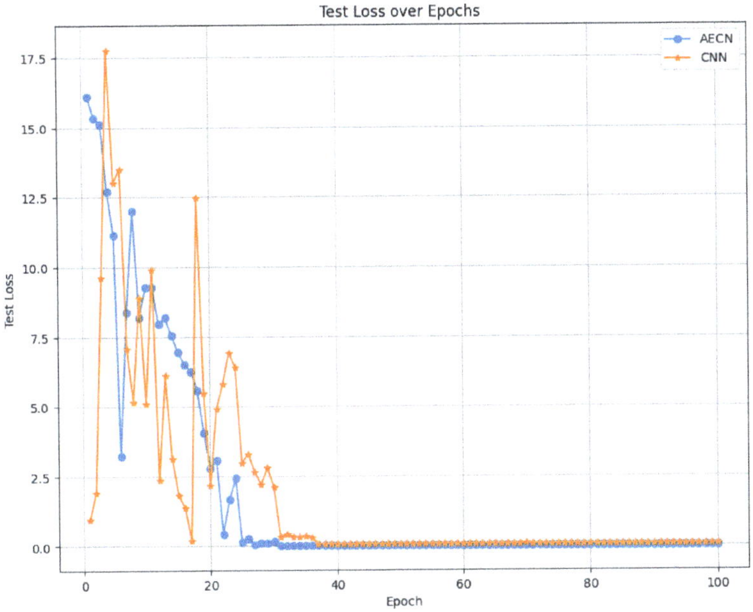

Figure 5. Loss of AECN and CNN.

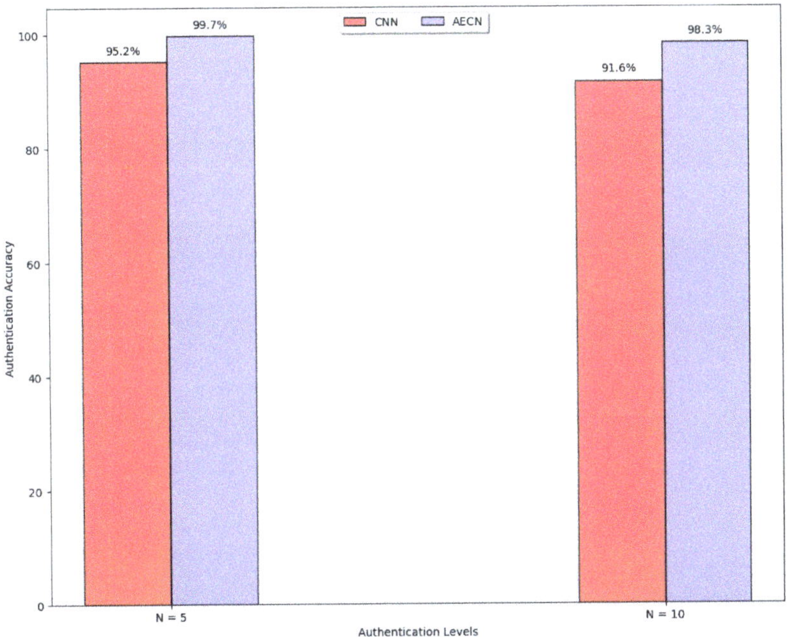

Figure 6. Authentication accuracy of AECN and CNN at authentication level N = 5 and N = 10.

Figure 7 shows the accuracy of the CNN and AECN when the number of authentication level is 5. In the first 20 epochs, the accuracy of the CCN fluctuated sharply, while the fluctuation of the AECN in this stage was significantly smaller than that of the CNN, indicating that the AECN is superior to the CNN in learning CSI features. After the 20th epoch, with the increase in epoch, the precision rate of both models shows an upward trend, and finally the precision rate of AECN converged to 99.7% and that of CNN converged to 92.8%.

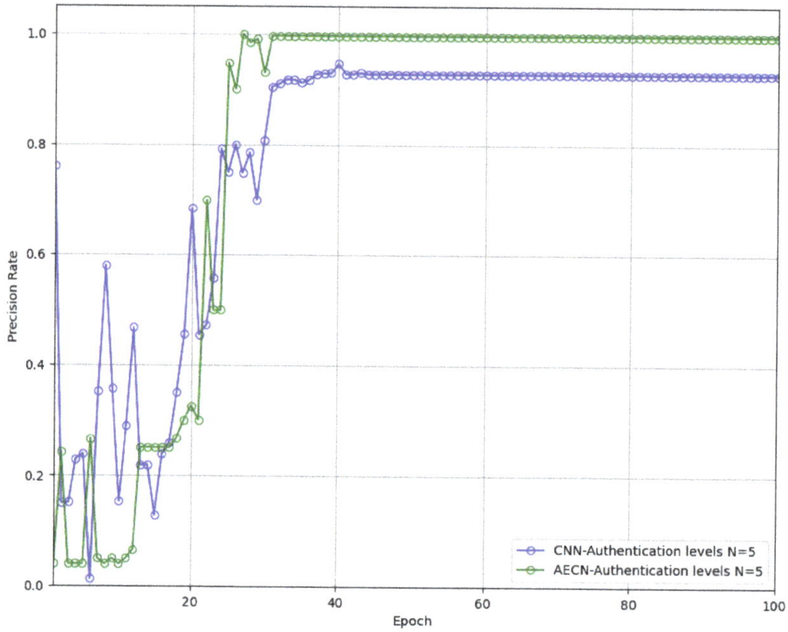

Figure 7. Precision rate of AECN and CNN at authentication level N = 5.

Figure 8 illustrates the recall rates of the CNN and AECN models with the authentication level fixed at 5. As the number of epochs increases, the recall rate of the AECN shows a consistent upward trend. Prior to the 20th epoch, the recall rate of the CNN exhibited significant oscillation. In terms of convergence speed, the AECN outperformed the CNN, converging more quickly. As the epochs increase, the recall rate of the AECN approaches 1, while the CNN converges at 96.3%. This indicates that our proposed AECN model demonstrates enhanced performance in distinguishing legitimate users.

Figures 9 and 10 illustrate the precision and recall rates for an authentication level of 10, respectively. Figure 9 shows that, during the initial 30 epochs, the CNN model experiences greater oscillations, ultimately converging at a precision rate of 90.4%. In comparison, the AECN model exhibits relatively minor fluctuations in its precision rate, eventually reaching a value of 99.3%. Throughout the training process, the precision rate of the AECN remains stable, showing no significant upward or downward trend. This suggests that the AECN model is better able to maintain its generalization ability.

With the authentication level set at 10, the recall rates of the CNN and AECN models are presented in Figure 10. As the number of epochs increases, the recall rates for both the AECN and CNN demonstrate a consistent upward trend. The fluctuations in the recall of the AECN are less pronounced than those of the CNN, and the AECN converges more quickly than the CNN prior to the convergence of both models. Notably, once the models have converged, the CNN achieves a recall rate of 93.2%, while the AECN attains a significantly higher recall rate of 99.3%. This indicates that our proposed AECN model, which includes an attention module, exhibits strong performance and generalization ability, even when the security authentication level is increased to 10.

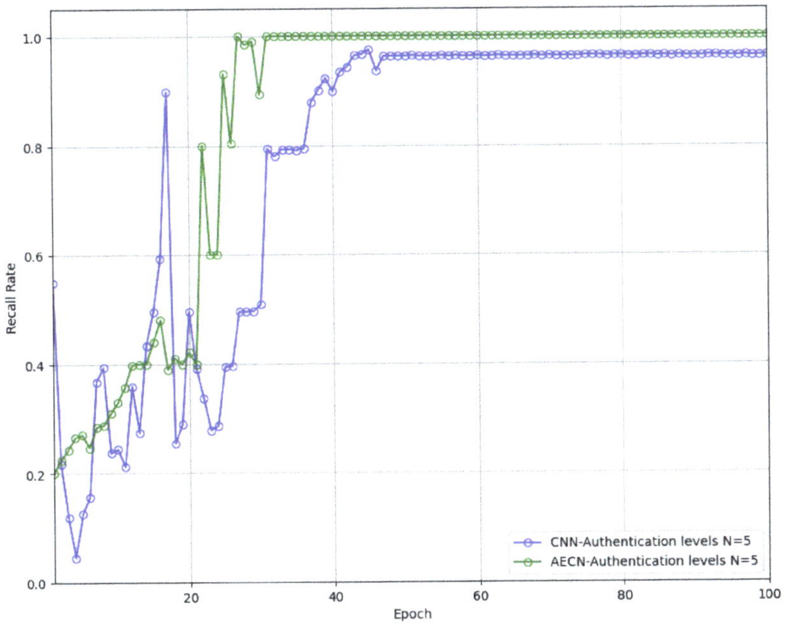

Figure 8. Recall rate of AECN and CNN at authentication level N = 5.

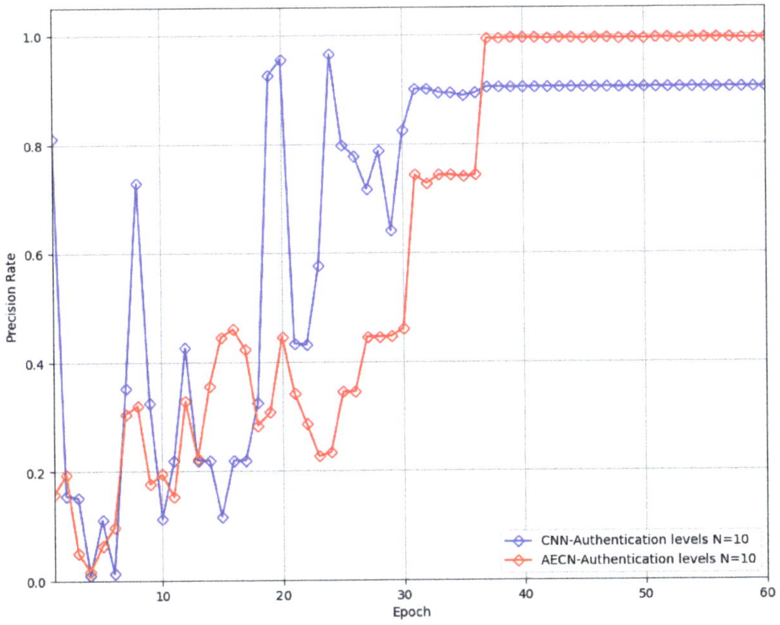

Figure 9. Precision rate of AECN and CNN at authentication level N = 10.

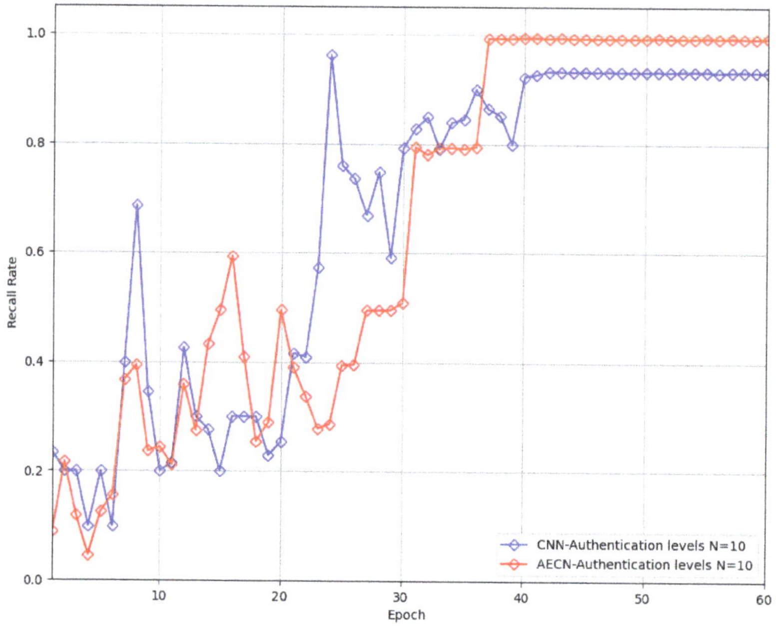

Figure 10. Recall rate of AECN and CNN at authentication level N = 10.

5. Discussion and Future Work

We designed a hierarchical security authenticator for IoT devices. Firstly, we proposed the concept of hierarchical security authentication, which enables multi-level access control by transforming the hierarchical security problem into a multi-classification problem, thereby enhancing the flexibility of security authentication for IoT devices. Secondly, the confidence score branch employs a sigmoid function to generate a confidence score between 0 and 1, indicating the degree of trust the receiver assigns to the transmitter's identity prediction. This eliminates the necessity for a fixed decision threshold in traditional authentication, thereby enhancing reliability in dynamic environments. Thirdly, an attention module comprising a bottleneck structure and a depth-separable convolution is devised for integration into the AECN model. The AECN model utilises an attention module that can capture key CSI features, generate attention weights and feature maps, and improve the classification performance of the network and the accuracy of the authentication.

However, our scheme has some aspects that require further improvement. For example, the performance of the model may be affected when dealing with different network conditions, especially in environments where noise and interference levels fluctuate. For future work, we will continue to optimize the performance of the model under different network conditions. Specifically, by utilizing data from both the simulated environment and the real environment for training, the generalization ability and robustness of the model are planned to be enhanced. In addition, we will explore methods of model optimization to reduce the computational complexity of the model without affecting its performance.

6. Conclusions

A hierarchical security authentication mechanism that integrates an AECN with a confidence score branch is presented. The AECN includes an attention mechanism module, which uses bottleneck structures and depth-wise separable convolution to accurately learn and focus on the crucial CSI features. This approach generates efficient feature maps and significantly enhances the network's classification performance. Additionally, we eliminate the conventional reliance on threshold detection and integrate a confidence score component to evaluate the prediction probability. We introduce the hyperparameter λ as a tuning weight for the confidence loss to optimize the balance between the AECN's classification task and overall loss. Simulation results demonstrate that, at an authentication level of 5, the authentication accuracy of theAECN is 99.7%. When the authentication level is increased to 10, the accuracy remains high at 98.3%. Therefore, the proposed hierarchical security authentication scheme can serve as a solution for IoT security.

Author Contributions: X.Q.: Study Conception and Design, Writing—Review, Editing and Funding. G.Z.: Study Conception and Design, Coding, Writing—Original Draft, Writing—Review. J.Y.: Coding, Data Collection. W.J.: Writing—Review, Funding. Z.G.: Writing—Review, Funding, M.X.: Writing—Review, Funding. All authors have read and agreed to the published version of the manuscript.

Funding: This work was supported in part by the National Key R&D Program of China under grant no. 2022YFB2703000, in part by the Young Backbone Teachers Support Plan of BISTU under grant no. YBT202437, in part by the R&D Program of Beijing Municipal Education Commission under grant no. KM202211232012, and in part by the Educational Innovation Program of BISTU under grant no. 2025JGYB19.

Data Availability Statement: Data available upon request from the authors.

Conflicts of Interest: The authors declare no conflicts of interest to report regarding the present study.

Abbreviations

Abbreviation	Full Name
IoT	Internet of Things
PLA	Physical Layer Authentication
AECN	Attention-Enhanced Convolutional Network
RF	Radio Frequency
CFO	Carrier Frequency Offset
CSI	Channel State Information
IoV	Internet of Vehicles
SVM	Support Vector Machine
GMM	Gaussian Mixture Model
DNN	Deep Neural Network
BS	Base Station
OFDM	Orthogonal Frequency Division Multiplexing

.eferences

Javed, F.; Afzal, M.K.; Sharif, M.; Kim, B.S. Internet of Things (IoT) Operating Systems Support, Networking Technologies, Applications, and Challenges: A Comparative Review. *IEEE Commun. Surv. Tutor.* **2018**, *20*, 2062–2100. [CrossRef]

Amutha, B. IoT Revolutionizing Healthcare: A Survey of Smart Healthcare System Architectures. In Proceedings of the 2023 International Conference on Research Methodologies in Knowledge Management, Artificial Intelligence and Telecommunication Engineering (RMKMATE), Chennai, India, 1–2 November 2023; pp. 1–5. [CrossRef]

Eliş, B.; Çar, E.; Kasap, N.; Sarı, A.İ.; Rovshenov, A. Development of IoT-Based Smart Home Automation System with Open-Sourced Components. In Proceedings of the 2024 International Conference on Electrical, Computer and Energy Technologies (ICECET), Sydney, Australia, 25–27 July 2024; pp. 1–6. [CrossRef]

Chen, L.; Chen, Y.; Liang, W.; Li, X.; Li, K.C.; Wang, J.; Xiong, N. MASS: A Multi-Attribute Sketch Secure Data Sharing Scheme for IoT Wearable Medical Devices Based on Blockchain. *IEEE Internet Things J.* **2024**. [CrossRef]

Liu, Y.; Wang, J.; Yan, Z.; Wan, Z.; Jäntti, R. A Survey on Blockchain-Based Trust Management for Internet of Things. *IEEE Internet Things J.* **2023**, *10*, 5898–5922. [CrossRef]

Xie, N.; Li, Z.; Tan, H. A Survey of Physical-Layer Authentication in Wireless Communications. *IEEE Commun. Surv. Tutor.* **2021**, *23*, 282–310. [CrossRef]

Zhao, Y.; Hu, Y.; Zhang, X.; Ma, Y.; Li, Y. Design and Implementation of Industrial Internet Application Layer Protocol Integrating AES and RSA Encryption Algorithm. In Proceedings of the 2023 12th International Conference of Information and Communication Technology (ICTech), Wuhan, China, 14–16 April 2023; pp. 351–356. [CrossRef]

Luo, H.; Li, G.; Xing, Y.; Zhang, J.; Hu, A.; Wang, X. RelativeRFF: Multi-Antenna Device Identification in Multipath Propagation Scenarios. In Proceedings of the ICC 2023—IEEE International Conference on Communications, Rome, Italy, 28 May–1 June 2023; pp. 3708–3713. [CrossRef]

9. Feng, Z.; Boxuan, S.; Wenbao, J. Review of key technology and its application of blockchain. *Chin. J. Netw. Inf. Secur.* **2018**, *4*, 22–29.
10. Niu, S.; Chen, L.; Liu, W. Attribute-Based Keyword Search Encryption Scheme with Verifiable Ciphertext via Blockchains. In Proceedings of the 2020 IEEE 9th Joint International Information Technology and Artificial Intelligence Conference (ITAIC), Chongqing, China, 11–13 December 2020; Volume 9, pp. 849–853. [CrossRef]
11. Wang, T.; Wang, S.; Zhou, Z.H. Machine learning for 5G and beyond: From model-based to data-driven mobile wireless networks. *China Commun.* **2019**, *16*, 165–175. [CrossRef]
12. Lu, X.; Lei, J.; Shi, Y.; Li, W. Improved Physical Layer Authentication Scheme Based on Wireless Channel Phase. *IEEE Wirel. Commun. Lett.* **2022**, *11*, 198–202. [CrossRef]
13. Wang, H.M.; Fu, Q.Y. Channel-Prediction-Based One-Class Mobile IoT Device Authentication. *IEEE Internet Things J.* **2022**, *9*, 7731–7745. [CrossRef]
14. Soltani, N.; Reus-Muns, G.; Salehi, B.; Dy, J.; Ioannidis, S.; Chowdhury, K. RF Fingerprinting Unmanned Aerial Vehicles with Non-Standard Transmitter Waveforms. *IEEE Trans. Veh. Technol.* **2020**, *69*, 15518–15531. [CrossRef]
15. Senigagliesi, L.; Baldi, M.; Gambi, E. Comparison of Statistical and Machine Learning Techniques for Physical Layer Authentication. *IEEE Trans. Inf. Forensics Secur.* **2021**, *16*, 1506–1521. [CrossRef]
16. Shi, H.; Niu, M.; Teng, Y.; Zhang, P. Privacy-Preserving Physical Layer Authentication Exploiting Carrier Frequency Offset in UAV-aided Communication Systems. In Proceedings of the 2024 International Conference on Networking and Network Applications (NaNA), Yinchuan, China, 9–12 August 2024; pp. 247–251. [CrossRef]
17. Xu, Q.; Zheng, R.; Saad, W.; Han, Z. Device Fingerprinting in Wireless Networks: Challenges and Opportunities. *IEEE Commun. Surv. Tutor.* **2016**, *18*, 94–104. [CrossRef]
18. Xiao, L.; Greenstein, L.; Mandayam, N.; Trappe, W. Fingerprints in the Ether: Using the Physical Layer for Wireless Authentication. In Proceedings of the 2007 IEEE International Conference on Communications, New Orleans, LA, USA, 11–13 April 2007, pp. 4646–4651. [CrossRef]
19. Lu, X.; Lei, J.; Shi, Y.; Li, W. Physical-Layer Authentication Based on Channel Phase Responses for Multi-Carriers Transmission. *IEEE Trans. Inf. Forensics Secur.* **2023**, *18*, 1734–1748. [CrossRef]
20. Xie, N.; Zhang, Q.; Chen, J.; Tan, H. Privacy-Preserving Physical-Layer Authentication for Non-Orthogonal Multiple Access Systems. *IEEE J. Sel. Areas Commun.* **2022**, *40*, 1371–1385. [CrossRef]
21. Xiao, L.; Li, Y.; Han, G.; Liu, G.; Zhuang, W. PHY-Layer Spoofing Detection with Reinforcement Learning in Wireless Networks. *IEEE Trans. Veh. Technol.* **2016**, *65*, 10037–10047. [CrossRef]
22. Xiao, L.; Chen, T.; Han, G.; Zhuang, W.; Sun, L. Game Theoretic Study on Channel-Based Authentication in MIMO Systems. *IEEE Trans. Veh. Technol.* **2017**, *66*, 7474–7484. [CrossRef]
23. Tian, S.; Jiang, W. Blockchain Traceability Process for Hairy Crab Based on Cuckoo Filter. *Appl. Sci.* **2024**, *14*, 8027. [CrossRef]
24. Fang, H.; Zhu, Y.; Zhang, Y.; Wang, X. Decentralized Edge Collaboration for Seamless Handover Authentication in Zero-Trust IoV. *IEEE Trans. Wirel. Commun.* **2024**, *23*, 8760–8772. [CrossRef]
25. Pei, C.; Zhang, N.; Shen, X.S.; Mark, J.W. Channel-based physical layer authentication. In Proceedings of the 2014 IEEE Global Communications Conference, Austin, TX, USA, 8–12 December 2014; pp. 4114–4119. [CrossRef]
26. Liu, H.; Wang, Y.; Liu, J.; Yang, J.; Chen, Y.; Poor, H.V. Authenticating Users Through Fine-Grained Channel Information. *IEEE Trans. Mob. Comput.* **2018**, *17*, 251–264. [CrossRef]
27. Fang, H.; Wang, X.; Xu, L. Fuzzy Learning for Multi-Dimensional Adaptive Physical Layer Authentication: A Compact and Robust Approach. *IEEE Trans. Wirel. Commun.* **2020**, *19*, 5420–5432. [CrossRef]
28. Wang, S.; Li, N.; Xia, S.; Tao, X.; Lu, H. Collaborative Physical Layer Authentication in Internet of Things Based on Federated Learning. In Proceedings of the 2021 IEEE 32nd Annual International Symposium on Personal, Indoor and Mobile Radio Communications (PIMRC), Helsinki, Finland, 13–16 September 2021; pp. 714–719. [CrossRef]
29. Wang, N.; Jiang, T.; Lv, S.; Xiao, L. Physical-Layer Authentication Based on Extreme Learning Machine. *IEEE Commun. Lett.* **2017**, *21*, 1557–1560. [CrossRef]
30. Pan, F.; Pang, Z.; Wen, H.; Luvisotto, M.; Xiao, M.; Liao, R.F.; Chen, J. Threshold-Free Physical Layer Authentication Based on Machine Learning for Industrial Wireless CPS. *IEEE Trans. Ind. Inform.* **2019**, *15*, 6481–6491. [CrossRef]
31. Qiu, X.; Jiang, T.; Wu, S.; Hayes, M. Physical Layer Authentication Enhancement Using a Gaussian Mixture Model. *IEEE Access* **2018**, *6*, 53583–53592. [CrossRef]
32. Xiao, L.; Wan, X.; Han, Z. PHY-Layer Authentication with Multiple Landmarks with Reduced Overhead. *IEEE Trans. Wirel. Commun.* **2018**, *17*, 1676–1687. [CrossRef]
33. Meng, R.; Xu, X.; Sun, H.; Zhao, H.; Wang, B.; Han, S.; Zhang, P. Multiuser Physical-Layer Authentication Based on Latent Perturbed Neural Networks for Industrial Internet of Things. *IEEE Internet Things J.* **2023**, *10*, 637–652. [CrossRef]
34. Liao, R.F.; Wen, H.; Chen, S.; Xie, F.; Pan, F.; Tang, J.; Song, H. Multiuser Physical Layer Authentication in Internet of Things with Data Augmentation. *IEEE Internet Things J.* **2020**, *7*, 2077–2088. [CrossRef]

electronics

MDPI

Article

Deep Learning for Cybersecurity Classification: Utilizing Depth-Wise CNN and Attention Mechanism on VM-Obfuscated Data

Sicheng Han, Heeheon Yun and Yongsu Park *

Department of Computer Science, Hanyang University, Wangshimriro 222, Seongdong-gu, Seoul 04763, Republic of Korea
* Correspondence: yongsu@hanyang.ac.kr

Abstract: With the increasing use of sophisticated obfuscation techniques, malware detection remains a critical challenge in cybersecurity. This paper introduces a novel deep learning approach to classify malware obfuscated by virtual machine (VM) code. We specifically explore the application of depth-wise convolutional neural networks (CNNs) combined with a spatial attention mechanism to tackle VM-protected cybersecurity datasets. To address the scarcity of obfuscated malware samples, the dataset was generated using VMProtect to ensure the models were trained on real examples of modern obfuscated malware. The effectiveness of our approach is demonstrated through extensive experiments on both regular malware and obfuscated malware, where our model achieved accuracies of nearly 100% and 93.55% in classifying the regular malware and the obfuscated malware, respectively.

Keywords: malware detection; code obfuscation; depth-wise CNN; attention; cybersecurity

1. Introduction

Malware detection has become more challenging with the rapidly evolving domain of cybersecurity, compounded by the increasingly sophisticated evasion techniques employed by adversaries. Among these, virtual machine (VM) code obfuscation stands out as a particularly complex method of evasion. By transforming executable malware into forms which are harder to analyze while preserving their functionality, VM code obfuscation significantly boosts the effectiveness of traditional detection systems. This paper introduces a novel approach to tackling the intricate problem of detecting VM code-obfuscated malware, leveraging the synergistic capabilities of depth-wise convolutional neural networks (CNNs) enhanced with spatial attention mechanisms.

VM code obfuscation alters executable code into a format which, while operational, becomes more challenging for both human analysts and automated tools to interpret. This can effectively shield malware from detection by conventional antivirus systems, posing a significant risk to cybersecurity infrastructures. Our work addresses this challenge by developing a robust deep learning model which precisely discerns various types of obfuscated malware. We utilize VMProtect, a leading software tool for code obfuscation, to create a diverse dataset of malware images. Our dataset comprises 10 classes of obfuscated malware, each represented by at least 1000 images derived from executable files. Notably, these classes include high-profile malware families such as Dark Hotel, Energetic Bear, Equation Group, and Gorgon Group. Given the restricted availability of malware samples and the rarity of specific variants, we applied data augmentation techniques through ImageDataGenerator.

Our methodology employs depth-wise CNNs to exploit the spatial hierarchies in the image data, alongside an attention mechanism which concentrates on the informative features of the images. This combination allows for effective and efficient feature extraction, which is essential for the classification of intricately obfuscated malware. The attention mechanism in particular enhances the model's ability to focus selectively on areas of the image most likely to contain obfuscation artifacts. The effectiveness of our approach is demonstrated by a notable classification success rate of 93.55%, achieved through meticulous training and validation of our model. This success sets a new benchmark in the field and highlights the potential of combining depth-wise convolutions with attention mechanisms to advance the state of the art in malware detection. To the best of our knowledge, this is the first attempt to use CNNs to classify VM-based, code-obfuscated malware. Our dataset and the proposed method are available at https://github.com/AHSCone/Mal_CNN (accessed on 15 July 2024).

This paper is organized as follows. Section 2 reviews the related literature on malware detection. Section 3 details the dataset, the architecture of our attention-enhanced CNN, and our data augmentation strategy. Section 4 describes our experimental set-up and the metrics used for evaluation. Section 5 discusses the results and outlines potential areas for future research.

The principal contributions of this paper are as follows:

1. We utilize the commercial software VMProtect, available online at https://vmpsoft.com/products/vmprotect/ (accessed on 15 July 2024) to generate an unprecedented dataset of VM code-obfuscated malware specifically tailored for our analysis.
2. Faced with limited access to diverse malware samples, we employ advanced data augmentation and image enhancement techniques to ensure a comprehensive dataset.
3. Our model integrates a depth-wise CNN with a spatial attention mechanism designed to effectively identify and classify a wide range of VM code-obfuscated malware.

2. Related Work

2.1. VM-Based Code Obfuscation

VM-based code obfuscation protects software by transforming executable code into a form that is difficult to analyze while maintaining its original functionality. This method provides a robust shield against reverse engineering and unauthorized modifications, which is crucial in maintaining software integrity and security. VMProtect exemplifies this approach by converting standard bytecode into a proprietary virtual instruction set, which is decipherable only with its custom virtual machine [1,2]. This conversion process involves multiple layers of transformation, each introducing additional complexity and making the deobfuscation process challenging for attackers.

Historically, both legitimate software protection and malware developers aiming to evade detection have widely adopted VM-based obfuscation. Studies have demonstrated that VM obfuscated code can significantly hinder the efforts of static and dynamic analysis techniques, typically requiring specialized tools and expertise for reversal [3,4].

Further research has targeted the detection and analysis of VM-based obfuscated malware, uncovering patterns and weaknesses exploitable by security experts. These studies often involve a combination of machine learning techniques and manual analysis to identify the characteristic features of obfuscated code [5,6].

2.2. CNN and Attention Mechanism

Convolutional neural networks (CNNs) have revolutionized image processing and classification by prioritizing the most informative image parts. This capability has established CNNs as the cornerstone of numerous sophisticated visual recognition systems, being extensively applied in diverse fields such as medical imaging and autonomous vehicle technology [7,8]. The integration of attention mechanisms has further propelled the capabilities of CNNs, thereby improving a model's performance and interpretation ability [9,10].

A significant development in the CNN architecture is the creation of MobileNets, which utilize depth-wise separable convolutions. This design significantly reduces the computational cost and model size, making them particularly suitable for mobile and embedded vision applications where resources are constrained [11]. Following this, MobileNetV2 introduced an inverted residual structure which uses lightweight depth-wise convolutions to filter features in the intermediate expansion layer, boosting accuracy and efficiency in mobile vision tasks [12].

In the context of malware detection, attention-based CNNs represent a pivotal enhancement. Wang et al. illustrated how incorporating attention mechanisms can substantially improve the reliability of malware detection systems [13]. These models intensively focus on regions potentially containing malicious content, enabling the detection of subtle anomalies which might elude conventional CNNs. Furthermore, the introduction of the transformer architecture by Vaswani et al. marked a significant evolution in sequence modeling [14]. Transformers utilize self-attention mechanisms to recognize dependencies within data regardless of the positional distance in the input sequence.

2.3. Obfuscated Malware Detection and Classification

Detecting and classifying obfuscated malware presents significant challenges due to the complexity and variety of obfuscation techniques designed to bypass standard detection methods [15,16]. Advances in deep learning have demonstrated significant potential in detecting obfuscated malware by deciphering complex patterns and anomalies which indicate malicious behavior [17–19]. Nataraj et al. pioneered the use of image representations of binary malware for analysis, noting that visual textures in these images can distinguish malicious software from benign software [20].

In our previous works, we used the classic CNN for symmetric key-encrypted malware detection [21]. Recent research has investigated hybrid approaches. Suarez-Tangil et al. combined CNNs with random forests to analyze malware images, devising a detection system which capitalizes on the strengths of both techniques [22]. Li et al. employed generative adversarial networks (GANs) to generate synthetic malware images for training, thus bolstering a CNN's robustness against emerging malware types [23].

Efforts to enhance model interpretability and resilience against adversarial attacks have included studies on neural network robustness [24] and training on adversarial examples to augment model generalization and fortify defense mechanisms [25]. Lei et al. proposed a transfer learning method with feature fusion to achieve software defect detection [26]. Furthermore, recent works used MobileNets for IoT malware detection with opcode features [27]. These developments represent a significant advancement in malware detection strategies, utilizing sophisticated CNN architectures and image processing technologies. This work seeks to build upon these innovations and advance the field of malicious software detection and analysis.

3. Methods

3.1. Dataset Generation with VMProtect

This section introduces the methodology to develop a specialized dataset designed for the classification of VM-based obfuscated malware, as illustrated in Figure 1. Our dataset includes 10 distinct malware classes, with each containing at least 1000 variant samples, which is crucial for training a robust model and ensuring a diverse range of data.

The initial stage in the dataset creation process involves using VMProtect to obfuscate executable malware files. VMProtect analyzes the binary code and employs multiple obfuscation techniques, including code virtualization. This process transforms the original code into a pseudo-code that is only executable by VMProtect's proprietary virtual machine, concealing the malware's true characteristics from analytical tools.

To manage the obfuscation process, an automated script sets up directories for each malwarre category, such as "Dark Hotel", "Energetic Bear", "Equation Group", "Gorgon Group", and "Winnti". We use scripts for generation and execute VMProtect's obfuscation commands within the Linux system's shell, also logging each operation to facilitate monitoring and troubleshooting.

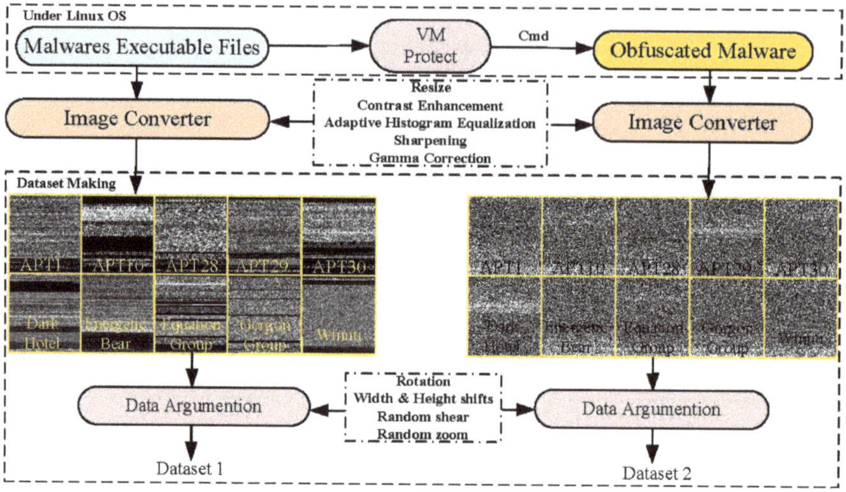

Figure 1. Illustration of the dataset generation procedure.

3.2. *Image Conversion and Data Augmentation*

Following obfuscation, binary files are converted into grayscale images. The conversion size s is determined as follows:

$$s = \max(\lceil \sqrt{L} \rceil, 128) \tag{1}$$

where L is the length of the binary file and the minimum dimension is set to 128 pixels. Padding is applied to ensure the binary data conform to $s \times s$ dimensions, reshaping the zero-padded array into a two-dimensional grid. These images are then standardized across the dataset, optimizing clarity and uniformity.

The images are subsequently enhanced to improve their analytical quality by employing several mathematical operations:

$$I' = (I - \mu) \times 3.0 + \mu \tag{2}$$

where I is the image intensity and μ is the mean intensity. This adjustment increases the contrast by a factor of three. Additionally, normalization scales the pixel values to a standard range of 0–255:

$$I_{\text{norm}} = \frac{I - \min(I)}{\max(I) - \min(I)} \times 255 \tag{3}$$

Adaptive histogram equalization is applied to enhance the contrast in localized areas:

$$I_{\text{eq}} = \text{equalize}(I) \tag{4}$$

Gamma correction is utilized to modify the luminance, and sharpness enhancement is achieved by increasing the edge definition:

$$I_{\gamma} = 255 \times \left(\frac{I}{255}\right)^{1.2} \tag{5}$$

$$I_{\text{sharp}} = \text{sharpen}(I, \text{factor} = 3.0) \tag{6}$$

Each processed image is then systematically archived and ready for model training.

To augment the diversity and volume of our dataset, we employed a script which enhanced the original set of images through various transformations. The script starts by duplicating existing images if their count is below the desired threshold. Then, we apply transformations including rotation, width and height shifts, shear, zoom, and horizontal flipping during model training. This method ensures that the dataset is uniformly extensive and varied across all classes. Our goal was to create a dataset that was not only comprehensive but also meticulously optimized for the effective training of deep learning models.

3.3. Depth-Wise Convolutional Neural Networks with Spatial Attention Mechanism (Mal-CNN)

This subsection describes the architecture of the malware classification convolutional neural network (Mal-CNN), a hybrid deep learning model which synergistically integrates depth-wise CNNs with spatial attention mechanisms. Designed to enhance discriminatory power while maintaining computational efficiency, the Mal-CNN excels at processing complex image data derived from VM code-obfuscated malware, as depicted in Figure 2.

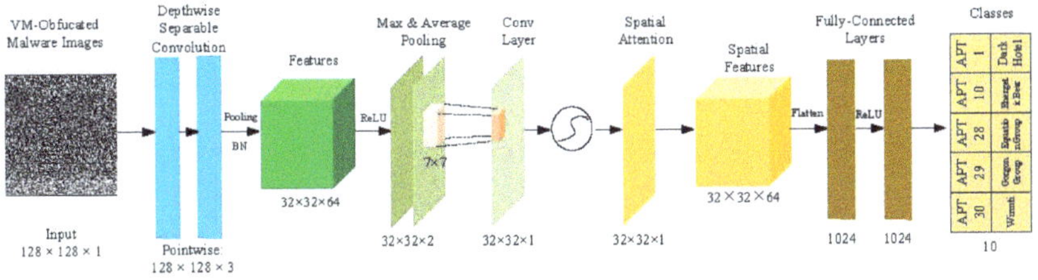

Figure 2. Our proposed Mal-CNN network structure.

Depth-wise convolution is an efficient adaptation of the standard convolution operation. Unlike traditional convolutions which combine inputs across all channels, depth-wise convolutions perform a separate convolution for each input channel, thereby significantly reducing both the computational load and the number of model parameters:

$$\text{Output}_k = \text{DepthConv}(\text{Input}_k) * \text{Filter}_k \quad (7)$$

Here, DepthConv signifies the depth-wise convolution applied to the kth channel of the input, Input_k, using the corresponding convolutional filter, Filter_k. Following this, a point-wise convolution aggregates these channel-wise outputs into comprehensive feature maps, effectively maintaining the network's capacity for sophisticated feature extraction.

By augmenting the efficiency of depth-wise convolutions, the Mal-CNN incorporates a spatial attention mechanism which selectively refines feature representations. This mechanism generates an attention map which highlights critical features for accurate classification while diminishing less important ones:

$$\text{Attention Map} = \sigma(\text{Conv}(\text{Concat}(\max(\text{Input}, \text{axis} = 3), \text{mean}(\text{Input}, \text{axis} = 3)))) \quad (8)$$

In this expression, σ represents the sigmoid activation function, Conv is a convolutional operation, and Concat denotes the concatenation of the channel-wise maximum and average of the input feature map. This focused mechanism directs the learning process toward the most informative elements within the feature map.

The integrated structure of the Mal-CNN optimizes both the spatial and channel-wise features of the input data:

$$\text{Enhanced Features} = \text{Attention Map} \odot \text{Depth-wise Convolved Features} \quad (9)$$

where $\odot$ indicates the element-wise multiplication of the depth-wise convolved features with the attention map, enhancing the model's responsiveness to critical features while diminishing the influence of irrelevant background noise.

The integration of depth-wise convolutions and spatial attention mechanisms positions the Mal-CNN as a significant advancement. Empirical evaluations highlight the Mal-CNN's effectiveness in precisely classifying VM code-obfuscated malware, showcasing superior performance and operational efficiency.

In the following Algorithm 1 N is the batch size, C is the channel count, and H and W are height and width, respectfully.

Algorithm 1 Depth-wise convolutional neural networks with spatial attention mechanism

1: **Input:** Image batch of size $N \times C \times H \times W$
2: **Output:** Class scores for each image in the batch
3: Initialize the network with the specified number of classes and input dimensions
4: $\text{DepthOutput}_k = \text{DepthConv}(\text{Input}_k) * \text{Filter}_k$
5: Apply point-wise convolution to combine channel outputs
6: $\text{Output} = \text{PointConv}(\text{DepthOutput})$
7: Calculate average and max pooling across channels
8: Apply convolution and sigmoid activation to obtain the attention map
9: $\text{Attention Map} = \sigma(\text{Conv}(\text{ConcatOutput}))$
10: Apply attention map to the original input by element-wise multiplication
11: $\text{Refined Output} = \text{Input} \odot \text{Attention Map}$
12: **return** Class probabilities for each image

4. Experiment and Decision

4.1. Dataset Description

The experimental evaluation utilized two distinct datasets to assess the efficacy of the proposed Mal-CNN model. The first dataset comprised images converted from original malware executable files, as depicted in Figure 3. The second dataset consisted of the images converted from the VM-obfuscated malware executable files (see Figure 4). These datasets were meticulously structured into 10 categories representative of various notable malware families. These categories were APT 1, APT 10, APT 28, APT 29, APT 30, Dark Hotel, Energetic Bear, Equation Group, Gorgon Group, and Winnti.

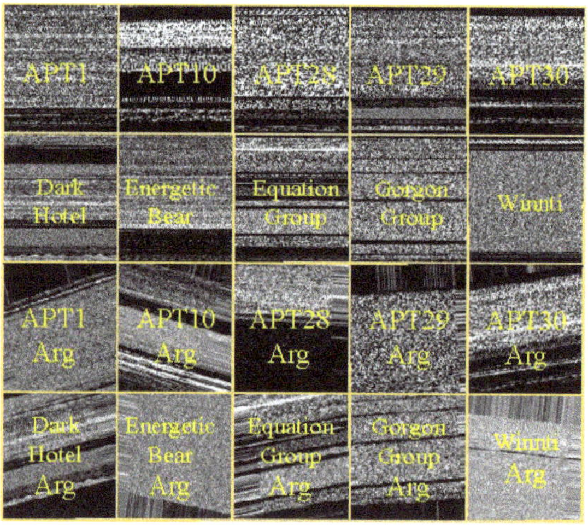

Figure 3. Dataset comprising original malware executable files, featuring a variety of malware families such as APT1, APT10, APT28, APT29, and APT30 enhanced through data augmentation to improve model training and robustness.

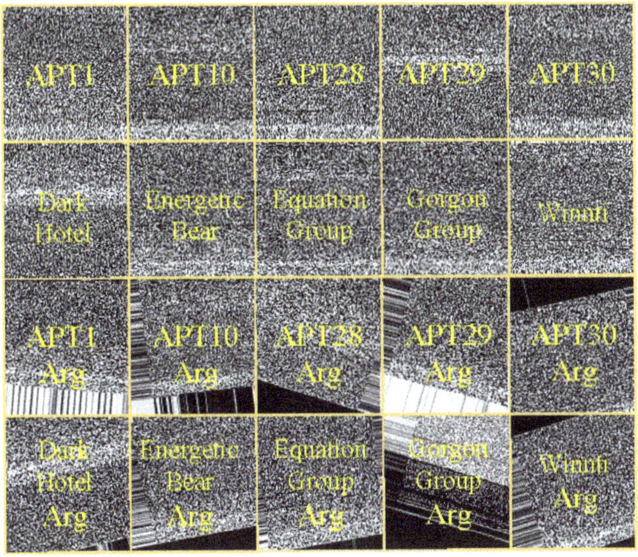

Figure 4. Dataset consisting of malware executable files processed through obfuscation techniques including VMProtect, encompassing malware families like APT1 and APT10, among others. This dataset was enhanced through data augmentation to improve model training and robustness.

Both datasets comprised a total of 10,000 images, with a division of 8000 images for training and 2000 for testing purposes. To ensure robustness and generalizability in the model's performance, each category within the datasets was augmented to contain at least 10,000 samples. This augmentation facilitated comprehensive training and testing, thereby enhancing the predictive capabilities of the Mal-CNN model in real-world scenarios.

The employment of two distinct datasets in our experimental framework served two purposes. The primary objective here was to assess the baseline performance of the model under controlled conditions with well-defined, non-obfuscated data. Moreover, the use of these datasets facilitated a direct and illustrative comparison between the feature representations of VM-obfuscated malware and their original counterparts.

4.2. Experimental Set-Up

The CNN architecture used in our experiments is detailed in the table below. The hyperparameters table (Table 1) outlines the specific settings used during the training phase of our model. The architecture of our CNN is detailed in the accompanying table, which specifies the optimizer, learning rate, batch size, and the choice of loss function, each of which is crucial for effective training. The reduction ratio for the spatial attention mechanism indicates the degree of compression applied in the attention layer to balance performance and computational cost. To mitigate the risk of overfitting, we incorporated dropout layers within the network to prevent co-adaptation of neurons by randomly dropping units during training. Additionally, we augmented the training dataset with transformations such as rotations and scaling to enhance the model's generalization capability. Early stopping was also employed to halt training once the improvement in model performance plateaued, ensuring the model did not continue to learn the idiosyncrasies of the training data. Without a dedicated validation set, hyperparameter tuning was approached by informally splitting the training set to allow for internal validation. A range of values for each hyperparameter was tested iteratively to find the optimal settings which resulted in the best performance on these informal validation trials.

Table 1. Training hyperparameters.

Parameter	Value
Optimizer	Adam
Learning Rate	0.0005
Batch Size	32
Number of Epochs	200
Loss Function	SGD
Reduction Ratio (Spatial Attention)	16

Additionally, the reduction ratio for the spatial attention mechanism specified the degree of compression in the attention layer, balancing performance and computational cost.

We present a structured overview of the Mal-CNN architecture specifically designed for effective malware detection (see Table 2). Each layer is described in terms of its type, input and output channels, kernel size, stride, and activation function.

Table 2. Detailed architecture of Mal-CNN.

Layer Type	Input	Output	Kernel Size	Stride	Activation
Depth-Wise Separable Conv.	1	32	3×3	1	ReLU
Batch Normalization	32	32	-	-	-
Max Pooling	-	-	2×2	2	-
Depth-Wise Separable Conv.	32	64	3×3	1	ReLU
Batch Normalization	64	64	-	-	-
Max Pooling	-	-	2×2	2	-
Depth-Wise Separable Conv.	64	128	3×3	1	ReLU
Batch Normalization	128	128	-	-	-
Max Pooling	-	-	2×2	2	-
Depth-Wise Separable Conv.	128	256	3×3	1	ReLU
Batch Normalization	256	256	-	-	-
Max Pooling	-	-	2×2	2	-
Spatial Attention	-	-	-	-	Sigmoid
Fully Connected	16,384	1024	-	-	ReLU
Fully Connected	1024	10	-	-	-

Figure 5 depicts a series of feature maps generated by the first convolutional layer of our CNN. Each map is a visual representation of the different filters' responses to a malware binary image. The variations in texture and intensity across these maps highlight the diverse aspects of the data which the network deemed significant for classification purposes. Some maps may show pronounced lines or stripes, possibly related to executable code segments or data definitions. In contrast, other maps appear more scattered and less uniform, suggesting areas where the binary structure might be employing obfuscation or encryption techniques to conceal its true nature.

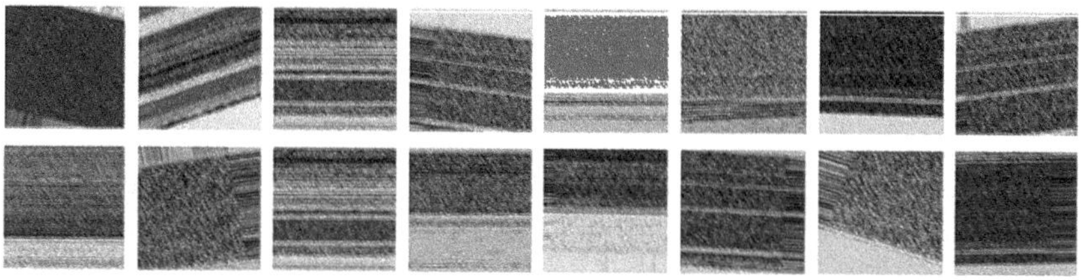

Figure 5. Feature maps extracted from a malware binary image by the first convolutional layer of the CNN.

Furthermore, the brightness within these maps indicates regions with higher neural activity, where the CNN detected features strongly indicative of malicious content. Such features might include unusual binary structures, specific sequences of bytes, or anomalies which differentiate malware from benign software. The ability of the CNN to detect these features and highlight them across various feature maps confirms the network's capacity to focus on pertinent aspects of the data, enhancing its effectiveness in malware detection.

4.3. Evaluation on Original Malware Dataset

The evaluation of the Mal-CNN model was meticulously performed using a dataset composed of images converted from original, non-obfuscated malware executables. This analysis involved a comparative assessment against a baseline CNN model which, while having a similar network depth, lacked the advanced features of depth-wise convolutional and spatial attention mechanisms present in the Mal-CNN. Furthermore, the Mal-CNN was also compared with MobileNetV2 [12], which also uses depth-wise convolutional layers.

The data reveal that the Mal-CNN achieved a training accuracy of 100.0%, indicative of its exceptional capability to capture and internalize the discriminative features inherent in the malware images (see Figure 6). Both the Mal-CNN and the baseline CNN exhibited similarly high training accuracies, evidencing that the inclusion of advanced architectural enhancements does not compromise the model's fit to the training data.

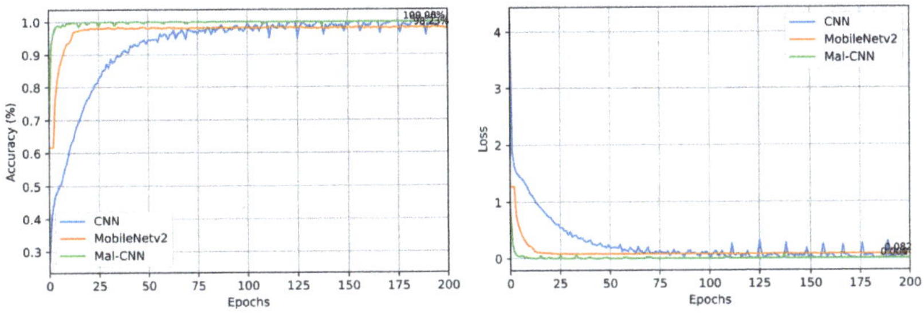

(a) (b)

Figure 6. Learning performance of the Mal-CNN on the original malware dataset, demonstrating the model's capacity for effective feature extraction and robust learning. (**a**) Learning curve for the training accuracy on the original dataset. (**b**) Learning curve for the training losses on the original dataset.

However, significant differences emerged in the testing phase. The Mal-CNN recorded a testing accuracy of 98.39% on the original dataset, substantially surpassing the baseline CNN, which achieved an accuracy of only 91.74% (see Figure 7). This disparity highlights the advantages conferred by the depth-wise convolutional layers and spatial attention mechanisms, which proves the Mal-CNN's generalization capabilities compared with a standard CNN. MobileNetV2 achieved an accuracy of 96.90%, higher than that of the CNN but slightly lower than that of the Mal-CNN. This phenomenon demonstrates the effectiveness of using depth-wise convolutional layers for regular malware detection. The marked improvement in testing accuracy reflects the Mal-CNN's superior ability to adapt and perform under varied conditions, affirming the architectural enhancements as crucial for dealing with complex real-world data.

Analysis of the features extracted by the CNN from malware binary images revealed efficient learning of distinctive textual patterns and shapes associated with different malware types. For instance, specific gradient patterns and texture changes indicative of malicious code were successfully recognized. The depth-wise convolutions helped capture nuanced variations within the malware images, which are often overlooked by simpler architectures.

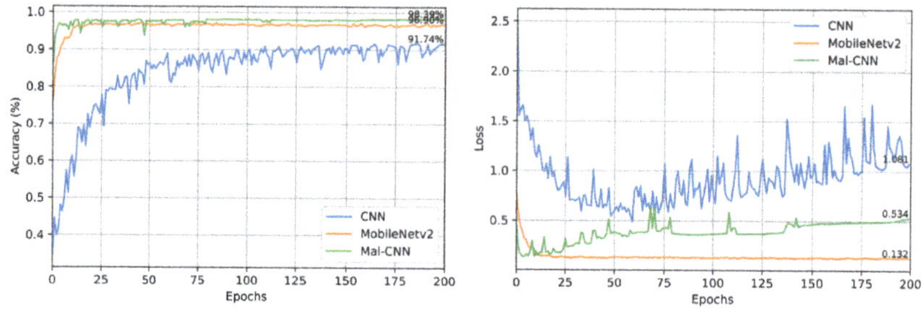

(a) (b)

Figure 7. Testing results of the Mal-CNN using the original malware dataset, showcasing the model's resilience under operational conditions. (**a**) Testing accuracy curve. (**b**) Testing loss curve.

4.4. Evaluation on VM-Obfuscated Malware Dataset

Building upon the initial findings with the original dataset, we further explored the robustness and adaptability of the Mal-CNN model by testing it against a dataset composed of VM-obfuscated malware images. This dataset presents a more challenging environment designed to test the model's effectiveness against sophisticated evasion techniques.

The training phase for the VM-obfuscated dataset revealed that the Mal-CNN achieved an impressive accuracy of nearly 100% (99.99%) at the culmination of the training epochs, as demonstrated in Figure 8a. The rapid convergence of the training loss to a minimal value (Figure 8b) further confirms the model's efficient learning capabilities in the face of obfuscated data.

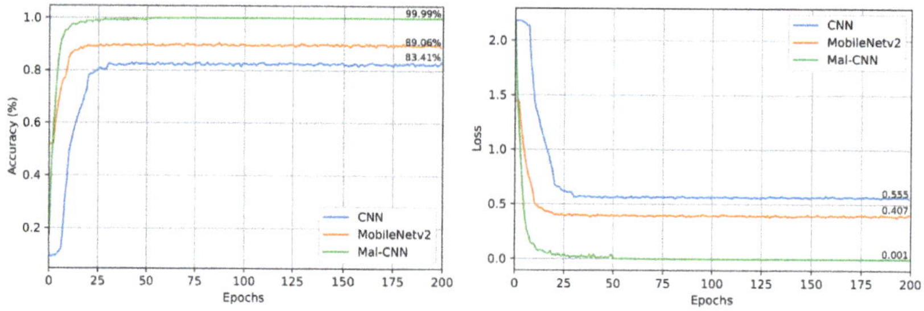

(a) (b)

Figure 8. Learning performance of the proposed method using the obfuscation-processed malware dataset. This figure illustrates the model's ability to effectively adapt and learn under the added complexity introduced by VM obfuscation. (**a**) Curve for the training accuracy on the VM-obfuscated dataset. (**b**) Learning curve for the training losses on the VM-obfuscated dataset.

During testing, the Mal-CNN exhibited a robust accuracy of 93.55%, significantly outperforming the standard CNN, which managed only 73.80% under the same conditions (Figure 9a). To better explore how the Mal-CNN held up against existing solutions in the field, we choose MobileNetV2 as another baseline. However, MobileNetV2 only achieved an accuracy of 79.40%, despite the similar network structure. Notably, both the Mal-CNN and MobileNetV2 utilize depth-wise convolutional methods, and therefore, it can be concluded that the attention mechanism contributes greatly to the detection of VM-obfuscated malware. This stark contrast in testing performance, particularly in a complex scenario marked by VM obfuscation, underscores the efficacy of the depth-wise convolution and spatial attention mechanisms integrated within the Mal-CNN. Furthermore, the reduction in loss over epochs (Figure 9b) demonstrates the model's ability to generalize well, suggesting that it can effectively handle the intricacies and challenges posed by obfuscation techniques.

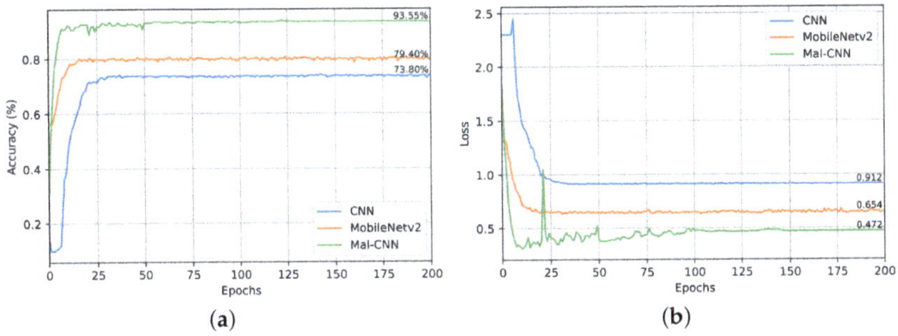

Figure 9. Testing results for the proposed method using the obfuscation-processed malware dataset. The results highlight the Mal-CNN's capacity to maintain a high level of performance, even when confronted with complex obfuscation techniques. (**a**) Testing accuracy curve for the VM-obfuscated dataset. (**b**) Testing loss curve for the VM-obfuscated dataset.

These findings articulate the substantial advantage conferred by the Mal-CNN architecture when dealing with advanced malware threats which employ obfuscation to evade detection. The model's superior performance in both the training and testing phases highlights its potential as a highly effective tool in cybersecurity capable of detecting even the most elusive threats. This phase of testing not only reinforced the model's robustness but also validated its applicability in real-world settings, where VM obfuscation is a prevalent challenge.

4.5. Evaluation Metrics

This evaluation covered two distinct datasets. The first dataset comprised images directly converted from the original malware executables, and the second dataset included images which were further processed using VM obfuscation techniques (see Table 3).

Table 3. Test recall and precision for CNN and Mal-CNN across two datasets.

Model	First Dataset		Second Dataset	
	Recall	**Precision**	**Recall**	**Precision**
CNN	82.74%	92.58%	73.80%	74.04%
MobileNetV2	89.85%	97.26%	79.39%	79.09%
Mal-CNN	93.65%	98.56%	93.55%	93.56%

The results from the datasets, as presented in Table 3, illustrate a distinct performance hierarchy among the evaluated models. The traditional CNN set-up, while performing well with a precision of 92.58% on unobfuscated malware, demonstrated considerable performance degradation when faced with the VM-obfuscated malware dataset. This highlights its limitations in coping with sophisticated obfuscation techniques. Meanwhile, MobileNetV2 not only showed enhanced efficiency but also better resilience against obfuscation compared with the traditional CNN, evidenced by its precision of 79.09% in the VM-obfuscated dataset. This improvement, particularly the precision reaching 79.39%, showcases the benefits of the depth-wise separable convolutions in dealing with complex malware forms.

In contrast, the Mal-CNN markedly outstripped the other models by combining both the depth-wise separable convolutions and the spatial attention mechanism. This model achieved the highest precision rates of 98.56% and 93.56% across the respective datasets.

The addition of the attention mechanism allowed the Mal-CNN to focus more adeptly on the relevant features within obfuscated malware images, substantially enhancing its detection capabilities.

These comparative results underscore the significant advantages of incorporating advanced architectural features such as spatial attention mechanisms alongside depthwise convolutions, particularly in environments where obfuscation techniques complicate traditional detection methods.

4.6. Discussion

4.6.1. Dateset Limitations

Our dataset was assembled from a variety of sources which are known to encounter and catalog extensive ranges of malware threats. By incorporating data from multiple channels such as established malware repositories, real-time blacklists, and anonymized network traffic from corporate security perimeters, we gathered a dataset which is diverse and representative of the global threat landscape. Notably, this research primarily concentrated on a subset of well-known, high-profile malware families. This focus was driven by the availability of detailed behavioral data and the significant impact these malware types have on current threats. However, this emphasis may limit the model's ability to generalize to less-common or emerging malware types which exhibit different behavioral patterns or employ novel obfuscation techniques.

Our dataset comprised 10,000 images, each derived from executable malware files. Of these, a significant portion underwent various transformations to augment the dataset effectively and introduce variability which challenged the robustness of our models. Specifically, transformations such as rotation, scaling, and translation were applied to approximately 60% of the dataset. These transformations were intended to simulate variations in malware signatures which might occur due to changes in compilation environments or minor code alterations, thus providing a more rigorous test bed for our Mal-CNN model. The malware images in our dataset were categorized into 10 distinct classes, each representing a unique family of malware with specific characteristics and behaviors. Each category exhibited unique payload delivery mechanisms, propagation methods, and evasion techniques. For instance, ransomware typically encrypts user data and demands payment, while worms autonomously spread across networks. By training the Mal-CNN across such varied categories, the model learns to recognize and differentiate between complex patterns and signatures, enhancing its practical utility in real-world applications where diverse malware attacks are prevalent.

The use of image transformations on malware binaries, particularly rotations, may initially seem counterintuitive, since binary executable files are not naturally subject to orientation changes. However, the rationale behind such transformations is grounded in enhancing the model's ability to generalize from visual patterns rather than specific binary configurations. This approach is supported by the literature, which advocates for robust feature learning in visual recognition tasks [25], where models trained on varied orientations demonstrate improved performance in recognizing objects across different views [28]. In the context of malware detection, although the actual binary content remains orientation-invariant, the transformation encourages the model to focus on the invariant features within the data, thereby mitigating overfitting and improving the model's ability to generalize from complex, obfuscated malware samples [29].

4.6.2. Obfuscation Techniques and Limitations of Mal-CNN

The effectiveness of the Mal-CNN in dealing with VM-based obfuscation has been demonstrated throughout this study. However, VM-based techniques represent just one facet of the diverse obfuscation landscape. In VM-based obfuscation, the original executable's code is transformed into a form which can only be interpreted by a specific virtual machine. While the Mal-CNN has shown proficiency in learning and recognizing these transformed representations, it is essential to consider how it performs against other obfuscation methods, such as packing. Packing is a prevalent obfuscation technique wherein the executable's code is compressed or encrypted and then decompressed or decrypted at runtime by a stub. This method significantly alters the appearance of binary content when viewed as an image, posing different challenges from those presented by VM-based obfuscation. The ability of the Mal-CNN to detect malware obfuscated by packing was not the primary focus of this research, and thus it remains an area for further investigation.

The current configuration of the Mal-CNN was optimized for detecting VM-obfuscated malware, which might limit its effectiveness against other sophisticated obfuscation techniques like advanced packing, encryption, or polymorphic and metamorphic malware. These limitations highlight the necessity for continuous model evaluation and adaptation to incorporate a broader range of obfuscation techniques into the training regime. To address these challenges, future work will involve extending the training dataset to include a wider variety of obfuscated malware samples. Additionally, enhancing the Mal-CNN with adaptive learning capabilities to dynamically adjust to new obfuscation methods as they evolve remains a critical research direction.

Furthermore, the Mal-CNN utilizes depth-wise separable convolutions coupled with spatial attention mechanisms, which inherently increase the computational complexity of the model. This complexity manifests in longer training times and higher computational resource requirements compared with simpler models. However, the use of depth-wise separable convolutions optimizes the number of computations and parameters compared with standard convolutions, making it a more efficient choice for high-dimensional data processing. Despite these advantages, the real-time deployment of the Mal-CNN in systems with limited computational resources could be challenging. To mitigate this, model quantization techniques can be applied to reduce the precision of the numerical calculations, thereby decreasing the model size and speeding up inference without significantly sacrificing accuracy.

5. Conclusions

The experimental results from this study highlight the advanced capabilities of the Mal-CNN model, which notably exceeded the performance of a traditional CNN in both original and VM-obfuscated malware detection scenarios. Through the strategic incorporation of depth-wise convolutional layers and spatial attention mechanisms, the Mal-CNN demonstrated a robust ability to discern intricate patterns typical of sophisticated malware obfuscation techniques. This superior performance underscores the Mal-CNN's potential as an invaluable tool in the cybersecurity arsenal, particularly in environments where complex and evolving threats are prevalent.

Moreover, the Mal-CNN's efficacy in adapting to and accurately classifying data from diverse and challenging datasets confirms its architectural strengths and suitability for practical deployment in real-world settings. The success of the Mal-CNN in these tests encourages further exploration into its application across broader malware types and attack vectors.

Future research could focus on extending the model's architecture to incorporate multi-modal data sources and exploring the integration of additional neural network innovations to enhance its predictive accuracy and efficiency. Additionally, evaluating the Mal-CNN under real-time detection scenarios could provide insights into its performance and scalability in operational cybersecurity environments.

Author Contributions: Conceptualization, Y.P.; data curation, S.H.; formal analysis, S.H.; funding acquisition, S.H.; investigation, S.H.; methodology, S.H.; project administration, Y.P.; resources, S.H.; software, S.H.; supervision, H.Y. and Y.P.; validation, S.H. and H.Y.; visualization, S.H.; writing—original draft, S.H.; writing—review and editing, S.H. All authors have read and agreed to the published version of the manuscript.

Funding: This research received no external funding.

Data Availability Statement: The datasets and proposed Mal-CNN can be found at https://github.com/AHSCone/Mal_CNN (accessed on 15 July 2024).

Conflicts of Interest: The authors declare no conflicts of interest.

References

1. Liu, Z.; Zheng, D.; Wu, X.; Chen, J.; Tang, X.; Ran, Z. VABox: A virtualization-based analysis framework of virtualization-obfuscated packed executables. In Proceedings of the 7th International Conference of the Advances in Artificial Intelligence and Security (ICAIS 2021), Dublin, Ireland, 19–23 July 2021; Proceedings, Part III 7; Springer: Cham, Switzerland, 2021; pp. 73–84.
2. Bang, C.H.; Suk, J.H.; Lee, S.J. VMProtect operation principle analysis and automatic deobfuscation implementation. *J. Korea Inst. Inf. Secur. Cryptol.* **2020**, *30*, 605–616.
3. Li, S.; Jia, C.; Qiu, P.; Chen, Q.; Ming, J.; Gao, D. Chosen-instruction attack against commercial code virtualization obfuscators. In Proceedings of the 29th Network and Distributed System Security Symposium, San Diego, CA, USA, 24–28 April 2022.
4. Zhu, H.; Kong, Q.; Xu, Z.; Chen, J.; Li, X. Research on Software Protection Technology Based on Driver. *Am. J. Inf. Sci. Technol.* **2020**, *4*, 46–50.
5. Lee, G.; Kim, M.; Yi, J.H.; Cho, H. Pinicorn: Towards Automated Dynamic Analysis for Unpacking 32-Bit PE Malware. *Electronics* **2024**, *13*, 2081. [CrossRef]
6. Abrath, B.; Coppens, B.; Broeck, J.V.D.; Wyseur, B.; Cabutto, A.; Falcarin, P.; Sutter, B.D. Code renewability for native software protection. *ACM Trans. Priv. Secur. TOPS* **2020**, *23*, 1–31. [CrossRef]
7. Alzubaidi, L.; Zhang, J.; Humaidi, A.J.; Al-Dujaili, A.; Duan, Y.; Al-Shamma, O.; Santamaría, J.; Fadhel, M.A.; Al-Amidie, M.; Farhan, L. Review of deep learning: Concepts, CNN architectures, challenges, applications, future directions. *J. Big Data* **2021**, *8*, 1–74.
8. Kattenborn, T.; Leitloff, J.; Schiefer, F.; Hinz, S. Review on Convolutional Neural Networks (CNN) in vegetation remote sensing. *ISPRS J. Photogramm. Remote Sens.* **2021**, *173*, 24–49. [CrossRef]
9. Salehi, A.W.; Khan, S.; Gupta, G.; Alabduallah, B.I.; Almjally, A.; Alsolai, H.; Siddiqui, T.; Mellit, A. A study of CNN and transfer learning in medical imaging: Advantages, challenges, future scope. *Sustainability* **2023**, *15*, 5930. [CrossRef]
10. Lu, J.; Tan, L.; Jiang, H. Review on convolutional neural network (CNN) applied to plant leaf disease classification. *Agriculture* **2021**, *11*, 707. [CrossRef]
11. Howard, A.G.; Zhu, M.; Chen, B.; Kalenichenko, D.; Wang, W.; Weyand, T.; Andreetto, M.; Adam, H. MobileNets: Efficient Convolutional Neural Networks for Mobile Vision Applications. *arXiv* **2017**, arXiv:1704.04861.
12. Sandler, M.; Howard, A.; Zhu, M.; Zhmoginov, A.; Chen, L.C. MobileNetV2: Inverted Residuals and Linear Bottlenecks. In Proceedings of the IEEE Conference on Computer Vision and Pattern Recognition, Salt Lake City, UT, USA, 18–22 June 2018, pp. 4510–4520.
13. Yakura, H.; Shinozaki, S.; Nishimura, R.; Oyama, Y.; Sakuma, J. Malware analysis of imaged binary samples by convolutional neural network with attention mechanism. In Proceedings of the Eighth ACM Conference on Data and Application Security and Privacy, Tempe, AZ, USA, 19–21 March 2018; pp. 127–134.
14. Vaswani, A.; Shazeer, N.; Parmar, N.; Uszkoreit, J.; Jones, L.; Gomez, A.; Kaiser, L.; Polosukhin, I. Attention is all you need. In Proceedings of the Advances in Neural Information Processing Systems, Long Beach, CA, USA, 4–9 December 2017; pp. 6000–6010.
15. Kim, J.Y.; Cho, S.B. Obfuscated malware detection using deep generative model based on global/local features. *Comput. Secur.* **2022**, *112*, 102501. [CrossRef]
16. Alani, M.M.; Mashatan, A.; Miri, A. XMal: A lightweight memory-based explainable obfuscated-malware detector. *Comput. Secur.* **2023**, *133*, 103409. [CrossRef]
17. Gopinath, M.; Sethuraman, S.C. A comprehensive survey on deep learning based malware detection techniques. *Comput. Sci. Rev.* **2023**, *47*, 100529.
18. Bensaoud, A.; Kalita, J.; Bensaoud, M. A survey of malware detection using deep learning. *Mach. Learn. Appl.* **2024**, *16*, 100546 [CrossRef]
19. Lu, T.; Du, Y.; Ouyang, L.; Chen, Q.; Wang, X. Android malware detection based on a hybrid deep learning model. *Secur. Commun. Netw.* **2020**, *2020*, 8863617. [CrossRef]
20. Nataraj, L.; Karthikeyan, S.; Jacob, G.; Manjunath, B. Malware Images: Visualization and Automatic Classification. In Proceedings of the 8th International Symposium on Visualization for Cyber Security, Pittsburgh, PA, USA, 20–21 July 2011.
21. Yang, W.; Park, Y. Identifying symmetric-key algorithms using CNN in Intel processor trace. *Electronics* **2021**, *10*, 2491. [CrossRef]
22. Suarez-Tangil, G.; Stringhini, G.; Cavallaro, L. Droids on Roids: Fortifying Scalable Malware Detection against Adversarial Attacks. *arXiv* **2019**, arXiv:1902.02354.
23. Li, Y.; Li, B. Enhancing Malware Detection via Generative Adversarial Networks. In Proceedings of the IEEE International Conference on Communications, Dublin, Ireland, 7–11 June 2020.
24. Papernot, N.; McDaniel, P.; Wu, X.; Jha, S.; Swami, A. Distillation as a defense to adversarial perturbations against deep neural networks. In Proceedings of the 2016 IEEE Symposium on Security and Privacy, San Jose, CA, USA, 22–26 May 2016; pp. 582–597

5. Goodfellow, I.J.; Shlens, J.; Szegedy, C. Explaining and harnessing adversarial examples. In Proceedings of the International Conference on Learning Representations, Banff, AB, Canada, 14–16 April 2014.
6. Lei, T.; Xue, J.; Man, D.; Wang, Y.; Li, M.; Kong, Z. SDP-MTF: A Composite Transfer Learning and Feature Fusion for Cross-Project Software Defect Prediction. *Electronics* **2024**, *13*, 2439. [CrossRef]
7. Mai, C.; Liao, R.; Ren, J.; Gong, Y.; Zhang, K.; Zhang, C. MobileNet-Based IoT Malware Detection with Opcode Features. *J. Commun. Inf. Netw.* **2023**, *8*, 221–230. [CrossRef]
8. Krizhevsky, A.; Sutskever, I.; Hinton, G.E. Imagenet classification with deep convolutional neural networks. In Proceedings of the Advances in Neural Information Processing Systems, Lake Tahoe, NV, USA, 3–6 December 2012; Volume 25.
9. Szegedy, C.; Zaremba, W.; Sutskever, I.; Bruna, J.; Erhan, D.; Goodfellow, I.; Fergus, R. Intriguing properties of neural networks. *arXiv* **2013**, arXiv:1312.6199.

electronics

Article

Research on the Teaching of Laser Chaotic Communication Based on Optisystem and Matlab Software

Xuefang Zhou *, Minjun Li, Meihua Bi, Guowei Yang and Miao Hu

School of Communication Engineering, Hangzhou Dianzi University, Hangzhou 310018, China;
222080108@hdu.edu.cn (M.L.); bmh@hdu.edu.cn (M.B.); 40909@hdu.edu.cn (M.H.)
* Correspondence: zhouxf@hdu.edu.cn

Abstract: The utilization of chaotic optical communication, a physical layer security technology, has the potential to enhance the security of optical fiber networks. In this paper, we take knowledge acquired while teaching "A chaotic security system based on phase-intensity (P-I) electro-optic feedback" as an example and, in detail, introduce a teaching implementation process based on the combination of Optisystem and Matlab. Firstly, based on the Lang–Kobayashi (L-K) laser equation, the generation mechanism of electro-optic feedback chaos was explained. Secondly, the P-I electro-optic feedback chaos was analyzed theoretically with the help of Matlab. Finally, a laser chaotic optical communication system based on electro-optic feedback was built with the help of Optisystem (15.0.0) software, and the performance of the communication was simulated and analyzed through the design of system parameters. The teaching design model and facilitate the concretization of the abstract theory of "the principle of chaos generated by electro-optic feedback, the composition of chaotic optical communication system and the performance index of chaotic communication system". Through after-class exercises and questionnaire surveys, it was verified that the teaching method is widely recognized by students and that it effectively improves the teaching effect of the course of laser chaotic communication and the students' academic research ability.

Keywords: electro-optical feedback; light chaos; secure communications; Optisystem; teaching research

1. Introduction

Laser chaotic communication is a form of hardware encryption that utilizes physical layer principles [1], specifically leveraging the unique characteristics of chaotic signals, such as their ergodicity, aperiodicity, continuous broadband spectrum, and noise-like properties [2]. This method involves embedding the transmitted signal within a chaotic signal or assigning distinct chaotic waveforms to different information sequences through symbolic dynamic analysis. The receiver then demodulates the transmitted information by exploiting the synchronization properties of chaos or the characteristics of chaotic waveforms. Chaotic systems exhibit numerous practical applications within the realm of information technology. For instance, within the domain of communication [3], the implementation of synchronous chaotic systems at both the transmitting and receiving ends can facilitate the generation of cryptographic keys or masks through the utilization of chaotic signals produced by the system, thereby enabling secure communication. Otherwise, chaotic signals can serve as entropy sources for the generation of random numbers in computational tasks [4], such as Monte Carlo simulation and reinforcement learning, by leveraging the initial value sensitivity of chaotic systems across various disciplines. Chaotic signals possess significant utility in various fields, being used in super-resolution imaging technology [5], multiple-input multiple-output (MIMO) radar applications [6], and random modulation continuous wave (RMCW) lidar applications [7] utilizing chaotic lasers. The laser chaotic system exhibits characteristics such as high bandwidth, low attenuation, complex dynamic behavior, high sensitivity to parameters, and enhanced security performance, rendering it well suited for high-speed remote secure communication. Laser chaos and chaos synchronization are fundamental aspects and challenges within the realm of Laser Chaos Communication. The presence of numerous intricate formulas poses a significant obstacle to students' comprehension of abstract and objective concepts, while the costly experimental equipment further constrains the advancement of the course.

With the rapid development of computer technology, Optisystem, machine learning, neural networks, and other technologies have been developed rapidly and widely used in the communication industry, specifically in quality of service (QoS) quality prediction [8,9], laser chaos synchronization judgment [10,11], optical amplifier gain equalization processing [12,13], and fiber laser spectrum prediction [14,15]. In 2020, Khurram [16] proposed a radio-over-fiber (ROF) front-end communication link scheme utilizing Optisystem to achieve a ROF communication system with a transmission rate of 5 Gb/s and a transmission distance of 90 km, resulting in a system Q factor of 30.8. In 2021, Gaurav Pandey [17] conducted an analysis and study of a wavelength division multiplex–radio-over-fiber (WDM-ROF) transmission system employing low-cost direct-modulated lasers for next-generation 5G networks by utilizing simulation and experimental verification methods, with the results demonstrating strong agreement between the two approaches. In this context, we started to modify the teaching mode of laser chaotic communication in 2021, relying on Matlab (2023) and Optisystem (15.0.0) software, and implemented project practice based on the course platform. Herein, the effect of this new teaching method is analyzed and discussed with the goal of "taking students as the center" and improving students' independent learning and problem-solving abilities. The results show that the teaching reform and experience improve students' ability to analyze and solve problems and stimulate students' creativity and interest in scientific research.

2. Basic Information of Laser Chaotic Communication Course

The laser chaotic communication course is designed to effectively support the three graduation requirements of engineering knowledge, research, and communication for the professional certification of engineering education in communication engineering majors and to imbue students with analytical and design capabilities. We identified the knowledge, competence, and quality objectives for this course, as shown in Figure 1.

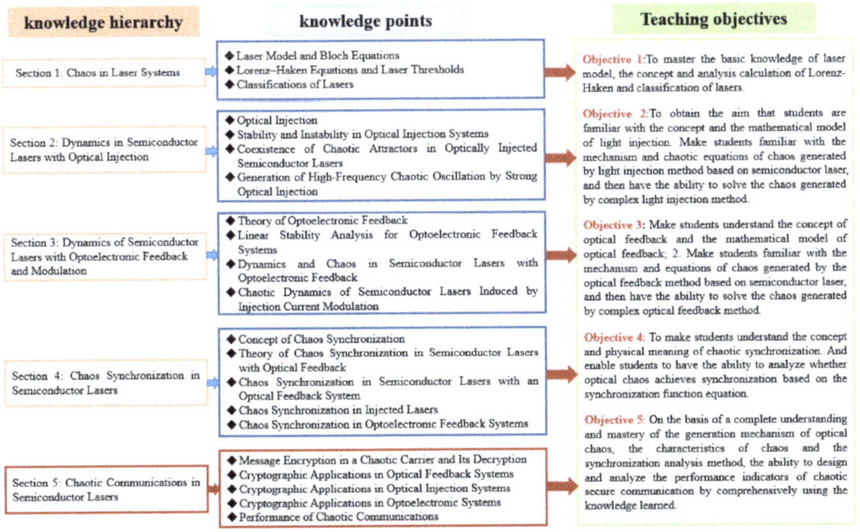

Figure 1. Teaching content and teaching objectives of laser chaotic communication.

There are two major pain points in the current teaching of this course. (1) Teaching concept: Many knowledge points in the course are abstract mathematical models and complex mathematical equations. The traditional teaching mode lacks personalization and innovation, and it does not sufficiently support the cultivation of students' ability to solve complex engineering problems. (2) Teaching methods: In the classroom, we often see "stub" information and silence. Teachers carry out detailed theoretical derivation and concept explanations. If there is no appropriate method, such as the use of software or experiments, for demonstration, it is not conducive to the cultivation of students' thinking ability, software application skills, and innovation ability.

Aiming to solve the problems posed by the above teaching pain points, we combine the five teaching objectives of the course to integrate resources. Firstly, with the help of the MOOC/SPOC teaching platform, high-quality resources are gathered through self-construction and sharing, the scale and quality of resources are improved, the online teaching resources network of the course is constructed, the project research activities inside and outside the classroom are activated, the open sharing of the course inside and outside the school is realized, and the smooth implementation of the cultivation of students' scientific research ability and innovation ability is guaranteed. Secondly, the four-in-one teaching mode of "understanding in learning, strengthening in practice, consolidating in practice, breaking through and innovating" is proposed and adopted. In classroom teaching, heuristic, comparative methods; teaching and practice with Matlab or Optisystem software; questioning and answering; discussion; and other teaching methods are used to achieve "learning while understanding". In the after-class section, the homework is carefully designed for students to complete through the course network platform in order to realize "consolidation and innovation while practicing". Teachers judge whether students can learn the subsequent course content through the feedback of students' test results, which can also be used as a reliable basis for teachers to modify course teaching plans and teaching methods.

Electro-optical phase chaos and electro-optical intensity chaos are frequently employed methods for generating chaos, but they exhibit limitations in terms of their effectiveness in time-delayed-signature (TDS) concealment and complexity enhancement. To meet the advanced teaching requirements of the course, the teaching design of the "electro-optic cascade phase feedback loop" is elaborated based on the students' learning of "electro-optic phase modulation" and "electro-optic intensity modulation". The teaching effect of this method is studied from the aspects of program design, theoretical derivation, software simulation analysis, testing, and, finally, through exercises and questionnaires after class. The results show that this method has been recognized by students and that it has good potential for development.

3. Teaching Implementation of "Laser Chaotic Communication Based on P-I Electro-Optic Cascade Phase Feedback" Course

To gain a more thorough and detailed understanding of the characteristics of chaos, this study discusses the electro-optical feedback chaos teaching approach, focusing specifically on the phase–intensity conversion process. The study considers the integration of Optisystem and Matlab to construct and analyze a secure communication system characterized by chaotic behavior. Initially, a theoretical model of phase-to-intensity (P-I) electro-optical feedback optical chaos was developed, and its mathematical expression was derived. Subsequently, the performance of the optical chaos system, including aspects of security, confidentiality, robustness, and synchronization, was numerically analyzed using Matlab. Finally, the simulation link was established within the Optisystem software, followed by the design of device parameters and subsequent simulation and analysis of the constructed system. This approach aids students in developing the "model-analysis-optimization" thought process, enhancing the efficacy of the course instruction, and offering potential applicability to other laser chaotic secure communication teaching materials. The specific teaching implementation process is shown in Figure 2.

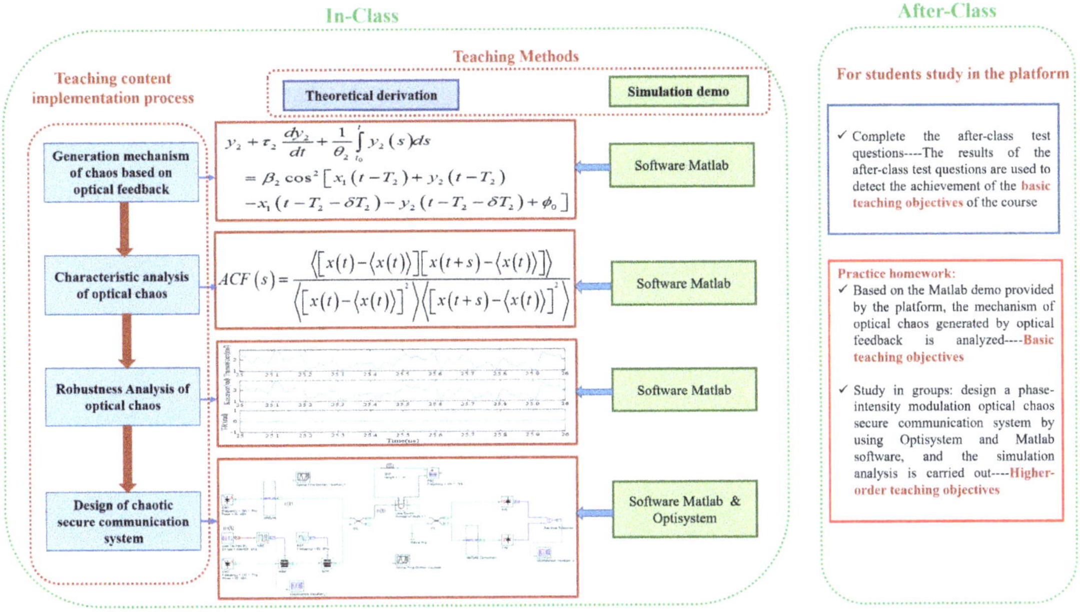

Figure 2. "Laser chaotic communication with electro-optic phase-intensity modulation" teaching implementation process.

3.1. Model of Electro-Optic Cascade-Phase Feedback Laser Chaotic Communication System

Figure 3 illustrates electro-optical cascade-phase feedback laser chaotic communication utilizing a phase-to-intensity conversion mechanism. In contrast to an intensity feedback chaos source, the laser chaos system incorporates a phase modulator (PM) in place of a Mach–Zehnder interferometer (MZI) and integrates an MZI within the feedback loop. Following PM modulation, the optical signal exhibits chaotic behavior in phase, which is subsequently converted into chaos in intensity by the MZI. The MZI generates a chaotic optical signal which is subsequently converted into an electrical signal by the photodetector (PD) and amplified by an amplifier, driving the PM to produce more intricate chaotic signals. In this system model, the laser chaotic signal maintains a constant light intensity and chaotic phase. Due to the difficulty of interfering with the nonlinear fiber during transmission, this system is commonly employed for ensuring the security of long-distance information transmission using chaotic signals.

In the transmitter, the PM1 modulator modulates the signal onto a continuous optical carrier produced by slave laser1 (SL1), and the resulting PM1 output is evenly divided by an optical coupler1 (OC1). A portion of the signal goes through the dispersion module (fiber Bragg grating (FBG1) with a 1200 ps/nm dispersion coefficient) for a phase-to-intensity conversion process, resulting in time–domain-waveform-stretching spectrum diffusion and random noise-like reflection, and is then sent to the receiver via standard single-mode fiber (SSMF). The other part of the signal is input into PM2, delayed by T2 through delay line 2 (DL2), and split into two paths via an OC2. One path enters the inner phase feedback loop, becoming the input for MZI2, which is converted into an electrical signal by PD1 and amplified by RF (Radio Frequency) to generate a signal $x_2(t)$ as the driver of PM2. The other path enters the external loop, delayed by T1 through DL1 and MZI1, and is converted into an electrical signal by PD2 and amplified to become the drive signal $x_1(t)$ of PM1, thus forming the internal and external feedback loops. After traveling through SSMF, the signal reaches the receiver, which mirrors the transmitter's parameters. The OC3 splits the signal into two parts. One part includes two feedback loops for synchronization. The output from PM3 goes through a dispersion module (FBG2 with −1200 ps/nm dispersion), compressing it in the time domain to counteract FBG1's effects, and is then converted into an electrical signal by PD5. The second signal is converted into an electrical signal by PD6, and the original plaintext signal is accurately reconstructed by subtracting the two signals with a low-pass filter.

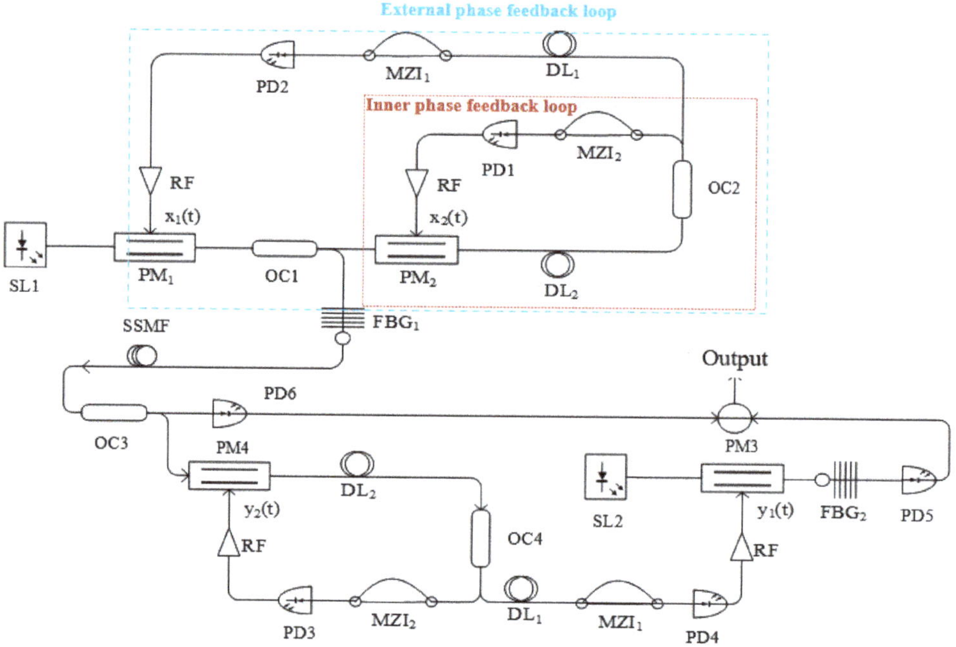

Figure 3. Schematic of P-I electro-optical cascade-phase feedback chaotic communication system. SL: slave laser; PM: phase modulator; MZI: Mach–Zehnder interferometer; OC: optical coupler; DL: delay line; FBG: fiber Bragg grating; RF: Radio Frequency; PD: photodetector; SSMF: standard single-mode fiber.

3.2. Theoretical Model

As shown in Figure 3, a linear filter is an important device for generating chaotic signals. τ and θ represent the high and low cutoff frequencies of the linear filter, respectively. Additionally, $v_i(t)$ denotes the output voltage of the linear filter, v_π represents the half-wave voltage of the PM modulator, and $x_i(t) = \pi v_i(t)/2v_\pi$ signifies the signal variable at the transmitter. It can be inferred that the dynamic mathematical models of the P-I electro-optical cascade-phase feedback chaotic communication system can be characterized by the subsequent system of integral differential equations:

$$x_1 + \tau_1 \frac{dx_1}{dt} + \frac{1}{\theta_1} \int_{t_0}^{t} x_1(s)ds = \beta_1 \cos^2[x_1(t - T_1 - T_2) + x_2(t - T_1 - T_2) - x_1(t - T_1 - T_2 - \delta T_1) - x_2(t - T_1 - T_2 - \delta T_1) + \phi_0] \quad (1)$$

$$x_2 + \tau_2 \frac{dx_2}{dt} + \frac{1}{\theta_2} \int_{t_0}^{t} x_2(s)ds = \beta_2 \cos^2[x_1(t - T_2) + x_2(t - T_2) - x_1(t - T_2 - \delta T_2) - x_2(t - T_2 - \delta T_2) + \phi_0] \quad (2)$$

$$y_1 + \tau_1 \frac{dy_1}{dt} + \frac{1}{\theta_1} \int_{t_0}^{t} y_1(s)ds = \beta_1 \cos^2[x_1(t - T_1 - T_2) + y_2(t - T_1 - T_2) - x_1(t - T_1 - T_2 - \delta T_1) - y_2(t - T_1 - T_2 - \delta T_1) + \phi_0] \quad (3)$$

$$y_2 + \tau_2 \frac{dy_2}{dt} + \frac{1}{\theta_2} \int_{t_0}^{t} y_2(s)ds = \beta_2 \cos^2[x_1(t - T_2) + y_2(t - T_2) - x_1(t - T_2 - \delta T_2) - y_2(t - T_2 - \delta T_2) + \phi_0] \quad (4)$$

where the subscript $i = 1$ represents the external feedback phase loop, $i = 2$ represents the internal feedback phase loop, ϕ_0 is the static offset phase of the PM modulator, T_1 and T_2 are the delay of the fiber delay line DL_i, δT_1 and δT_2 are the coherence time introduced by the two Mach–Zehnder interferometers (MZIs), and β_i is the coefficient of the phase feedback loop:

$$\beta_i = \frac{\pi AgGP_0}{2V_\pi} \quad (5)$$

where Equations (1) and (2) are mathematical models at the transmitter, and Equations (3) and (4) are mathematical models at the receiver. The Runge–Kutta algorithm can be used to solve the integral differential mathematical equation with delay [18]. Only by ensuring that the PM, DL, PD, and RF parameters at both ends are set the same can the chaotic student system achieve complete synchronization.

The chaotic signal output from the cascaded phase feedback loop undergoes dispersion compensation via module FBG, which results in the original chaotic signal being disturbed again in phase and amplitude, thus producing a more complex chaotic signal. The mathematical representation of FBG in the frequency domain is provided in Ref. [19]:

$$H(\omega) = \exp\left(j\frac{B}{2}(\omega - \omega_0)^2\right) \quad (6)$$

where B is the dispersion coefficient of the dispersion compensation module FBG, and ω_0 is the center angular frequency of the semiconductor laser. Upon passing through the dispersion compensation module FBG, the complex amplitude of the resulting optical chaotic signal becomes more intricate, and it can be shown as follows:

$$E_{FBG}(t) = F^{-1}(F(E_{interfer}(t))H(\omega)) \quad (7)$$

where $F(\cdot)$ is the Fourier transform, and F^{-1} is the inverse Fourier transform.

3.3. *Analysis of Chaotic Characteristics in Matlab Software*

3.3.1. Bifurcation Diagram

A bifurcation diagram illustrates the variation in the number of stable points of a nonlinear system as its parameters are altered. The dynamic characteristics of a chaotic laser source are significantly influenced by changes in the bifurcation coefficient, specifically in terms of alterations to the phase space. This includes modifications to the solutions of the dynamic mathematical equation, impacting both the quantity and stability of the solutions, thereby manifesting as bifurcation phenomena within the phase space. By modifying the bifurcation coefficient, the nonlinear behavior of the laser chaotic system can be altered, leading the system to transition from a stable state to a period-doubling state and, ultimately, a chaotic state. The bifurcation diagram index elucidates the progression of the system towards chaotic behavior as the bifurcation coefficient increases.

The parameter values used in our simulation are shown in Table 1. As depicted in Figure 4, when the feedback strength coefficient $\beta_1 = \beta_2$, the phase bifurcation diagram of the P-I electro-optical cascade-phase feedback chaotic system closely resembles that of the conventional electro-optical cascade-phase feedback chaotic system. As the feedback strength coefficient increases, the system transitions from its initial state to a chaotic state, gradually losing stability.

Table 1. Parameter values used in our simulation.

Symbol	Parameter	Values
τ_1	The time of the high-pass cutoff frequency in the external phase feedback loop	20 ns
θ_1	The time of the low-pass cutoff frequency in the external phase feedback loop	16.6 ms
T_1	The delay of the phase-modulated branch	300 ns
δT_1	The coherence time of phase-modulated branch MZI1	600 ps
τ_2	The time of the high-pass cutoff frequency in the inner phase feedback loop	12.2 ns
θ_2	The time of the low-pass cutoff frequency in the inner phase feedback loop	16.6 ms
T_2	The delay of phase-modulated shunt	500 ns
δT_2	The coherence time of phase-modulated branch MZI2	400 ps
Φ_0	The static offset phase introduced by the two-phase feedback loops	$\pi/4$
B	Dispersion	1200 ps/km
β_i	The feedback coefficient	[0, 5]

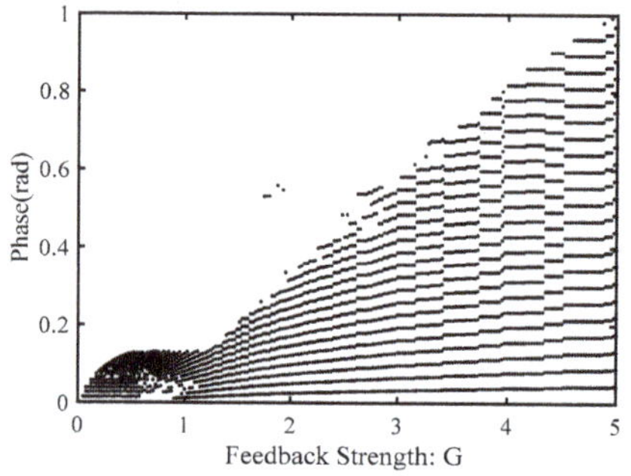

Figure 4. Phase bifurcation diagram of P-I electro-optical cascade-phase feedback chaotic system.

The optical power time-series waveforms of chaotic signals at the transmitter and receiver are shown in Figure 5. It can be seen from Figure 5 that the signals at the transmitter and the receiver enter the chaotic state at the same time and have good synchronization.

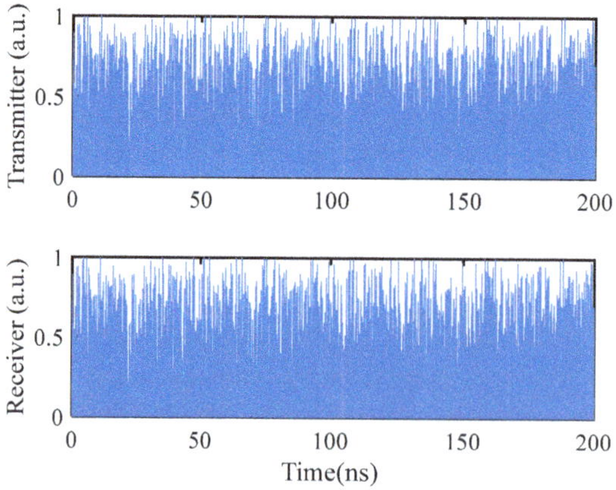

Figure 5. Optical power time-series waveforms of chaotic signals at transmitter and receiver.

3.3.2. Probability Density Distribution

The assessment of system complexity relies heavily on the probability density distribution of chaotic signal output, with a Gaussian noise signal serving as the benchmark for an ideal chaotic state. A Gaussian-like distribution in the probability density of a chaotic signal indicates a high level of complexity, as it suggests a close resemblance to noise. The probability density distributions of the P-I Phase Feedback System (P-I-TPFS) and traditional phase feedback system (TPFS), discussed in reference [20], for when the feedback intensity coefficient $\beta_1 = \beta_2 = 3$ are depicted in Figure 6. It can be seen from Figure 6 that the Gaussian distribution is symmetric concerning $x = 0$. When $x > 0$, the probability density distribution of the P-I electro-optical cascade-phase feedback chaotic system exhibits a faster decrease compared to that of the traditional electro-optical cascade-phase feedback chaotic system. The P-I electro-optical cascade-phase feedback chaotic system exhibits increased complexity, resembling a Gaussian distribution. Numerical simulations conducted in MATLAB demonstrate that the incorporation of the P-I dispersion module enhances the chaotic signal generated by this system, making it more suitable for communication systems in the 5G front-end network compared to traditional electro-optical cascade-phase feedback chaotic systems.

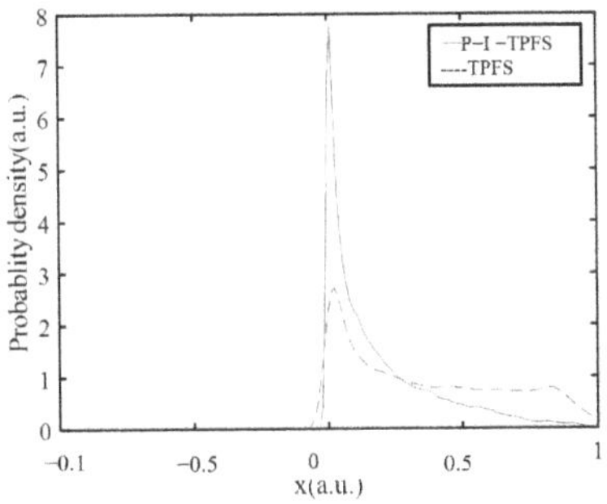

Figure 6. Probability distribution of P-I and traditional electro-optical cascade-phase feedback chaotic systems.

3.3.3. ACF and CCF

The autocorrelation function (*ACF*) describes and quantifies the degree of correlation between observations of a time series at different lags. The mathematical expression for the *ACF* is given by the following formula [8]:

$$ACF(s) = \frac{\langle [x(t) - \langle x(t) \rangle][x(t+s) - \langle x(t) \rangle] \rangle}{\left\langle [x(t) - \langle x(t) \rangle]^2 \right\rangle \left\langle [x(t+s) - \langle x(t) \rangle]^2 \right\rangle} \quad (8)$$

The operator symbol $\langle \cdot \rangle$ represents the average value of $\cdot$, and s is the delay of the signal. In the context of a random signal, correlation peaks are exclusively observed $s = 0$. Conversely, in a delayed electro-optical feedback chaotic source, correction peaks are present at the delay parameters of the feedback loop and their integer multiples. The absence of a discernible correlation peak in the ACF curve suggests that the delay parameters are effectively concealed.

The ACF of the P-I electro-optical cascade-phase feedback chaotic system will be calculated using Matlab to analyze the TDS hiding effect, and it will be compared with the traditional electro-optical cascade-phase feedback chaotic system. The autocorrelation functions of both systems for when the feedback intensity coefficient $\beta_1 = \beta_2 = 3$ are shown in Figure 7a,b.

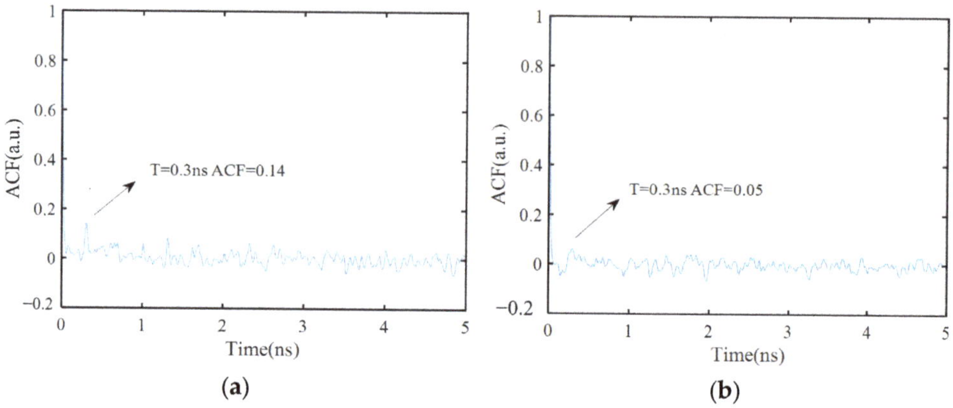

Figure 7. Autocorrelation function of electro-optic cascade-phase feedback chaotic system. (**a**) Traditional system and (**b**) P-I system.

Figure 7a illustrates that the ACF of the traditional electro-optical cascade-phase feedback chaotic system exhibits a sharp peak when the delay parameter $T_1 = 0.3$ns. The results indicate that the chaotic signal output correlation in the phase feedback loop delay of the traditional electro-optical cascade chaotic system has not been adequately mitigated, thereby ensuring the system's security. Figure 7b demonstrates that the ACF of the P-I electro-optical cascade-phase feedback chaotic system does not exhibit significant peaks at $T_1 = 0.3$ns, $T_2 = 0.5$ns, $T_1 + T_2 = 0.8$ns integer multiples of the delay parameter. This demonstrates that the traditional electro-optical cascaded phase feedback chaotic system can successfully mitigate the temporal correlation of chaotic signals within the delay parameters of the two feedback loops utilizing a dispersion module, leading to the effective concealment of TDS. Consequently, unauthorized users are unable to reconstruct the chaotic dynamic equation of the transmitter or decipher the transmitted plaintext signal by acquiring TDS information, thereby guaranteeing security and the confidentiality of communication.

The cross-correlation function (CCF) typically quantifies the degree of synchronization between the chaotic signal at the transmitter and receiver, as well as the correlation between the transmitted information and the chaotic signal. The mathematical formula for the CCF is as follows [9]:

$$CCF(t) = \frac{\langle [x_1(t) - \langle x_1(t)\rangle][x_2(t+s) - \langle x_2(t)\rangle]\rangle}{\left\langle [x_1(t) - \langle x_1(t)\rangle]^2 \right\rangle \left\langle [x_2(t+s) - \langle x_2(t)\rangle]^2 \right\rangle} \quad (9)$$

where $x_1(t)$ and $x_2(t)$ represent the two time series for which the degree of cross-correlation needs to be calculated. A peak value below 0.3 on the CCF curve indicates a very low correlation between the time series. Conversely, a peak value exceeding 0.8 suggests a strong correlation between the two time series. In a synchronous system of chaotic signals, a peak value exceeding 0.95 on the CCF curve indicates a high level of synchronization within the system.

The power CCF of the P-I electro-optical cascade-phase feedback chaotic system is shown in Figure 8. Figure 8 illustrates that in the absence of external disturbances, the maximum peak value of CCF is equal to 1, as referenced in Ref. [21], where the CCF's maximum peak value exceeds 0.95, indicating a high degree of synchronization within the system. Consequently, the transmitter and receiver are synchronized.

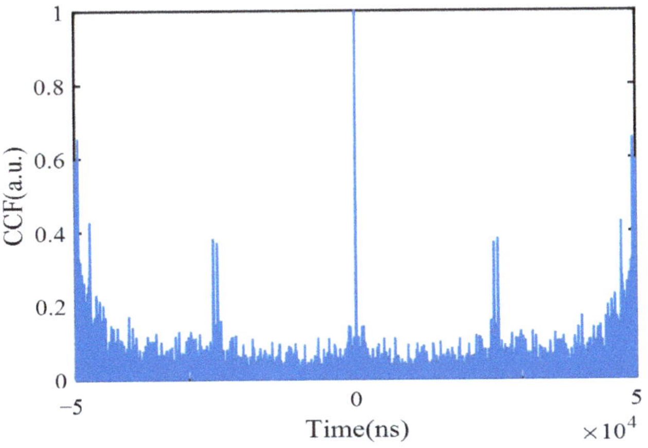

Figure 8. Power cross-correlation function of P-I electro-optic cascade-phase feedback chaotic system.

3.3.4. Robustness

The term "Robustness" pertains to the ability of a system to maintain consistent performance in the face of disturbances or uncertainties. When all system parameters at the transmitter and receiver are identical, the optical power and optical phase time waveforms at both ends are observed to be consistently within the range of 25 to 26 ns, as shown in Figures 9 and 10. Consequently, it can be inferred that the waveforms at the transmitter and receiver of the P-I electro-optical cascade-phase feedback chaotic system remain consistent. Simultaneously, it is demonstrated that the P-I electro-optical cascade-phase feedback chaotic system exhibits high synchronization.

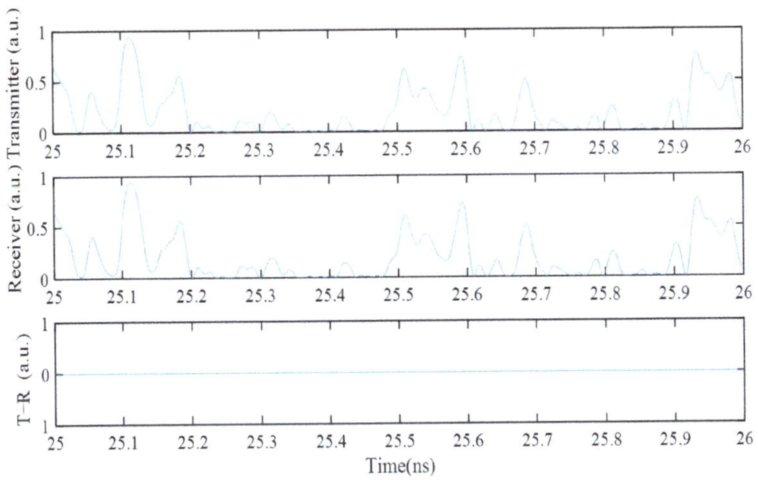

Figure 9. A time trajectory diagram of the optical power at the transmitter and receiver at a certain time.

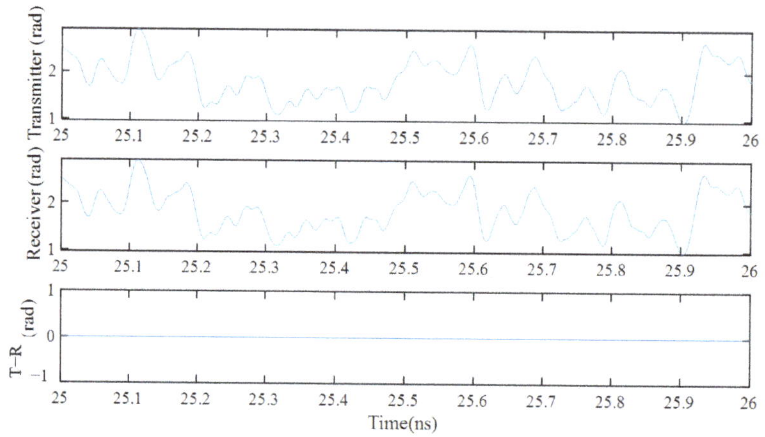

Figure 10. A time trajectory diagram of the optical phase at the transmitter and the receiver at a certain time.

To further illustrate the robustness of the system, Optisystem and MATLAB are used for joint simulation. In the Optisystem, a customized binary signal generator is employed to produce the rectangular pulse shown in Figure 11. Disturbances occur when $t = 100\text{ns}$, and the disturbance is canceled when $t = 162\text{ns}$. The optical power synchronization error between the transmitter and receiver is shown in Figure 12. The results demonstrate that the system's synchronization performance deteriorates upon the application of a rectangular pulse to the transmitter, but a high level of synchronization is achieved once the disturbance ceases. This confirms that the P-I electro-optic cascade-phase feedback chaotic system proposed in this study exhibits strong resilience to external interference.

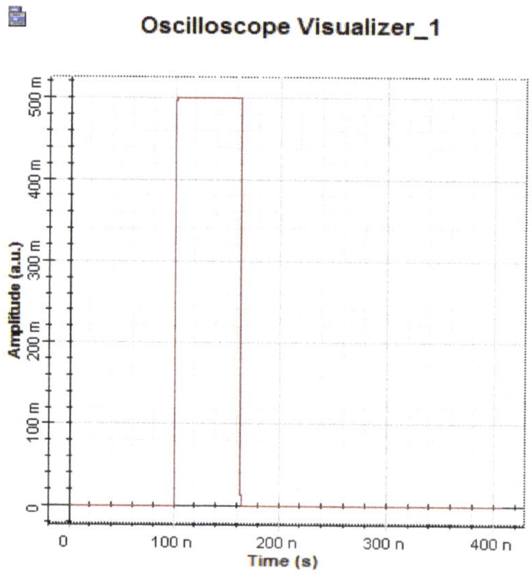

Figure 11. Rectangular disturbed signal.

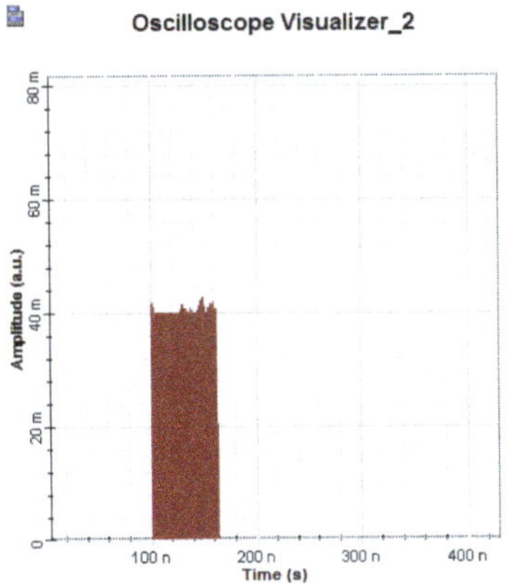

Figure 12. The optical power synchronization error between the transmitter and receiver.

The research on synchronization robustness discussed above is crucial, as it demonstrates that aligning the parameters of the transmitter and receiver in the secure communication system of the 5G front-end network enables the P-I electro-optical cascade-phase feedback chaotic dynamics to achieve full synchronization, and it shows good robustness in the case of external interference. Thus, it can realize the encryption and decryption process of the plaintext signals transmitted on the 5G front-end network system.

3.4. P-I Electro-Optic Cascade-Phase Feedback Laser Chaotic Synchronization Communication System Based on Matlab and Optisystem

The simulation of the P-I electro-optical cascade-phase feedback chaotic system in the context of a 5G front-end network is shown in Figure 13 through a co-simulation using Matlab and Optisystem. The generation of chaotic signals through the P-I electro-optical cascade-phase feedback chaotic source is achieved in Matlab, while the encryption, transmission through fiber, and decoding of plaintext signals are carried out in Optisystem. This approach allows for a more comprehensive simulation of the P-I electro-optical cascade-phase feedback chaotic system within the 5G front-end network. Radio-over-fiber (ROF) signals operating at a frequency of 60 GHz can facilitate the transmission of plaintext signals at speeds of up to 10 Gbit/s within the 5G front-end network. Additionally, chaotic signals employ a straightforward and cost-effective code shift keying (CSK) loading technique for ensuring secure communication [22].

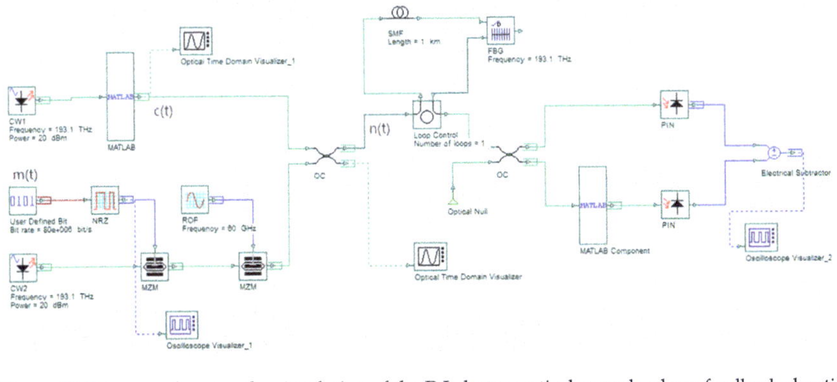

Figure 13. Diagram showing the simulation of the P-I electro-optical cascade-phase feedback chaotic system of a 5G front-end network co-simulated by Matlab and OptiSystem.

In the transmitter, an 80 Mbit/s binary plaintext signal is generated using the user-defined signal rate in Optisystem. The plaintext signal is then modulated into a binary non-return-to-zero code $m(t)$ through a non-return-to-zero (NRZ) encoder. Subsequently, the optical intensity signal $m_1(t)$ is modulated by an optical carrier with a frequency of 193.1 THz, and the ROF signal with a frequency of 60 GHz is further modulated by MZM to make $m_2(t)$. Finally, the plaintext signal $m_2(t)$ chaotic signal $c(t)$ and the encrypted signal $n(t)$ are transmitted via 50/50 OC coupling into the optical fiber channel with a transmission distance of 1 km, utilizing FBG for dispersion compensation. At the receiver, the original plaintext signal is reconstructed through the use of PD to convert the received signal $n(t)$ into an electrical signal by subtracting the same $c(t)$. By comparing the transmitter's signal and the receiver's signal, as shown in Figure 14, it can be observed that the original plaintext signal is successfully recovered.

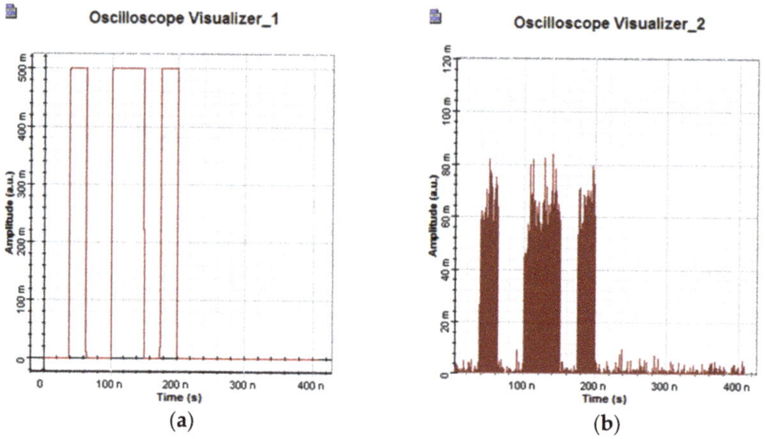

Figure 14. The signal waveform: (**a**) original plaintext signal; (**b**) the plaintext signal waveform after decryption.

3.5. Teaching Effect Analysis Based on Matlab and Optisystem Software

To understand the students' achievement of the teaching objectives of this knowledge point in time, an after-class test and questionnaire survey are carried out to track and improve the teaching effect of the course.

The test questions and specific responses to the after-class survey are shown in Table A1 in the Appendix A. These questions are designed around the basic teaching objectives of this knowledge point. From the statistical results, the correct rate of each question is more than 90%, and the correct rate of the first and the second questions is 100%. The results showed that the students' basic teaching objectives regarding this knowledge point were completely achieved.

Table A2 in the Appendix A shows the contents and statistical results of the questionnaire survey. According to the survey and the corresponding statistics, 91.12% of the students believed that the application of software in class-based teaching was beneficial, helping them to understand the course knowledge points. This suggests that the teaching design was highly valued by the students, that it improved their scientific research ability, and that they were willing to invest time and energy into their studies. Overall, 84.84% of the students hope that they will be offered an opportunity to complete homework by using Matlab and Optisystem software, which would improve their software application ability and operation ability. Students believe that the proposed system helped to cultivate interest in learning, deepen their understanding of theoretical knowledge, and improve their practical operation and teamwork abilities. Therefore, 73.34% of the students hope that subsequent courses will also provide the opportunity to use Matlab and Optisystem to solve problems related to chaotic communication. Regarding the system's application to scientific research projects, 84.44% of the students hope to have the opportunity to apply the system to course-related scientific research projects.

4. Conclusions

Considering the problems of the laser chaotic communication course being abstract and difficult to understand and the shortage of experimental equipment, we improved the course via the construction of curriculum resources and reforming teaching methods and created a mathematical model of each knowledge point in the teaching content with Matlab code. By using Optisystem software to design and simulate the optical link of the laser chaotic communication system, considering the method of combining theoretical analysis and software demonstration in class, and through perusing online resources and completing course-related practice assignments after class, students can consolidate the knowledge points and become better prepared, helping to cultivate students' ability to solve complex engineering problems in the field of communication engineering.

This paper explored the objective of teaching laser chaotic communication by proposing a P-I electro-optical cascade-phase feedback chaotic system, comprising two cascaded phase feedback loops and two dispersion encryption modules. The bifurcation diagram and probability density distribution of the P-I electro-optical cascade-phase feedback chaotic system were computed through Matlab numerical simulation, demonstrating that a feedback coefficient within a specific range can generate intricate chaotic signals. The ACF of the system was determined through numerical simulation using Matlab. The absence of prominent peaks in the delay parameter and its integer multiples suggests that the system is capable of effectively concealing TDS, thereby safeguarding the 5G front-end network communication system against unauthorized access and enhancing its confidentiality. When the system parameters of both the transmitter and receiver are identical, the Matlab numerical simulation calculates a maximum peak value of 1 for the CCF, indicating a high level of synchronization within the system. Despite the presence of external interference, the system demonstrates robust synchronization capabilities.

Finally, relying on the online platform of the course, the learning effect of the "P-I electro-optic cascade phase feedback chaotic system" was tested and surveyed. The results of the after-class test indicated that the students had a better understanding of each knowledge point. The results of the questionnaire survey showed that the students felt that the implementation of teaching based on Matlab and Optisystem software had improved their interest in learning, research ability, and teamwork spirit, and they also expressed their hope to encounter the use of this method in their following courses.

Author Contributions: Conceptualization, M.B. and G.Y.; formal analysis, X.Z. and M.H.; investigation, M.L.; data curation, M.L.; writing—original draft preparation, M.L.; writing—review and editing, X.Z.; visualization, M.H. All authors have read and agreed to the published version of the manuscript.

Funding: This research was supported by Zhejiang Province general undergraduate universities "14th Five-Year" teaching reform project (JG20220215); the Primary Research and Development Plan of Zhejiang Province (No. 2023C03014) and the Key Research and Development Program of Zhejiang Province (No. 2022C03037).

Data Availability Statement: Data will be made available upon request to the corresponding author.

Conflicts of Interest: The authors declare no conflicts of interest.

Appendix A

Table A1. Test questions after class and answers (45 students in the test group).

Questions	Results	Answers
1. The chaotic system based on optical feedback can make the laser output a chaotic signal by increasing the laser bias current or setting the appropriate feedback coefficient—( ) Yes or No?	Yes (45) No (0)	Yes
2. Based on the chaotic system of light injection, the response laser can be brought from the stable state to the chaotic state by modulating the phase or intensity of the perturbed light by external injection—( ) Yes or No?	Yes (45) No (0)	Yes
3. The correlation coefficient can analyze the synchronization degree of the chaotic signal at the transmitter and the chaotic signal at the receiver, and the larger the correlation coefficient is, the better the synchronization of the chaotic system is—( ) Yes or No?	Yes (42) No (3)	Yes
4. $\sigma = \frac{\langle \lvert P_t(t) - P_r(t) \rvert \rangle}{\langle \lvert P_t(t) \rvert \rangle}$ Synchronization error σ can reflect a similar degree of output chaotic signal amplitude. The smaller the value is, the worse the synchronization degree of the system is—( ) Yes or No?	Yes (2) No (43)	No
5. The properties of chaotic systems can be characterized by the following indicators: A. bifurcation diagram; B. Lyapunov exponent; C. fractal dimension; D. convergence.	A (45) B (45) C (41) D (44)	ABCD

Table A2. Feedback obtained from the questionnaire designed for the students in the test group.

Questions	Strongly Agree, n (%)	Agree, n (%)	Neutral, n (%)	Disagree, n (%)	Strongly Disagree, n (%)
Matlab and Optisystem software help you better understand the theoretical knowledge of the course.	16 (35.56%)	25 (55.56%)	4 (8.88%)	0 (0.00%)	0 (0.00%)
Matlab and Optisystem software improve your ability to design and analyze projects.	20 (44.44%)	25 (55.56%)	0 (0.00%)	0 (0.00%)	0 (0.00%)
Teaching based on Matlab and Optisystem software improves your scientific research ability.	18 (40.00%)	19 (42.22%)	7 (15.56%)	1 (2.22%)	0 (0.00%)
The practice homework improved your team's cooperation ability.	25 (55.56%)	20 (44.44%)	0 (0.00%)	0 (0.00%)	0 (0.00%)
This kind of teaching mode stimulates your interest in learning the course.	22 (48.89%)	20 (44.44%)	3 (6.67%)	0 (0.00%)	0 (0.00%)
It is hoped that the follow-up courses will also offer an opportunity to practice homework by using Matlab or Optisystem software.	19 (42.22%)	19 (42.22%)	7 (15.56%)	0 (0.00%)	0 (0.00%)
The practical homework improves your software application ability and operation ability.	23 (51.11%)	20 (44.44%)	2 (4.44%)	0 (0.00%)	0 (0.00%)

Table A2. *Cont.*

Questions	Strongly Agree, n (%)	Agree, n (%)	Neutral, n (%)	Disagree, n (%)	Strongly Disagree, n (%)
If you had another chance, would you hope to make the project more perfect?	17 (37.78%)	16 (35.56%)	10 (22.22%)	2 (4.44%)	1 (2.22%)
Do you want to apply for a research project related to the course?	20 (44.44%)	18 (40.00%)	5 (11.11%)	1 (2.22%)	1 (2.22%)

eferences

Qiao, L.; Wang, X.; Hao, Y.; Zhang, M. Progress of Chaotic Semiconductor Lasers and Their Applications. *Laser Optoelectron. Prog.* **2024**, *61*, 0114008.

Yi, L.; Ke, J. Research progress of chaotic secure optical communication. *J. Commun.* **2020**, *41*, 168–178.

Li, Z.Y.; Wang, H.X.; Ji, Y.F. Hardware fingerprint construction of optical transmitters based on permutation entropy spectrum of chaos for secure authentication. *Opt. Laser Technol.* **2023**, *171*, 109947. [CrossRef]

Don, S.H.G.M.; Inui, Y.; Kako, S.; Yamamoto, Y.; Aonishi, T. Mean-field coherent Ising machines with artificial Zeeman terms. *J. Appl. Phys.* **2023**, *134*, 234901.

Kanwal, S.; Inam, S.; Quddus, S.; Hajjej, F. Research on color image encryption approach based on chaotic Duffing map. *Phys. Scr.* **2023**, *98*, 125252. [CrossRef]

Shajin, F.H.; Rajesh, P. FPGA Realization of a Reversible Data Hiding Scheme for 5G MIMO-OFDM System by Chaotic Key Generation-Based Paillier Cryptography Along with LDPC and Its Side Channel Estimation Using Machine Learning Technique. *J. Circuits Syst. Comput.* **2022**, *31*, 2250093. [CrossRef]

Dong, Y.X.; Li, J.C.; Li, Y.-L.; Shi, Y.; Xiao, J.-L.; Yang, Y.-D.; Huang, Y.-Z.; Chen, Y. Feedback insensitivity in a self-chaotic microcavity laser. *Opt. Lett.* **2023**, *49*, 69–72. [CrossRef] [PubMed]

Ayassi, R.; Triki, A.; Crespi, N.; Minerva, R.; Laye, M. Survey on the Use of Machine Learning for Quality of Transmission Estimation in Optical Transport Networks. *J. Light-Wave Technol.* **2022**, *40*, 5803–5815. [CrossRef]

Sahu, S.; Clement, J.C.; Indhumathi, S.; Evelyn Ezhilarasi, I.; Chandrasekaran, D.S. BER and OSNR Based Quality Estimation in Optical Networks using Machine Learning Algorithms. In Proceedings of the 2023 2nd International Conference on Vision Towards Emerging Trends in Communication and Networking Technologies (ViTECoN), Vellore, India, 5–6 May 2023. [CrossRef]

0. Lin, C.M.; Pham, D.H.; Huynh, T.T. Encryption and Decryption of Audio Signal and Image Secure Communications Using Chaotic System Synchronization Control by TSK Fuzzy Brain Emotional Learning Controllers. *IEEE Trans. Cybern.* **2023**, *52*, 13684–13698. [CrossRef]

1. Li, N.; Wu, Z.M.; Lin, X.D.; Tang, X.; Xia, G.; Deng, T. Bidirectional digital image secure transmission and recognition based on a long-distance chaos synchronization system with machine learning capability. *Nonlinear Dyn.* **2023**, *104*, 2745–2758. [CrossRef]

2. Wang, Z.; Kilper, D.C.; Chen, T. Open EDFA gain spectrum dataset and its applications in data-driven EDFA gain modeling. *J. Opt. Commun. Netw.* **2023**, *15*, 588–599. [CrossRef]

3. Freire, M.; Sengupta, D.; Lavignotte, A.; Tremblay, C.; Lepers, C. Learning for Compensating Power Excursions in Amplified WDM Systems. *J. Light. Technol.* **2023**, *39*, 6805–6813. [CrossRef]

4. Kuprikov, Y.; Kokhanovskiy, A.; Serebrennikov, K.; Turitsyn, S. Deep reinforcement learning for a self-tuning laser source of dissipative solitons. *Sci. Rep.* **2022**, *12*, 7185. [CrossRef] [PubMed]

5. Jiang, M.; Wu, H.; An, Y.; Hou, T.; Chang, Q.; Huang, L.; Li, J.; Su, R.; Fiber, P.Z. laser development enabled by machine learning: Review and prospect. *PhotoniX* **2022**, *3*, 16. [CrossRef]

5. Qureshi, K.K.; Qureshi, A.R.; Magam, M.G.; Jamal, L. Radio-over-fiber front-haul link design using Optisystem. *J. Opt. Commun.* **2020**, *15*, 1–6. [CrossRef]

7. Pandey, G.; Choudhary, A.; Dixit, A. Wavelength Division Multiplexed Radio over Fiber links for 5G Fronthaul Networks. *IEEE J. Sel. Areas Commun.* **2021**, *99*, 2789–2803. [CrossRef]

3. Alcin, M. The Runge Kutta-4 based 4D hyperchaotic system design for secure communication applications. *Chaos Theory Appl.* **2020**, *2*, 23–30.

9. Suárez-Vargas, J.J.; Márquez, B.A.; González, J.A. Highly complex optical signal generation using electro-optical systems with non-linear, non-invertible transmission functions. *Appl. Phys. Lett.* **2012**, *101*, 071115. [CrossRef]

). Chen, D.; Li, Q.; Bao, Q. Bidirectional communication with time-delay concealment in a system combining all-optical intensity and electrooptical phase chaos. *Opt. Commun.* **2020**, *465*, 124962. [CrossRef]

21. Zhan, M.; Wang, X.; Gong, X.; Wei, G.W.; Lai, C.-H. Complete synchronization and generalized synchronization of one-way coupled time-delay systems. *Phys. Rev. E* **2003**, *68*, 036208. [CrossRef] [PubMed]
22. Ali, A.; Naveed, H.; Qamar, F.; Shahzadi, R.; Ali, M.; Qamar, N.; Shahzadi, R. Design and analysis of secure RoF based communication in 5G fronthaul. In Proceedings of the 2020 International Conference on Cyber Warfare and Security (ICCWS), Islamabad, Pakistan, 20–21 October 2020; pp. 1–6.

electronics

MDPI

Article

A Secure Data-Sharing Model Resisting Keyword Guessing Attacks in Edge–Cloud Collaboration Scenarios

Ye Li [1], Mengen Xiong [1,*], Junling Yuan [1], Qikun Zhang [1] and Hongfei Zhu [2]

1 School of Computer Science and Technology, Zhengzhou University of Light Industry, Zhengzhou 450001, China; liye_ie@126.com (Y.L.); yuanjunling@foxmail.com (J.Y.); zhangqikun04@163.com (Q.Z.)
2 Key Laboratory of Big Data Intelligent Computing, Chongqing University of Posts and Telecommunications, Chongqing 400065, China; zhuhf@cqupt.edu.cn
* Correspondence: zzuli33112619@163.com

Abstract: In edge–cloud collaboration scenarios, data sharing is a critical technological tool, yet smart devices encounter significant challenges in ensuring data-sharing security. Attribute-based keyword search (ABKS) is employed in these contexts to facilitate fine-grained access control over shared data, allowing only users with the necessary privileges to retrieve keywords. The implementation of secure data sharing is threatened since most of the current ABKS protocols cannot resist keyword guessing attacks (KGAs), which can be launched by an untrusted cloud server and result in the exposure of sensitive personal information. Using attribute-based encryption (ABE) as the foundation, we build a secure data exchange paradigm that resists KGAs in this work. In our paper, we provide a secure data-sharing framework that resists KGAs and uses ABE as the foundation to achieve fine-grained access control to resources in the ciphertext. To avoid malicious guessing of keywords by the cloud server, the edge layer computes two encryption session keys based on group key agreement (GKA) technology, which are used to re-encrypt the data user's secret key of the keyword index and keyword trapdoor. The model is implemented using the JPBC library. According to the security analysis, the model can resist KGAs in the random oracle model. The model's performance examination demonstrates its feasibility and lightweight nature, its large computing advantages, and lower storage consumption.

Keywords: attribute-based keyword search; secure data sharing; group key agreement; keyword guessing attacks

1. Introduction

Since the edge–cloud collaboration scenario is developing so quickly, its data-sharing technology has been applied to the Industrial Internet of Things [1], intelligent transportation systems [2], and the Medical Internet of Things [3]. Additionally, resource-constrained intelligent terminals in the edge–cloud collaboration scenario can realize improved computing power elasticity, and the core data-sharing technology satisfies the entity users in the scenario to carry out high-precision, fast-response, low-latency transmission, and safe information exchange. In an edge–cloud scenario, data users can efficiently lower terminal communication costs and realize resource rationalization by outsourcing data to the cloud server. However, sensitive data are contained in the stored data [4–6], and data security is readily jeopardized. As a result, maintaining data security becomes an important and difficult responsibility [7].

Sensitive data must first be encrypted before being uploaded to the cloud to enable secure data sharing in edge–cloud scenarios. Users who meet the requirements for keyword information matching can then access the relevant ciphertext information. Unfortunately, fine-grained access control to cloud-stored data cannot be achieved by using public key encryption with keyword search. This is because when more users access cloud-stored data, the cloud generates a significant volume of private data simultaneously. Additionally, there is a greater frequency of information interaction between data users and the cloud. To access the relevant data, users must jointly negotiate a session key, which consumes a lot of computational power and results in inefficient access authorization from the users. The scheme in [8] suggests using ABE in conjunction with keyword search to address this issue. In this method, the data owner encrypts private information using an access policy, creates a secure index for the keyword, and then, outsources the work to the cloud. Only authorized data users who comply with the access policy can verify the keyword trapdoor on the cloud server. Upon successful verification, the cloud server retrieves the corresponding ciphertext and calculation parameters and sends them directly to the authorized data user for decryption. However, a semi-trusted cloud server that uses protocols with keyword-searchable encryption is vulnerable to internal and external KGAs [9,10]. In these attacks, adversaries with probabilistic polynomial-time capabilities can use the captured query message to learn more about a particular keyword and use that information to launch KGAs during a data user's search.

Thus, it is necessary to pay attention to resist KGAs to safeguard the privacy of sensitive data stored in the cloud. This paper aims to tackle the issue of privacy leakage by developing a secure data-sharing model that withstands KGAs in edge–cloud collaboration scenarios. To achieve this goal, the edge layer generates two inversely related session keys based on GKA technology. One is used to re-encrypt the data owner's secret key of the keyword index to prevent tampering during the upload to the cloud, and the other is used to re-encrypt the keyword trapdoor information to prevent its leakage to the cloud server. The data owner transmits the ciphertext and keyword index parameters to the edge layer, where the edge server managing the domain has the corresponding attribute permissions of the data owner and computes the data user's decryption key factor based on these permissions. The edge layer uses one of its session keys to re-encrypt the secret key of the keyword index, and then, sends the ciphertext and other parameters to the cloud for secure storage and data sharing. To prevent the cloud server from launching KGAs, the keyword trapdoor is re-encrypted by the edge server managing the domain after the data user computes and sends the keyword trapdoor to it. Only when the keyword trapdoor of the data user, who meets the access policy, successfully matches the keyword index stored in the cloud, does the data user have the authority to access the ciphertext resources. The cloud server searches the ciphertext and sends it along with the decryption key factor to the data user based on their ip address. The data user then uses the decryption key factor and the Lagrange interpolating polynomial to compute the decryption key and decrypt the ciphertext, thereby obtaining the corresponding resources and completing flexible and secure cross-domain data sharing. The re-encrypted keyword trapdoor can resist KGAs initiated by the cloud server in this model and prevent sensitive privacy leakage and tampering. The simplified process of the appeal is shown in Figure 1.

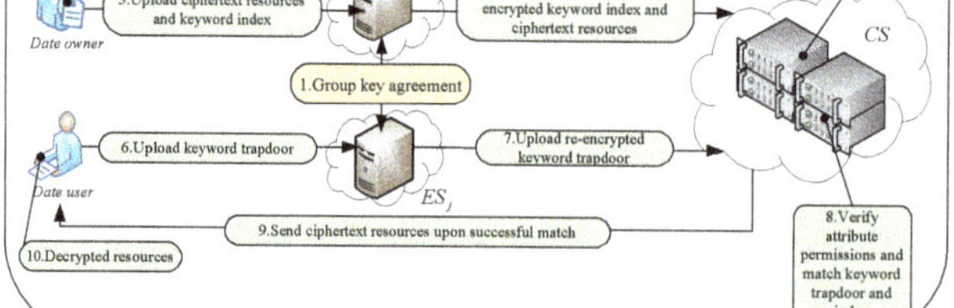

Figure 1. Simplified process for our model.

2. Related Work

Song et al. [11] were the first to propose the keyword-searchable encryption (SE) technique, which allows data users to securely search ciphertexts stored in the cloud while providing concealed keyword querying. Building on Song's scheme, Li et al. [12] introduced searchable symmetric encryption (SSE) with forward search privacy. This approach enhances security by enabling the addition of new documents without revealing any information about previous queries, proving to be more effective than previous techniques according to test data. To counteract adversaries with arbitrary background knowledge, Chen et al. [13] developed a framework for SSE systems based on differential privacy approaches, offering verifiable security guarantees. However, experimental investigations have shown that even advanced leakage suppression techniques in SSE schemes are insufficient to defend against new inference attacks. Gui et al. [14] proposed a novel inference attack capable of performing efficient, scalable, and accurate query reconstruction against end-to-end SSE systems, revealing that the existing SSE framework cannot prevent such attacks.

Public-key encryption with keyword search (PEKS) was introduced by Boneh et al. [15] to facilitate data exchange between users. In this scheme, the data provider encrypts the chosen keyword within the ciphertext before outsourcing it to the cloud for storage. The data user generates a list of keywords, searches for them on the cloud server, and utilizes a test function in the cloud to verify the presence of the keywords in each ciphertext. If a match is found, the corresponding ciphertext can be returned to the data user. With this technique, security and privacy could be readily jeopardized if the cloud server is hostile. Most current PEKS systems cannot simultaneously achieve high search efficiency and robust security. To address this challenge, Chen et al. [16] proposed a method for parallel and forward private searchable encryption with cloud data sharing. This approach ensures forward privacy and parallelism, with experimental results demonstrating its effectiveness and applicability. Through comparative analysis and experimental results, Lu et al. [17] proposed an effective PKES scheme featuring flexible keyword-free domain multi-keyword search, and forward ciphertext retrieval. This scheme effectively guards against KGAs and unauthorized ciphertext retrieval, demonstrating security in the random oracle model and outperforming existing schemes. Cheng et al. [18] introduced a server-assisted public-key authentication searchable encryption scheme with constant ciphertext and constant trapdoor sizes, combining sender and receiver servers. In this scheme, the sender only needs to encrypt the keyword once, and the constant sizes of the ciphertext and trapdoor ensure scalability, enabling multi-scenario applications.

Bethencourt, Sahai, and Waters [19] initially introduced ABE with a ciphertext policy to establish access control for cloud data. In this approach, data users determine access based on the specified access policy. Goyal [20] proposed a key-policy attribute-based encryption (KP-ABE) method, featuring a key-associative access control structure. Waters et al. [21] later introduced a ciphertext-policy attribute-based encryption (CP-ABE) approach, enabling one-to-many fine-grained sharing. Subsequently, numerous traditional ABE systems and variations were proposed [22]. To prevent dishonest searches by the data user's cloud, Zheng and Xu et al. [23] proposed VABKS (verifiable attribute-based keyword search) for outsourced encrypted data. This method can verify whether the cloud has performed honest searches. Combining ABE with SE, ABSE offers advantages over traditional PKES. However, as the cloud is not entirely trustworthy, Liu et al. [24] proposed a key-policy attribute-based searchable encryption (KP-ABSE) method to enhance practicality. This approach can successfully verify the accuracy and integrity of data files stored in the cloud. Since the cloud holds a public key for re-encrypting keyword ciphertexts, it can effectively fend off offline KGAs. Nevertheless, hostile adversaries can fabricate the cloud's public key, compromising user data privacy.

Liang and Susilo [25] employed attribute-based proxy re-encryption capabilities and ABKS to facilitate data sharing and keyword upgrading. The approach verifies that it is chosen-ciphertext-safe in the random oracle and guarantees that the ciphertexts' keyword search functionality can be maintained after ciphertext sharing. A verifiable keyword search for encrypted cloud data in smart cities was proposed by Miao [26]. This allows the data user to confirm the search results and also demonstrates the security of the scheme against targeted keyword attacks (CKAs). A verified attribute-based keyword search with fine-grained owner-enforced search authorization in the cloud was proposed by Sun et al. [27] Multiple data owners and users are supported by this method. Large-scale systems may scale more easily thanks to the user owner's enforced search authorization, and the user revocation process is more effective and resilient to targeted keyword attacks.

Cui et al. [28] proposed an attribute-based keyword search with an effective revocation scheme (AKSER). AKSER achieves fine-grained authorization of search under a distributed multi-attribute authority institution. It also ensures keyword semantic security, keyword confidentiality, trapdoor unlinkability, and collision resistance. In contrast to ciphertext-policy attribute-based encryption schemes, Wang et al. [29] introduced the first hierarchical attribute-based encryption scheme for document collections, which uses fewer ciphertext storage resources. They also developed a depth-first search algorithm for ARF trees, enhancing search efficiency, which can be further improved through parallel computing. The search algorithm only requires one keyword to be the same in two keyword sets to output the corresponding correlation, reflecting the number of identical keywords in these sets. Meng et al. [30] proposed an attribute-based encryption and dynamic keyword search method in fog computing that shifts the majority of computational overhead from resource-constrained users to fog nodes, reducing the computational load on the endpoints. Current CP-ABKS methods are designed for non-shared multi-owner configurations and are not immediately applicable to shared multi-owner configurations.

To improve monitoring of hostile users for selective security and resistance to offline keyword guessing attacks, Miao et al. [31] presented privacy-preserving attribute-based keyword searches in shared owner settings. Most earlier techniques are vulnerable to offline KGAs when the keyword space is polynomial. To address these issues, Zhang et al. [32] proposed an attribute-based encryption scheme with searchable and verifiable multiple keywords based on cloud data. Their experimental results demonstrate the scheme's effectiveness, achieving selective security against offline keyword guessing attacks and ensuring the unforgeability of signatures.

Li et al. [33] proposed an attribute-based keyword search strategy that prevents keyword guessing attacks by signing the keyword with the data owner's private key before generating the keyword ciphertext. To combat data tampering, Zhang et al. [34] introduced a blockchain-based anonymous attribute searchable encryption scheme for data sharing. This scheme leverages blockchain technology to conceal the attributes of the access policy while ensuring tamper resistance, integrity verification, and non-repudiation. Experimental results demonstrate the scheme's practicality and efficiency. Ge et al. [35] proposed an attribute-based proxy re-encryption scheme with a direct revocation mechanism for data sharing in the cloud. This mechanism allows the cloud server to directly revoke users in the original shared set involved in the re-encryption key. Additionally, Ge et al. [36] proposed a secure keyword search and data-sharing mechanism for cloud computing, addressing the need for users to quickly search and return results without compromising data confidentiality. This mechanism supports attribute-based keyword search and attribute-based data sharing simultaneously, and it has been shown to be secure against chosen-ciphertext attacks in random oracle models and CKAs.

Upon perusing the above references, it is evident that researchers have made significant contributions to the attainment of secure data sharing. However, there exist certain limitations. Specifically, the majority of schemes are susceptible to KGAs, and in the event of a probabilistic polynomial-time adversary of a semi-trusted cloud server, they can obtain specific keyword information through the captured query information, thereby compromising privacy. In the edge–cloud collaboration scenario, we propose a secure data-sharing model based on an anti-keyword guessing attack to counter the appeal attack. The model is lightweight and highly appropriate for resource-constrained smart terminals, as it achieves resistance to keyword guessing attacks through key negotiation at the edge layer, and safe in terms of privacy for end users. Comparative investigations indicate that this model performs better than existing schemes.

Methodology

We propose a secure data-sharing model that resists keyword guessing attacks in edge–cloud collaboration scenarios (SDSM-KGA). The methodology of this paper is as follows, and the problems addressed are illustrated in Figure 2.

(1) This paper extends the traditional attribute-based keyword search (ABKS) model by proposing a new flexible, fine-grained access control mechanism. This mechanism allows data users with identical attribute permissions to perform fine-grained searches on ciphertext based on specific access policies, enabling flexible and secure data sharing. If a data user's attribute permissions do not meet the requirements of the access policy, they are not able to access the shared ciphertext. This access control strategy enhances the efficiency and security of data sharing among users.

(2) The ABKS model we propose supports cross-domain data sharing and can effectively resist KGAs initiated by cloud servers. In traditional models, keyword trapdoor information is public in the cloud, and is therefore vulnerable to attacks by external attackers or malicious cloud servers. To prevent such attacks, we implement a key negotiation method at the edge layer. This allows the edge layer to re-encrypt the keys of the data owner's keyword index and keyword trapdoor key stored in the cloud to prevent other entities from identifying them.

(3) We define a new security model and prove its ability to resist KGAs under the random oracle model, and implement our scheme using the JPBC library. The experimental evaluation proves the practicality and high performance of the scheme compared with other traditional schemes.

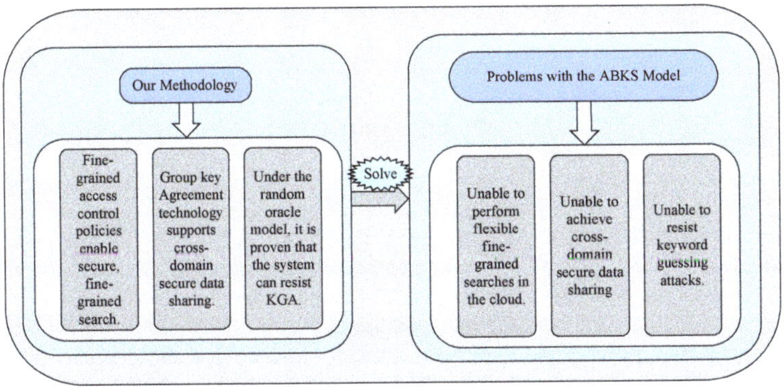

Figure 2. Problems solved by the methodology.

3. Basic Knowledge

3.1. Bilinear Map

Let $\mathbb{G}_1$ be an additive group and g be a $\mathbb{G}_1$ generator. $\mathbb{G}_T$ represents a multiplicative cyclic group. $\mathbb{G}_1$ and $\mathbb{G}_T$ have the same prime order q. We can say $e : \mathbb{G}_1 \times \mathbb{G}_1 \rightarrow \mathbb{G}_T$ is a bilinear pairing if it meets the following properties:

(1) Bilinearity: For all $\forall a, b \in \mathbb{Z}_q^*$ and $g_1, g_2 \in \mathbb{G}_1$, we have $e(ag_1, bg_2) = e(g_1, g_2)^{ab}$.

(2) Non-degenerate: $\exists g_1 \in \mathbb{G}_1, e(g_1, g_1) \neq 1$.

(3) Computability: $\forall g_1, g_2 \in \mathbb{G}_1$; there exist efficient algorithms in polynomial time that can compute the $e(g_1, g_2)$.

3.2. Access Structure

Let $P = \{P_1, P_2, \ldots, P_n\}$ denote the set of participants, and let $2^P = \{A | A \subseteq P = \{P_1, P_2, \ldots, P_n\}\}$. For $\forall B, C \subseteq P$, if $B \subseteq \mathbb{A}$ and $B \subseteq C$, then $C \subseteq \mathbb{A}$. If $\mathbb{A}$ is a non-empty subset of $P = \{P_1, P_2, \ldots, P_n\}$, then $\mathbb{A}$ is called an access structure. For any set D, if $D \subseteq \mathbb{A}$, then D is an authorized set; otherwise, it is an unauthorized set.

3.3. Linear Secret-Sharing Scheme

The set of participants is $P = \{P_1, P_2, \ldots, P_n\}$, where the access structure is $\mathbb{A} =< M, F >$. Here, M is a matrix with n rows and m columns. For all $\forall 1 \leq i \leq n$, F_i is a mapping function that maps each row of the matrix to different attributes. If Π satisfies the following conditions, then Π is a linear secret-sharing scheme (LSSS) defined over P.

(1) Given a secret value $s \in \mathbb{Z}_q^*$, randomly select $l_2, l_3, \ldots, l_n \in \mathbb{Z}_q^*$; construct the column vector $\vec{v} = (s, l_2, l_3, \ldots, l_n)^T$. Then, compute $h_i = (M\vec{v})_i$, where h_i represents the secret share held by F_i.
(2) There exists a set of vectors $\{\omega_i \in \mathbb{Z}_q^*\}_{i \in I}$ such that $\sum_{i \in I} \omega_i M_i = (1, 0, \ldots, 0)$. The secret value s can be reconstructed as $s = \sum_{i \in I} \omega_i M_i \cdot \vec{v} = \sum_{i \in I} \omega_i h_i$, where $\{h_i\}(1 \leq i \leq r)$ are valid secret shares of the secret value.

This scheme is based on the algorithm idea of scheme [37], using the elements in the access matrix to encrypt the information, and decrypting according to $\sum_{i \in I} \omega_i M_i = (1, 0, \ldots, 0)^T$, which can ensure that $\prod_{j=1}^{n} \sum_{i \in I} M_{i,j} \omega_i = 1$.

3.4. Decisional Bilinear Diffie–Hellman Assumption

Considering the bilinear mapping elements $\mathbb{G}_1, \mathbb{G}_T, g, e, q$ and random elements $a, b, c \in \mathbb{Z}_q^*$, we see that adversary $\mathcal{B}$ is unable to discriminate between the tuples (ag, bg, cg, Z) and $(ag, bg, cg, abcg)$, where Z is chosen at random from $\mathbb{G}_1$. Consequently, there is no probabilistic polynomial time (PPT). The advantage ε of $\mathcal{B}$ in resolving the DBDH problem is described as follows, assuming the following equations hold.

$$|\Pr[\mathcal{B}((ag, bg, cg, abcg)) = 1]| - |\Pr[\mathcal{B}((ag, bg, cg, Z)) = 1]| < \varepsilon. \quad (1)$$

3.5. Security Model

Init: The simulator $\mathcal{B}$ ensures that the keyword index secret key s_0 remains secret. The value $s_0 g$ is sent by $\mathcal{B}$ to the attacker $\mathcal{A}$. Attacker $\mathcal{A}$ challenges the access structure $\mathbb{A}$ and randomly selects attributes to form a set $\{att_1^*, att_2^*, \ldots, att_r^*\}$, which is then sent to the simulator $\mathcal{B}$. The simulator $\mathcal{B}$ computes the corresponding attribute permissions $\{\rho_1^*, \rho_2^*, \ldots, \rho_r^*\}$ and sends them to $\mathcal{A}$. The attacker $\mathcal{A}$ subsequently computes the attribute permission key $s_1^* = \sum_{i=1}^{r} H_2(\rho_i^*) \bmod q$ for the challenge.

Phase 1: $\mathcal{A}$ executes a polynomially limited number of queries in an adaptive manner, which means that each query may depend on the response to previous queries.

(1) Attribute permissions secret-key extraction query: $\mathcal{A}$ chooses an attribute permissions secret key $s_{1,i}^*$, then sends $s_{1,i}^*$ to simulator $\mathcal{B}$ to verify whether the private key is legal or not; the verification succeeds in computing the key E_i, then runs the re-encryption attribute permissions private key to obtain $E_i^{`}$, and then, returns $E_i^{`}$ to $\mathcal{A}$.
(2) Keyword trapdoor extraction query: $\mathcal{A}$ randomly selects a keyword kw_i from the keyword dictionary, then $\mathcal{A}$ sends kw_i to $\mathcal{B}$; simulator $\mathcal{B}$ calculates the keyword trapdoor Y_i of the searchable keyword kw_i, then runs to re-encrypt the trapdoor $Y_i^{'}$ and returns $Y_i^{'}$ to $\mathcal{A}$.

Challenge: $\mathcal{A}$ decides when the first stage will end. $\mathcal{A}$ generates two keywords kw_1 and kw_0 of the same length that it wants to be challenged. The simulator $\mathcal{B}$ randomly selects bits $coin \in \{0, 1\}$, computes the trapdoor for keyword kw_* as Y_i^*, and then, runs the re-encryption trapdoor to obtain $Y_i^{*`} =< \beta, Y_i^* >$. $\mathcal{B}$ re-encrypts the attribute permissions private key $E_i^*$ to obtain $E_i^{*`} =< \alpha, E_i^* >$, and sends $(Y_i^{*`}, E_i^{*`})$ as the challenged parameters to $\mathcal{A}$. If the encryption of the trapdoor for the target keyword kw_* fails, then $\mathcal{A}$ aborts the game.

Phase 2: $\mathcal{A}$ can make a polynomially bounded number of adaptive queries as in phase 1, except that it cannot make private-key extraction queries and trapdoor extraction queries for s_1^* and kw_1, kw_0.

$\mathcal{A}$ outputs the result $coin'$, if $coin' = coin$ will win the game. We define the advantage of $\mathcal{A}$ in attacking the scheme as $Adv_{\mathcal{A}}^{IND-KGA} = \left|\Pr[coin' = coin] - 1/2\right|$.

4. System Model and Initialization

In this paper, we propose a secure data-sharing model to resist keyword guessing attacks in the edge–cloud collaboration scenario. The system model is shown in Figure 3, which mainly has certification authority, cloud layer, edge layer, and data user layer.

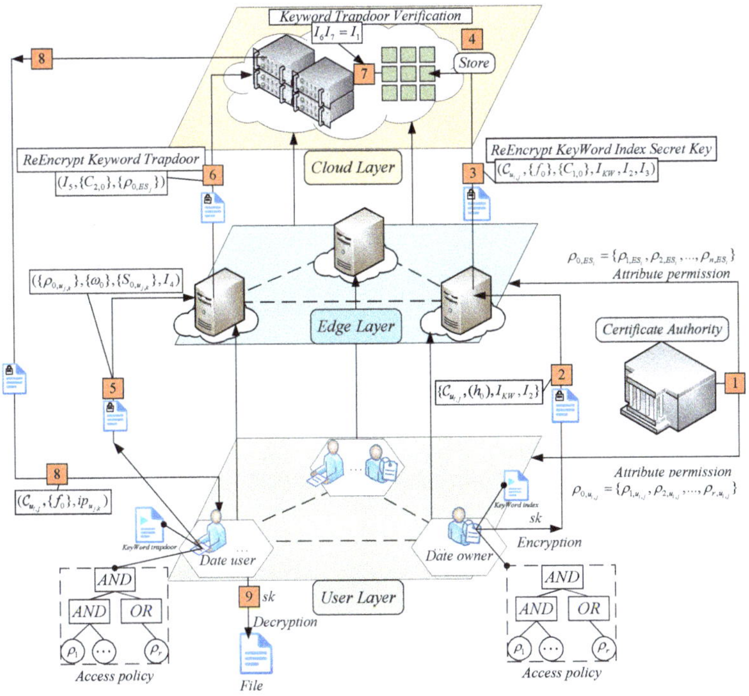

Figure 3. System model.

4.1. System Model

CA Authentication Center: The center is responsible for implementing system parameter settings, generating the system's master and public keys, registering user attributes, determining attribute permissions, and distributing attributes to data users and edge servers.

Cloud service layer: Comprised of a cloud server, the primary purpose of this layer is to store and validate the private key and re-encrypted keyword trapdoor data sent by the edge layer. Upon successful verification, ciphertext resources are sent to data users who comply with the access policy. This layer also offers higher storage capacity, high scalability, and flexibility, while handling complex calculations and tasks from the edge layer and providing a secure channel for data sharing.

Edge layer: The edge layer primarily handles the negotiation of session keys, one is used to re-encrypt the data owner's secret key of the keyword index to prevent tampering during the upload to the cloud, and the other is used to re-encrypt the keyword trapdoor information to prevent its leakage to the cloud server. This layer facilitates collaborative computation, enhances data resource-sharing security, and reduces processing times. By decreasing latency and improving security, it ensures efficient collaborative computation.

User layer: This layer consists of mobile data users and data owners. The data owner is the one who uploads the shared resources. For a data user to access the decrypted key factor and ciphertext resources, their attribute permission set must match the access policy. Additionally, only when the keyword index and trapdoor are successfully verified by the cloud server will ciphertext resources be accessible.

4.2. System Initialization

The CA authentication center generates a bilinear mapping $e : \mathbb{G}_1 \times \mathbb{G}_1 \rightarrow \mathbb{G}_T$, where $\mathbb{G}_1$ is an addition group, $\mathbb{G}_T$ is a multiplicative cyclic group, the prime order is q, and g is a generating element of $\mathbb{G}_1$. Then, it selects a random number $sk_{CA} \in \mathbb{Z}_q^*$, and computes $pk_{CA} = sk_{CA}g$, where (pK_{CA}, sk_{CA}) is the CA's public/private key pair, and the CA selects a hash function $H_1 : \{0,1\}^* \rightarrow \mathbb{Z}_q^*, H_2 : \mathbb{G}_1 \rightarrow \mathbb{Z}_q^*, H_3 : \mathbb{Z}_q^* \rightarrow \mathbb{G}_1$, and the CA sets the system's public parameters $\{g, q, \mathbb{G}_1, \mathbb{G}_T, e, H_1, H_2, H_3, PK_{CA}\}$.

4.3. System Entity Key Generation

Assume there are N edge servers $ES_i (1 \leq i \leq N)$, each edge server manages ES_i the corresponding domain and the number of data users in each domain is at most n. For example, data user $u_{i,j}$ is the j-th user in the i-th domain, and the identity set of data users in the i-th domain is $ID_i = \{id_{u_{i,1}}, id_{u_{i,2}}, id_{u_{i,j}}, \ldots, id_{u_{i,n}}\}$. Using data user $u_{i,j}$ who is controlled by edge server ES_i as an example, the CA broadcasts system parameters $\{g, q, \mathbb{G}_1, \mathbb{G}_T, e, H_1, H_2, H_3, pk_{CA}\}$ in the following ways:

1. The data user $u_{i,j}$, whose identity is $id_{u_{i,j}}$, receives the system parameters $\{g, q, \mathbb{G}_1, \mathbb{G}_T, e, H_1, H_2, H_3, pk_{CA}\}$ that the CA broadcasts, $u_{i,j}$ chooses a positive number $sk_{u_{i,j}} \in \mathbb{Z}_q^*$ at random, $u_{i,j}$ computes public key $pk_{u_{i,j}} = sk_{u_{i,j}}g$ and $\eta_0 = H_1(id_{u_{i,j}}||pk_{u_{i,j}})pk_{CA}$. After that, the CA receives argument $\{u_{i,j}, id_{u_{i,j}}, \eta_0, pk_{u_{i,j}}\}$.
2. After receiving the parameter $\{u_{i,j}, id_{u_{i,j}}, \eta_0, pk_{u_{i,j}}\}$, the CA checks whether the public key $pk_{u_{i,j}}$ and the user's identity $id_{u_{i,j}}$ correspond using equation $e(pk_{u_{i,j}}, \eta_0) = e(sk_{CA}pk_{u_{i,j}}, H_1(id_{u_{i,j}}||pk_{u_{i,j}})g)$ to verify its legitimacy. If valid, the CA publishes the valid public key $pk_{u_{i,j}}$ of $u_{i,j}$. The procedure mentioned above provides the identified public-key information to the data user $u_{i,j}$, enabling them to create their own public/private key pair $(pk_{u_{i,j}}/sk_{u_{i,j}})$.

The process of creating the public/private key pair for the cloud server (CS) and the edge server $ES_i (1 \leq i \leq N)$ is the same. The entity's CS generated the public/private key pair (pk_{CS}, sk_{CS}) through the above process. The ES_i of the i management domain generated the public/private key pair (pk_{ES_i}, sk_{ES_i}).

4.4. Acquisition of Data User Attribute Permissions

For network resource access, the CA authentication center defines the system attribute set $SA_{set} = \{Att_1, Att_2, \ldots, Att_n\}$. The attribute serial number corresponding to each attribute is $\{S_1, S_2, \ldots, S_n\}$. It also generates the corresponding attribute parameter $b_i \in \mathbb{Z}_q^* (1 \leq i \leq n)$ for each attribute to form the attribute parameter set $Att_{set} = \{b_1, b_2, \ldots, b_n\}$, and the terminal members receive the attribute set that is available for authentication. Assuming that the attribute set of $u_{i,j} (1 \leq i \leq N, 1 \leq j \leq n)$ is expressed as $\{att_{1,u_{i,j}}, att_{2,u_{i,j}}, \ldots, att_{r,u_{i,j}}\} \subseteq SA_{set} (1 \leq r \leq n)$, where $att_{r,u_{i,j}} \subseteq SA_{set} (1 \leq r \leq n)$, attribute registration for arbitrary terminals and acquisition of attribute privileges are as follows:

1. $u_{i,j}$ When carrying out the process of attribute authentication, the terminal $u_{i,j}$ obtains the set SA of authentication attributes announced by the CA, randomly chooses $\gamma_{1,u_{i,j}} \in \mathbb{Z}_q^*$, computes $o_{1,u_{i,j}} = \gamma_{1,u_{i,j}}g$, $\vartheta_{1,u_{i,j}} = H_1(att_{1,u_{i,j}})pk_{CA}$, $\vartheta_{2,u_{i,j}} = H_1(att_{2,u_{i,j}})pk_{CA}, \ldots, \vartheta_{r,u_{i,j}} = H_1(att_{r,u_{i,j}})pk_{CA} (1 \leq r \leq n)$, $\eta_{1,u_{i,j}}$ as the signature message, $\eta_{1,u_{i,j}} =$

$sk_{u_{i,j}}^{-1}\gamma_{1,u_{i,j}}H_1(att_{1,u_{i,j}}||att_{2,u_{i,j}}||\ldots||att_{r,u_{i,j}}||pk_{u_{i,j}})g$, where $\vartheta_{0,u_{i,j}} = \{\vartheta_{1,u_{i,j}}, \vartheta_{2,u_{i,j}}, \ldots, \vartheta_{r,u_{i,j}}\}$, and then, sends the parameters $\{o_{1,u_{i,j}}, \{\vartheta_{0,u_{i,j}}\}, \eta_{1,u_{i,j}}, pk_{u_{i,j}}\}$ to the CA.

2. After receiving the parameters $\{o_{1,u_{i,j}}, \{\vartheta_{0,u_{i,j}}\}, \eta_{1,u_{i,j}}, pk_{u_{i,j}}\}$ from $u_{i,j}$, the CA computes $l_1 = sk_{CA}^{-1}\vartheta_{1,u_{i,j}}, l_2 = sk_{CA}^{-1}\vartheta_{2,u_{i,j}}, \ldots, l_r = sk_{CA}^{-1}\vartheta_{r,u_{i,j}}(1 \leq r \leq n)$ and $L_1 = H_1(Att_1)g$, $L_2 = H_1(Att_2)g, \ldots, L_r = H_1(Att_r)g$ by comparing the sets $l_0 = \{l_1, l_2, \ldots l_r\}$ and $L_0 = \{L_1, L_2, \ldots, L_r\}$ to see if they are equal; the CA can determine the set of attributes and the corresponding attribute sequence numbers of the attributes $S_0 = \{S_1, S_2, \ldots, S_r\}$. The CA computes $\eta_2 = H_1(Att_1||Att_2\ldots||Att_r||pk_{u_{i,j}})g$, verifies the signature of $u_{i,j}$ by Equation $e(\eta_{1,u_{i,j}}, pk_{u_{i,j}}) = e(\eta_2, o_{1,u_{i,j}})$, and determines whether the equation is valid. The CA can determine $\{att_1^{u_{i,j}}, att_2^{u_{i,j}}, \ldots, att_r^{u_{i,j}}\}$ the set of attributes $u_{i,j}$ has, and the CA selects the corresponding attribute parameters according to the corresponding attributes to compute for $u_{i,j}$ the set of attribute authority factors for the set $\chi_{1,u_{i,j}} = b_1H_2(att_{1,u_{i,j}})pk_{u_{i,j}}, \chi_{2,u_{i,j}} = b_1H_2(att_{2,u_{i,j}})pk_{u_{i,j}}\cdots\chi_{r,u_{i,j}} = b_rH_2(att_{r,u_{i,j}})pk_{u_{i,j}}$, $\chi_{0,u_{i,j}} = \{\chi_{1,u_{i,j}}, \chi_{2,u_{i,j}}, \ldots, \chi_{r,u_{i,j}}\}$. The CA chooses $\gamma_2 \in \mathbb{Z}_q^*$ randomly, computes $o_2 = \gamma_2 g$, $\eta_{3,u_{i,j}} = \gamma_2 sk_{CA}^{-1}H_2(\chi_{1,u_{i,j}}||\chi_{2,u_{i,j}}||\ldots||\chi_{r,u_{i,j}}||pk_{CA})g$, and then, sends the parameters $(\{\chi_{0,u_{i,j}}\}, \eta_{3,u_{i,j}}, o_2, pk_{CA})$ to $u_{i,j}$.

3. $u_{i,j}$ receives the public parameters $(\{\chi_{0,u_{i,j}}\}, \eta_{3,u_{i,j}}, o_2, pk_{CA})$ sent by the CA, computes $\eta_{4,u_{i,j}} = H_2(\chi_{1,u_{i,j}}||\chi_{2,u_{i,j}}||\ldots||\chi_{r,u_{i,j}}||pk_{CA})g$, verifies if the CA's signature is valid through equation $e(\eta_{3,u_{i,j}}, pk_{CA}) = e(o_2, \eta_{4,u_{i,j}})$, accepts the parameters if valid, and then, calculates the attribute permissions through the attribute factor $\rho_{1,u_{i,j}} = sk_{u_{i,j}}^{-1}\chi_{1,u_{i,j}}$, $\rho_{2,u_{i,j}} = sk_{u_{i,j}}^{-1}\chi_{2,u_{i,j}}, \ldots, \rho_{r,u_{i,j}} = sk_{u_{i,j}}^{-1}\chi_{r,u_{i,j}}$. Thus, the set of attribute permissions is $\rho_{0,u_{i,j}} = \{\rho_{1,u_{i,j}}, \rho_{2,u_{i,j}}, \ldots, \rho_{r,u_{i,j}}\}$, where $\rho_{i,u_{i,j}} = b_iH_1(att_{i,u_{i,j}})g(1 \leq i \leq r)$. The attribute permissions set $\{\rho_{1,u_{i,j}}, \rho_{2,u_{i,j}}, \ldots, \rho_{r,u_{i,j}}\}$ corresponds to the attribute set $\{att_{1,u_{i,j}}, att_{2,u_{i,j}}, \ldots, att_{r,u_{i,j}}\}$.

The edge server $ES_i(1 \leq i \leq n)$ is specialized and is considered to have all the attributes of the system attribute set $SA_{set} = \{Att_1, Att_2, \ldots, Att_n\}$ as well as the attribute sequence numbers $\{S_1, S_2, \ldots, S_n\}$ corresponding to the attributes, and all the attribute permission sets $\rho_{0,ES_i} = \{\rho_{1,ES_i}, \rho_{2,ES_i}, \ldots, \rho_{r,ES_i}\}$ are obtained according to the above process, where $\rho_{i,ES_i} = b_iH_1(Att_i)g(1 \leq i \leq r)$. The CA carries out the division of the management domain according to the $u_{i,j}$ address of $u_{i,j}$ and the ip_{ES_i} of the edge server $ES_i(1 \leq i \leq N)$.

4.5. Edge Server Session Key Establishment

Each edge server in the system manages different domains. In order to enable secure cross-domain data access, the edge servers use a ring data structure. This structure facilitates the negotiation of the session private key α and the calculation of the inverse session private key β by the edge server based on GKA technology. Each edge server is connected to its neighboring edge servers, and authentication is performed through signing and calculating the session key factor. The specific steps are as follows:

1. Using the edge server ES_1 as an example, ES_1 computes the session factor about the key to the neighboring edge server ES_2. ES_1 randomly selects $\gamma_{3,ES_1} \in \mathbb{Z}_q^*$, and computes parameters $ssk_1 = sk_{ES_1}$, $T_{1,ES_1} = \gamma_{3,ES_1}g$, ssk_1g, and the signature $\theta_{1,ES_1} = \gamma_{3,ES_1}H_3(T_{1,ES_1}||\rho_{1,ES_1}||\rho_{2,ES_1}||\ldots||\rho_{r,ES_1}||pk_{ES_1}||ip_{ES_1}||ssk_1g)sk_{ES_1}^{-1}g$. The parameter set $(\theta_{1,ES_1}, T_{1,ES_1}, pk_{ES_1}, ip_{ES_1}, ssk_1g)$ is sent to the edge server ES_2.
2. Edge server ES_2 receives the parameters $(\theta_{1,ES_1}, T_{1,ES_1}, pk_{ES_1}, ip_{ES_1}, ssk_1g)$, ES_2 computes $\xi_{1,ES_2} = H_3(T_{1,ES_1}||\rho_{1,ES_2}||\rho_{2,ES_2}||\ldots||\rho_{r,ES_2}||pk_{ES_1}||ip_{ES_1}||ssk_1g)g$ and verifies the signature through equation $e(\theta_{1,ES_1}, pk_{ES_1}) = e(\xi_{1,ES_2}, T_{1,ES_1})$, if the equation holds ES_2 computes the session key factor ssk_2ssk_1g, in which $ssk_2 = sk_{ES_2}$. ES_2 randomly selects $\gamma_{4,ES_1} \in \mathbb{Z}_q^*$ and computes $\theta_{2,ES_2} = \gamma_{4,ES_1}H_3(T_{2,ES_2}||\rho_{1,ES_2}||\rho_{2,ES_2}||\ldots||\rho_{r,ES_2}||pk_{ES_2}||ip_{ES_2}||ssk_2ssk_1g)sk_{ES_2}^{-1}g$.

3. Following the steps of the appeal, ES_n sends message $(\theta_{n,ES_n}, T_{n,ES_n}, pk_{ES_n}, ip_{ES_n}, ssk_n \ldots ssk_2 ssk_1 g)$ to ES_1. Then, ES_1 computes $\xi_{n,ES_1} = H_3(T_{n,ES_n}||\rho_{1,ES_1}||\rho_{2,ES_1}||\cdots||\rho_{r,ES_1}||pk_{ES_n}||ip_{ES_n}||ssk_n \ldots ssk_2 ssk_1 g)g$, where $ssk_0 = ssk_n \ldots ssk_2 ssk_1 g$, ES_1 verifies the signature by equation $e(\theta_{n,ES_n}, pk_{ES_n}) = e(\xi_{n,ES_1}, T_{n,ES_n})$, and if the equation holds ES_1 computes $\alpha = H_2(H_2(ssk_0)g)$ as the session key for the system edge servers layer, then ES_1 sends the parameters $\{(H_2(ssk_0)pk_{ES_2}, ip_{ES_2}), (H_2(ssk_0)pk_{ES_3}, ip_{ES_3}), \ldots (H_2(ssk_0)pk_{ES_n}, ip_{ES_n})\}$ to the corresponding edge servers based on the ip address. When the edge servers $ES_i (2 \leq i \leq n)$ have all accepted the parameter to compute $\alpha = H_2(sk_{ES_i}^{-1} H_2(ssk_0)pk_{ES_i}) = H_2(H_2(ssk_0)g)$, there exists $\alpha\beta = 1 \bmod q$.

5. The Construction of Our Model

Taking the data owner $u_{i,j}$ in the management domain of the edge server ES_i as an example, the related algorithm interaction process is depicted in Figure 4.

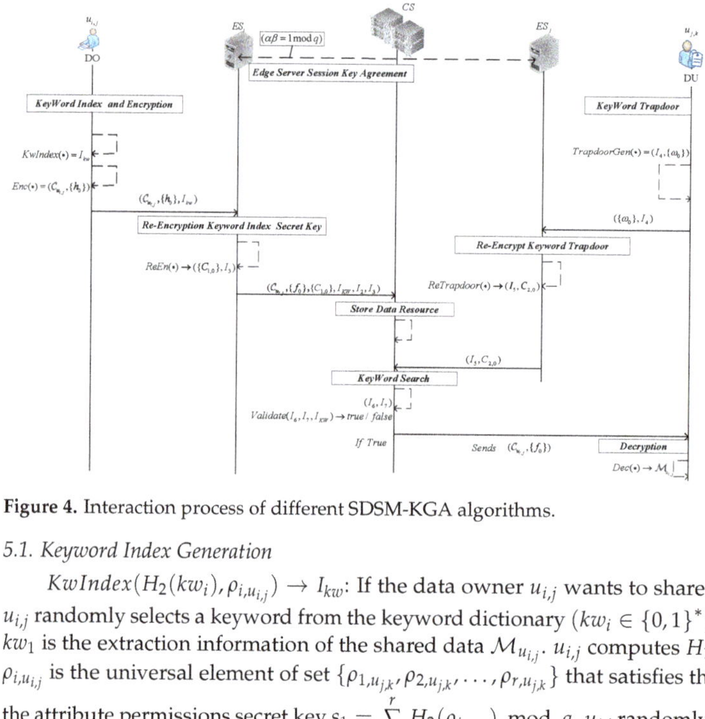

Figure 4. Interaction process of different SDSM-KGA algorithms.

5.1. Keyword Index Generation

$KwIndex(H_2(kw_i), \rho_{i,u_{i,j}}) \to I_{kw}$: If the data owner $u_{i,j}$ wants to share the data $\mathcal{M}_{u_{i,j}}$, $u_{i,j}$ randomly selects a keyword from the keyword dictionary $(kw_i \in \{0,1\}^*)$. The keyword kw_1 is the extraction information of the shared data $\mathcal{M}_{u_{i,j}}$. $u_{i,j}$ computes $H_1(kw_1)g$, where $\rho_{i,u_{i,j}}$ is the universal element of set $\{\rho_{1,u_{j,k}}, \rho_{2,u_{j,k}}, \ldots, \rho_{r,u_{j,k}}\}$ that satisfies the access policy, the attribute permissions secret key $s_1 = \sum_{i=1}^{r} H_2(\rho_{i,u_{i,j}}) \bmod q$. $u_{i,j}$ randomly selects $s_0, z_1 \in \mathbb{Z}_q^*$ and computes the signature parameters $\psi_1 = z_1 g$, $\psi_2 = pk_{ES_i} z_1$. The keyword index of $u_{i,j}$ is $I_{KW} = e(H_2(kw_1)g, H_3(s_1)s_0)e(g, s_0 g)$, with s_0 as the secret key of the keyword index.

5.2. Data Owner Encryption

$Enc(\mathcal{M}_{u_{i,j}}, H_2(z_1 g), F(.)) \to (C_{u_{i,j}}, \{h_0\})$: Data owner $u_{i,j}$ computes $I_2 = s_0 g$. According to Section 3.3, $u_{i,j}$ randomly selects $l_i \in \mathbb{Z}_q^* (2 \leq i \leq r)$ to combine into secret vectors $\vec{v} = [s_0, l_2, l_3, \ldots l_n]^T$. $u_{i,j}$ to encrypt the plaintext message $\mathcal{M}_{u_{i,j}}$, to obtain the ciphertext $C_{u_{i,j}} = e(g, H_2(z_1 g)g)\mathcal{M}_{u_{i,j}}$. $u_{i,j}$ computes the share of the randomized secret value from this matrix $h_i = M_i \vec{v} = M_i [s_0, l_2, l_3, \ldots l_n]^T (1 \leq i \leq r)$, the secret key of the keyword index share parameter and the signature information $h_0 = \{h_1 g, h_2 g, \ldots h_r g\}$ and $\sigma_{1,u_{i,j}} = z_1 H_1(C_{u_{i,j}}||S_0||\psi_2||pk_{u_{i,j}}||h_1 g||h_2 g||\ldots||h_r g||I_{KW}||I_2)pk_{ES_i}$. The attribute sequence number is $S_{0,u_{i,j}} = \{S_1, S_2, \ldots, S_r\}$, whose parameters $(\sigma_{1,u_{i,j}}, C_{u_{i,j}}, \{h_0\}, \psi_2, I_{KW}, I_2, pk_{u_{i,j}}, S_{0,u_{i,j}})$ will be sent over a secure channel to the edge server that manages the domain ES_i.

5.3. Edge Server ES_i Re-Encrypts Secret Key of Keyword Index

$ReEnc(\alpha, \{h_0\}, I_2) \rightarrow (\{C_{1,0}\}, I_3)$: When the edge server ES_i receives the parameters $(\sigma_{1,u_{i,j}}, C_{u_{i,j}}, \{h_0\}, \psi_2, I_{KW}, I_2, pk_{u_{i,j}}, S_{0,u_{i,j}})$, it computes $\phi_{1,ES_i} = H_1(C_{u_{i,j}}||S_{0,u_{i,j}}||\psi_2||pk_{u_{i,j}}||h_1 g|| h_2 g|| \ldots h_r g||I_{KW}||I_2)g$, determines whether the equation is valid by $e(\sigma_{1,u_{i,j}}, sk_{u_{i,j}}^{-1} g) = e(\phi_{1,ES_i}, \psi_2)$, and accepts the parameters if it is valid, and computes $\psi_3 = sk_{ES_i}^{-1}\psi_2$, $d_0 = H_2(\psi_3)$. ES_i obtains the corresponding attribute permissions based on the set of permission numbers $S_{0,u_{i,j}}$ sent by $u_{i,j}$ to access the ciphertext, constructs a polynomial $P_1(x) = d_{r-1}x^{r-1} + d_{r-2}x^{r-2} + \ldots + d_1 x + d_0$ of degree $r-1$, and then, substitutes the attribute values $\{H_2(\rho_{1,ES_i}) \bmod q, H_2(\rho_{1,ES_i}) \bmod q, \ldots, H_2(\rho_{1,ES_i}) \bmod q\}$ into the polynomial $P_1(x)$. Respectively, ES_i obtains the r function value $f_0 = \{f_1, f_2, \ldots, f_r\}$, the encryption factor of the key reconstruction. ES_i re-encrypts the secret key of keyword index $I_3 = \alpha I_2$ and re-encrypts the secret key of keyword index share $C_{1,0} = \{C_{1,1} = \alpha h_1 g, C_{1,2} = \alpha h_2 g, \ldots C_{1,r} = \alpha h_r g\}$. Then, ES_i randomly selects $z_2 \in \mathbb{Z}_q^*$ and computes $\psi_4 = z_2 g$ and $\sigma_{2,ES_i} = z_2 H_2(f_1||f_2|| \ldots ||f_r||I_{KW}|| I_2||I_3||pk_{ES_i}||\psi_4)pk_{CS}$. Then, ES_i sends the parameters $(C_{u_{i,j}}, \sigma_{2,ES_i}, \psi_4, \{f_0\}, I_{KW}, I_2, I_3, \{C_{1,0}\}, pk_{ES_i})$ to the cloud server for storage.

5.4. Cloud Server Ciphertext Resource Store

The cloud server receives the parameters $(C_{u_{i,j}}, \sigma_{2,ES_i}, \psi_4, \{f_0\}, \{C_{1,0}\}, I_{KW}, I_2, I_3, pk_{ES_i})$, CS computes $\phi_{2,CS} = H_3(f_1||f_2|| \ldots ||f_r||I_{KW}||I_2||I_3||pk_{ES_i}||\psi_4)g$ and verifies the equation $e(\sigma_{2,ES_i}, sk_{CS}^{-1} g) = e(\phi_{2,CS}, \psi_4)$. If the equation holds, CS stores the ciphertext and keyword index.

5.5. Data User's Trapdoor Generation

$TrapdoorGen(\Pi, \{\rho_{0,u_{j,k}}\}, s_1) \rightarrow I_4$: Taking the data user demander $u_{j,k}$ in the management domain of ES_j as an example, assume that $u_{j,k}$ has the attribute permission of $\rho_{0,u_{j,k}} = \{\rho_{1,u_{j,k}}, \rho_{2,u_{j,k}}, \ldots, \rho_{r,u_{j,k}}\}$ and the corresponding attribute sequence of $S_{0,u_{j,k}} = \{S_1, S_2, \ldots, S_r\}$. According to the corresponding access policy to obtain the matrix M, according to Section 3.3, we can obtain $\sum_{i=1}^{r} \omega_i M_i = [1,0,0,\ldots,0]^T$; $u_{j,k}$ obtains $\{\omega_1, \omega_2, \ldots, \omega_r\}$. $u_{j,k}$ computes $\omega_0 = (\omega_1 g, \omega_2 g, \ldots, \omega_r g)$ and attribute permissions secret $s_1 = \sum_{i=1}^{r} H_2(\rho_{i,u_{j,k}})$, mod q, where $\rho_{i,u_{j,k}}$ is the universal element of set $\{\rho_{1,u_{j,k}}, \rho_{2,u_{j,k}}, \ldots, \rho_{r,u_{j,k}}\}$ that satisfies the access policy. $u_{j,k}$ randomly selects $z_3, z_4 \in \mathbb{Z}_q^*$ and computes $\psi_5 = z_3 g$. Then, $u_{j,k}$ selects the keyword from the keyword dictionary and computes the parameter of the keyword trapdoor $I_4 = H_3(s_1)H_1(kw_{i,u_{j,k}})$. The signature information is $\sigma_{3,u_{j,k}} = z_3 pk_{ES_j} H_3(\rho_{1,u_{j,k}}||\rho_{2,u_{j,k}}|| \ldots ||\rho_{r,u_{j,k}}||\omega_1 g||\omega_2 g|| \ldots ||\omega_r g||pk_{u_{j,k}})$, $u_{j,k}$ sends the parameters $(\sigma_{3,u_{j,k}}, \{\rho_{0,u_{j,k}}\}, \{\omega_0\}, \{S_{0,u_{j,k}}\}, pk_{u_{j,k}}, ip_{u_{j,k}}, I_4)$ to the edge server managing the domain ES_j.

5.6. Edge Server ES_j Re-Encrypts Keyword Trapdoor

$ReTrapdoor(\beta, I_4) \rightarrow I_5$: ES_j according to the serial number $S_{0,u_{j,k}} = \{S_1, S_2, \ldots, S_r\}$ to find the corresponding attribute permissions, and then, computes $\phi_{3,ES_j} = H_3(\rho_{1,ES_j}||\rho_{2,ES_j}|| \ldots ||\rho_{r,ES_j}||\omega_1 g||\omega_2 g|| \ldots ||\omega_r g||pk_{u_{j,k}})g$ based on the serial number sent. If the equation $e(\sigma_{3,u_{j,k}}, sk_{ES_j}^{-1} g) = e(\phi_{3,ES_j}, \psi_5)$ holds, ES_j re-encrypts the keyword trapdoor $I_5 = \beta I_4$ and the keyword index secret-key share parameter $C_{2,0} = (C_{2,1} = \beta\omega_1 g, C_{2,2} = \beta\omega_2 g, \ldots, C_{2,r} = \beta\omega_r g)$. ES_j computes parameters $\psi_6 = z_4 g$ and $\phi_{4,ES_j} = z_4 H_3(C_{2,1}||C_{2,2}|| \ldots ||C_{2,r}|| \rho_{1,ES_j}||\rho_{2,ES_j}|| \ldots ||\rho_{r,ES_j}||pk_{ES_j})g$. Then, ES_j sends parameters $(\{C_{2,0}\}, \{\rho_{0,ES_j}\}, pk_{ES_i}, ip_{u_{i,j}}, \phi_{4,ES_j}, \psi_6, I_5)$ to the CS.

5.7. Cloud Server Keyword Search

$Verify(I_6, I_7, I_{KW}) \rightarrow true/false$: After the CS receives parameters $(\{C_{2,0}\}, \{\rho_{0,ES_j}\}, pk_{ES_i}, ip_{u_{i,j}}, \phi_{4,ES_j}, \psi_6, I_5)$, the CS computes $\phi_{5,ES_j} = H_3(C_{2,1}||C_{2,2}||\ldots||C_{2,r}||\rho_{1,ES_j}||\rho_{2,ES_j}||\ldots||\rho_{r,ES_j}||pk_{ES_j})g$ if the equation $e(\phi_{5,ES_j}, \psi_6) = e(\phi_{4,ES_j}, g)$ is true. And, if it is true CS computes $I_6 = e(C_{1,1}, C_{2,1})e(C_{1,2}, C_{2,2})\ldots e(C_{1,r}, C_{2,r}) = e(g,g)^{\sum_{i=1}^{r} h_i\omega_i} = e(g, s_0 g)$ and $I_7 = e(I_5, I_3)$. CS matches the keyword trapdoor information by equation $I_6 I_7 = I_{KW}$. CS verifies if the equation holds true, if the equation holds it means that the keyword information is matched successfully. Then, the CS retrieves the corresponding ciphertext resources and computes $\sigma_{4,CS} = H_2(f_1||f_2||\ldots||f_r||ip_{u_{j,k}}||pk_{u_{j,k}})pk_{u_{j,k}}$, the ciphertext parameters $(C_{u_{i,j}}\sigma_{4,CS}, \{f_0\}, ip_{u_{j,k}})$ are sent directly to $u_{j,k}$ through the $ip_{u_{j,k}}$.

5.8. Data User Decryption

$Dec(C_{u_{i,j}}, \{f_0\}, P_1(x)) \rightarrow \mathcal{M}_{u_{i,j}}$: After receiving the parameters $\{C_{u_{i,j}}\sigma_4^{CS}, (f_0), ip_{u_{j,k}}\}$, $u_{j,k}$ decrypts and computes $\phi_6^{u_{j,k}} = H_2(f_1||f_2||\ldots||f_r||ip_{u_{j,k}}||pk_{u_{j,k}})g$. By verifying the equation $e(\sigma_4^{CS}, sk_{u_{j,k}}^{-1}g) = e(\phi_6^{u_{j,k}}, g)$, if true, the decryption key is then computed. $u_{j,k}$ uses the encryption key factors $(f_1, f_2, \ldots, f_r)$ of $C_{u_{i,j}}$, along with the attribute permissions $\{\rho_1^{u_{j,k}}, \rho_2^{u_{j,k}}, \ldots, \rho_r^{u_{j,k}}\}$ it possesses, and parameters $\{x_1, x_2, \ldots, x_r\}$, where $x_i = H_2(\rho_i^{u_{j,k}}) \bmod q$ (for $1 \leq i \leq r$). For data users $u_{j,k}$ who satisfy the access policy, based on the Lagrange interpolation theorem they reconstruct the polynomial $P_1(x)$ using the parameters $\{(x_1, f_1), (x_2, f_2), \ldots, (x_r, f_r)\}$ and the equation $P(x) = \sum_{i=1}^{r} f_i \ell_i(x)$, where $\ell_i(x) = p_i(x) = \prod_{j=1, j\neq i}^{r} \frac{x - x_j}{x_i - x_j}$. The polynomial $P_1(x) = d_{r-1}x^{r-1} + d_{r-2}x^{r-2} + \ldots + d_1 x + d_0$ is reconstructed. $P_1(0) = d_0$ serves as the decryption key for the shared resource. The data user decrypts the resource $\mathcal{M}_{u_{i,j}}$ as $\mathcal{M}_{u_{i,j}} = C_{u_{i,j}}/e(g, d_0 g)$ to obtain the plaintext data.

6. Security Analysis

This scheme proposes a cross-domain secure data-sharing model to resist keyword guessing attacks. To demonstrate the correctness and security of the model, this section discusses the security analysis of the model.

Theorem 1. *If a probabilistic polynomial-time (PPT) adversary $\mathcal{A}$ can break the KGA security of our scheme with non-negligible advantage, then the simulator $\mathcal{B}$ can break the assumption of the DBDH problem with advantage ε.*

Proof of Theorem 1. We are assuming the existence of an adversary $\mathcal{A}$ that can break our protocol in polynomial time t by a non-negligible advantage ε (t, ε) in the IND-KGA security model; we construct a simulator $\mathcal{B}$ to solve the DBDH problem. Given an instance (g, ag, bg, cg, Z) of the problem on a bilinear pair of groups $\mathbb{PG}$, where g is a generator of an additive group $\mathbb{G}_1$, $a, b \in \mathbb{Z}_q^*$ is randomly chosen, and let $coin$ be a random bit 0 or 1, when $coin = 0$, Z in this case can be equal to $abcg$ and when $coin = 1$, Z is a random element in $\mathbb{G}_1$; the interaction between the challenger and the adversary is as follows.

Init: Initialize the secret key of the keyword index as $s_0 = a$; the challenger enters the public parameters $[g, ag]$ to send to the attacker $\mathcal{A}$; the attacker selects the challenge access structure $\mathbb{A}$ and the set of challenged attributes $\{att_1^*, att_2^*, \ldots, att_r^*\}$ to send to $\mathcal{B}$; $\mathcal{B}$ randomly selects $t_i^* \in \mathbb{Z}_q^* (1 \leq i \leq r)$ and computes the attribute permissions $\rho_1^* = t_1^* H_1(att_1^*)g, \rho_2^* = t_2^* H_1(att_2^*)g, \ldots, \rho_r^* = t_r^* H_1(att_r^*)g, \rho_0^* = \{\rho_1^*, \rho_2^*, \ldots, \rho_r^*\}$ and sends them to $\mathcal{A}$.

Phase 1: $\mathcal{A}$ can query oracles that can be simulated by $\mathcal{B}$ as follows.

Hash query: The adversary performs a private-key hash query in this phase, the attacker computes the attribute permission secret key $s_1^* = \sum_{i=1}^{r} H_2(\rho_i^*) \bmod q (1 \leq i \leq r)$, using j to represent the number of queries, where $j \in [1, Q_{H_3}]$ and $k \in [1, Q_{H_1}]$, where Q_{H_1} and Q_{H_3} represent the number of queries to the random oracles H_1 and H_3, respectively. The simulator $\mathcal{B}$ creates two hash lists to record all queries and responses, and the hash lists are initialized to be empty.

1. Let the j-th query of H_3 be $s_{1,j}^*$; if the hash list already has $s_{1,j}^*$ corresponding options, the simulator $\mathcal{B}$ answers the query according to the hash list; otherwise, the simulator $\mathcal{B}$ randomly chooses $a_j \in \mathbb{Z}_q^*$, tosses a biased coin where $coin \in \{0,1\}$, where $\Pr[coin = 0] = \delta$, and when $coin = 1$, set $H_3(s_{1,j}^*) = a_j g$; when $coin = 0$, $H_3(s_{1,j}^*) = bg$. The simulator $\mathcal{B}$ then marks $H_3(s_{1,j}^*)$ as the should for that query and adds the corresponding tuple $< j, s_{1,j}^*, a_j, H_3(s_{1,j}^*) >$ to the hash table.
2. The adversary $\mathcal{A}$ randomly selects keyword kw_k from the keyword dictionary for each query; if there is already an item corresponding to kw_k in the hash list, simulator $\mathcal{B}$ answers the query based on the hash list; otherwise, simulator $\mathcal{B}$ randomly selects $Y_k \in \mathbb{G}_1$ (the k-th query $H_1(kw_k)$ of H_1 is y_k, when $coin = 1$, $y_k a_j g = Y_k$; when $coin = 0$, $y_k bg = Y_k$), and adds the tuple $< g, kw_k, Y_k >$ to the hash list.

Attribute permissions secret-key extraction query: The adversary performs private-key interrogation in this phase. $\mathcal{A}$ queries the attribute permissions secret key of $s_{1,j}^*$ such that $< j, s_{1,j}^*, a_j, H(s_{1,j}^*) >$ is the corresponding tuple; it randomly tosses a coin and aborts if $coin = 1$; otherwise, according to the simulation process, and computes $E_j = a_j ag = aH_3(s_{1,j}^*)$, so that $H_3(s_{1,j}^*)$ is a valid intermediate parameter, and randomly choosing $\alpha_j \in \mathbb{Z}_q^*$, computes the re-encryption attribute permissions secret key $E_j' = \alpha_j ag$ and adds E_j' to this tuple $< j, s_{1,j}^*, a_j, H_3(s_{1,j}^*), E_j, E_j' >$.

Keyword trapdoor extraction query: The adversary $\mathcal{A}$ makes a keyword trapdoor query in this phase to respond to the keyword trapdoor extraction query; the simulator $\mathcal{B}$ maintains a list keyword trapdoor $< g, y_k, kw_k >$; $\mathcal{A}$ selects the keyword kw_k to be queried, and if $coin = 0$, aborts; if $coin = 1$, the simulation $\mathcal{B}$ process calculates that $Y_k = y_k a_j g$, and therefore, Y_k is a valid trapdoor corresponding to the keyword, and selects $\beta_k \in \mathbb{Z}_q^*$, where $\alpha_j \beta_k = 1 \bmod q$, and re-encrypts the keyword trapdoor $Y_k' = \beta_k y_k a_j g$. $\mathcal{B}$ adds Y_k' to that tuple $< g, kw_k, Y_k, Y_k' >$.

Challenge phase: Challenge phase: the adversary $\mathcal{A}$ selects two equal-length keywords $kw_0, kw_1 \in \{0,1\}^*$ and a challenge attribute permission secret key $s_{1,j}^*$ in the H_3, H_1 hash list, $s_{1,j}^*$ corresponding to the tuple $< j, s_{1,j}^*, a_j, H_3(s_{1,j}^*), E_j', Y_k' >$, if $coin = 1$, it reports a failure and an abort; otherwise, if $coin = 0$, it can obtain $H_3(s_{1,i}^*) = bg$. kw_0 corresponding to the tuple $< g, kw_0, Y_0, Y_0' >$, kw_1 corresponding to the tuple $< g, kw_1, Y_1, Y_1' >$, and the simulator $\mathcal{B}$ randomly selects $coin \in \{0,1\}$ again, and if $coin = 1$, the simulator $\mathcal{B}$ reports a failure and an abort; if $coin = 0$, the simulator $\mathcal{A}$ can compute the challenge keyword information as $I^* = e(g, ag)Z$, where $Z \in \mathbb{G}_1$. If we make $H_1(kw_{coin}) = c$, we can compute $Z = e(E_k', Y_j') = e(\beta_k cbg, \alpha_j ag) = e(cbg, ag) = e(g,g)^{abc}$, then we can obtain the challenge keyword trapdoor information $I_{KW}^* = e(g,g)^a e(g,g)^{abc}$, and therefore, this challenge keyword parameter I^* is the correct parameter corresponding to the attribute permission ρ_0^* and keyword trapdoor information kw_{coin}.

Phase 2: $\mathcal{A}$ can adaptively interrogate queries for a polynomial a bounded number of times as in phase 1, but it cannot perform an attribute permissions secret-key extraction query for $s_{1,i}^*$ and a keyword trapdoor extraction query for kw_0 and kw_1, where $kw_* \neq \{kw_0, kw_1\}$.

Guess: Adversary $\mathcal{A}$ outputs a guess about the result of $coin$, $coin = coin'$, the simulator outputs *True*; otherwise, it outputs *False*. We use *event* to denote that the simulator reports failed and aborted events during the game, and from the process above we can see that there are two cases: $event_1$ denotes that $\mathcal{B}$ reports failed and aborted events during attribute permissions secret-key extraction queries and keyword trapdoor extraction queries, $event_2$ denotes that $\mathcal{B}$ reports failed and aborted events during the generation of challenge permissions during the challenge phase and during the challenge trapdoor, $\Pr(\overline{event_1}) = (1-\delta)^{Q_{H_3}+Q_{H_1}}$, $\Pr(\overline{event_2}) = 1-(1-\delta)^2$ because of $\Pr(\overline{event}) = \Pr(\overline{event_1}) \cdot \Pr(\overline{event_2})$. It can be computed when $\delta = 1 - \sqrt{\frac{Q_{H_3}+Q_{H_1}}{2+Q_{H_3}+Q_{H_1}}}$, $\Pr(\overline{event})_{\max} = (\frac{Q_{H_3}+Q_{H_1}}{Q_{H_3}+Q_{H_1}+2})^{\frac{Q_{H_3}+Q_{H_1}}{2}} \cdot \frac{Q_{H_3}+Q_{H_1}}{Q_{H_3}+Q_{H_1}+2} \approx \frac{1}{(Q_{H_3}+Q_{H_1})e}(e \approx 2.72)$. It can be shown that the $\Pr[\overline{event}]$ probability is non-negligible. □

The time cost of the simulation process is $T_s = O(Q_{H_1} + Q_{H_3})$. According to Equation (1), the probability that the simulator $\mathcal{B}$ can solve the DBDH problem is $|\Pr[coin = coin^`] - \frac{1}{2}| = \frac{\varepsilon}{2}\Pr[\overline{event}]$. If ε is non-negligible, simulator $\mathcal{B}$ will be able to solve the DBDH problem with $(t + T_s, \frac{\varepsilon}{2}\Pr[\overline{event}])$. Since the DBDH problem is difficult, no attacker can break the IND-KGA security of our protocol.

7. Performance Analysis

In this section, we evaluate the performance aspects of the scheme, which we compare with the most advanced schemes [30–33,38–41]. We evaluate the performance of our scheme. In terms of theoretical performance, we mainly analyze the aspect of computational complexity. Then, we perform experimental comparisons using real datasets to demonstrate the feasibility and effectiveness of our scheme.

7.1. Functional Comparison

Before analyzing the performance of our scheme, we first compare the functionality of our scheme with several state-of-the-art schemes in Table 1. All the schemes in Table 1 satisfy fine-grained keyword search; Refs. [30,33,38] are based on the structural construction of an access tree, Ref. [39] is based on the structural construction of a hidden AND-tree; Ref. [32] and the present scheme are based on the structural construction of LSSS; all the schemes are efficient in terms of expressiveness. Refs. [30,32,39] cannot resist keyword guessing attacks; Refs. [30,33,38,39] cannot realize cross-domain data sharing; and only the present scheme supports resisting keyword guessing attack and cross-domain data sharing of the above schemes.

Table 1. Functional comparison of various schemes.

Scheme	Function 1 [1]	Function 2 [2]	Function 3 [3]	Function 4 [4]
ABDKS [30]	✓	*Tree*	✗	✗
MKS-VABKS [32]	✓	*LSSS*	✗	✗
HP-CPABKS [39]	✓	*AND-gates*	✓	✗
LFGS [38]	✓	*Tree*	✗	✗
ABKS-SKGA [33]	✓	*Tree*	✓	✗
Ours	✓	*LSSS*	✓	✓

[1] Function 1: fine-grained keyword search. [2] Function 2: access structure. [3] Function 3: keyword guessing attacks. [4] Function 4: cross-domain data share.

7.2. Theoretical Performance

The existing schemes' computational times and storage costs are shown in Tables 2 and 3, respectively, taking into account certain time-consuming operations. The bilinear pairing operation is denoted by T_{bp}, the point addition operation is denoted by T_{pa} in the additive group $\mathbb{G}_1$, and the exponential operation is denoted by $T_{\exp}$ in the multiplication cyclic group $\mathbb{G}_T$. In addition, we consider $|\mathbb{Z}_q^*|$ to denote the length of an element in $\mathbb{Z}_q^*$, and $|\mathbb{G}_1|$ denotes the length of an element in group $\mathbb{G}_1$; $|\mathbb{G}_T|$ denotes the size of an element in group $\mathbb{G}_T$.

Table 2. Computational costs in various schemes.

Algorithm	Our Scheme	MKS-VABKS [32]	HP-CPABKS [39]	LFGS [38]	ABKS-SM [31]	ABCKS [40]	CABKS-CRF [41]
KeyGen	$(2r+6)T_{pa}$+$(2r+2)T_{inv}$+$6T_{bp}$	$(2r+6)T_{\exp}$	$(2r+2)T_{\exp}$	$(r+5)T_{\exp}$	$(6+2r)T_{\exp}$	$3rT_{\exp}$	$(r+1)T_{\exp}$
$r=40$	78.75 ms	854.07 ms	814.35 ms	446.90 ms	854.07 ms	1191.73 ms	407.18 ms
Encryption	$(r-1)T_{\exp}$+$(2r+11)T_{pa}$+$7T_{bp}$	$(2r+6)T_{\exp}$	$(2r+2)T_{\exp}$	$(r+5)T_{\exp}$+T_{bp}	$(7+2r)T_{\exp}$	$(r+5)T_{\exp}$	$(8T_{\exp}+3T_{bp})(r+1)$
$r=40$	477.24 ms	854.07 ms	814.35 ms	448.96 ms	864.01 ms	446.90 ms	4740.05 ms
Trapdoor Gen	$2T_{bp}$+$(2r+7)T_{pa}$	$(2r+1)T_{\exp}$	$(2r+1)T_{\exp}$	$(3r+2)T_{\exp}$	$(2r+1)T_{\exp}$	$(2r+3)T_{\exp}$	$(4r+2)T_{\exp}$
$r=40$	29.38 ms	804.42 ms	804.42 ms	1211.59 ms	804.42 ms	824.28 ms	1608.84 ms
Search	$(r+3)T_{bp}$+$2T_{pa}$	$(2r+1)T_{bp}$+$T_{\exp}$	$(2r+1)T_{bp}$+$T_{\exp}$	$(r+1)T_{bp}$+$2T_{\exp}$	$(1+2r)T_{bp}$+$T_{\exp}$	$(2r+3)T_{bp}$	$(r+1)T_{bp}+T_{\exp}$
$r=40$	518.60 ms	986.60 ms	986.60 ms	514.23 ms	986.60 ms	1000.80 ms	504.30 ms
Decryption	T_{pa}+$3T_{bp}$+$(r-1)T_{\exp}$	$(2r-1)T_{bp}$		$(r+3)T_{bp}$	$2rT_{\exp}$+$3T_{bp}$	$T_{\exp}$	
$r=40$	423.55 ms	976.67 ms		518.48 ms	830.66 ms	9.93 ms	

Table 3. Storage costs of various schemes.

Algorithm	Our Scheme	MKS-VABKS [32]	HP-CPABKS [39]	LFGS [38]	ABKS-SM [31]	ABCKS [40]	CABKS-CRF [41]
KeyGen	$(2r+4)\|\mathbb{G}_1\|+\|\mathbb{Z}_q^*\|$	$(2r+5)\|\mathbb{G}_T\|+(r+3)\|\mathbb{Z}_q^*\|$	$(2r+1)\|\mathbb{G}_1\|+(r+2)\|\mathbb{Z}_q^*\|$	$(3r+9)\|\mathbb{G}_T\|+2\|\mathbb{Z}_q^*\|$	$(2r+5)\|\mathbb{G}_T\|+(r+3)\|\mathbb{Z}_q^*\|$	$3r\|\mathbb{G}_T\|+r\|\mathbb{Z}_q^*\|$	$(\|\mathbb{G}_T\|+\|\mathbb{Z}_q^*\|)(r+1)$
$r=40$	5.27 kb	5.98 kb	5.72 kb	8.09 kb	5.98 kb	8.13 kb	3.20 kb
Encryption	$(2r+9)\|\mathbb{G}_1\|+(r+3)\|\mathbb{Z}_q^*\|+3\|\mathbb{G}_T\|$	$(2r+1)\|\mathbb{G}_T\|+2\|\mathbb{Z}_q^*\|$	$(2r+1)\|\mathbb{G}_T\|+(r+1)\|\mathbb{Z}_q^*\|$	$(2r+8)\|\mathbb{G}_T\|+(2r+1)\|\mathbb{Z}_q^*\|$	$(2r+6)\|\mathbb{G}_T\|+(r+2)\|\mathbb{Z}_q^*\|$	$(2r+2)\|\mathbb{G}_T\|+\|\mathbb{Z}_q^*\|$	$(5r+4)\|\mathbb{G}_T\|+2\|\mathbb{Z}_q^*\|$
$r=40$	6.42 kb	6.09 kb	5.70 kb	6.77 kb	6.03 kb	5.14 kb	12.78 kb
Trapdoor Gen	$2\|\mathbb{Z}_q^*\|+(2r+7)\|\mathbb{G}_1\|+2\|\mathbb{G}_T\|$	$(2r+1)\|\mathbb{G}_T\|+2\|\mathbb{Z}_q^*\|$	$(2r+1)\|\mathbb{G}_T\|+2\|\mathbb{Z}_q^*\|$	$(4r+3)\|\mathbb{G}_T\|+4\|\mathbb{Z}_q^*\|$	$(2r+1)\|\mathbb{G}_T\|+2\|\mathbb{Z}_q^*\|$	$3r\|\mathbb{G}_T\|+\|\mathbb{Z}_q^*\|$	$(2r+1)\|\mathbb{G}_T\|+2\|\mathbb{Z}_q^*\|$
$r=40$	5.59 kb	5.09 kb	5.09 kb	10.25 kb	5.09 kb	7.52 kb	5.09 kb
Search	$2\|\mathbb{G}_T\|+2\|\mathbb{G}_1\|$	$4\|\mathbb{G}_T\|$	$4\|\mathbb{G}_T\|$	$(r+1)\|\mathbb{G}_T\|$	$4\|\mathbb{G}_T\|$	$5\|\mathbb{G}_T\|$	$\|\mathbb{G}_T\|$
$r=40$	0.25 kb	0.25 kb	0.25 kb	2.56 kb	0.25 kb	0.3125 kb	0.0625 kb
Decryption	$2\|\mathbb{G}_1\|$	$2\|\mathbb{G}_T\|$		$(r+2)\|\mathbb{G}_T\|+\|\mathbb{Z}_q^*\|$	$(r+1)\|\mathbb{G}_T\|$	$\|\mathbb{G}_T\|$	
$r=40$	0.125 kb	0.125 kb		2.64 kb	2.56 kb	0.0625	

Key generation: Data users in our scheme need to obtain public and private key pairs and attribute permissions, and our scheme has a very significant reduction in computational overhead compared to the schemes in [31,32,38–41] . The data user obtains the corresponding attribute privileges by CA authentication computation for randomly selected attributes from the attribute collection, and our scheme significantly outperforms the compared schemes. Our scheme has slightly higher storage overhead compared to the scheme in [41], but it is superior to the schemes in [31,32,38–40]. It offers certain advantages in terms of storage overhead and shows significant advantages for data users with limited resources.

Encryption: Our scheme has a similar computational cost to the schemes in [38,40]. However, compared to the schemes in [31,32,39,41], our scheme has a lower overhead cost, making it more suitable for resource-constrained terminal devices. The storage overhead of our scheme is better than that of the schemes in [38,41], but higher than that of the schemes in [31,32,39]. However, since most of the storage overhead in our scheme is handled by the edge server, it does not impose any additional resource burden on data users.

Trapdoor generation: Our scheme has a lower overhead cost compared to the schemes in [31,32,38–41], because the trapdoor is generated based on the number of attribute permissions of the attribute endpoints that satisfy the access structure. In contrast, the schemes in [31,32,39,40] require $2r$ exponential operations, the scheme in [38] requires $(3r+2)$ exponential operations, and the scheme in [41] requires $(4r+2)$ exponential operations. The storage cost of our scheme is slightly higher than that of the schemes in [31,32,39,41], but better than the schemes in [38,40]. Additionally, at this stage our scheme offloads part of the computation to the edge server, thereby reducing the actual storage costs for data users.

Keyword search: Our scheme's efficiency in the search phase is comparable to the schemes in [38,41], but significantly better than the comparison schemes in [31,32,39,40]. This is because those comparison schemes incur time overhead due to $2r$ bilinear pair operations, whereas our scheme only requires r bilinear pair operations, resulting in less overhead during the verification process. In terms of storage overhead, our scheme is on par with the comparison schemes in [31,32,39], and all are lower than those of the schemes in [38,40]. Although the scheme in [41] has certain advantages, our scheme performs searches in the cloud, ensuring that no extra storage space is occupied.

Decryption: In our scheme, data users decrypt based on an interpolated polynomial reduction key during the decryption process. The time overhead in this phase is highly efficient compared to the comparison schemes in [31,32]. Although it is higher than the scheme in [40], the computational overhead remains acceptable. Our scheme has the same storage overhead as the comparison scheme in [32], is lower than the schemes in [31,38], and is slightly higher than the scheme in [40]. Additionally, it does not incur any extra storage overhead.

7.3. Actual Performance

In this section, we tested on an Android device with 8.0 GB + 2.0 GB (HONOR RAM Turbo) of RAM and 256 GB of storage space, using the JPBC encryption library (version JPBC-2.0.0) in Java to measure the computational time for the processes used, as shown in Tables 2 and 3. The process of testing the algorithm time is divided into two steps. First, the APK file is generated in Android Studio, and then, the APK file is run on the Android phone to obtain the corresponding algorithm time. The obtained calculation data are shown in Table 4.

We consider $|\mathbb{Z}_q^*|$ = 128 bit to denote the length of the elements in $\mathbb{Z}_q^*$, $|\mathbb{G}_1| = 512$ bit to denote the length of the elements in $\mathbb{G}_1$, $|\mathbb{G}_T|$ = 512 bit to denote the length of the elements in $\mathbb{G}_T$, and for ease of description, we assume that the range of the attributes is $r \in [10, 40]$. In this paper, we show the performance characteristics of some of the main algorithms, key generation, encryption, trapdoor generation, keyword search, and decryption.

Table 4. Time of operation execution.

Computation Type	Operational Time (ms)
T_{bp} [1]	$T_{bp} \approx 12.0577$
$T_{\exp}$ [2]	$T_{\exp} \approx 9.9311$
T_{pa} [3]	$T_{pa} \approx 0.0605$
T_{inv} [4]	$T_{inv} \approx 0.0146$

[1] Bilinear pair operation. [2] Exponential operations. [3] Point addition on elliptic curves. [4] Modular inversion operation.

In Figure 5, we present the computational costs of key generation algorithms, illustrating variations in time consumption across the comparison schemes with r set to 10, 20, 30, and 40. When the number of attributes is 40, our scheme consistently exhibits the lowest computational cost, approximately 78.75 ms. In contrast, the time consumption of the comparison schemes in [31,32,39] is around 850 ms, while the scheme in [40] has the highest time consumption at 1191.73 ms, and the scheme in [41] shows a time consumption of 407.18 ms. In Figure 6, we analyze the storage overhead of key generation algorithms. Our scheme demonstrates the lowest storage consumption at 5.27 kb, highlighting a clear advantage over the schemes in [31,32,38–40]. Although the scheme in [41] has a lower storage overhead of 3.20 kb in key generation, our scheme still has an advantage over the storage overhead of other algorithms.

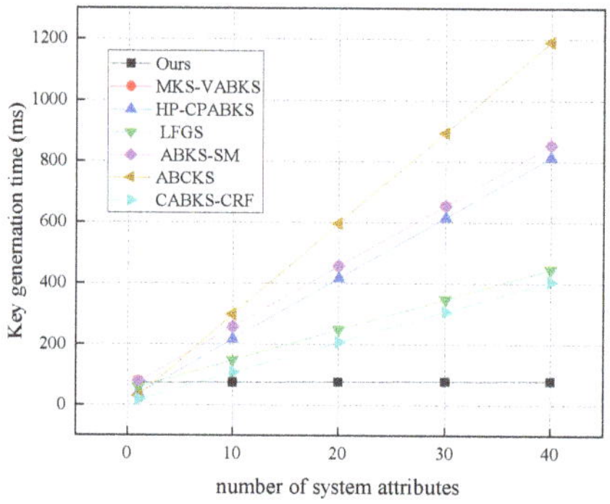

Figure 5. Computational costs in *KeyGen*. (The red line of MKS-VABKS overlaps with the purple line of ABKS-SM).

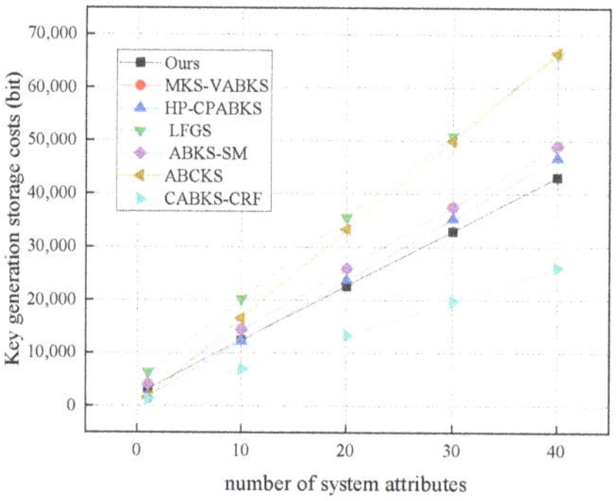

Figure 6. Storage costs in *KeyGen*. (The red line of MKS-VABKS overlaps with the purple line of ABKS-SM).

In Figure 7, we maintain *r* values from 10 to 40 to compare encryption algorithms. Our scheme demonstrates a time consumption of 477.24 ms, while the scheme from Ref. [38] shows 458.96 ms, and the scheme in [40] shows 446.89 ms. All of these schemes significantly outperform the schemes in [31,32,39,41]. In Figure 8, we analyze the storage overhead of the encryption algorithms. Our scheme has a storage consumption of 6.42 kb, which is slightly higher than the schemes in [31,32,39,40], but better than the storage overhead of the schemes in [38,41].

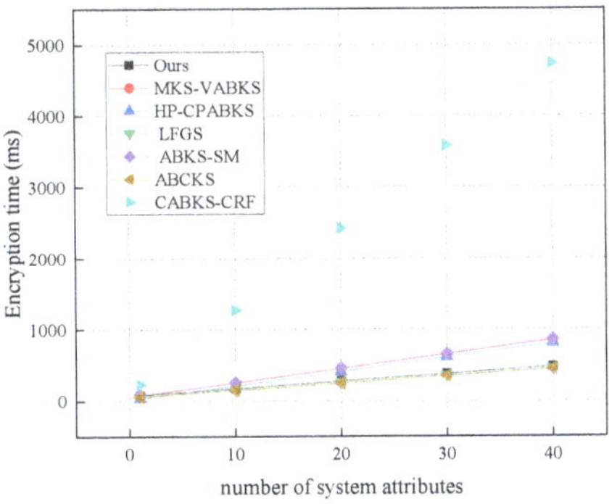

Figure 7. Computational costs in *Enc*.

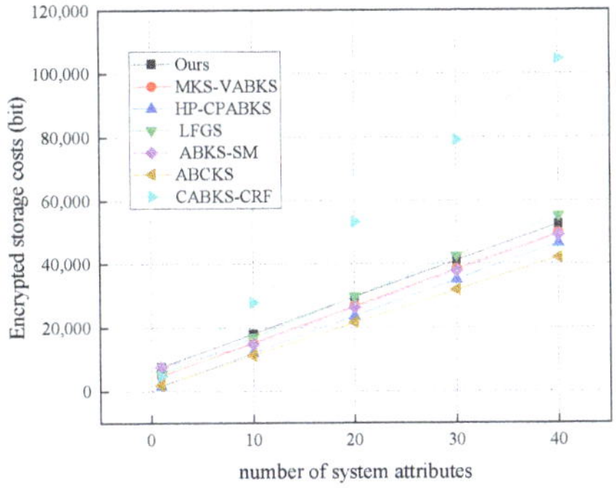

Figure 8. Storage costs in *Enc*.

In Figure 9, we compare the computational costs of the trapdoor generation algorithms among the schemes in [31,32,39]. The time consumption for these three schemes is consistently 804.42 ms, while the scheme in [41] exhibits the highest time expenditure at approximately 1608.84 ms. Our scheme, with a time overhead of only 29.38 ms, demonstrates a significant advantage. In Figure 10, we analyze the storage overhead of the trapdoor algorithms. Our scheme has a storage overhead of 5.59 kb, which is slightly higher than the 5.09 kb overhead of the comparison schemes in [31,32,39], and the scheme in [41], but lower than the 10.25 kb overhead of the scheme in [38].

In Figure 11, we analyze the computational overhead of the keyword search algorithms. The schemes in [31,32,39] all have a time overhead of 986.6 ms. Our scheme shows a time overhead of 518.60 ms, which is comparable to the scheme in [38] with 514.23 ms and the scheme in [41] with 504.30 ms. The scheme in [40] has the highest time overhead at 1000.79 ms, ensuring efficient search for ciphertext information by data users. In Figure 12, we analyze the storage overhead of keyword search algorithms. Our scheme and the comparison schemes in [31,32,39] all have a storage overhead of 0.25 kb. Although the scheme in [41] has a lower storage overhead of 0.0625 kb, our scheme overall provides better performance. The scheme in [38] has the highest storage overhead at 2.56 kb.

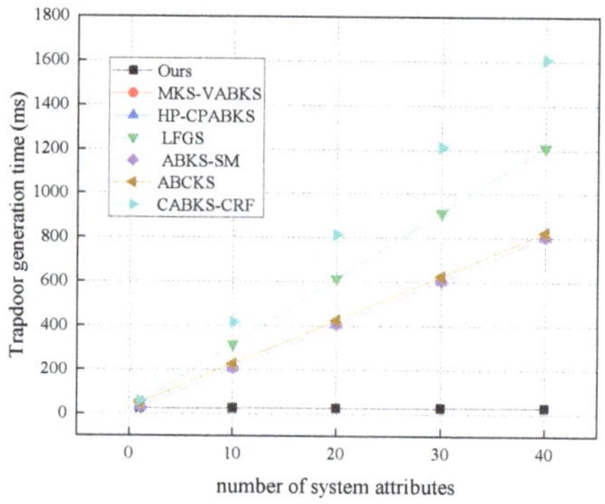

Figure 9. Computational costs in *TrapdoorGen*. (The red line of MKS-VABKS and the blue line of HP-CPABKS overlap with the purple line of ABKS-SM.)

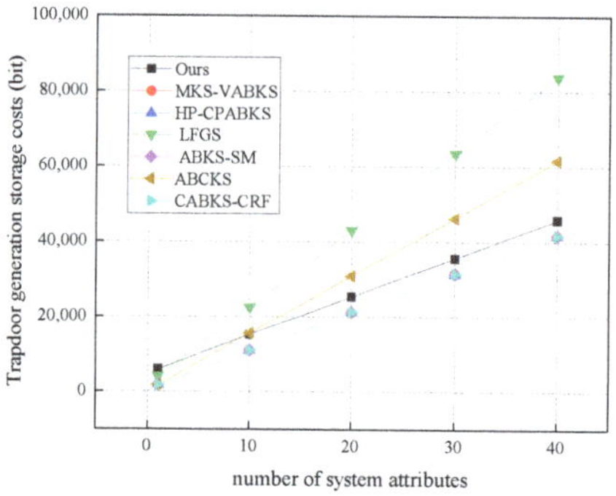

Figure 10. Storage costs in *TrapdoorGen*. (The red line of MKS-VABKS, the blue line of HP-CPABKS, and the purple line of ABKS-SM overlap with the cyan line of CABKS-CRF.)

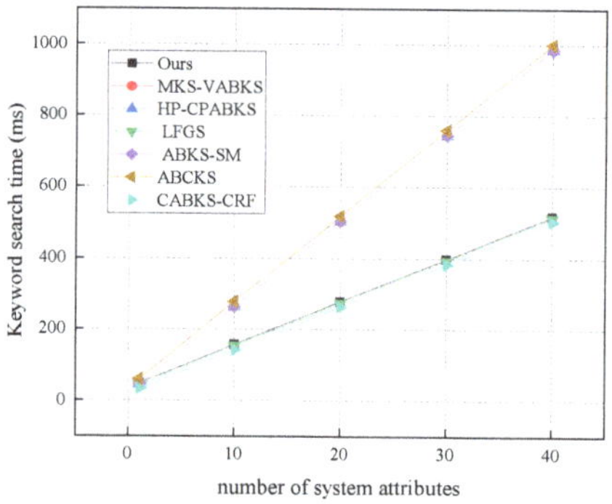

Figure 11. Computational costs in *Keyword Search*. (The red line of MKS-VABKS and the blue line of HP-CPABKS overlap with the purple line of ABKS-SM.)

In Figure 13, we analyze the computational overhead of the decryption algorithms. The scheme in [31] exhibits a computational overhead of 830.66 ms, while the schemes in [32,38] show time overheads of 976.67 ms and 518.48 ms, respectively. Our scheme achieves a time overhead of 423.55 ms, and although the scheme in [40] has a time overhead of 9.93 ms, our scheme still significantly outperforms it in overall computational cost. In Figure 14, we analyze the storage overhead of decryption algorithms with the number of system attributes set to 40. Both our scheme and the comparison scheme in [32] have the same storage overhead of 0.125 kb. In contrast, the schemes in [31,38] have storage overheads of 2.64 kb and 2.56 kb, respectively. Our scheme demonstrates a clear storage advantage in this phase, making it suitable for resource-constrained terminal devices.

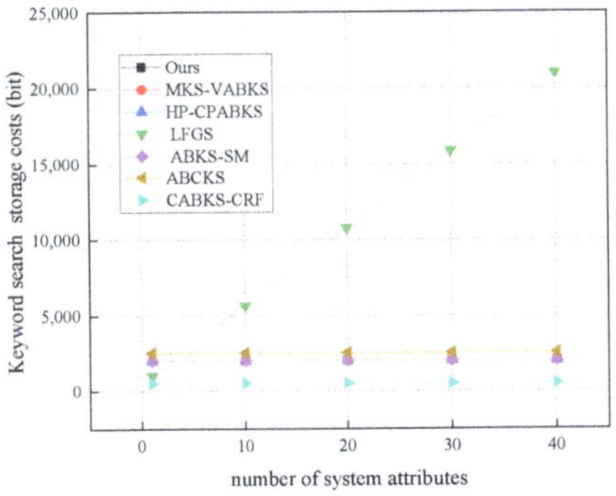

Figure 12. Storage costs in *Keyword Search*. (The gray line of our scheme, the red line of MKS-VABKS, and the blue line of HP-CPABKS overlap with the purple line of ABKS-SM.)

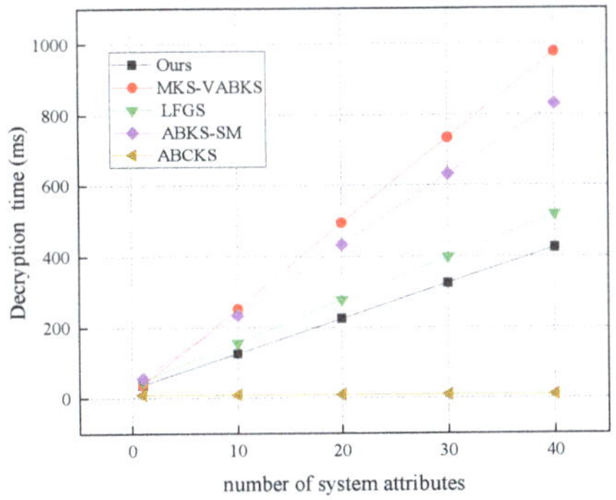

Figure 13. Computational costs in *Dec*.

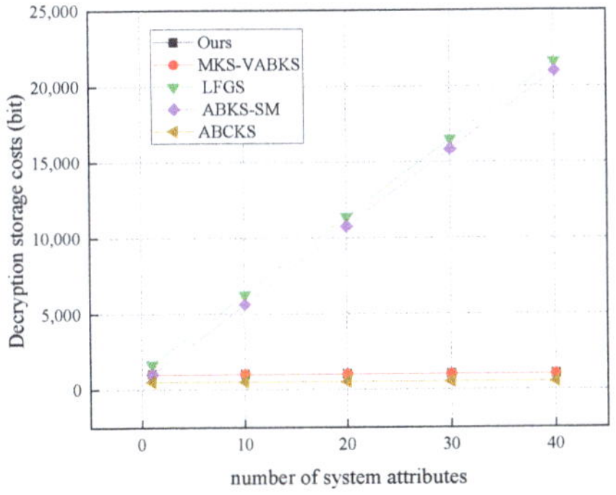

Figure 14. Storage costs in *Dec*. (The gray line of our scheme overlaps with the red line of MKS-VABKS.)

8. Discussion

We have designed a new secure data-sharing model that uses an edge–cloud server architecture to enable secret resource sharing between data users across different domains.

First, this model consists of algorithms with five stages, and compared to other schemes it shows significant advantages in terms of overall computational performance and storage consumption. The model supports fine-grained search characteristics during keyword searches in the cloud, and its lower computational overhead allows for faster responses in real-world environments. Second, the edge layer of the model uses group key agreement technology to re-encrypt ciphertext and keyword information, preventing keyword trapdoor guessing in the cloud and further enhancing security. Third, the model is based on the computational difficulty of the Decisional Bilinear Diffie–Hellman (DBDH) problem, and its security under the random oracle model is proven, ensuring theoretical completeness.

However, our model also has some drawbacks, such as handling attribute updates and revocations, updating and revoking data users, and whether it can allow data users to authenticate without a CA. A decentralized secure data-sharing model, where users authenticate themselves using their own public and private keys, could be explored. Currently, using a CA for authentication may impose a heavy computational burden on the CA. For future work, we will continue to explore attribute-based keyword search, focusing on flexible attribute updates, revocations, and traceability. In practical applications, both data users and attribute sets are dynamically changing. If user attributes are updated, how can secure data sharing be ensured? Thus, we need to address several challenges, such as revoking user permissions at specific attribute levels to allow secure data sharing and tracking malicious users' identities. If a user's identity is found to be malicious, it can be directly revoked to enhance the model's robustness. Additionally, we aim to develop a decentralized secure data-sharing model that does not rely on CA authentication centers. Therefore, we will further optimize our model to improve its efficiency and adaptability across various environments.

For future work, we will continue to work on attribute-based keyword search, including flexible attribute updates, revocations, and traceability. In practical applications, data users and attribute sets are dynamically changing. If user attributes are updated, how to ensure secure data sharing? Therefore, some challenges need to be addressed, such as revoking the permissions of a user at a specific attribute level so that the user can still share data securely, and tracking the identity of malicious users. If the user identity is malicious, it can be directly revoked to make the model more complete. Therefore, in the future, SDSM-KGA will be further optimized to improve efficiency so that it can be used in various environments.

9. Conclusions

In this work, we propose the secure data-sharing model resisting keyword guessing attacks in edge–cloud collaboration scenarios (SDSM-KGA). On the one hand, SDSM-KGA can greatly reduce the computation and storage burden through the edge layer without leaking sensitive information. On the other hand, the SDSM-KGA supports fine-grained keyword search and resists keyword guessing attacks in the cloud. Furthermore, standard security analyses demonstrate that it is capable of resisting keyword guessing attacks (KGAs) in the random oracle model. This empirical experiment using a cryptographic database illustrates the efficiency and feasibility of SDSM-KGA.

Author Contributions: Conceptualization, Y.L. and M.X.; methodology, M.X.; validation, M.X., Q.Z. and J.Y.; formal analysis, J.Y. and H.Z.; resources, Y.L.; data curation, M.X.; writing—original draft preparation, M.X.; writing—review and editing, Y.L.; visualization, Y.L.; supervision, J.Y. and H.Z; project administration, Y.L and H.Z. All authors have read and agreed to the published version of the manuscript.

Funding: This work is supported by the National Natural Science Foundation of China under Grant No. 61971380, 61772477, and the key technologies R&D Program of Henan Province (No. 242102211098), and the research funding of Key Laboratory of Big Data Intelligent Computing (No. BDIC-2023-B-006).

Data Availability Statement: Data are contained within the article.

Conflicts of Interest: The authors declare no conflicts of interest.

References

1. Pan, J.; McElhannon, J. Future edge cloud and edge computing for internet of things applications. *IEEE Internet Things J.* **2017**, *5*, 439–449. [CrossRef]
2. Arthurs, P.; Gillam, L.; Krause, P.; Wang, N.; Halder, K.; Mouzakitis, A. A taxonomy and survey of edge cloud computing for intelligent transportation systems and connected vehicles. *IEEE Trans. Intell. Transp. Syst.* **2021**, *23*, 6206–6221. [CrossRef]
3. Lakhan, A.; Sodhro, A.H.; Majumdar, A.; Khuwuthyakorn, P.; Thinnukool, O. A lightweight secure adaptive approach for internet-of-medical-things healthcare applications in edge-cloud-based networks. *Sensors* **2022**, *22*, 2379. [CrossRef]
4. Alouffi, B.; Hasnain, M.; Alharbi, A.; Alosaimi, W.; Alyami, H.; Ayaz, M. A systematic literature review on cloud computing security: Threats and mitigation strategies. *IEEE Access* **2021**, *9*, 57792–57807. [CrossRef]
5. Saxena, D.; Gupta, I.; Singh, A.K.; Lee, C.N. A fault tolerant elastic resource management framework toward high availability of cloud services. *IEEE Trans. Netw. Serv. Manag.* **2022**, *19*, 3048–3061. [CrossRef]
6. Gupta, I.; Singh, A.K. SELI: Statistical evaluation based leaker identification stochastic scheme for secure data sharing. *IET Commun.* **2020**, *14*, 3607–3618. [CrossRef]
7. Gupta, I.; Singh, A.K. GUIM-SMD: Guilty user identification model using summation matrix-based distribution. *IET Inf. Secur.* **2020**, *14*, 773–782. [CrossRef]
8. Wang, C.; Li, W.; Li, Y.; Xu, X. A ciphertext-policy attribute-based encryption scheme supporting keyword search function. In Proceedings of the Cyberspace Safety and Security: 5th International Symposium, CSS 2013, Zhangjiajie, China, 13–15 November 2013; pp. 377–386.
9. Byun, J.W.; Rhee, H.S.; Park, H.A.; Lee, D.H. Off-line keyword guessing attacks on recent keyword search schemes over encrypted data. In Proceedings of the Workshop on Secure Data Management, Seoul, Republic of Korea, 10–11 September 2006; pp. 75–83.
10. Yau, W.C.; Heng, S.H.; Goi, B.M. Off-line keyword guessing attacks on recent public key encryption with keyword search schemes. In Proceedings of the Autonomic and Trusted Computing: 5th International Conference, ATC 2008, Oslo, Norway, 23–25 June 2008; pp. 100–105.
11. Song, D.X.; Wagner, D.; Perrig, A. Practical techniques for searches on encrypted data. In Proceedings of the Proceeding 2000 IEEE Symposium on Security and Privacy, Berkeley, CA, USA, 14–17 May 2000; pp. 44–55.
12. Li, J.; Huang, Y.; Wei, Y.; Lv, S.; Liu, Z.; Dong, C.; Lou, W. Searchable symmetric encryption with forward search privacy. *IEEE Trans. Dependable Secur. Comput.* **2019**, *18*, 460–474. [CrossRef]
13. Chen, G.; Lai, T.H.; Reiter, M.K.; Zhang, Y. Differentially private access patterns for searchable symmetric encryption. In Proceedings of the IEEE INFOCOM 2018-IEEE Conference on Computer Communications, Honolulu, HI, USA, 16–19 April 2018; pp. 810–818.
14. Gui, Z.; Paterson, K.G.; Patranabis, S. Rethinking searchable symmetric encryption. In Proceedings of the 2023 IEEE Symposium on Security and Privacy (SP), San Francisco, CA, USA, 22–25 May 2023; pp. 1401–1418.
15. Boneh, D.; Di Crescenzo, G.; Ostrovsky, R.; Persiano, G. Public key encryption with keyword search. In Proceedings of the Advances in Cryptology-EUROCRYPT 2004: International Conference on the Theory and Applications of Cryptographic Techniques, Interlaken, Switzerland, 2–6 May 2004; pp. 506–522.
16. Chen, B.; Wu, L.; Li, L.; Choo, K.K.R.; He, D. A parallel and forward private searchable public-key encryption for cloud-based data sharing. *IEEE Access* **2020**, *8*, 28009–28020. [CrossRef]
17. Lu, Y.; Li, J. Privacy-preserving and forward public key encryption with field-free multi-keyword search for cloud encrypted data. *IEEE Trans. Cloud Comput.* **2023**, *11*, 3619–3630. [CrossRef]
18. Cheng, L.; Meng, F. Server-Aided Public Key Authenticated Searchable Encryption With Constant Ciphertext and Constant Trapdoor. *IEEE Trans. Inf. Forensics Secur.* **2023**, *19*, 1388–1400. [CrossRef]
19. Bethencourt, J.; Sahai, A.; Waters, B. Ciphertext-policy attribute-based encryption. In Proceedings of the 2007 IEEE Symposium on Security and Privacy (SP'07), Berkeley, CA, USA, 20–23 May 2007; pp. 321–334.
20. Goyal, V.; Pandey, O.; Sahai, A.; Waters, B. Attribute-based encryption for fine-grained access control of encrypted data. In Proceedings of the 13th ACM Conference on Computer and Communications Security, Alexandria, VA, USA, 30 October–3 November 2006; pp. 89–98.
21. Waters, B. Ciphertext-policy attribute-based encryption: An expressive, efficient, and provably secure realization. In Proceedings of the International Workshop on Public Key Cryptography, Taormina, Italy, 6–9 March 2011; pp. 53–70.
22. Lewko, A.; Waters, B. New proof methods for attribute-based encryption: Achieving full security through selective techniques. In Proceedings of the Annual Cryptology Conference, Santa Barbara, CA, USA, 9–23 August 2012; pp. 180–198.
23. Zheng, Q.; Xu, S.; Ateniese, G. VABKS: Verifiable attribute-based keyword search over outsourced encrypted data. In Proceedings of the IEEE INFOCOM 2014-IEEE Conference on Computer Communications, Toronto, ON, Canada, 23 April–2 May 2014; pp. 522–530.
24. Liu, P.; Wang, J.; Ma, H.; Nie, H. Efficient verifiable public key encryption with keyword search based on KP-ABE. In Proceedings of the 2014 Ninth International Conference on Broadband and Wireless Computing, Communication and Applications, Guangzhou, China, 8–10 November 2014; pp. 584–589.

25. Liang, K.; Susilo, W. Searchable attribute-based mechanism with efficient data sharing for secure cloud storage. *IEEE Trans. Inf. Forensics Secur.* **2015**, *10*, 1981–1992. [CrossRef]
26. Miao, Y.; Ma, J.; Jiang, Q.; Li, X.; Sangaiah, A.K. Verifiable keyword search over encrypted cloud data in smart city. *Comput. Electr. Eng.* **2018**, *65*, 90–101. [CrossRef]
27. Sun, W.; Yu, S.; Lou, W.; Hou, Y.T.; Li, H. Protecting your right: Verifiable attribute-based keyword search with fine-grained owner-enforced search authorization in the cloud. *IEEE Trans. Parallel Distrib. Syst.* **2014**, *27*, 1187–1198. [CrossRef]
28. Cui, J.; Zhou, H.; Zhong, H.; Xu, Y. AKSER: Attribute-based keyword search with efficient revocation in cloud computing. *Inf. Sci.* **2018**, *423*, 343–352. [CrossRef]
29. Wang, N.; Fu, J.; Bhargava, B.K.; Zeng, J. Efficient retrieval over documents encrypted by attributes in cloud computing. *IEEE Trans. Inf. Forensics Secur.* **2018**, *13*, 2653–2667. [CrossRef]
30. Meng, F.; Cheng, L.; Wang, M. ABDKS: Attribute-based encryption with dynamic keyword search in fog computing. *Front. Comput. Sci.* **2021**, *15*, 155810. [CrossRef]
31. Miao, Y.; Liu, X.; Choo, K.K.R.; Deng, R.H.; Li, J.; Li, H.; Ma, J. Privacy-preserving attribute-based keyword search in shared multi-owner setting. *IEEE Trans. Dependable Secur. Comput.* **2019**, *18*, 1080–1094. [CrossRef]
32. Zhang, Y.; Zhu, T.; Guo, R.; Xu, S.; Cui, H.; Cao, J. Multi-keyword searchable and verifiable attribute-based encryption over cloud data. *IEEE Trans. Cloud Comput.* **2021**, *11*, 971–983. [CrossRef]
33. Li, J.; Wang, M.; Lu, Y.; Zhang, Y.; Wang, H. ABKS-SKGA: Attribute-based keyword search secure against keyword guessing attack. *Comput. Stand. Interfaces* **2021**, *74*, 103471. [CrossRef]
34. Zhang, K.; Zhang, Y.; Li, Y.; Liu, X.; Lu, L. A blockchain-based anonymous attribute-based searchable encryption scheme for data sharing. *IEEE Internet Things J.* **2023**, *11*, 1685–1697. [CrossRef]
35. Ge, C.; Susilo, W.; Liu, Z.; Xia, J.; Szalachowski, P.; Fang, L. Secure keyword search and data sharing mechanism for cloud computing. *IEEE Trans. Dependable Secur. Comput.* **2020**, *18*, 2787–2800. [CrossRef]
36. Ge, C.; Susilo, W.; Liu, Z.; Baek, J.; Luo, X.; Fang, L. Attribute-Based Proxy Re-Encryption With Direct Revocation Mechanism for Data Sharing in Clouds. *IEEE Trans. Dependable Secur. Comput.* **2023**, *21*, 949–960. [CrossRef]
37. Agrawal, S.; Chase, M. FAME: Fast attribute-based message encryption. In Proceedings of the 2017 ACM SIGSAC Conference on Computer and Communications Security, Dallas, TX, USA, 30 October–3 November 2017; pp. 665–682.
38. Miao, Y.; Ma, J.; Liu, X.; Weng, J.; Li, H.; Li, H. Lightweight fine-grained search over encrypted data in fog computing. *IEEE Trans. Serv. Comput.* **2018**, *12*, 772–785. [CrossRef]
39. Qiu, S.; Liu, J.; Shi, Y.; Zhang, R. Hidden policy ciphertext-policy attribute-based encryption with keyword search against keyword guessing attack. *Sci. China Inf. Sci.* **2017**, *60*, 1–12. [CrossRef]
40. Zhang, D.; Wang, S.; Zhang, Q.; Zhang, Y. Attribute Based Conjunctive Keywords Search With Verifiability and Fair Payment Using Blockchain. *IEEE Trans. Serv. Comput.* **2023**, *16*, 4168–4182. [CrossRef]
41. Zhang, K.; Jiang, Z.; Ning, J.; Huang, X. Subversion-Resistant and Consistent Attribute-Based Keyword Search for Secure Cloud Storage. *IEEE Trans. Inf. Forensics Secur.* **2022**, *17*, 1771–1784. [CrossRef]

electronics MDPI

Article

SDP-MTF: A Composite Transfer Learning and Feature Fusion for Cross-Project Software Defect Prediction

Tianwei Lei [1], Jingfeng Xue [1], Duo Man [1,*], Yong Wang [1], Minghui Li [1] and Zixiao Kong [2]

[1] School of Computer Science and Technology, Beijing Institute of Technology, Beijing 100081, China; 3120195527@bit.edu.cn (T.L.); xuejf@bit.edu.cn (J.X.); wangyong@bit.edu.cn (Y.W.); minghuili@bit.edu.cn (M.L.)
[2] School of Cyber Science and Engineering, University of International Relations, Beijing 100091, China; kongzixiao@uir.edu.cn
* Correspondence: manduo@bit.edu.cn

Abstract: Software defect prediction is critical for improving software quality and reducing maintenance costs. In recent years, Cross-Project software defect prediction has garnered significant attention from researchers. This approach leverages transfer learning to apply the knowledge from existing projects to new ones, thereby enhancing the universality of predictive models. It provides an effective solution for projects with limited historical defect data. Nevertheless, current methodologies face two main challenges: first, the inadequacy of feature information mining, where code statistical information or semantic information is used in isolation, ignoring the benefits of their integration; second, the substantial feature disparity between different projects, which can lead to insufficient effect during transfer learning, necessitating additional efforts to narrow this gap to improve precision. Addressing these challenges, this paper proposes a novel methodology, SDP-MTF (Software Defect Prediction using Multi-stage Transfer learning and Feature fusion), that combines code statistical features, deep semantic features, and multiple feature transfer learning methods to enhance the predictive effect. The SDP-MTF method was empirically tested on single-source cross-project software defect prediction across six projects from the PROMISE dataset, benchmarked against five baseline algorithms that employ distinct features and transfer methodologies. Our findings indicate that SDP-MTF significantly outperforms five classical baseline algorithms, improving the F1-Score by 8% to 15.2%, thereby substantively advancing the precision of cross-project software defect prediction.

Keywords: cross-project software defect prediction; code statistical features; semantic features; feature fusion

1. Introduction

Software defect prediction is a pivotal automated technique aimed at forecasting bugs within software [1]. It aspires to pinpoint potentially flawed modules during the early development phases of a project. By channeling more resources into the scrutiny and testing of these modules, the approach seeks to safeguard software quality and security, fundamentally cutting down the costs associated with manual testing and condensing the development timeline.

In recent years, the domain of cross-project software defect prediction has attracted substantial attention from the research community as a means to bolster software quality assurance. Cross-project defect prediction (CPDP) is principally designed to circumvent the challenges associated with model construction and data paucity in new project defect predictions, as noted by [2]. It endeavors to apply the knowledge encapsulated in the predictive models of established projects (source projects) to predict defects in new ventures (target projects), offering novel solutions for developers to identify and rectify bugs in the nascent stages of the software development life-cycle.

Current cross-project software predictions grapple with two predominant issues. First, is the prevalent focus on single-feature utilization—either code statistics in isolation or semantic information gleaned solely through source code and deep learning techniques but without integrating both feature sets. Since both code statistics and deep semantic features are derived from source code, each provides a unique insight into the source program's characteristics. They are mutually enriching, not contradictory; their amalgamation could be key to amplifying prediction precision. Second, significant variations in the development processes, programming languages, and personnel coding habits across projects lead to distinct project data features and potentially wide disparities in data distributions. Thus, bridging the gap between varying projects and transferring knowledge from one project domain to another encapsulates the essence of cross-project defect prediction.

In response to these challenges, this paper introduces a novel cross-project software defect prediction approach rooted in compound transfer learning and feature fusion. Initially, a feature constructor is employed to distill code statistical features and deep semantic features from the Abstract Syntax Tree (AST), fusing them into an integrated feature set. Subsequently, a compound methodology that marries Transfer Component Analysis (TCA+) with domain adaption network is deployed on the feature to facilitate transfer learning, diminishing the distributional skew between source and target domains. The transformed features are then channeled into a classifier to conduct the ultimate categorization, culminating in the cross-project software defect prediction task. This methodology was validated on six projects within the PROMISE dataset and benchmarked against five baseline algorithms that employed diverse features and transfer strategies. The empirical findings corroborate that our proposed SDP-MTF method registers a substantial improvement in the F1-Score, ranging from 8% to 15.2% over baseline algorithms, thereby significantly bolstering the precision of cross-project software defect predictions.

The main contributions of this paper are as follows:

- We propose a cross-project software defect prediction method, SDP-MTF, based on compound transfer and feature fusion. Experiments conducted on two datasets demonstrate that our algorithm effectively enhances the effect of cross-project defect prediction methods.
- We utilize both code metric-based statistical features and source code features derived from AST to construct fused features, serving as the foundation for transfer learning and classification, and mining the relationship between projects and defects from multiple feature perspectives.
- We integrate two feature-level transfer learning methods, TCA+ and Deep Adaptation Network (DAN), to narrow the gap between source and target projects, ensuring the effect of cross-project defect prediction.

The subsequent organization of this paper is as follows: Section 2 reviews related work on cross-project software defect prediction; Section 3 primarily introduces our proposed SDP-MTF method, including the motivation and framework behind the method, feature construction, the process of the two transfer learning methods, and feature fusion; Section 4 details our experimental design, including research questions, baseline comparison algorithms, datasets used, and evaluation metrics; Section 5 presents the experimental results; Section 6 analyses and compares the results of the previous experiment and describes the validity threat and Section 7 concludes the paper with a summary and future outlook.

2. Related Work

Cross-Project Defect Prediction (CPDP) primarily addresses challenges in building new project models and data scarcity within project defect prediction [2]. The earliest studies on the feasibility of CPDP can be traced back to the work of [3], who constructed defect prediction models using different projects from the same development team to explore CPDP's feasibility. Their findings confirmed that the differences between projects in CPDP are non-negligible. Currently, most cross-project software defect prediction research employs transfer learning, applying models and knowledge established in source projects to target projects for new defect prediction tasks. Next, we briefly introduce research and content related to cross-project software defect prediction using code statistical features and deep semantic features.

2.1. Code Statistical Features

Code statistical features are used in the vast majority of research. These features, also known as software metric elements, are intrinsic attributes related to the external manifestations of code defects, typically associated with software testing and quality assurance, and provide valuable insights into the relationship between defects and software programs. Nam [4] leveraging feature mapping, improved the classic feature-based transfer method TCA [5] in transfer learning and proposed a TCA+ method. This approach maps code statistical feature information between projects to a common space for model building and data normalization, automatically selecting optimal data normalization methods. He [6] conducted research from the perspective of feature dimensions, using feature selection methods to choose different feature subsets, identifying the TOP K features, and analyzing their associations to remove redundant features, thereby ensuring the effectiveness of feature subsets. Ni [7] proposed a cross-project defect method based on feature and instance transfer, using feature clustering and the TrAdaBoost [8] method. They compared numerous classic methods and proved the effectiveness of their approach. Hosseini [9] used approximate methods like local sensitive hashing (LSH) to reduce computational costs in instance selection based on nearest neighbor information and proved the effectiveness of these approximate methods through optimizing hyperparameters. Lei [10] reduced the differences between projects from the perspective of feature engineering, introducing transfer learning technology to build cross-project defect prediction models WCM-WTrA and the multi-source model Multi-WCM-WTrA.

2.2. Deep Semantic Features

With the development of deep learning and natural language processing technologies, researchers have begun processing programming languages with NLP techniques, extracting program semantics to generate intermediate representations, and representing program semantics, syntax structures, and contextual relationships. Deep semantic feature-based code classification tasks can be seen as advanced abstraction tasks of NLP in programming languages, including code clone detection, code smell classification, and defect vulnerability detection. Chen [11] proposed a method to address the challenges of extracting and expressing rich semantics and relationships from error reports in code repair. This method combines neural network RNN with dependency parsers to automatically extract error entities and their relationships from error reports. Wang [12] extracted abstract syntax trees from source code and built FA-AST by enriching original ASTs with explicit control and data flow edges. They applied two different types of graph neural networks (GNNs) to assess the similarity of code pairs for clone detection. Li [13] proposed a method combining search-based automatic program repair with neural machine translation approaches, using redundant hypotheses and correct patch sequences for potential repair statements and introduced a new framework called ARJANMT for automatic Java program repair.

In cross-project software defect prediction, such features can also reveal connections between defect patterns and source code. Wang [14] et al., to bridge the gap between program semantics and defect prediction features, proposed leveraging the powerful representational learning algorithm of deep learning to automatically learn semantic representations from source code. Specifically, they used Deep Belief Networks (DBN) to learn semantic features automatically from token vectors extracted from programs' Abstract Syntax Trees (ASTs). Li [15] proposed the DP-CNN framework for defect prediction, which uses deep learning for effective feature generation and evaluated F1-Score in defect prediction across seven open-source projects, demonstrating superior results compared to DBN. Qiu [16] proposed the Transfer Convolutional Neural Network TCNN, which introduced a distribution matching layer into the process of mining semantic features with convolutional neural networks. By simultaneously minimizing empirical classification loss, cross-project data distribution differences, and manifold regularization, TCNN could extract transferable deep learning-generated features. Gupta [17] extracted seven unique features from programs, evaluated them using Cognitive Complexity Metrics (CCM), and combined the CCM results as node feature values in CFG to create a node vector matrix. This matrix was then fed into a Graph Convolutional Network (GCN) for intermediate representation and defect prediction.

3. Method

3.1. Motivation and Framework

Cross-project software prediction adeptly addresses the issue of missing historical data or the need for early life-cycle software forecasting and has garnered increasing attention from researchers in recent years. Current cross-project software predictions largely employ transfer learning methods, with researchers achieving notable results. However, two main challenges persist in cross-project software defect prediction: incomplete feature construction and significant probability distribution gaps between source and target projects.

In terms of feature construction, existing studies tend to choose either code statistical features or semantic features. Code statistical features are derived from metrics associated with the source code, measuring various indicators of software quality, while semantic features represent the theoretical units that convey the meanings of tokens in the code and their context. Code statistical and semantic features each represent different characteristics of the code from the perspectives of expert knowledge on software quality and the intrinsic structure of the code, respectively. Neglecting either aspect undoubtedly results in the loss of a wealth of rich information, diminishing the precision of predictions.

The gap between source and target projects poses another challenge: cross-project software defect prediction models are built on different projects and cannot directly use data for modeling. Consequently, transfer learning models that migrate knowledge from one domain to another are a common solution. On this premise, deciding what knowledge to transfer and how to further narrow the probability distribution gap between source and target projects to enhance the effect of defect prediction is the core issue in transfer learning-based cross-project software prediction.

Addressing these issues and with the goal of further enhancing the accuracy of cross-project software defect prediction, we propose SDP-MTF, a method that combines transfer learning with feature fusion. Our aim is to improve the final prediction effect from multiple perspectives by utilizing different types of features and suitable transfer learning. Our motivation is to mine as much information as possible from the source and target projects during the feature stage, then apply appropriate transfer learning methods to bridge the gap between the source and target projects, construct suitable transfer features, and ultimately perform defect prediction classification based on this foundation.

The framework of the method we propose is illustrated in Figure 1. The method mainly consists of a feature construction part and a transfer learning part. Firstly, in the feature construction part, we collect code statistical features and semantic features. We use transfer component analysis to transform and map the features of the code statistical features, after which the source code is converted into an intermediate representation of the abstract syntax tree AST, and the semantic features are extracted from the traversal sequences of the AST using Bi-LSTM with a self-attention mechanism. Finally, the two are feature fused to construct a richer and more comprehensive feature representation. This is followed by the transfer learning phase. In this phase, we introduce the domain-adaptive deep adaptive network DAN to train and classify the tasks in the two domains to accomplish the cross-project software defect prediction task. The algorithmic flow of SDP-MTF is shown in Algorithm 1. We will now delineate the details of our method in the subsequent sections.

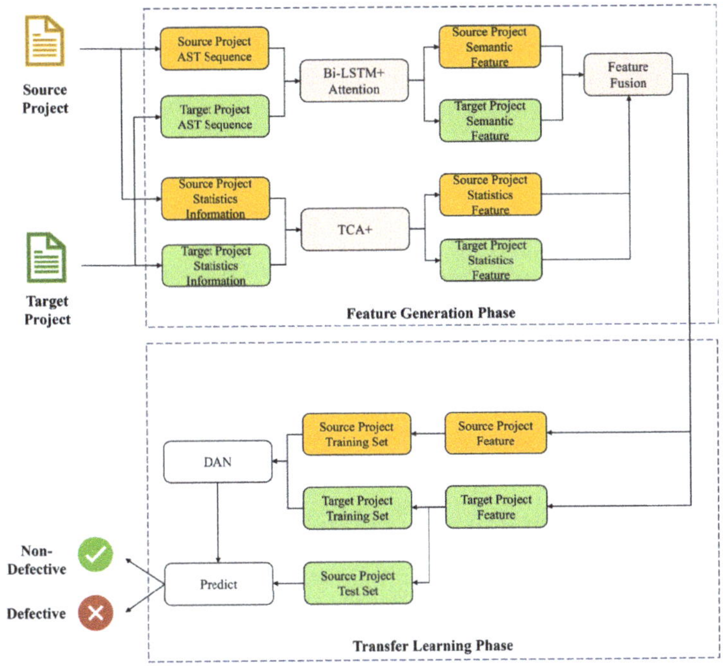

Figure 1. The framework of SDP-MTF.

Algorithm 1 SDP-MTF Methodology

Input:
S: Source project data
T: Target project data
Output:
M: Trained defect prediction model

1. Parse source code S to obtain code metrics
2. Apply TCA+ to normalize and transform code metrics
3. Parse source code S to obtain ASTs
4. Perform depth-first traversal on ASTs to obtain path sequences
5. Use Bi-LSTM with self-attention to extract semantic features from path sequences
6. Concatenate statistical features and semantic features to form a comprehensive feature set
7. Minimize classifier loss L_{task}: Binary cross-entropy on source domain data
8. Minimize adaptive loss L_D: MK-MMD to reduce distribution differences
9. Minimize streamform regularization L_M: Maintain local similarity structures
10. Train a classifier on the transformed features
11. Use the classifier to predict defects in the target project T

3.2. Feature Generation Phase

Next, we describe the details of the method in detail. Figure 2 illustrates the process of the feature construction phase. First, is the feature construction phase, which aims to construct fusion features with richer and more complete information. This phase consists of three steps, namely TCA+-based code statistics feature generation, AST-based semantic feature generation, and feature fusion.

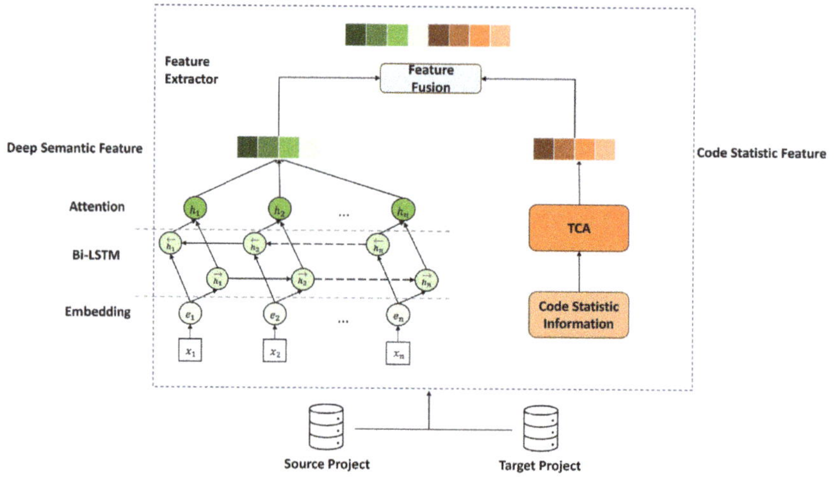

Figure 2. The framework of the feature generation phase.

Code statistical features are closely related to the external defects of the code and are another name for software metrics. Typically, each metric is related to certain functional features of a software project, such as coupling, cohesion, inheritance, and code modification [18], which characterize a software product macroscopically. They provide a basis for improving software quality and efficiency through data analysis. Metrics are crucial for cross-project software defect prediction, offering key data to identify patterns, predict high-risk areas, and help teams detect issues early, optimize testing, and enhance software quality.

Code statistical features are selected and extracted by humans, and their quality is directly related to a priori expert knowledge. We used some of the code statistics created by Jureczko et al. [19] and shared in PROMISE. Specific descriptions of the code statistics used by SDP-MTF are shown in Table 1.

After that, for the differences in code statistics between different projects, we use the classical transfer component analysis method, TCA+ [5], to find the migratable components between different projects, and reduce the differences between different projects while preserving the structural characteristics of the data. The core idea of TCA+ is to learn the transformation of mapping the data of the source and target projects into the Reproducing Kernel Hilbert Space (RKHS), which is the most efficient method to analyze the data of source and target projects. into the Reproducing Kernel Hilbert Space (RKHS) transformations. In this space, the maximum mean difference $Dist(\varphi(X_s), \varphi(X_T))$ between the source project's feature X_s and the target project's feature X_T is very small and the variance of the transformed data $Var(\varphi(X_s), \varphi(X_T))$ is very large, and the formula for the optimization objective can be abstracted as:

$$argmin_{\varphi} Dist(\varphi(X_S), \varphi(X_T)) + \lambda R(\varphi)$$

where $R(\varphi)$ is the regularization term to avoid overfitting, and $\lambda \geq 0$ is the tradeoff parameter that controls the effect of the regularization term in the target. We refer to the retained source and target project features after the TCA+ transformation as source project statistical features and target project code statistical features for subsequent feature fusion.

Table 1. The description of the code statistics used by the SDP-MTF.

Feature Name	Feature Description
amc	The average complexity of methods.
avg_cc	The average McCabe Cyclomatic Complexity in a file.
cam	The sum of the number of parameters of different types of methods.
cbm	The number of inter-method couplings.
cbo	The number of inter-object couplings.
ce	The number of outward coupling.
dam	The ratio of the number of private attributes to the total number of attributes.
dit	The depth of the inheritance tree.
ic	The number of inheritance couplings.
lcom	The number of lack of cohesion between methods.
lcom3	The another measure of the lack of method cohesion.
loc	The number of lines of code.
max_cc	The McCabe maximum cyclomatic complexity.
mfa	The number of function abstractions.
moa	The number of data declarations counted.
noc	The number of subclasses of a class.
npm	The number of public methods.
rfc	The number of methods called in response to a message.
wmc	The number of methods in a class (assuming all methods have a weight of 1).

In order to compensate for the problems of insufficient feature information mining and single feature type, we introduce semantic features of source code to supplement. Semantic features of source code refer to the meaningful aspects of code that convey its functionality and behavior. These include the types of nodes (such as variable declarations, function calls, and control structures), identifiers (names of variables, functions, and classes), operators (arithmetic, logical, and assignment operators), and constants (numerical values, strings, etc.). These features help in understanding the logic and intent of the code, making them crucial for tasks such as defect detection, code analysis, and optimization. By extracting these semantic features, we can enhance the comprehensiveness and accuracy of our analysis.

We extract semantic information of source and target projects based on the Abstract Syntax Tree (AST) sequence. First, we parse the source codes of different projects using JavaLang, obtain their ASTs and perform depth-first traversal to obtain the path sequences. The path sequence contains the global information of the source code with the syntactic structure features of the source code.

We use Bi-LSTM to learn the contextual features of the AST sequences. Bi-LSTM is a commonly used deep semantic model for contextual semantic capture and belongs to the RNN network. Compared with unidirectional LSTM, Bi-LSTM not only inherits the function of LSTM in capturing the semantics of long sequences, but also solves the limitation of LSTM in the coding from the back-to-front direction, and is able to capture the semantics between statements more effectively from the back-to-front direction to capture the semantic dependencies between utterances. Bi-LSTM at each position t can be described and computed by the following equation.

$$i_t = \sigma(W_i \cdot [h(t-1), x_t] + b_i) \tag{1}$$

$$f_t = \sigma(W_f \cdot [h(t-1), x_t] + b_f) \tag{2}$$

$$o_t = \sigma(W_o \cdot [h(t-1), x_t] + b_o) \tag{3}$$

where $\sigma(\cdot)$ represents the sigmoid function, x_t denotes the sequence of statements at position t and h_t represents the learning assumption of the hidden layer. The c_t represents the unit of the hidden layer with the learning assumption of the hidden layer h_t can be calculated by the following equation:

$$\widetilde{c_t} = tanh(W_c \cdot [h(t-1), x_t] + b_c) \tag{4}$$

$$c_t = f_t \odot c(t-1) + i_t \odot (c_t) \tag{5}$$

$$h_t = o_t \odot tanh(c_t) \tag{6}$$

Finally, Bi-LSTM performs forward and backward traversal of the inputs and sums the results, and the final result can be expressed by the following equation:

$$h_i = [\overrightarrow{h_i} \oplus \overleftarrow{h_i}] \tag{7}$$

After extracting the context information, we introduce the self-attention mechanism [20] to solve the dependency problem caused by the long distance of the context vocabulary and can effectively extract the internal connection between statements. The self-attention mechanism can be expressed by the following formula:

$$Attention(Q, K, V) = Softmax(\frac{QK^T}{\sqrt{d_k}})V \tag{8}$$

where d_k represents the dimension of the hidden representation and Q , K, V are linear functions of the previously hidden representation, generated from the embedding paths, that is, the

$$Q = H^{l-1}W_Q^l, Q \in R^{l \times d} \tag{9}$$

$$K = H^{l-1}W_K^l, K \in R^{l \times d} \tag{10}$$

$$V = H^{l-1}W_V^l, V \in R^{l \times d} \tag{11}$$

After obtaining the code statistical features and semantic features of the source and target projects through the above steps, the final fusion features are obtained by using the means of splicing, and the fusion features can be described as:

$$feature_{all} = concat(features_s, feature_c) \tag{12}$$

where $feature_s$, $feature_c$ represent the statistical features of the migrated code and the semantic features generated in depth based on the abstract syntax tree, respectively, and $contact$ is the splicing operation.

3.3. Transfer Learning Phase

After obtaining the fusion features, we enter the transfer learning stage. In this stage, we use the idea of Deep Adaptation Neural Network (DAN) [21] in deep transfer learning, and introduce the training model based on domain adaptation [22] for the construction of a cross-project defect prediction model. The schematic of the deep adaptive neural network we used can be shown in Figure 3.

The optimization objective of the DAN model is three complementary objective functions as follows:

(1) Minimize the classifier loss L_{task} for source domain data;
(2) Minimize the adaptive loss L_D between the source and target domains;
(3) Minimize the flow regularization term L_M between the source and target domains;

Therefore, the optimization objective of the deep adaptive neural network DAN can be expressed as:

$$L_{total} = min(L_{task} + \lambda L_D + \beta L_M) \tag{13}$$

where $\lambda > 0$ and $\beta > 0$ are two balancing parameters used to balance the effects of classifier loss and adaptive loss, respectively.

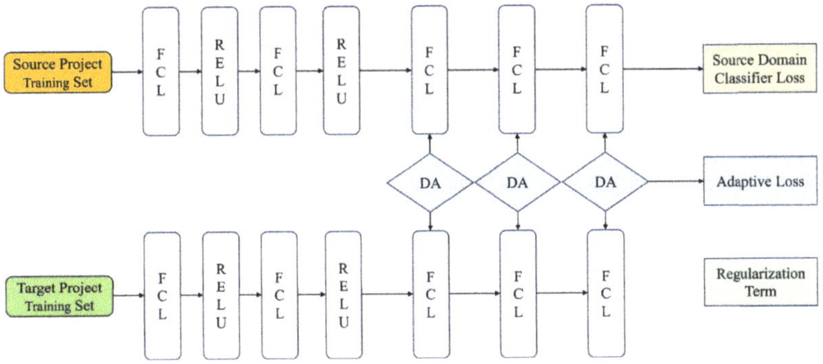

Figure 3. The schematic of DAN used in SDP-MTF.

The specific formulas for each of the three losses are given next. The first is the classifier loss L_{task} for the source domain data, which uses the binary cross entropy as the loss function for binary categorization, specifically:

$$L_{task} = -\frac{1}{N_S}\sum_{i=1}^{N}[y_i log(\hat{y}_i) + (1 - y_i) log(1 - \hat{y}_i)] \tag{14}$$

where N_s is the number of source domain samples, y_i is the true label of the ith sample, and $\hat{y}_i$ is the result of the ith sample predicted by the model.

Next, is the adaptive loss L_D between the source and target domains, which is performed in the last three layers using the multi-kernel maximum mean difference MK-MMD [23] for the difference in distribution between the source and target projects, and the resulting adaptive loss. The adaptive loss for each adaptive layer is as follows:

$$L_{MMD} = \left\| \frac{1}{N_S}\sum_{i=1}^{N_s}\phi(x_i^s) - \frac{1}{N_t}\sum_{j=1}^{N_t}\phi(x_j^t) \right\|_{\mathcal{H}_{||}}^2 \tag{15}$$

where N_s and N_t represent the number of samples in the source and target domains, respectively, and $\phi(\cdot)$ is the mapping function that maps the input data into the Hilbert space; x_i^s and x_j^t are the samples in the source and target domains, respectively, and $\mathcal{H}$ denotes the regenerated kernel Hilbert space RKHS, MK- MMD losses are computed in this space. The k represents a linear combination of multiple kernel functions, as follows:

$$k(x, x') = \sum_{q=1}^{Q} d_q k_q(x, x') \tag{16}$$

where d_q is the weight of the kernel k_q, which is used to optimize the distance measure between the two distributions during learning.

In addition, since three adaptive layers are used, the total adaptive loss is as follows:

$$L_D = \sum_{i=1}^{3} L_{MMD} \tag{17}$$

Finally, there is the stream-form regularization term. The basic assumption of stream-form regularization is that local similarities between data points may not be apparent in a high-dimensional space, but are significant on some low-dimensional stream-form. Based on this premise, stream-form regularization attempts to maintain the local neighborhood structure between data points during the learning process, even when dealing with high-dimensional data [24]. Thus, the stream shape regularization term can be expressed as follows:

$$\begin{aligned} L_M &= \frac{1}{2}\sum_{q=1}^{Q} d_q \left(\sum_{i,j} W_{ij} \|\Phi_q(x_i) - \Phi_q(x_j)\|^2 \right) \\ &= \frac{1}{2}\sum_{q=1}^{Q} d_q \left(\mathrm{Tr}(\Phi_q^T L \Phi_q) \right) \end{aligned} \tag{18}$$

where $\phi(x_i)$ and $\phi(x_j)$ denote the points x_i and x_j mapped to the low-dimensional manifolds, respectively, while W_{ij} is the similarity matrix representing the similarity between the points x_i and x_j, and L is the normalized Laplace matrix. d_q is the kernel weight used to weigh the contribution of different kernel functions in MK-MMD and Q is the number of different kernel functions used. The k_q represents the kernel functions, each of which provides a view from a different feature space and is used to learn and compare the difference in distribution between the source and target domains.

Finally, the similarity matrix W_{ij} is computed as follows:

$$W_{ij} = \begin{cases} \cos(x_i, x_j) & \text{if } x_i \in N_k(x_j) \vee x_j \in N_k(x_i) \\ 0 & \text{otherwise} \end{cases} \tag{19}$$

where $cos(x_i, x_j)$ denotes the cosine similarity between the vector x_i and the vector x_j. $(N_k(x_j)$ denotes the set of k vectors that are most similar to vector x_j, i.e., the k nearest neighbors of x_j. The weight W_{ij} is set to the cosine similarity between x_i and x_j when x_i and x_j are k-nearest neighbors, otherwise, it is set to 0. This approach, which considers only the similarity between each point and its k-nearest neighbors, helps to focus on the local structure of each data point when constructing the network and ignores the relatively distant and less relevant points.

Therefore, the total loss function optimization of the prediction model can be expressed as:

$$\begin{aligned} \Theta &= \arg\min_{\Theta} L_{\text{task}} + \lambda L_D + \beta L_M \\ &= -\frac{1}{N_s}\sum_{i=1}^{N_s} [y_i \log(\hat{y}_i) + (1 - y_i)\log(1 - \hat{y}_i)] \\ &\quad + \lambda \sum_{i=1}^{3} \left\| \frac{1}{N_s}\sum_{i=1}^{N_s} \phi(x_i^s) - \frac{1}{N_t}\sum_{j=1}^{N_t} \phi(x_j^t) \right\|_{mathcalH}^2 \\ &\quad + \frac{\beta}{2}\sum_{i,j} W_{ij} \|\phi(x_i) - \phi(x_j)\|^2 \end{aligned} \tag{20}$$

We input the output of the DAN to a fully connected layer that, along with the project label columns, serves as the input to the classifier to accomplish the final prediction of cross-project defects. We chose SVM as the classifier, which has some advantages in handling high-dimensional data.

4. Experiments Design

In this section, we will introduce the research questions, dataset, experimental baselines, and evaluation metrics that our experiments will explore.

4.1. Research Questions

Our experimental motivation is to investigate the effectiveness of our method in various aspects. Therefore, we propose the following questions and conduct experiments around them.

RQ1: How does our proposed method compare to the baseline algorithms in cross-project software defect prediction? RQ1 is our most critical research question, aimed at exploring the comparison between our method and the baseline approach. For baseline algorithms, we examined classical methods in cross-project software defect prediction, with their names and descriptions provided in Section 4.3. In Section 5.1, we will compare the performance of our proposed SPD-MTF method with the baseline algorithms based on evaluation metrics.

RQ2: Does our method of using fused features effectively enhance the predicted effect of cross-project software defect prediction? RQ2 aims to explore whether our proposed method of feature fusion truly improves the effect of cross-project software defect prediction. Our approach suggests using both code statistical features and deep semantic features simultaneously, merging them into a new feature set to mine more information within projects to enhance the final prediction effect. We will conduct experiments around RQ2 to compare the impact of using code statistical features alone, semantic features alone, and our method on defect prediction effect. Section 5.2 presents specific data and conclusions of these experiments.

RQ3: How does the dimensionality of the fused features of SDP-MTF affect cross-project software defect prediction effect? RQ3 aims to explore the impact of the dimensionality of the fused features of SDP-MTF on the model effect. The fused features used in SDP-MTF consist of two parts, namely, the coded statistical features with feature transfer and the AST-based semantic features, and the two features are connected to form the final fused features using the *contact* operation, and we will explore the impact of the dimensionality of the two feature vectors on the final effect, respectively. The results and analysis of this RQ are shown in Section 5.3.

RQ4: Does our proposed compound method based on domain multiple transfer learning effectively improve the effect of cross-project software defect prediction? In RQ4, we investigate the impact of our proposed method combining domain adaptation transfer learning and feature transfer on the final defect prediction effect. In this research question, we will compare methods that do not use a discriminator and directly use fused features for defect prediction, with methods that use a discriminator but do not perform feature transfer on code statistical features, and the performance of SDP-MTF. Section 5.4 elucidates the specific performance of these experiments.

4.2. Dataset and Evaluation Metrics

We use the commonly used PROMISE dataset in software defect prediction as our dataset [19]. The PROMISE dataset contains open-source project codes, collected by Jureczko and Madeyski and available from the PROMISE data repository. We selected six projects, all written in JAVA, and obtained the source code and code statistical features from the dataset. Table 2 shows the names, versions, sizes, and defect rates of the projects used.

Table 2. The Dataset.

Project	Version	Amount	Defect Percentage
Camel	1.6	935	20.10%
Poi	3.0	438	64.10%
Xerces	1.4.4	508	76.80%
Lucene	2.4	330	61.50%
Xalan	2.6	875	53.10%
Log4j	1.2	194	95.90%

On the evaluation indicators of the supervised classification model, we used the F1-Score. Its formula is as follows:

$$F1\text{-}Score = \frac{2 \times Precision \times Recall}{Precision + Recall} \quad (21)$$

Among them, Precision represents the accuracy of the positive predictions made by the model, while Recall refers to the proportion of actual positive cases that were correctly identified by the model. The formulas for these metrics are as follows:

$$Precision = \frac{TP}{TP + FP} \quad (22)$$

$$Recall = \frac{TP}{TP + FN} \quad (23)$$

Finally, in order to assess the generalization ability and stability of the algorithm over different cross-project pairs, this paper also uses the IQR Range (IQR) in statistical learning to qualitatively assess the algorithmic metrics in terms of dispersion, outliers, and consistency. The IQR is the difference between the third quartile (Q3) and the first quartile (Q1) and is given by the equation:

$$IQR = Q3 - Q1 \quad (24)$$

Regarding the composition of cross-project software defect prediction tasks, we first select one project from the dataset as the target project and then use the remaining five projects as source projects, forming 30 pairs of cross-project software defect prediction tasks with six open-source projects.

4.3. Baseline

In selecting baseline methods, we chose to compare various representative cross-project software prediction methods, including algorithms that solely use code statistical features like TCA [4] and NNFilter [25], algorithms that exclusively use deep semantic features like DBN [26] and AC-GAN [27], and an algorithm that combines both types of features, CNN-THFL [16] and BATM [28]. Table 3 lists the selected baseline algorithms and their brief information.

Table 3. The information of baseline algorithm.

Algorithm	Author	Year	Features	Training Model
NNFilter	[25]	2009	Statistic feature	Naive Bayes
TCA	[5]	2013	Statistic feature	Transfer Component Analysis (TCA)
DBN	[26]	2018	Deep sematic feature	Deep Belief Network (DBN)
AC-GAN	[27]	2022	Deep sematic feature	Generative Adversarial Network (GAN)
CNN-THFL	[16]	2019	Statistic feature and deep semantic feature	TCA + CNN
BATM	[28]	2024	Statistic feature and deep semantic feature	Adversarial Learning

TCA and NNFilter are classic methods for cross-project software defect prediction using only code statistical features, laying a solid foundation for this prediction approach. TCA+ is a variant of the classic feature transfer algorithm TCA, adapted for prediction tasks, aiming to extend the application of the TCA algorithm using custom data preprocessing rules and regularization terms. NNFilter applies instance transfer in software defect prediction, filtering out source project data unrelated to the target project to make the data distribution between projects more similar.

For algorithms using only deep semantic features, we selected DBN and AC-GAN. DBN utilizes Deep Belief Networks (DBN) to automatically learn semantic features from token vectors extracted from program abstract syntax trees and source code changes. AC-GAN, after extracting semantic word vectors from the abstract syntax tree of the source code, employs adversarial learning for feature extraction and data transfer to complete defect prediction tasks.

Finally, as mentioned earlier, there are a few methods that fuse code statistical and deep features. We selected two algorithms for comparison. CNN-THFL mines deep learning-generated features from token vectors extracted from program abstract syntax trees through convolutional neural networks, then adds code statistical features for feature fusion and utilizes TCA for transferable joint features. BATM also employs a method that uses both types of features simultaneously. They introduce pseudo-labels and an auxiliary classifier, ensuring the model's predictive performance across different projects through adversarial training.

To ensure the validity of our experiments, we ran the above methods under the same experimental conditions as our proposed SDP-MTF, adjusting according to the parameters described in the papers to ensure that the experimental data are recorded when each model is in its optimal state.

5. Experimental Results

In this chapter, we will explore the four research questions (RQs) proposed in Section 4.1, demonstrating the effectiveness of our model from various perspectives.

5.1. Model Prediction Result

In response to the question raised in RQ1, we compare our method with the baseline algorithms mentioned in Section 4.3, using the F1-Score as the evaluation metric, as specified in Section 4.2. For each experiment, we use one project as the target project and each of the other five projects as the source project, conducting single-source cross-project defect prediction experiments. The results of all single-source cross-project software defect predictions are presented in Table 4. We used a bold font to indicate the best-case scenario for this cross-project prediction.

In all the comparison experiments, our proposed SDP-MTF method achieves the highest average F1-Score of 0.7061, which is on average 8% to 15.2% better than other algorithms. Meanwhile, in all but three cross-project pair experiments, "Lucene → Camel", "Camel → Log4j" and "Xalan → Log4j", SDP-MTF achieves the highest average F1-Score of 0.7061, which is 8% to 15.2% higher than other algorithms. SDP-MTF achieves the highest precision and F1-Score. Specifically, SDP-MTF improves F1-Score by up to 28.2% and 13.8% on average compared to the NNFilter algorithm; it improves F1-Score by up to 35.8% and 13.7% on average compared to the TCA+ algorithm; compared to the DBN algorithm, SDP-MTF improves F1-Score by up to 25.6% of F1-Score, with an average improvement of 15.2% of F1-Score; for AC-GAN, SDP-MTF improves up to 30.5% of F1-Score, with an average improvement of 8% of F1-Score, and the algorithm outperforms SDP-MTF on three project pairs, making it the best performing algorithm among the compared algorithms. Finally, CNN-THFL and BATM, similar to SDP-MTF, use the idea of combining statistical features with semantic features, and in terms of F1-Score, SDP-MTF improves 23.6% to CNN-THFL, with an average of 10.3%, and vs. BATM, SDP-MTF improves up to 30%, with an average of 5.6% on average.

Figure 4 shows the stability of each algorithm's F1-Score on different target projects. We show the maximum, minimum, and median values of each algorithm's F1-Score under different source projects when each project is the target project, as well as the stability of different algorithms in terms of IQR. The boxplots with different projects as target projects are separated by dashed lines, where the six different algorithms are distinguished by different colors. In this case, Figure 4a shows the performance of the algorithms when the target project is Camel, Log4j and Lucene, while Figure 4b demonstrates the case of the algorithms when the target project is Poi, Xalan and Xerces.

Combining the information from the above pictures, Camel has a large difference in F1-Score from the other projects, so in the subsequent discussion, we will focus on the cross-project pairs with the other projects as the target projects, and the reasons for the poor performance of Camel's project will be discussed in the final analysis section. In the cross-project prediction except Camel, the SDP-MTF algorithm shows the best results with the smallest IQR, i.e., the best stability, and has the highest rankings on the majority of the project pairs, and the IQR is small on each target project, and the IQR for the F1-Score is

0.02, which is ranked the second best among all algorithms, and has a good stability and generalization ability.

Table 4. The F1-Score of SDP-MTF with baseline algorithm.

Source Project	Target Project	SDP-MTF	NNFilter	TCA+	DBN	AC-GAN	CNN-THFL	BATM
Log4j	Camel	**0.3988**	0.2044	0.2208	0.2477	0.3100	0.2690	0.3045
Lucene		0.3969	0.3204	0.3040	0.2765	0.4256	0.3565	0.4453
Poi		**0.3459**	0.2871	0.3160	0.3272	0.3384	0.2782	0.3339
Xalan		**0.3497**	0.3033	0.3057	0.2746	0.3180	0.3302	0.3502
Xerces		**0.4296**	0.3146	0.2882	0.2917	0.3546	0.3142	0.4245
Camel	Log4j	0.7660	0.6065	0.5758	0.6034	**0.7699**	0.6679	0.7286
Lucene		0.7851	0.5925	0.5833	0.6100	0.7603	0.6323	0.7961
Poi		**0.8016**	0.5771	0.6422	0.6308	0.7592	0.6208	0.6586
Xalan		0.7593	0.8303	0.8040	0.8018	**0.8125**	0.7835	0.7229
Xerces		**0.7852**	0.5923	0.6895	0.6295	0.7045	0.7069	0.7187
Camel	Lucene	**0.7466**	0.5142	0.6024	0.5691	0.7434	0.6100	0.7259
Log4j		**0.7424**	0.5914	0.5379	0.5408	0.6532	0.5605	0.6606
Poi		**0.7268**	0.5620	0.6404	0.5617	0.7011	0.6829	0.6037
Xalan		**0.7935**	0.7063	0.7158	0.6543	0.4886	0.6903	0.6065
Xerces		**0.7783**	0.6141	0.5962	0.5401	0.6260	0.6756	0.7193
Camel	Poi	**0.7396**	0.4576	0.5752	0.5735	0.7058	0.6590	0.5847
Log4j		**0.7561**	0.6570	0.3981	0.5670	0.6907	0.5205	0.6950
Lucene		**0.7796**	0.6195	0.7343	0.5516	0.6575	0.6324	0.6151
Xalan		**0.7966**	0.7704	0.5981	0.6858	0.7243	0.7455	0.7764
Xerces		**0.7555**	0.7254	0.5081	0.5811	0.7195	0.5864	0.6688
Camel	Xalan	**0.7592**	0.5686	0.5454	0.6182	0.4930	0.6858	0.6771
Log4j		**0.7822**	0.7089	0.6278	0.7447	0.7542	0.7424	0.6503
Lucene		**0.7984**	0.6100	0.6024	0.6142	0.5576	0.6495	0.6708
Poi		**0.7816**	0.5004	0.6026	0.6266	0.7312	0.6364	0.7066
Xerces		**0.7325**	0.5844	0.7068	0.6268	0.5815	0.6823	0.6747
Camel	Xerces	**0.7663**	0.5039	0.5595	0.5609	0.6168	0.6521	0.7139
Log4j		**0.7825**	0.7128	0.7107	0.5470	0.6864	0.6535	0.7081
Lucene		**0.7701**	0.6886	0.6563	0.5113	0.7029	0.6904	0.6544
Poi		**0.7908**	0.5858	0.6389	0.5551	0.7655	0.7158	0.6716
Xalan		**0.7864**	0.7310	0.7849	0.7023	0.6295	0.6517	0.6720
	Avg	**0.7061**	0.5680	0.5690	0.5542	0.6261	0.6028	0.6290

For the other six comparative baseline algorithms. BATM, which uses two features with adversarial learning, was ranked second with an F1-Score of 0.6290. It is ranked fourth for stability with an IQR of 0.1082. And then is followed by AC-GAN, which employs the idea of adversarial learning, and is ranked third in terms of average F1-Score performance, while the algorithm is generally stable, with an IQR of 0.15 for the F1-Score, and is ranked fifth overall. The algorithm that ranked fourth in prediction effectiveness is CNN-THFL, an algorithm that also uses statistical features and semantic features of the code, and the algorithm has an IQR of 0.06, for the F1-Score, and ranks third in stability. The fifth and sixth-ranked algorithms are TCA+ and NNfilter which use coded statistical features and transfer learning of statistical features from the perspective of features and instances, respectively, and both perform poorly in terms of stability performance, with an IQR of 0.24 for the F1-Score of NNFliter, and 0.23 for the TCA+ algorithm, respectively. The final algorithm that performs poorly in our experiments is DBN which uses semantic features alone, with an IQR of 0.06, and ranked third in terms of stability. The algorithm that performed less well in our experiments was DBN with semantic features alone, with an average F1 value of 0.594, but this algorithm was the most stable with an IQR of 0.01 for the F1-Score.

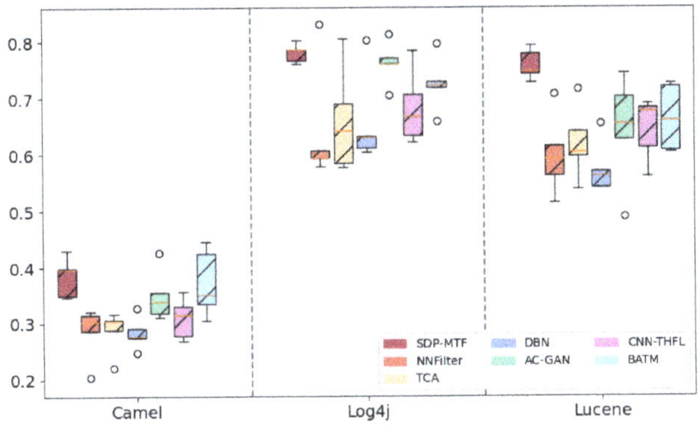

(**a**) Target projects are Camel, Log4j and Lucene

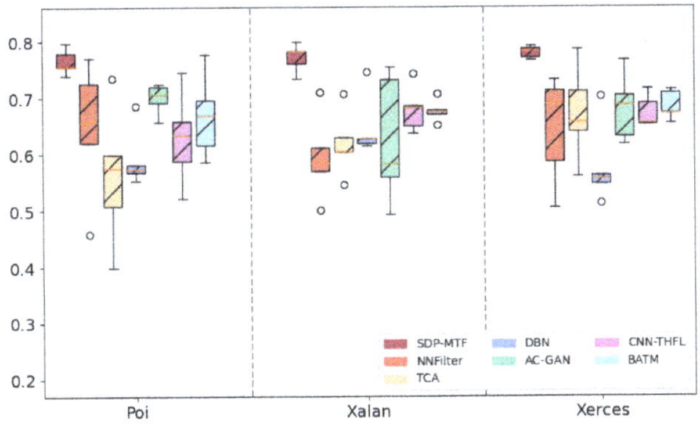

(**b**) Target projects are Poi, Xalan and Xerces

Figure 4. The stability of F1-Score of SDP-MTF and baseline algorithms on different target projects.

The performance of the baseline algorithms also gives some useful information: first, the first and second-ranked algorithms are SDP-MTF and AC-GAN, while the DBN method using semantic features alone is slightly insufficient in terms of F1-Score, which side by side indicates that the semantic features need to be learned and processed further during the transfer process, and also need to be supplemented with deep transfer learning for cross-project coordination; second, the same as SDP- MTF also using the method BATM CNN-THFL that combines code statistical features and semantic features performs better than NNfilter, TCA+ algorithm that uses code statistical features alone and DBN algorithm that uses semantic features alone, which proves that the use of the combination of code statistical features and semantic features can improve the F1-Score and validates the motivation of our proposed method. We will discuss the project and algorithm effects in more depth in the subsequent analysis.

RQ1 Results: Our proposed SDP-MTF method outperformed the baseline algorithms in terms of F1-Score, ranking second in stability among all algorithms.

5.2. Impact of Fusion Features on the Experimental Model

This subsection develops ablation experiments for RQ2, aiming to explore whether our proposed feature fusion approach improves the effect of cross-project software defect prediction.

Table 5 shows the F1-Score of the algorithm for SDP-MTF versus the algorithm using a feature alone. SDP-MTF uses a combination of code statistical features and semantic features to fuse them into new features that mine more information within the project to improve the final prediction effect. We compare the performance of the algorithms SDP-DS (Deep-learning based Semantic Feature) using semantic features alone, SDP-CS (Code Statistic Feature) using code statistical features alone, and SDP-MTF with fused features through ablation experiments. The first two columns of the table represent the source and target projects, the third to last column is the F1-Score, and the last row represents the average performance of each algorithm.

Table 5. The F1-Score for SDP-MTF and algorithms using features alone.

Source Project	Target Project	SDP-MTF	SDP-DS	SDP-CS
Log4j	Camel	**0.3988**	0.3805	0.3668
Lucene		**0.3969**	0.3648	0.3668
Poi		**0.3459**	0.3319	0.3213
Xalan		0.3497	0.3249	**0.4063**
Xerces		**0.4296**	0.3842	0.3901
Camel	Log4j	**0.7660**	0.7063	0.7335
Lucene		**0.7851**	0.7057	0.6918
Poi		**0.8016**	0.6554	0.7208
Xalan		**0.7593**	0.6780	0.6169
Xerces		**0.7852**	0.6685	0.6531
Camel	Lucene	**0.7466**	0.7287	0.6735
Log4j		**0.7424**	0.6628	0.6031
Poi		**0.7268**	0.6609	0.6115
Xalan		**0.7935**	0.7190	0.6630
Xerces		**0.7783**	0.7013	0.6555
Camel	Poi	**0.7396**	0.6552	0.5919
Log4j		**0.7561**	0.7394	0.6268
Lucene		**0.7796**	0.7016	0.6432
Xalan		**0.7966**	0.7302	0.6804
Xerces		**0.7555**	0.6989	0.6564
Camel	Xalan	**0.7592**	0.6564	0.5793
Log4j		**0.7822**	0.6940	0.6278
Lucene		**0.7984**	0.6883	0.6058
Poi		**0.7816**	0.6376	0.5037
Xerces		**0.7325**	0.6535	0.5943
Camel	Xerces	**0.7663**	0.6605	0.7212
Log4j		**0.7825**	0.6622	0.6402
Lucene		**0.7701**	0.7036	0.6537
Poi		**0.7908**	0.7253	0.6762
Xalan		**0.7864**	0.6546	0.6941
Avg		**0.7061**	0.6311	0.5990

It is easy to see that SDP-MTF using fused features outperforms SDP-DS using semantic features alone and SDP-CS using code statistical features alone, while comparing SDP-DS and SDP-CS, they perform similarly, with SDP-DS using only semantic features slightly outperforming SDP-CS using code statistical features alone. The average SDP-DS F1-Score using only semantic features is 0.6311, which is 7.4 percentage points lower than the SDP-MTF algorithm. The average F1-Score of the SDP-CS algorithm using code statistical features alone is 0.5990, which is 10.7 percentage points lower than the SDP-MTF algorithm using fused features. On the algorithm using code semantic and statistical features alone, the semantic features are slightly better but still have a large gap with the fusion features, which proves the effectiveness of the fusion features, and verifies that a single type of feature will lead to a lower effect, and also verifies our view that there is a need for complementary information between the two features.

The bars in Figure 5 represent, from left to right, the fusion feature algorithm SDP-MTF, the semantic feature alone SDP-DS, and the code statistical feature alone SDP-CS. From the figure, we can see that the stability of SDP-MTF is better than that of SDP-DS with the semantic feature alone and SDP-CS with the code statistical feature alone. CS, with the smallest IQR, which we believe is related to the introduction of multiple types of features, compensates for the feature information while improving the generalization ability of the model. The four-digit scores of SDP-DS and SDP-CS are similarly spaced, specifically, the IQR of the SDP-DS F1-Score with semantic features only is 0.07, while the IQR of the SDP-CS with code statistical features only is 0.08.

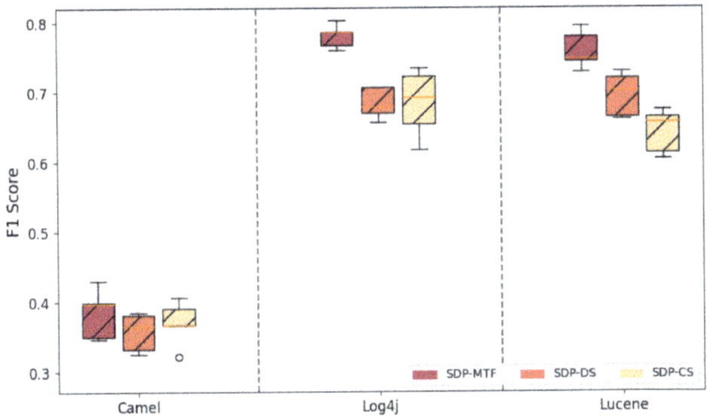

(**a**) Target projects are Camel, Log4j and Lucene

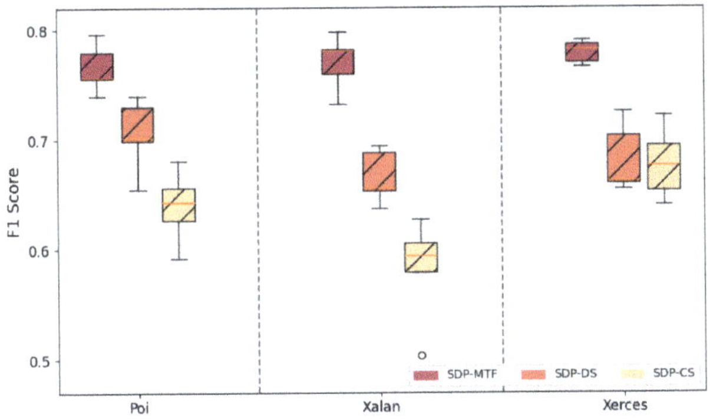

(**b**) Target projects are Poi, Xalan and Xerces

Figure 5. The stability of F1-Score of SDP-MTF and comparison algorithms using feature alone on different target projects.

From the comparison in RQ2, we can draw the following informative conclusion: the prediction effect using fused features is higher than the result of using a feature alone while keeping other experimental conditions constant. Meanwhile, our experiments also answer RQ2 that the use of fusion features can effectively improve the prediction effect of the model, and under the same experimental conditions, the prediction effect is better than the effect of the model that uses semantic features and code statistics features alone. Fusion features can be more effective in solving the problem of a single type of feature, and at the same time, the introduction of fusion features can make the feature information more comprehensive, effectively making up for the problem of insufficient feature information mining.

RQ2 Result: Our proposed method of using fusion features is effective and can significantly improve the prediction effect of cross-project defects when comparing the models using code statistical features alone and semantic features alone.

5.3. Impact of Feature Dimensions on Model Result

This subsection conducts experiments for RQ3 with the aim of exploring the impact of the dimension of the fusion features of SDP-MTF on the effect of the model. The fusion features we use consist of two parts, the coded statistical features with feature transfer and the AST-based semantic features, in this subsection, the generated dimensions of the semantic features are directly generated using Bi-LSTM control, whereas the dimensions of the statistical features are usually reduced or unchanged after feature transfer, and we will use a fully connected layer to control the length of the statistical features. We use Statistic to represent the code statistical features for the upper part of the fusion features, and Deep Semantic to represent the semantic features for the lower part of the fusion features and use the F1-Score as the judging metrics for this experiment.

First, we make the two parts of the features to be generated using 16, 32, 64, 96, 128, 160, 192, 224 and 256 dimensions for all the data for the experiment. Figure 6a,b are the 3D plots of the F1-Score of the SDP-MTF using different combinations of dimensions and the corresponding contour schematics.

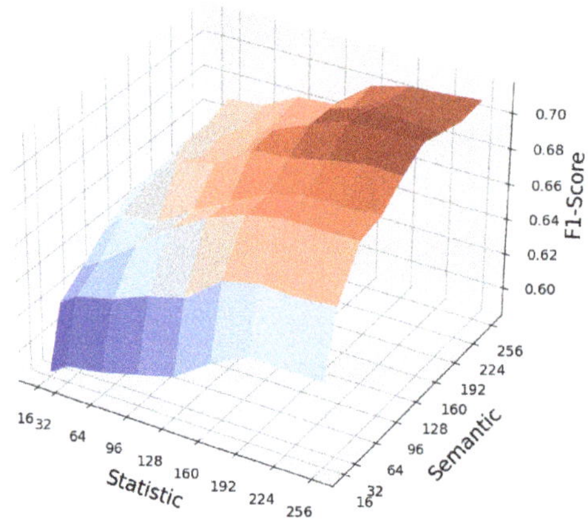

(**a**) The 3D plot of F1-Score

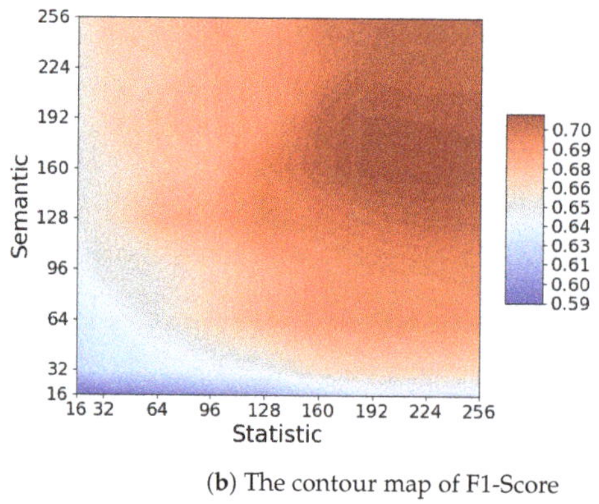

(**b**) The contour map of F1-Score

Figure 6. The effect of feature dimensions on the F1-Score of the SDP-MTF.

The closer the color to red in Figure 6 represents a higher F1-Score for that combination of dimensions, and the closer the color to blue indicates a lower F1-Score. We can see that the F1-Score of the model is low when the generated dimensions of both embeddings are low, and the F1-Score of the model starts to improve with the increase in feature dimensions, but when both embeddings are in high dimensions, the model dimensions gradually level off and no longer rise, and even have a tendency to fall. When the difference between the dimensions of the statistical feature dimension and the semantic feature is large, the model will tend to use the feature with a large dimension more for classification, resulting in the failure of the fusion feature, and the F1-Score tends to be closer to the performance of the feature alone. When the semantic feature dimension is low, Bi-LSTM cannot adequately capture the complexity of the utterance structure, leading to information loss, which affects the final task performance, so it is important to ensure the dimension of the semantic features, and it also restricts the statistical feature dimension not to differ too much from it. When the vector dimension is high, although the embedding vectors contain rich information, it may lead to overfitting, and also increase the computational complexity and memory requirements, which is the reason why the final F1-Score in Figure 6 has leveled off or even decreased. The model achieved the best average results at 160 dimensions for statistical features and 192 dimensions for semantic features, so we chose this parameter for model prediction in subsequent experiments and other research questions.

Next, we will explore the effect of each of the two feature lengths on the model's effectiveness. Since the best results of the model were obtained when the statistical features were 160 dimensions and the semantic features were 192 dimensions, we will control the dimension change in a single variable in the next experiments while setting the other vector dimension to the above dimensions as a way to ensure the validity and reliability of the experiments. Figure 7 shows the performance of F1-Score of SDP-MTF on cross-project prediction when the dimension of a single vector is varied and the other vector is fixed to the nearest dimension, in which the red curve Statistic indicates the change in F1 value produced by the method when the dimension of the statistically based feature vectors is varied, in which case the dimension of the deep semantic vectors generated based on the Bi-LSTM is fixed at 192 dimensions; similarly, the gray Deep Semantic curve represents the change in the F1 value of the model caused by the change in the dimension of the semantic features, at which time the dimension of the statistical features is fixed to be unchanged at 160 dimensions. We can see that in all the experiments, the F1-Score of SDP-MTF is affected by the fusion feature dimensions, and the trend is that the F1-Score is lower in low dimensions, and as the vector dimensions increase, the F1-Score increases, and then tends to stabilize, and a smooth trend occurs after high dimensions. Among the two types of vectors, the model is more sensitive to changes in the dimension of the semantic features generated by Bi-LSTM, and the slopes of the folds are relatively larger.

Therefore, it can be concluded that the dimension size of the fused features has an effect on the final prediction results of the model, which is manifested in the fact that the F1-Score of the model firstly increases with the dimension of the two types of vectors, and then it tends to be stable or slightly fluctuates; therefore, the selection of appropriate generation dimension for the two types of vectors is necessary, and both types of vectors have an effect on the prediction results of the model. Meanwhile, the generating dimensions of 160 dimensions and 192 dimensions that we chose for the two features achieved the best results in our experiments, which also proved the effectiveness of our experiments.

RQ3 Results: The dimension of the fused features has an effect on the prediction effect of SDP-MTF, which is shown as follows: (1) when the dimension of the fused features is low, the prediction effect is low; (2) as the dimension of the fused features increases, the prediction effect appears to increase firstly and then stabilize; (3) when the dimension of the two vectors in the fused features has a large difference, the prediction effect tends to be the effect of the feature with larger dimension alone; (4) the model reaches the best result at 160 dimensions for the code statistical features and 192 dimensions for the semantic features, which is the final choice of the fusion feature dimension in our model.

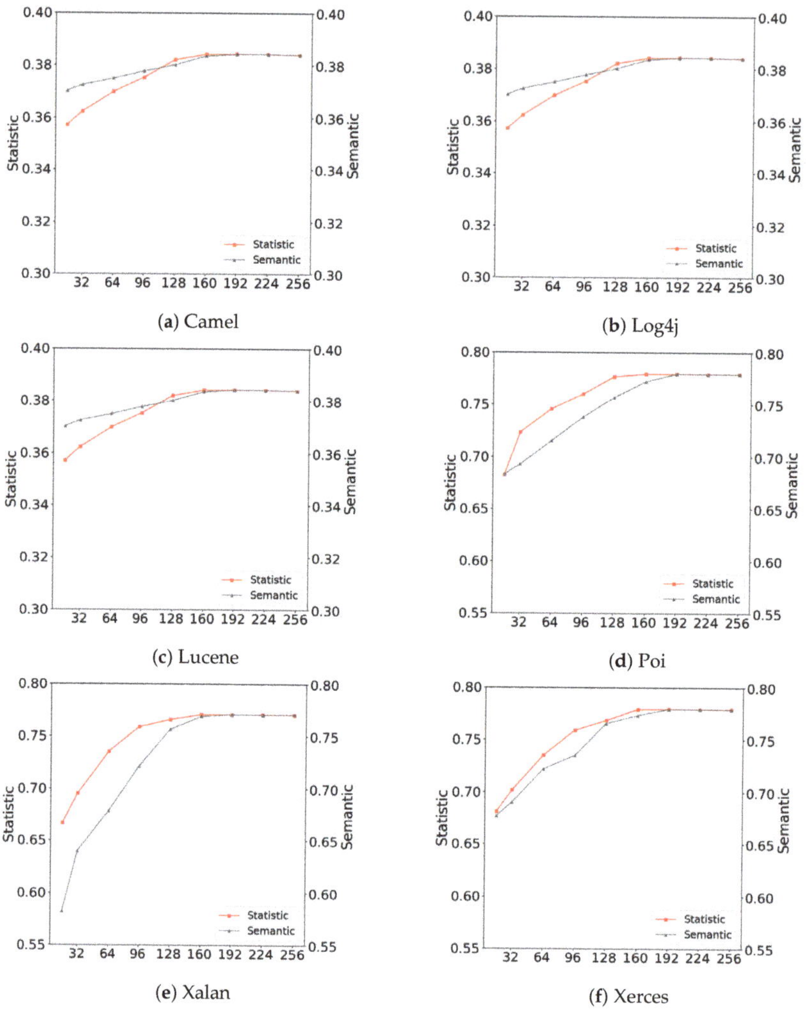

(**a**) Camel (**b**) Log4j (**c**) Lucene (**d**) Poi (**e**) Xalan (**f**) Xerces

Figure 7. The mean F1-Score performance of SDP-MTF when using a single transformed feature dimension.

5.4. *Effectiveness of Multiple Transfer Learning*

This subsection develops the ablation experiment for RQ4. This research question aims to investigate the effectiveness of multiple transfer learning methods for feature transfer and deep transfer learning, which refer to the method applied to statistical feature TCA+ and the method applied to deep adaptive neural networks with fused features, respectively. Table 6 shows the effect and F1-Score performance of the algorithmic model.

We set up the following ablation experiments: SDP-ND (Non-Domain Adaptation based), which uses fusion features generated by feature transfer but does not use a domain adaptation layer, SDP-NT (Non-TCA+ based), which is a method that uses the domain adaptation idea but does not use TCA+ for the code statistics features in the fusion features, and the original model SDP-MTF, i.e., the method that uses the multiple transfer learning idea.

Table 6. The F1-Score for SDP-MTF and algorithms using transfer learning alone.

Source Project	Target Project	SDP-MTF	SDP-UD	SDP-UT
Log4j	Camel	0.3988	0.2301	**0.4058**
Lucene		0.3969	0.3881	**0.4382**
Poi		0.3459	0.3186	**0.4381**
Xalan		0.3497	0.3454	**0.3582**
Xerces		**0.4296**	0.2826	0.4053
Camel	Log4j	**0.7660**	0.6233	0.6319
Lucene		**0.7851**	0.6281	0.6030
Poi		**0.8016**	0.5835	0.6565
Xalan		**0.7593**	0.5387	0.6854
Xerces		**0.7852**	0.6058	0.6775
Camel	Lucene	**0.7466**	0.5682	0.6596
Log4j		**0.7424**	0.6176	0.7127
Poi		**0.7268**	0.6104	0.6706
Xalan		**0.7935**	0.5702	0.6486
Xerces		**0.7783**	0.5271	0.6981
Camel	Poi	**0.7396**	0.5247	0.6937
Log4j		**0.7561**	0.4809	0.6456
Lucene		**0.7796**	0.5715	0.7233
Xalan		**0.7966**	0.5178	0.7005
Xerces		**0.7555**	0.4534	0.6393
Camel	Xalan	**0.7592**	0.6202	0.6666
Log4j		**0.7822**	0.5226	0.5857
Lucene		**0.7984**	0.5535	0.6464
Poi		**0.7816**	0.6076	0.6443
Xerces		**0.7325**	0.5653	0.5931
Camel	Xerces	**0.7663**	0.5016	0.6003
Log4j		**0.7825**	0.6029	0.5732
Lucene		**0.7701**	0.4671	0.602
Poi		**0.7908**	0.5766	0.6856
Xalan		**0.7864**	0.5699	0.5726
Avg		**0.7061**	0.6311	0.5990

From the table, we can learn that the SDP-MTF algorithm effectively improves the F1-Score using the transfer learning idea, which confirms the effectiveness of our proposed multiple transfer idea. In addition to this, the method SDP-NT without TCA+ outperforms the SDP-ND method without a domain adaptation layer. The SDP-NT method achieves an F1-Score of 0.6087, which is a 9.7% percentage difference compared to the SDP-MTF method; whereas, the SDP-ND method performs poorly in cross-project prediction due to the lack of a domain adaptation layer, with an average F1-Score of 0.5191, which is lower than the SDP-MTF method by 18.7%. This validates the need for transfer learning and the effectiveness of multiple transfer learning.

Figure 8 shows the stability effect of different algorithms. From left to right in the figure are SDP-MTF, SDP-ND without Domain Adaptation Layer and SDP-NT without TCA+. In terms of stability, SDP-UT has a similar IQR as SDP-MTF, with an IQR of 0.03 for the F1-Score, which indicates that both have similar generalization-ability and both have good stability. While the stability of SDP-UD is poorer, the IQR is 0.14, respectively, and the data fluctuate more. The comparison of the three suggests that multiple migration learning does not have a large impact on the fluctuation of the prediction effect.

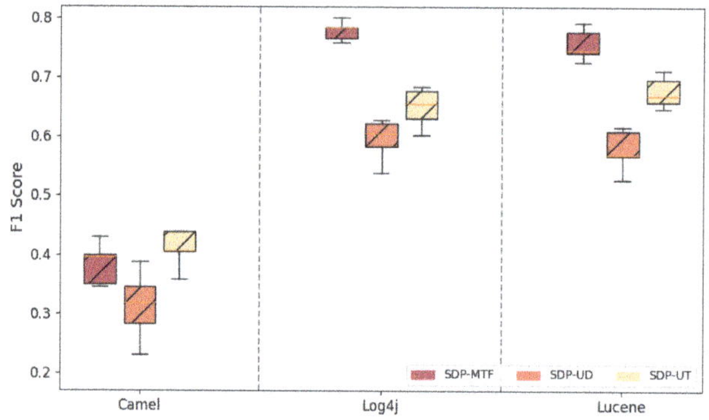

(**a**) Target projects for Camel, Log4j and Lucene

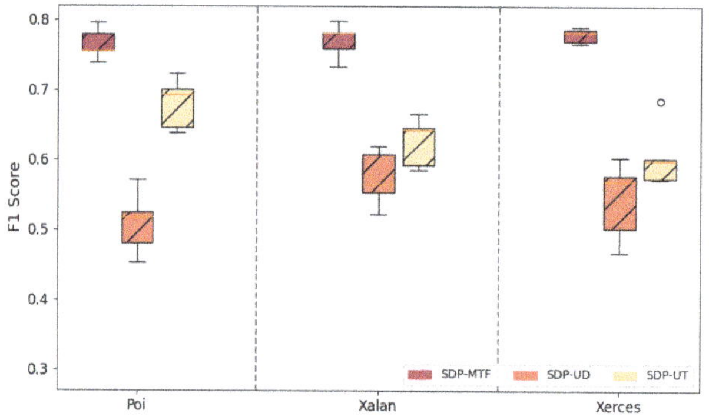

(**b**) Target projects for Poi, Xalan and Xerces

Figure 8. The stability of F1-Score of algorithms for SDP-MTF and single transfer learning on different target projects.

We can infer the following information from this experiment: first, the idea of multiple transfer learning used by the method is effective, and our SDP-MTF method shows sufficient advantages, whether comparing algorithms that do not use the domain adaptation layer or methods that do not use feature transfer learning. Second, in terms of the stability of the algorithm, the use of multiple transfer learning does not cause large fluctuations in the predictors. Finally, the domain adaptation layer of deep transfer learning can effectively improve the prediction effect using semantic features and is an effective deep transfer method.

RQ4 Results: The idea of transfer learning method with deep adaptive neural network and multiple transfer learning with feature transfer that we use is effective, and under the same experimental conditions, SDP-MTF shows advantages in F1-Score over the algorithm without feature transfer and without domain adaptation layer, which improves the prediction.

6. Result Analysis and Discussion

6.1. Analysis and Comparison

From the above four RQs, we show the effectiveness of the model, the effectiveness of the fused features, the influence of feature dimensions on the prediction effect, and the effectiveness of the multiple transfer learning idea from multiple perspectives. In this subsection, we will explore the model effect in general and summarize the phenomena and conclusions observed in the above experiments.

Firstly, the model effectiveness. SDP-MTF shows different improvements in average F1-Score than the other six comparative baseline algorithms in all the 6-project, 30 cross-project pairs experiments. The use of fused features can fruitfully improve model prediction compared to algorithms that use statistical or semantic features of the code alone, as can be seen in the baseline algorithms BATM and CNN-THFL, which, as methods that also use two types of fused features, we can see that they are more effective than algorithms that use a particular type of feature alone, and they are ranked the second and the fourth out of all the algorithms. In addition, the poor performance of the DBN algorithm side-steps the fact that semantic features alone may not work very well for mining defective patterns, and that further work is needed to close the gap between projects or to include traditional features for information remediation. Finally, we also briefly assessed the stability of the individual algorithms, mainly by comparing the variance of the two metrics of each algorithm on all projects. The SDP-MTF algorithms show good stability on all F1-Score except for the Camel project. All these performances prove the effectiveness of our proposed SDP-MTF model.

This is followed by the evaluation of the SDP-MTF feature construction phase. In our experiments, it can be seen that the low cross-project prediction accuracy with the Camel project as the target project is directly related to the fact that the characteristics of the Camel project are significantly different from other projects and have a low defect rate. Differences in features between projects pose a significant challenge to cross-project defect prediction. Changes in feature distribution can lead to mismatches, which can degrade the model performance as the model may overfit the features of the source item or fail to generalize to the target item; therefore, in this paper, we abate the feature differences between items by two methods, TCA and DAN, as a way to provide a better feature space for migration learning. In order to test the effectiveness of feature-to-feature fusion, we designed RQ2 and RQ3 to test the model. We use Research Question 2 experiments to evaluate the effectiveness of fused features and to verify whether fusing code statistical features and semantic features can compensate for the problem of insufficient feature information mining. The experiments demonstrate that fused features have a higher prediction effect than using one type of feature alone. Moreover, the effect of SDP-DS using only semantic features is lower than that of SDP-CS, which also side by side confirms that a single type of feature and the use of deep features alone may not bring good results and that the introduction of code statistical features to complement the information from another perspective of the procedure is beneficial to the mining and correlation of defective patterns.

RQ3 explores the effect of the dimensionality of fusion features on the prediction effectiveness. The dimensionality of fusion features is determined by the dimensions of both statistical and semantic features. The dimensionality of a feature vector is closely related to its information representation capability, which represents how much information and intrinsic relationships can be captured by the vector. Longer feature vectors tend to capture more complex and detailed features, but at the same time, excessively long generating dimensions for feature vectors may also lead to problems such as model complexity, sparsity of high-dimensional space, and excessive computational overhead of the model. In our experiments, we first used multiple sets of generating dimensions to make the dimensions of two vectors change at the same time and record the model performance; after that, we searched for the point where the lengths of two vectors are most suitable, fixed the generating dimension of one vector, respectively, and changed the lengths of the other vector to record the model changes. The experimental results show that the dimension of the fused features will have a non-negligible impact on the final prediction of the model, and when the feature dimension is low, there will be a phenomenon of insufficient feature information capture leading to low model effect, while with the increase in the generation dimension, the model effect will first increase and then converge to a stable state. In the experiment of single generation length change, the semantic feature length change generated by the Bi-LSTM model is more likely to cause the change in the whole model effect, which is related to the characteristic that Bi-LSTM is not good at dealing with long sequence information. Therefore, finally, we choose the feature dimension of 352 dimensions of fused features (160 dimensions of statistical features and 192 dimensions of semantic features) as the criterion for the experiment.

RQ4 focuses on verifying the effectiveness of multiple migration learning. In our model, two modes of feature migration and deep adaptive neural network are used, corresponding to the code statistical features and the fused features incorporating the semantic features, and the two parts are used in combination to reduce the inter-item variance and improve the prediction results. The core idea of both means is to reduce the variability of features across items. TCA+-based feature migration focuses more on mapping the features of different items into a unified space to reduce the variance and achieve feature dimension alignment. Deep adaptive neural networks, on the other hand, focus more on the adaptive processing of source and target domain data through adaptive layers. This adaptive layer design makes the data distributions in the source and target domains closer to each other, thus improving the efficiency and effectiveness of data migration. From the experimental results, both of the means we used successfully improved the prediction effect.

Finally, we explore the similarities and differences between SDP-MTF and baseline algorithms. We have chosen six comparison algorithms, which can be divided into three categories according to the different use of features, namely NNFilter and TCA+ which use coded statistical features alone, DBN and AC-GAN which use semantic features alone, and CNN-THFL which uses a combination of coded statistical and semantic features. For the two algorithms of coded statistical features, NNFilter and TCA+ The difference is that the former focuses on instance migration, while the latter takes in feature migration, and in terms of effect TCA+ gives better results than NNFilter, which also inspired our algorithms and CNN-THFL. Algorithms DBN and AC-GAN, which use semantic features alone, both mine information from token sequences and ASTs, respectively, while AC-GAN employs the idea of adversarial learning for the latter step of migration, which improves the model effect and gives better results than DBN. The two algorithms CNN-THFL and BATM are the rare methods we found to combine two features. Compared with CNN-THFL, the biggest difference of our algorithm is the introduction of a deep adaptive neural network in the migration learning model of the fused features; while comparing with BATM, our algorithm uses multiple migration learning to weaken the item differences, which makes the model further improve the prediction effect.

6.2. Potential Risks and Future Prospects

We next discuss potential threats to our approach. Firstly, the construction factor, the representative algorithms in the controlled experiments used in this paper cannot be traced back to the source code, and thus methods reproduced according to the article's introduction are used, and the implementation of these methods may not be exactly the same as that of the original authors. Especially in the methods involving deep learning CNN-THFL and adversarial learning AC-GAN and BATM, although this paper adopts the parameter settings recommended by the original authors, it is not possible to reproduce the experimental environment and algorithmic constructions completely, and thus there may be some bias in the prediction results. In addition, this paper adopts the F1 score index as a comprehensive evaluation index to evaluate the model and lacks the index evaluation index in the unbalanced scenario.

Next, are the internal factors. The method proposed in this paper does not do the treatment of imbalance, and there is no guarantee that the method will achieve the same effect for samples with imbalanced defects. At the same time, this paper uses the method of combining code statistical features with deep semantic features to make up for the problem of a single type of feature, but in terms of the fusion means, this section only uses *contact* splicing operation and does not give enough consideration to other means of feature fusion, which may affect the model's final prediction accuracy, and the use of different feature fusion methods to better combine the two types of features is a future. The use of different feature fusion methods and the better combination of the two types of features are the key perspectives for further mining of feature information.

Finally, there are external factors. This paper uses the PROMISE dataset as the experimental dataset, these datasets are written in Java language, the defects contained in these datasets may be with tendency, and these datasets are small in size, this paper can not guarantee that the model achieves the same effect on other languages written in a larger scale project.

Looking forward, in response to these challenges, we plan to test our model on samples written in various programming languages and apply it in more realistic, real-world scenarios [29,30]. Additionally, we aim to delve deeper into the relationship between various representations of deep semantic features and defect patterns. Exploring alternative representations such as control flow graphs and data flow diagrams could enhance prediction effect [31,32]. Moreover, while our current methodology concentrates on single-source cross-project software defect prediction, exploring multi-source scenarios represents a compelling direction for future research [33]. In addition, To ensure the reliability of AI-based defect prediction models, formal methods can be employed for rigorous verification. By applying formal methods, we can verify that AI models adhere to predefined specifications and perform consistently across different projects, thus ensuring accurate and reliable defect predictions [34,35]. Finally, how to introduce interpretable analyses into cross-project software defect prediction research and use the results of cross-project software defect prediction and these interpretable analyses to be extracted and transformed into something that testers can accept and recognize and use for deeper guidance on software security [36] is a theme that we will continue to focus on.

7. Conclusions

Cross-project software defect prediction addresses the cold start problem and early data scarcity in software defect prediction, representing a critical approach to software quality assurance. However, current methodologies predominantly grapple with two challenges: inadequate feature information mining and significant probabilistic distribution gaps between projects, leading to reduced effect. To tackle these issues, we propose the SDP-MTF method, which integrates feature fusion and composite transfer learning. By merging code statistical features with deep semantic features, we mine source code information from diverse perspectives, addressing the problem of incomplete feature information. Additionally, our approach employs a composite transfer learning strategy combining feature transfer based on TCA+ with DAN, effectively narrowing the gap between projects and concluding with defect prediction via the SVM classifier. We evaluated SDP-MTF on six projects from the PROMISE dataset, demonstrating its efficacy across various dimensions. The results show that SDP-MTF significantly outperforms six advanced baseline algorithms employing different feature methods, with an average improvement of 8% to 15.2% on the F1-Score. Future work will extend this research to real-world projects and explore multi-source cross-project defect prediction through further experimental studies.

Author Contributions: Conceptualization, T.L. and J.X.; methodology, T.L. and Y.W.; software, T.L. and D.M.; validation, T.L., D.M. and Z.K.; data curation, M.L. and Z.K.; writing—original draft preparation, T.L. and Y.W.; writing—review and editing, J.X., D.M. and Y.W.; visualization, T.L., M.L. and Z.K.; supervision, J.X. and Y.W.; project administration, J.X. and Y.W.; funding acquisition, J.X. All authors have read and agreed to the published version of the manuscript.

Funding: This work was supported by Major Scientific and Technological Innovation Projects of Shandong Province (2020CXGC010116) and the National Natural Science Foundation of China (No. 62172042).

Data Availability Statement: Data is contained within the article.

Conflicts of Interest: The authors declare no conflicts of interest.

References

1. Hall, T.; Beecham, S.; Bowes, D.; Gray, D.; Counsell, S. A Systematic Literature Review on Fault Prediction Performance in Software Engineering. *IEEE Trans. Softw. Eng.* **2012**, *38*, 1276–1304. [CrossRef]
2. Chen, X.; Wang, L.P.; Gu, Q.; Wang, Z.; Ni, C.; Liu, W.S.; Wang, Q.P. A Survey on Cross-Project Software Defect Prediction Methods. *Jisuanji Xuebao Chin. J. Comput.* **2018**, *41*, 254–274.
3. Briand, L.C.; Melo, W.L.; Wust, J. Assessing the applicability of fault-proneness models across object-oriented software projects. *IEEE Trans. Softw. Eng.* **2002**, *28*, 706–720. [CrossRef]
4. Nam, J.; Pan, S.J.; Kim, S. Transfer defect learning. In Proceedings of the 2013 35th International Conference on Software Engineering (ICSE), San Francisco, CA, USA, 18–26 May 2013; pp. 382–391.
5. Pan, S.J.; Tsang, I.W.; Kwok, J.T.; Yang, Q. Domain adaptation via transfer component analysis. *IEEE Trans. Neural Netw.* **2010**, *22*, 199–210. [CrossRef]
6. He, P.; Li, B.; Liu, X.; Chen, J.; Ma, Y. An empirical study on software defect prediction with a simplified metric set. *Inf. Softw. Technol.* **2015**, *59*, 170–190. [CrossRef]
7. Ni, C.; Chen, X.; Liu, W.; Gu, Q.; Huang, Q.; Li, N. Cross-project defect prediction method based on feature transfer and instance transfer. *J. Softw.* **2019**, *30*, 1308–1329.
8. Yao, Y.; Doretto, G. Boosting for transfer learning with multiple sources. In Proceedings of the 2010 IEEE Computer Society Conference on Computer Vision and Pattern Recognition, San Francisco, CA, USA, 13–18 June 2010; pp. 1855–1862.
9. Hosseini, S.; Turhan, B. A comparison of similarity based instance selection methods for cross project defect prediction. In Proceedings of the 36th Annual ACM Symposium on Applied Computing, Virtual Event, Republic of Korea, 22–26 March 2021; pp. 1455–1464.
10. Lei, T.; Xue, J.; Wang, Y.; Niu, Z.; Shi, Z.; Zhang, Y. WCM-WTrA: A Cross-Project Defect Prediction Method Based on Feature Selection and Distance-Weight Transfer Learning. *Chin. J. Electron.* **2022**, *31*, 354–366. [CrossRef]
11. Chen, D.; Li, B.; Zhou, C.; Zhu, X. Automatically identifying bug entities and relations for bug analysis. In Proceedings of the 2019 IEEE 1st International Workshop on Intelligent Bug Fixing (IBF), Hangzhou, China, 24 February 2019; pp. 39–43.
12. Wang, W.; Li, G.; Ma, B.; Xia, X.; Jin, Z. Detecting code clones with graph neural network and flow-augmented abstract syntax tree. In Proceedings of the 2020 IEEE 27th International Conference on Software Analysis, Evolution and Reengineering (SANER), London, ON, Canada, 18–21 February 2020; pp. 261–271.
13. Li, D.; Wong, W.E.; Jian, M.; Geng, Y.; Chau, M. Improving search-based automatic program repair with Neural Machine Translation. *IEEE Access* **2022**, *10*, 51167–51175. [CrossRef]
14. Wang, S.; Liu, T.; Tan, L. Automatically learning semantic features for defect prediction. In Proceedings of the 38th International Conference on Software Engineering, Austin, TX, USA, 14–22 May 2016; pp. 297–308.
15. Li, J.; He, P.; Zhu, J.; Lyu, M.R. Software defect prediction via convolutional neural network. In Proceedings of the 2017 IEEE International Conference on Software Quality, Reliability and Security (QRS), Prague, Czech Republic, 5–29 July 2017; pp. 318–328.
16. Qiu, S.; Lu, L.; Cai, Z.; Jiang, S. Cross-Project Defect Prediction via Transferable Deep Learning-Generated and Handcrafted Features. In Proceedings of the SEKE, Lisbon, Portugal, 10–12 July 2019; pp. 431–552.
17. Gupta, M.; Rajnish, K.; Bhattacharjee, V. Cognitive Complexity and Graph Convolutional Approach Over Control Flow Graph for Software Defect Prediction. *IEEE Access* **2022**, *10*, 108870–108894. [CrossRef]
18. Hamer, P.G.; Frewin, G.D. MH Halstead's Software Science-a critical examination. In Proceedings of the 6th International Conference on Software Engineering, Tokyo, Japan, 13–16 September 1982; pp. 197–206.
19. Jureczko, M.; Madeyski, L. Towards identifying software project clusters with regard to defect prediction. In Proceedings of the 6th International Conference on Predictive Models in Software Engineering, Timişoara, Romania, 12–13 September 2010; pp. 1–10.
20. Vaswani, A.; Shazeer, N.; Parmar, N.; Uszkoreit, J.; Jones, L.; Gomez, A.N.; Kaiser, Ł.; Polosukhin, I. Attention is all you need. *Adv. Neural Inf. Process. Syst.* **2017**, *30*.
21. Long, M.; Cao, Y.; Wang, J.; Jordan, M. Learning transferable features with deep adaptation networks. In Proceedings of the 25th International Conference on Machine Learning (ICML), Lille, France, 6–11 July 2015; pp. 97–105.
22. Wang, J.; Chen, Y.; Hao, S.; Peng, X.; Hu, L. Deep learning for sensor-based activity recognition: A survey. *Pattern Recognit. Lett.* **2019**, *119*, 3–11. Deep Learning for Pattern Recognition. [CrossRef]
23. Gretton, A.; Borgwardt, K.M.; Rasch, M.J.; Schölkopf, B.; Smola, A. A kernel two-sample test. *J. Mach. Learn. Res.* **2012**, *13*, 723–773.
24. Belkin, M.; Niyogi, P.; Sindhwani, V. Manifold regularization: A geometric framework for learning from labeled and unlabeled examples. *J. Mach. Learn. Res.* **2006**, *7*, 2399–2434.
25. Turhan, B.; Menzies, T.; Bener, A.B.; Di Stefano, J. On the relative value of cross-company and within-company data for defect prediction. *Empir. Softw. Eng.* **2009**, *14*, 540–578. [CrossRef]
26. Wang, S.; Liu, T.; Nam, J.; Tan, L. Deep semantic feature learning for software defect prediction. *IEEE Trans. Softw. Eng.* **2018**, *46*, 1267–1293. [CrossRef]
27. Xing, Y.; Qian, X.; Guan, Y.; Zhang, S.; Zhao, M.; Lin, W. Cross-project Defect Prediction Method Using Adversarial Learning. *J. Softw.* **2022**, *33*, 2097–2112.

8. Jiang, S.; Zhang, J.; Guo, F.; Ouyang, T.; Li, J. Balanced Adversarial Tight Matching for Cross-Project Defect Prediction. *IET Softw.* **2024**, *2024*, 1561351. [CrossRef]
9. Tang, L.; Bao, L.; Xia, X.; Huang, Z. Neural SZZ algorithm. In Proceedings of the 2023 38th IEEE/ACM International Conference on Automated Software Engineering (ASE), Luxembourg, 11–15 September 2023; pp. 1024–1035.
0. Yang, Y.; Xia, X.; Lo, D.; Grundy, J. A survey on deep learning for software engineering. *ACM Comput. Surv.* **2022**, *54*, 1–73. [CrossRef]
1. Xu, J.; Wang, F.; Ai, J. Defect prediction with semantics and context features of codes based on graph representation learning. *IEEE Trans. Reliab.* **2020**, *70*, 613–625. [CrossRef]
2. Ni, C.; Wang, W.; Yang, K.; Xia, X.; Liu, K.; Lo, D. The best of both worlds: Integrating semantic features with expert features for defect prediction and localization. In Proceedings of the 30th ACM Joint European Software Engineering Conference and Symposium on the Foundations of Software Engineering, Singapore, 14–18 November 2022; pp. 672–683.
3. Ryu, D.; Baik, J. Effective multi-objective naïve Bayes learning for cross-project defect prediction. *Appl. Soft Comput.* **2016**, *49*, 1062–1077. [CrossRef]
4. Krichen, M.; Mihoub, A.; Alzahrani, M.Y.; Adoni, W.Y.H.; Nahhal, T. Are Formal Methods Applicable to Machine Learning and Artificial Intelligence? In Proceedings of the 2022 2nd International Conference of Smart Systems and Emerging Technologies (SMARTTECH), Riyadh, Saudi Arabia, 9–11 May 2022; pp. 48–53.
5. Raman, R.; Gupta, N.; Jeppu, Y. Framework for Formal Verification of Machine Learning Based Complex System-of-Systems. *Insight* **2023**, *26*, 91–102. [CrossRef]
6. Dam, H.K.; Tran, T.; Ghose, A. Explainable software analytics. In Proceedings of the 40th International Conference on Software Engineering: New Ideas and Emerging Results, Gothenburg, Sweden, 27 May–3 June 2018; pp. 53–56.

electronics

Article

Delving Deep into Reverse Engineering of UEFI Firmwares via Human Interface Infrastructure

Siyi Chen [1], Yu-An Tan [2], Kefan Qiu [2], Zheng Zhang [2], Yuanzhang Li [1] and Quanxin Zhang [1,*]

[1] School of Computer Science & Technology, Beijing Institute of Technology, Beijing 100081, China; chensiyi@bit.edu.cn (S.C.); popular@bit.edu.cn (Y.L.)
[2] School of Cyberspace Science & Technology, Beijing Institute of Technology, Beijing 100081, China; tan2008@bit.edu.cn (Y.-A.T.); kfqiu@bit.edu.cn (K.Q.); zhangzheng@bit.edu.cn (Z.Z.)
* Correspondence: zhangqx@bit.edu.cn

Abstract: The Unified Extensible Firmware Interface (UEFI) provides a specification of the software interface between an OS and its underlying platform firmware. UEFI UI is an interactive interface that allows users to configure and manage UEFI settings, which is closely related to HII (Human Interface Infrastructure). In practice, HII provides a mechanism that allows developers to create UI elements with HII-related protocols. In this paper, we provide a comprehensive analysis of the UEFI combined with a case study. We proposed a protocol-centered static analysis method to obtain UEFI's password policy, using HII-related protocols to find password implementation. Existing static analyses are ineffective in detecting such password policy in stripped UEFI firmware images. By reverse-engineering the IFR (Internal Forms Representation) in HII, we located where much sensitive information is stored. Lastly, we studied hardware port configurations, using Secure Boot as a case in point. We analyzed how UEFI uses the HII protocol to set relevant information in the UEFI UI. This paper is the first to offer a reverse-engineering systematic analysis of exploring UEFI via HII, providing valuable insights into its structure and potential enhancements for firmware security.

Keywords: UEFI firmware; HII; UEFI UI; password policy; sensitive information; hardware configuration

1. Introduction

The Unified Extensible Firmware Interface (UEFI) [1] is currently the most popular industry standard, defining the software interface between an operating system and its underlying platform firmware. Many industry-leading technology companies have created the UEFI Forum, which defines the specifications of the interfaces [2] used by operating systems and Platform Initialization (PI) specifications. Now, manufacturers provide UEFI-compatible firmware images as a replacement for the Basic Input/Output System (BIOS). Compared to BIOS, UEFI has a better extensibility, a more flexible configuration, and a more standard boot process. The UEFI firmware [3], commonly named the UEFI BIOS on x86 platforms for historic reasons, is the main component of system firmware. The UEFI operating system runs on top of the UEFI firmware and can usually be viewed as a tandem of a UEFI application, serving as an operating system bootloader and a UEFI-compatible kernel, which is aware of the features brought by the UEFI firmware via the UEFI specification. Alongside UEFI, alternative open-source projects such as coreboot [4], libreboot [5], linuxboot [6], and u-boot [6] offer different approaches and philosophies to firmware initialization, focusing on modularity, security, and the freedom to customize the boot process to specific needs and hardware configurations.

HII (Human Interface Infrastructure) [7,8] is a part of the UEFI specification, which provides a standard framework for managing user interfaces based on UEFI systems. More specifically, HII provides a unified way to create and display user interfaces for BIOS settings, system configurations, boot options, etc. Beyond this, it also offers a mechanism to manage these user interfaces, including how to gather user input, how to change system configurations, and how to display the results of the changes. By providing a standard interface and framework, it simplifies the work of hardware manufacturers and operating system developers in creating user interfaces within the UEFI environment, thereby improving development efficiency and reducing development costs. In order to provide more possibilities in system booting, hardware configuration, and system-level management, the UEFI Management System User Interface (UEFI UI) based on HII came into being. This is an interactive interface that allows users to configure and manage UEFI settings. This user interface can be provided by manufacturers and may vary depending on the manufacturer and device. Typically, users can access this user interface by pressing a specific key (such as F2, F10, or Delete) when the computer starts up. In the UEFI UI, users can adjust various hardware and boot options, such as modifying the boot order, enabling or disabling devices, enabling Secure Boot [9], etc. Therefore, it is a very important tool that allows users to customize and adjust their computer systems.

By delving into the boot process of UEFI, we find that the UEFI UI is intimately connected with the BDS (Boot Device Select) phase. For example, changing the boot device sequence will impact the order in which boot devices are selected during the BDS phase. During the BDS phase, the system introduces the HII (Human Interface Infrastructure) framework, which facilitates the design of elegant human–computer interaction interfaces and even the extension of the functionality of the UEFI UI by maintenance personnel. This enables UEFI to offer a wealth of features compared to the traditional BIOS. These features could potentially lead to unauthorized access. Moreover, the complexity of the UEFI UI might lead to configuration errors, thereby affecting system security. Therefore, this paper focuses on a reverse-engineering exploration of the implementation details of the UEFI UI, conducts an in-depth, comprehensive analysis of it, and ultimately aims to enhance manufacturers' awareness of the security aspects of the UEFI.

However, the complexity and proprietary nature of UEFI binary images make reverse engineering challenging. To address this issue, researchers have used many specialized tools, such as the UEFI Tool [10] and IDA Pro [11]. These tools can help researchers understand and analyze the structure and content of UEFI binary images. However, these tools alone are far from sufficient for analyzing the user interface. To achieve this goal, this paper will use reverse engineering tools, like the UEFI Tool and IDA Pro, and delve deeply into the crucial role that the HII framework plays in the analysis of the UEFI UI. By applying existing reverse engineering techniques to the analysis of the UEFI UI, we reveal key information hidden in the firmware as well as some design flaws.

In this paper, we systematically investigate the password policy of UEFI. For systems that have set a UEFI password, we need to enter the correct password to gain access when we power on the system or enter the UEFI UI. Therefore, the UEFI password often becomes our first interaction with the user interface, sparking our intense interest to deeply analyze the implementation of the password policy. However, in many UEFI firmware, manufacturers have implemented various protection measures such as code obfuscation techniques, making it challenging for us to find the password implementation program via direct reverse engineering. Hence, to address this situation, we propose a protocol-centric static analysis method to analysis the UEFI password policy.

In addition, we aim to find the actual location of the password within the flash chip. Therefore, by analyzing the HII framework and combining it with the open-source tool Universal-IFR-Extractor [12], we reverse-engineered the VFR language that implements the UEFI UI. As a result, we found the storage locations of the password and other variables. Moreover, during this process, by validating all the modules of the Dell r730 firmware against the manufacturer's standard firmware, we found that not only is the UEFI password stored within the firmware, but previously used passwords are also recorded. This is because NVRAM variables were stored in the UEFI firmware by developers, which undeniably presents a significant security risk.

Finally, regarding the richer configuration options provided by UEFI, we studied the hardware port configurations, using secure boot as a case study. Additionally, combining the HII framework and IDA, we analyzed the logic of the UEFI UI in setting hardware interfaces.

In summary, we make the following contributions:

- We analyzed the UEFI password policy of different manufacturers, using HII protocols. For the first time, from a reverse engineering perspective, we found the way that the AMI standard protocol implements password policy. We proposed a protocol-centered static analysis method for password policies.
- We deeply analyzed the role of the VFR language in the UEFI UI from a reverse engineering perspective. we found the storage locations of some sensitive information in the UEFI firmware image. Ultimately, during the analysis, we discovered that the UEFI firmware used by a series of models exposes the encrypted password content and salt value in the binary firmware and even records previously used passwords and salt values.
- Compared to traditional BIOS, UEFI offers richer features. We analyzed how UEFI configures hardware ports by reverse engineering the VFR language.

The rest of this work is structured as follows: Section 2 provides a comprehensive background; Section 3 describes the HII framework and its related technologies; Section 4 provides implementation details of the UEFI management Interface analysis process; Section 5 describes related work; Section 6 discusses additional research questions; and Section 7 concludes.

2. Background

2.1. Visual Forms' Representation

Another innovation of UEFI over Legacy BIOS is in the specification of building blocks for user interfaces [8]. There are various scenarios where a platform component might want to interact in some fashion with the user. Examples of this are when presenting a user with several choices of information, sending information to the display, or offering a user menus for configuring the system, such as the BIOS Setup program shown in Figure 1. The potentially arduous task of managing user interface elements is simplified for UEFI modules requiring such functionality by UEFI providing some basic graphical elements like forms, strings, images, and fonts.

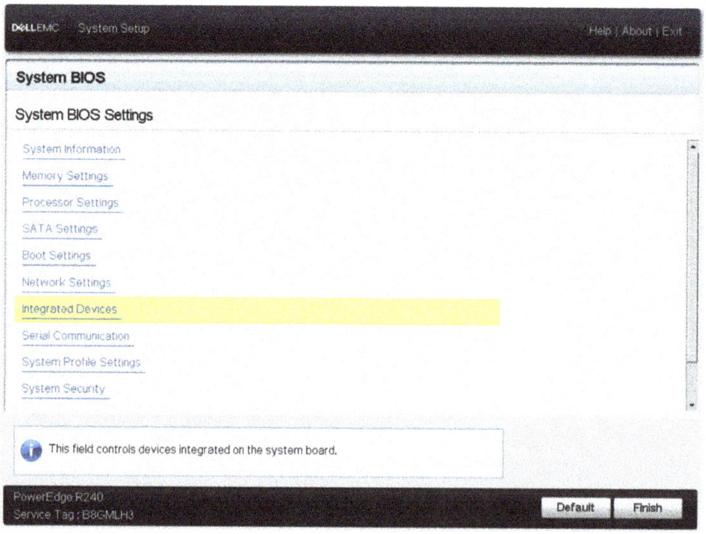

Figure 1. UEFI Management System User Interface.

UEFI calls this user interface support Human Interface Infrastructure (HII). HII is a set of protocols that allows for a UEFI module to register user interface and configuration content with the BIOS.

The implementation of the UEFI user interaction interface involves various types of files, such as VFR (Visual Forms Representation) and UNI. The strings of the UEFI interactive interface come from the UNI files, while the framework of the entire form is derived from the VFR files. In UEFI, there are roughly four components that constitute such a form: Strings, Forms, Fonts, and Images, as shown in Figure 2.

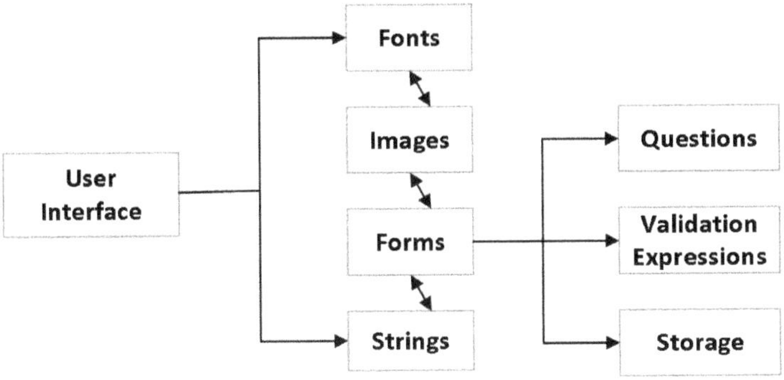

Figure 2. UEFI User Interface Components.

Strings are provided by UNI files, while Forms are supplied by VFR files. Forms describe the organization of the window, offer methods for user interaction, and dictate how the interactive content is stored. It is provided in a binary format, which, within the EDK framework, is referred to as IFR (Internal Forms Representation). IFR is generated by compiling VFR. Therefore, we define the organizational structure, interaction methods, and related content of the UEFI interactive interface by writing VFR files.

2.2. Static Code Analysis

Static Code Analysis refers to a code analysis technique where the program code is scanned using lexical analysis, syntax analysis, control flow analysis, data flow analysis, and other technologies without executing the code. This is performed to verify whether the code meets specifications, security, reliability, maintainability, and other metrics.

Programmers often make minor mistakes, such as missing a semicolon here or adding an extra parenthesis there. Most of the time, these oversights do not result in serious consequences: the compiler flags these errors, programmers correct the code, and the development process continues. However, this rapid feedback and response loop typically does not apply to most security vulnerabilities, which might lurk undetected for extended periods. As mentioned earlier, the longer software defects go unnoticed, the higher the cost to remedy them. The objective of static analysis is to inspect a program's text without attempting to execute it. Theoretically, static analysis tools can examine either the program's source code or its compiled form, with both offering similar advantages, although decoding the latter might be somewhat challenging [13].

Manual review or auditing is a form of static analysis and is highly time-consuming. For it to be effectively executed, human code auditors first need to know which types of mistakes they should be looking for, before rigorously examining the code. Reviewing the application code can be performed at any stage of software development, but it is most effective when undergone early, as detecting and rectifying security vulnerabilities and quality deficiencies might be high in cost and risk later in the software development process. When these errors slip into the market and are discovered by customers, they can impact profits and tarnish a company's reputation. Reviews encompass not just the code, but all documentation, requirements, and designs generated by developers, as every step in software development can harbor mistakes. Essentially, human-performed static code analysis can be categorized into two main types: self-review and third-party review, both of which are closely related to individual software processes and team software processes [14].

Static analysis tools have advantages over manual reviews because they operate faster, meaning they can assess programs more frequently. They encapsulate some of the knowledge required to perform such code analysis in a way that the tool operator does not need the same expertise level as a human auditor. Just as programmers can rely on compilers to consistently handle the nuances of language syntax, operators of good static analysis tools can effectively use the tool without delving into the finer details of more elusive errors.

2.3. Password Policy

In today's era, the ubiquity of passwords is an indisputable fact. Authentication is often executed via a combination of usernames and passwords [15]. As a result, passwords often serve as the sole barrier between potential attackers and the victim's information. Knowing someone's password allows an attacker to impersonate that individual in an online environment or access sensitive data intended only for that person. As society's reliance on password security deepens, it also becomes increasingly vulnerable to threats of password breaches.

Previous studies have shown that when given a choice, users tend to create simple passwords [16,17]. However, simple passwords are particularly easy for attackers [15–17]. As a result, many groups and organizations implement password policies, imposing restrictions on the passwords users can create and how they use them. A well-crafted policy might enhance the security of an organization [15,17–19].

Much of a password policy typically relates to the creation of passwords. For instance, a password creation policy might require passwords to be at least six characters long and contain at least one numerical character. However, there are several other aspects in the lifecycle of a password where password policies are relevant.

When designing password policies, it is crucial to consider human factors in addition to technical ones. While password policies might specify the encryption methods to be used on passwords, overly complex passwords might end up being written down by users because they cannot remember them [17]. Likewise, many password policies outline with whom users can share passwords and under what circumstances they should contact the administrator.

Today's formulation of password policies seems to be based more on experience and heuristics than on science or computation. While many organizations use passwords for security, there is not a universally accepted unified framework under which all these password policies can be understood and compared. Such a unified framework would promote better creation and understanding of password policies.

2.4. NVRAM

Modern memory hardware is either fast but volatile (DRAM) or persistent but slow (SSD/HDD). As a result, to prevent data loss, applications expend significant effort to persist runtime information onto non-volatile storage mediums. In this process, data structures in main memory often undergo costly transformations to reflect the distinct access characteristics of block storage devices and better utilize limited bandwidth. Non-Volatile Random Access Memory (NVRAM) is the latest advancement in memory technology, representing a unique opportunity to simplify the persistence we know. Unlike DRAM, NVRAM cells do not require periodic refreshes to maintain their state, allowing them to retain content even when power is lost. Performance analysis currently places NVRAM between DRAM and NAND-flash, but with ongoing research and development, its performance is expected to eventually meet or even surpass DRAM. By allocating data structures on NVRAM instead of DRAM, the application state can ultimately be persisted in-place without sacrificing speed or increasing software complexity [20].

UEFI provides booting and system management, relying on data stored in UEFI NVRAM. The UEFI environment itself may be susceptible to malware attacks. Moreover, the existence of UEFI NVRAM introduces certain security concerns, such as UEFI NVRAM often being bypassed by security software and computer forensics frequently overlooking the vast data stored in UEFI NVRAM [21]. Attackers could exploit the UEFI NVRAM storage space to stash illicitly obtained data (like credit card details) on the victim's/attacker's computer between the communication lines, without any traditional high-capacity storage access. Another example is data exfiltration in malware scenarios, which can be used to store encryption keys in use, or even for leaking personal, private data, leading to privacy issues. The data would only appear as highly volatile data in memory and network data streams, making it hard to capture for IT forensic purposes unless strategically prepared in advance. Vulnerabilities in NVRAM also pose threats to UEFI itself. Given the rich configuration capabilities of UEFI, attackers might attempt to exploit any vulnerabilities in NVRAM to alter configurations [22]. Unauthorized configuration changes could expose the system to additional risks or allow attackers to bypass security controls.

2.5. Challenges in Firmware Analysis

Low-power, single-purpose embedded devices (such as routers and IoT devices) are ubiquitous. While they have automated and simplified many aspects of users' lives, recent large-scale attacks have demonstrated that they pose a serious threat to the internet infrastructure due to their vast numbers. Unfortunately, the software on these systems relies on hardware and typically runs in unique, minimized environments with non-standard configurations, making security analysis particularly challenging. In the field of reverse engineering, the correct image base of firmware has very important significance for the reverse engineers to understand the firmware by building accurate cross references. However, for a large number of embedded system firmwares, the format is nonstandard and the image base is unknown. Thus, [23] presents a two-step method to determine the image base of firmwares for ARM-based devices. First, based on the storage characteristic of string in the firmware files and the encoding feature of literal pools that contain string addresses, we propose an algorithm called FIND-LP to recognize all possible literal pools in firmware. Second, we propose an algorithm called Determining image Base by Matching Literal Pools (DBMLP) to determine the image base. Addressing the non-standardized firmware formats, Ref. [24] describes a methodology for automatically determining the image base of firmware of ARM-based industrial control systems. Two algorithms, FIND-String and FIND-LDR, are presented that obtain the offsets of strings in firmware and the string addresses loaded by LDR instructions, respectively. Ref. [25] introduced Karonte, a static analysis approach capable of analyzing embedded device firmware by modeling and tracking multi-binary interactions. This method propagates tainted information between binary files to detect insecure interactions and identify vulnerabilities. Ref. [26] designed and implemented a new tool named FIE, which builds on the KLEE symbolic execution engine to provide a scalable platform for detecting errors in firmware programs of the popular MSP430 series microcontrollers. FIE incorporates new symbolic execution techniques, enabling it to verify the security properties of simple firmware common in practice. Ref. [27] designed a software framework that continuously executes given firmware binary files while bootstrapping inputs from off-the-shelf fuzzers, achieving hardware-independent and scalable firmware testing. This framework employs a novel technique called P2IM, which abstracts various peripherals and processes firmware I/O in real-time based on automatically generated models. P2IM is agnostic to peripheral designs and generic to firmware implementations, making it applicable to a wide range of embedded devices. Ref. [28] introduced FIRMSCOPE, an innovative static analysis system that analyzes Android firmware to expose unwanted functionalities in pre-installed applications using efficient and practical context-sensitive, flow-sensitive, field-sensitive, and partially object-sensitive taint analysis.

For UEFI, existing static analyses fail to effectively detect such vulnerabilities in stripped COTS UEFI firmware images, which are developed based on a custom callback mechanism that organizes callable functions into protocols identified by GUIDs. Leveraging this callback-based programming paradigm, Ref. [29] introduced the first static detection framework, SPENDER, built upon a novel protocol-centric analysis for efficiently and accurately discovering potential SMM privilege escalation vulnerabilities in UEFI firmware. The calling conventions in UEFI are so unusual that existing reverse engineering tools cannot handle them natively. Therefore, Ref. [30] developed an extension for Ghidra [31] to better analyze UEFI modules.

3. Understanding HII Framework and Related Technologies

3.1. HII Overview

HII is a set of protocols that allow a UEFI driver to provide the ability to register user interface and configuration content with the platform firmware. Unlike legacy option ROMs, the configuration of drivers and controllers is delayed until a platform management utility chooses to use the services of these protocols. UEFI drivers are not allowed to perform setup-like operations outside the context of these protocols. This means that a driver is not allowed to interact with the user outside the context of this protocol.

Figure 3 shows a basic platform configuration or "setup" model. The drivers and applications install elements (such as fonts, strings, images, and forms) into the HII Database, which acts as a central repository for the entire platform. The Forms Browser uses these elements to render the user interface on the display devices and receive information from the user via HID devices. When complete, the changes made by the user in the Forms Browser are saved, either to the UEFI global variable storage—(GetVariable() and SetVariable())—or to the variable storage provided by the individual drivers.

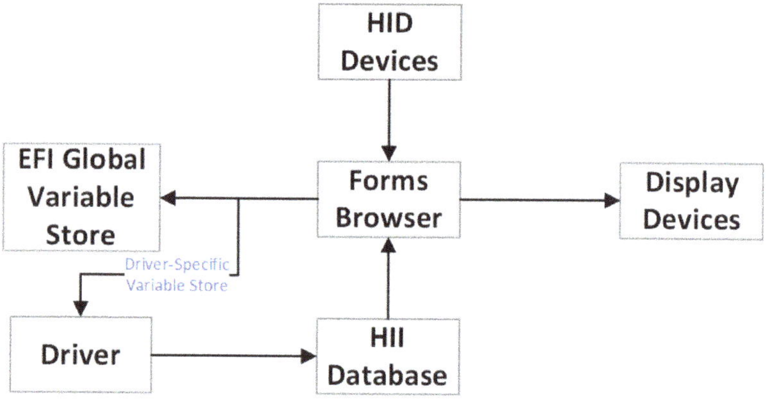

Figure 3. UEFI Platform Configuration Overview.

3.2. HII Elements

3.2.1. HII Databas

The HII database is the resource that serves as the repository of all the form, string, image, and font data for the system. Drivers that contain information destined for the end user will store their data in the HII database. For example, one UEFI module might implement the BIOS Setup program, allowing the user to configure motherboard component settings. Additionally, add-in cards may contain their own UEFI drivers, which, in turn, have their own BIOS Setup-related data. All the UEFI modules that contain BIOS Setup-related data can include their information in the HII database. This architecture is summarized in Figure 4.

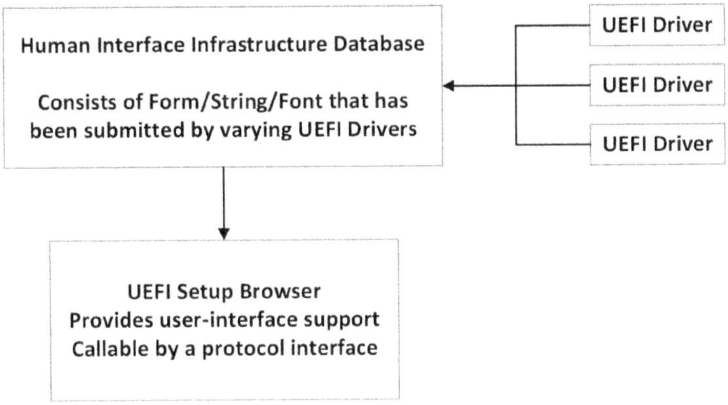

Figure 4. HII architecture.

3.2.2. Forms

The UEFI specification describes how a UEFI module can present a forms-based interface to a user and a UI element akin to Windows'CFrameWnd or Java's JFrame. This forms-based interface assumes that each window or screen consists of some window overhead, such as a title and buttons, and a list of user interface controls. For example, these controls could represent individual configuration settings for a UEFI application or driver. Associated with the notion of a form is a Forms Browser—the entity that reads the form data and presents a graphical representation on the display. The Forms Browser provides a forms-based renderer which understands how to read the contents of the forms, interact with the user, and save any resulting values. The Forms Browser uses forms data installed by UEFI modules in the HII database. The Forms Browser organizes the forms so that a user can navigate between the forms, select individual controls, and change the values using a keyboard, touch digitizer, or mouse. When the user has finished making modifications, the Forms Browser saves the values to NVRAM.

3.2.3. Strings

Strings in the UEFI environment are defined using the 16-bit UCS-2 character encoding. Strings are another one of the types of resources installed into the HII Database. In order to facilitate localization, programmers reference each string via a unique identifier defined as part of the strings package installed by the UEFI image. Each identifier may have several translations associated with it, e.g., English, French, and Traditional Chinese. When displaying a string, the Forms Browser selects the text to display based on the current platform language setting. The actual text for each language is stored in a separate file, which makes it possible to add and remove language support just by including or excluding language-specific files. Moreover, each string may have font information, including the font family name, font size, and font style, associated with it.

3.2.4. Images

UEFI supports storing images in the HII database. The format of images stored in the HII database was created to conform to the industry standard 1-bit, 4-bit, 8-bit, and 24-bit video memory layouts.

3.2.5. Fonts

UEFI specifies a standard font which is required for all systems that support text display on bit-mapped output devices. The standard font, named "system", is a fixed pitch font where all characters are either narrow (8×19 pixels) or wide (16×19 pixels). UEFI also allows for the display of other fonts, both fixed-pitch and variable-pitch. Platform support for fonts beyond the system is optional.

3.3. HII Protocol

HII Protocol is a set of protocols and services used for constructing and managing user interfaces. Its primary purpose is to provide a standardized way to describe and manage user interfaces in the UEFI management interface, including everything from BIOS setup menus to full-featured graphical user interfaces.

Through the analysis of these protocols, we propose a method to analyze the UEFI password policy produced by AMI vendors. To ascertain the storage location of the password policy in UEFI, we first need to be aware of protocols related to keyboard input, such as the EFI SIMPLE TEXT INPUT PROTOCOL. Due to the customizability of UEFI, many manufacturers redefine the keyboard input protocol based on this protocol. For instance, the AMI firmware manufacturer defines a keyboard input protocol named AMI EFIKEYCODE PROTOCOL as follows:

```
struct AMI_EFIKEYCODE_PROTOCOL{
AMI_RESET_EX Reset;
AMI_READ_EFI_KEY ReadEfikey;
EFI_EVENT WaitForKeyEx;
EFI_SET_STATE SetState;
EFI_REGISTER_KEYSTROKE_NOTIFY RegisterKeyNotify;
EFI_UNREGISTER_KEYSTROKE_NOTIFY UnregisterKeyNotify;
}
```

Based on the GUID of AMI EFIKEYCODE PROTOCOL as follows:

```
#define AMI_EFIKEYCODE_PROTOCOL_GUID{
   0x0ADFB62D, 0xFF74, 0x484C,
      {0x89, 0x44, 0xF8, 0x5C, 0x4B, 0xEA, 0x87, 0xA8}
}
```

We can accurately pinpoint the location in AMI firmware where this protocol is invoked. Subsequently, by analyzing the context and considering the characteristics of the password input, we can identify the password input location. After that, based on the program's execution logic, we can extract the UEFI password policy as illustrated in Figure 5.

Figure 5. UEFI Password Input Box Model.

In HII, there is a protocol known as the HII Configuration Processing and Browser Protocol, which encompasses two other protocols: EFI FORM BROWSER2 PROTOCOL and EFI HII CONFIG ROUTING PROTOCOL. EFI FORM BROWSER2 PROTOCOL is used for displaying pages, and HII Drivers can retrieve information from current HII Driver configuration options that users have modified but not yet stored via its BrowserCallback function. EFI HII CONFIG ROUTING PROTOCOL is a global protocol that handles interactions on the Setup interface. We can implement some UEFI interface elements, such as drop-down boxes, based on these two protocols. Using the GUIDs of these two protocols, we can also locate their invocation points within the firmware as shown in Figure 6.

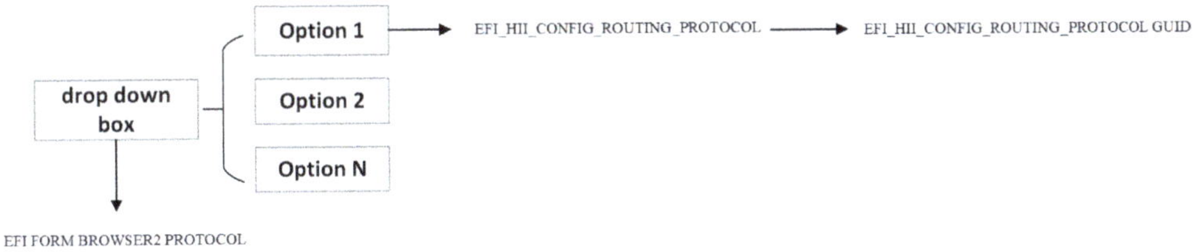

Figure 6. UEFI Dropdown Box Model.

3.4. Reverse Engineering of VFR

VFR (Visual Forms Representation) is a high-level descriptive language used to define the layout and behavior of the UEFI settings' interface. It is closer to source code, providing developers with a convenient way to design and describe forms, controls, and related actions. When VFR is compiled, it is transformed into IFR. IFR is the binary representation of VFR, stored in the UEFI firmware and parsed at runtime to display the corresponding user interface. Since it is in a binary format, directly reading or editing it is challenging; thus, we resort to VFR reverse engineering techniques to convert IFR back to VFR for easier comprehension. The reverse process from IFR to VFR can be employed to view or modify the UEFI firmware settings interface. The basic steps to transition from IFR to VFR are shown in Figure 7. Using tools like UEFITool, one can extract the IFR binary segment from the UEFI firmware image. As IFR is the compiled form of VFR, you need a decompiler to convert IFR back to VFR. Such tools might not be as common as forward compilers, but the community offers some, such as the Universal IFR Extractor. Once the VFR representation of the IFR is obtained, one can start analyzing it to understand the user interface layout, options, and behavior of the UEFI firmware.

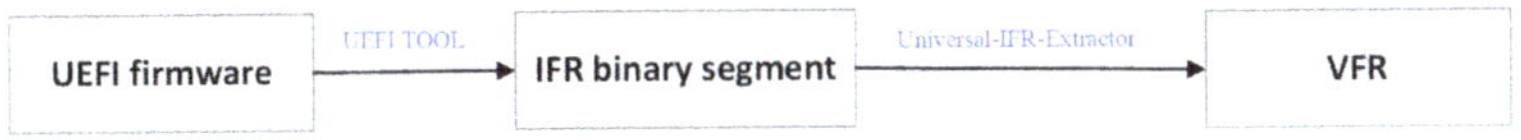

Figure 7. VFR Reverse Analysis Steps.

4. Case Studies

We have observed that the keyboard protocols associated with user input differ significantly among various vendors, so our approach to finding the password policy differs for firmware from different vendors. This paper initially uses Dell r240 as a case study to illustrate the simplest method for identifying the password policy. Then, taking SuperServer 6028U-TR4T+ as an example, this paper introduces a protocol-centric static analysis method to determine the password policy. Concerning the sensitive information of the UEFI UI, the primary focus of this paper is on the location of the password. By reverse analyzing VFR files, we pinpointed the location where the UEFI password is stored in NVRAM. Considering security aspects, the UEFI firmware has instituted protective measures for the location of the password. For instance, NVRAM variables are typically not stored within the UEFI firmware. However, this paper has discovered that for Dell r730 and r630 series models, the UEFI password is stored in the UEFI firmware file, verified via the integrity check of UEFI modules. Employing the rainbow table method, this paper has successfully retrieved the UEFI password. As for the implementation method of the hardware interface, referencing the aforementioned form implementation protocols, we can discern the program logic of the implemented interface by locating where these protocols are invoked in the firmware using IDA.

4.1. Password Policy Analysis

4.1.1. Analysis of Dell r240 UEFI Password Policy

In the Dell r240, we extracted the BdsDxe module, which is the driver that loads the UEFI UI and contains the program implementing the logic of the UI. We analyzed this module via IDA and found strings related to the password, as shown in Figure 8. We then entered the function sub 2D0D0 that references this string for inspection as shown in Figure 9. We found there is a condition 'v22 $\geq$ 3'. Using the context information, we can understand that this 'v22' represents the number of password inputs. Therefore, we can determine that the number of inputs for this UEFI password cannot exceed three times; otherwise, the system will be locked.

```
aEnterSetupPass:                        ; DATA XREF: sub_2D0D0+1B8↑o
                text "UTF-16LE", 'Enter Setup Password: ',0
                align 10h
aPasswordInvali:                        ; DATA XREF: sub_2D0D0:loc_2D330↑o
                                        ; sub_2D500:loc_2D808↑o
                text "UTF-16LE", 0Ah
                text "UTF-16LE", '*** Password Invalid. ***',0Dh,0Ah,0
                align 10h
```

Figure 8. Password Strings in UEFI UI. We can find it by searching for strings in IDA.

```
if ( v22 >= 3 )
{
  v16 = L"\nNumber of unsuccessful password attempts:";
  v23 = sub_3C9E0(L"\nNumber of unsuccessful password attempts:");
  v26 = *(_QWORD *)(qword_75170 + 64);
  (*(void (__fastcall **)(_QWORD, unsigned __int64, __int64))(v26 + 56))(
    *(_QWORD *)(qword_75170 + 64),
    40 - v23 / 2,
    16i64);
  (*(void (__fastcall **)(_QWORD, const __int16 *))(*(_QWORD *)(qword_75170 + 64) + 8i64))(
    *(_QWORD *)(qword_75170 + 64),
    v16);
  sub_4B5F0(L" %d ", v22);
  v16 = L"\n*** Maximum number of password attempts exceeded. System halted. ***";
  v23 = sub_3C9E0(L"\n*** Maximum number of password attempts exceeded. System halted. ***");
  v27 = *(_QWORD *)(qword_75170 + 64);
  (*(void (__fastcall **)(_QWORD, unsigned __int64, __int64))(v27 + 56))(
    *(_QWORD *)(qword_75170 + 64),
    40 - v23 / 2,
    17i64);
  (*(void (__fastcall **)(_QWORD, const __int16 *))(*(_QWORD *)(qword_75170 + 64) + 8i64))(
    *(_QWORD *)(qword_75170 + 64),
    v16);
  sub_41660();
}
```

Figure 9. System Locked In Dell R240. The v22 contains the count of password entry attempts; when the number exceeds 3, the system gets locked.

4.1.2. Analysis of SuperServer 6028U-TR4T+ UEFI Password Policy

The UEFI firmware of SuperServer 6028U-TR4T+ is different from that of r240 in that there is no way to find the function that implements the UEFI password input via the same string search method. Therefore, this paper proposes a targeted method to solve this situation. The steps of this method are as follows:

- Obtain the GUID of the protocol that implements the keycode input. In this paper, we obtained the AMI EFIKEYCODE PROTOCOL GUID 0x0ADFB62D, 0xFF74, 0x484C, {0x89, 0x44, 0xF8, 0x5C, 0x4B, 0xEA, 0x87, 0xA8}.
- Retrieve the module that implements the password logic from the UEFI image. In this paper, we obtained AMISetup, which in some firmware is known as BdsDxe.
- Considering the impact of endianness, we need to search for the GUID in the module using both big-endian and little-endian formats.
- After locating the GUID, we validate whether this protocol has been invoked here.
- After determining that there is an input operation on the interface, we check the context to confirm if it is the part where a password is being entered. For example, we can look to see if there is an operation that converts characters into asterisks (*).
- After confirming that it is the part where a password is entered, we iteratively examine the original function to observe the program's logic.

Through searching for the AMI EFIKEYCODE PROTOCOL GUID, we locate this line of code as shown in Figure 10.

```
while ( 1 )
{
  (*(void (__fastcall **)(_QWORD, __int64, __int64))(*(_QWORD *)byte_40 + 56i64))(*(_QWORD *)byte_40, v10, a4);
  LOBYTE(v11) = 1;
  (*(void (__fastcall **)(_QWORD, __int64))(*(_QWORD *)byte_40 + 64i64))(*(_QWORD *)byte_40, v11);
  do
  {
    v12 = (*(__int64 (__fastcall **)(_QWORD, __int64 *, __int64 *))&byte_40[88])(*(_QWORD *)word_28, qword_1AB8, &v19);
    if ( v12 >= 0 )
    {
      v12 = (*(__int64 (__fastcall **)(__int64, int *))(v19 + 8))(v19, &v20);
      if ( (v21 & 0x40) != 0 && v12 >= 0 && !v20 )
        v12 = 0x8000000000000006ui64;
      v17 = v20;
    }
  }
```

Figure 10. System Calls The AMI EFIKEYCODE PROTOCOL. We located this spot by tracing the GUID.

We find that qword 1AB8 indeed matches 2D B6 DF 0A 74 FF 4C 48 89 44 F8 5C 4B EA 87 A8. So, we continue to confirm this point. By translating this code into assembly language as demonstrated in Figure 11, we identify a call instruction, of which we suspect this instruction calls the HandleProtocol function. Further analysis of this assembly instruction reveals an offset of 98 h. We searched the UEFI specification and discovered that the EFI BOOT SERVICES structure is defined within it, containing numerous function pointers. These function pointers are arranged in a specific order in the UEFI firmware. Hence, each function has an offset corresponding to its position in the structure. The offset of the HandleProtocol function in the EFI BOOT SERVICES structure under the X64 architecture is precisely 98 h. Therefore, this code is calling AMI EFIKEYCODE PROTOCOL.

```
loc_3A410:
mov     rcx, cs:qword_4AC48
mov     rax, cs:qword_4AC50
lea     r8, [rsp+88h+var_48]
mov     rcx, [rcx+28h]
lea     rdx, qword_1AB8
call    qword ptr [rax+98h]
cmp     rax, rbx
mov     r11, rax
jl      short loc_3A47B
```

Figure 11. Assembly Code Representation.

Then, we start looking for the context of this code and find some keyboard code information and the implementation of converting characters into asterisks, as shown in Figures 12 and 13.

```
if ( HIWORD(v17) == 8 )
{
  if ( v9 )
  {
    --v9;
    --v7;
    a1[v9] = 0;
  }
  goto LABEL_23;
}
if ( HIWORD(v17) == 13 )
{
  (**(void (__fastcall ***)(_QWORD, _QWORD))&word_28[4])(*(_QWORD *)&word_28[4], 0i64);
  sub_69B8(&v18);
  goto LABEL_32;
}
```

Figure 12. Keyboard Code Information. HIWORD(v17) == 8′ means that when the keyboard code of the character entered by the user is equal to 8, then the backspace operation is executed. HIWORD(v17) == 13′ means that when the keyboard code of the character entered by the user is equal to 13, the system performs a confirmation operation.

```
for ( i = 0i64; i < 0x14; ++i )
  *(_WORD *)(v14 + 2 * i) = i < v9 ? 42 : 32;
```

Figure 13. Converting The Password Input Chars With The Hidden Mark '*'.

We conclude that this part of the code is the part that implements the password logic and then we start looking at the original function that calls this part of the code, as shown in Figure 14.

```
while ( 1 )
{
  v12 = sub_3A300(v9, 20i64, v74, v73);
  if ( v12 != 0x8000000000000015ui64 )
  {
    if ( v12 == 0x8000000000000012ui64 )
      goto LABEL_23;
    v10 = v11 & (unsigned int)sub_39604(v9);
    if ( !*v9 )
    {
      if ( v10 )
        goto LABEL_23;
      if ( (v11 & 1) == 0 && (a1 & 1) != 0 )
        v10 = 1i64;
      if ( (v11 & 2) == 0 && (a1 & 2) != 0 )
        v10 = 2i64;
    }
    if ( v10 )
    {
EL_23:
      v6 = v72[0];
      break;
    }
    if ( *a2 == 1i64 )
      sub_3A1B0(20, 19, v74, v73, 0);
    else
      sub_3A1B0(20, 19, v74, v73, 1);
    --*a2;
  }
  if ( !*a2 )
    goto LABEL_23;
}
```

Figure 14. 'sub 3A300' is the function where Figures 12 and 13 are located. Upon entering the original function, it was found that 'sub 3A300' is within a 'while' loop.

In the original function, sub 3A300 is nested inside a while loop, which ends when the value of *a2 is 0. We observe that *a2 is passed as an argument to int64 fastcall sub 39AA4(char a1, QWORD *a2), so we continue to jump to the original function that calls this while loop, as shown in Figure 15. We can see that v4 is passed to the parameter position where *a2 is located. Since the value of v4 is 3, we can conclude that the maximum number of password attempts is 3. Finally, we find the number of password attempts using this protocol-centric static analysis method. All the AMI standard interface UEFI firmware we have tried can find the maximum number of password attempts using this method.

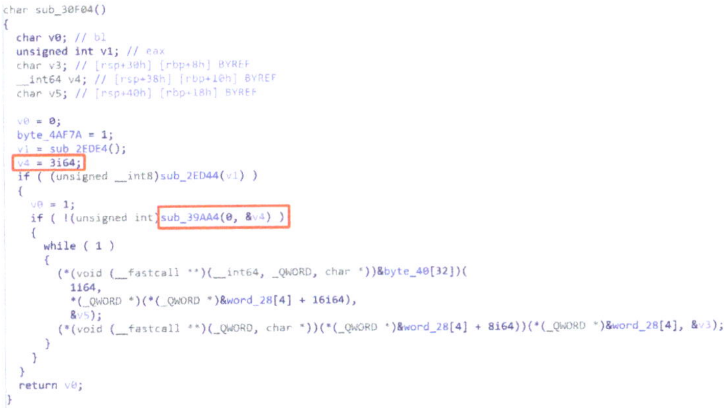

Figure 15. v4 is passed as an argument into 'sub 39AA4', which is the original function of Figure 14. In Figure 14, a2 inherits the value of v4. With each loop, the value of a2 decreases by 1. Therefore, v4 stores the number of password attempts.

4.2. Sensitive Information Localization

Using SuperServer 6028U-TR4T+ as an example, the steps for locating sensitive information are as follows:

- Extract the corresponding module from the UEFI firmware using the UEFI TOOL; here, we are extracting the Setup module.
- Use the Universal-IFR-Extractor tool to decompile the Setup module into VFR language.
- From this VFR language information, we can retrieve the content of different sensitive information, taking the password as an example, as shown below.
- Find the corresponding NVRAM variable name and storage offset from these contents.
- Afterwards, we can view the NVRAM variables in the UEFI Shell for verification.

```
Gray Out If{19 82}
QuestionId: 0x224 equals value 0x1{12 06 24 02 01 00}
password: Administrator Password,
        VarStoreInfo(VarOffset/VarName): 0x28,
        VarStore: 0x6, QuestionId: 0x1B3,
        MinSize: 0x3, MaxSize 0x14{08 91 CB 04 CC 04 B3 01 06 00 28 00 00 03 00
            ↪ 14 00}
End{29 02}
End If{29 02}
```

From the example above, we can see that in the NVRAM variable with VarStore 0x6, the administrator password is stored at an offset of 0x28. We further discover that the NVRAM variable with VarStore 0x6 is named AMITSESetup. However, a variable named AMITSESetup usually does not exist in UEFI firmware, as passwords are typically not stored within UEFI firmware. By verifying a computer that uses this UEFI firmware, we can locate the actual storage location of the AMITSESetup variable. After clearing the AMITSESetup variable, the administrator password is removed.

However, not all firmware will store the password in other locations on the chip. By verifying the Dell r730 firmware module file with the standard firmware module file provided by the manufacturer, we found that the Dell r730 firmware that has set the password will store password-related information in a padding file, including the ciphertext, salt value, and even previously used passwords will be saved, as shown in Figure 16.


```
203C0 00 00 00 00 00 03 2F 00 00 00 FE FF 01 00 08 00 | ....../...þÿ....
203D0 00 00 10 00 53 79 73 50 61 73 73 77 6F 72 64 53 | ....SysPasswordS
203E0 61 6C 74 00 63 EA 95 D9 AB 89 35 3B 67 F9 0B EB | alt.cê Ù«5;gù.ë
203F0 CF 9E 5A 0A 03 3B 00 00 00 FE FF 01 00 08 00 00 | Ï Z..;...þÿ.....
20400 00 20 00 53 79 73 50 61 73 73 77 6F 72 64 00 40 | . .SysPassword.@
20410 72 CF 61 4E 22 8F E2 EC A9 86 9A 7C 14 EA EA 96 | rÏaN" âì©  |.êê
20420 DB F8 5E 5B 74 CC 65 73 EA A0 C1 5A 51 3B 57 03 | Ûø^[tÌesê ÁZQ;W.
20430 31 00 00 00 FE FF 01 00 08 00 00 00 10 00 53 65 | 1...þÿ........Se
20440 74 75 70 50 61 73 73 77 6F 72 64 53 61 6C 74 00 | tupPasswordSalt.
20450 36 40 C0 73 FE 23 60 91 32 53 5E 41 9A 34 0F A0 | 6@Àsþ#`'2S^A 4.
20460 03 3D 00 00 00 FE FF 01 00 08 00 00 00 20 00 53 | .=...þÿ...... .S
20470 65 74 75 70 50 61 73 73 77 6F 72 64 00 35 64 78 | etupPassword.5dx
20480 E5 64 36 D1 50 AE 86 74 7F E3 E0 9D D4 DA 11 42 | åd6ÑP®¶t ãà ÔÚ.B
20490 12 97 57 15 85 FA A8 8E 02 F9 F9 DA EF 03 2F 00 | . W.…ú¨ .ùùÚï./.
204A0 00 00 FE FF 01 00 08 00 00 00 10 00 53 79 73 50 | ..þÿ........SysP
204B0 61 73 73 77 6F 72 64 53 61 6C 74 00 F0 23 71 AB | asswordSalt.ð#q«
204C0 92 15 7B 1C F4 30 EF 99 F6 02 14 2D 03 3B 00 00 | '.{.ô0ï ö..-.;..
204D0 00 FE FF 01 00 08 00 00 00 20 00 53 79 73 50 61 | .þÿ...... .SysPa
204E0 73 73 77 6F 72 64 00 83 16 16 8C 44 65 6C B2 B2 | ssword.ƒ..ŒDel²²
204F0 60 11 9D 5B 70 BB 86 64 D7 69 F5 83 F4 DE 9D 54 | `. [p»†d×iõƒôÞ T
20500 86 D2 46 D6 96 97 7A 03 31 00 00 00 FF FF 01 00 | †ÒFÖ––z.1...ÿÿ..
20510 08 00 00 00 10 00 53 65 74 75 70 50 61 73 73 77 | ......SetupPassw
20520 6F 72 64 53 61 6C 74 00 85 99 2C 05 C5 BE AE F6 | ordSalt.…™,.Å¾®ö
20530 81 8A B2 37 A1 A9 C1 C7 03 3D 00 00 00 FF FF 01 | Š²7¡©ÁÇ.=...ÿÿ.
20540 00 08 00 00 00 20 00 53 65 74 75 70 50 61 73 73 | ..... .SetupPass
20550 77 6F 72 64 00 FB E7 C0 19 9B F7 05 65 F5 F6 5D | word.ûçÀ.›÷.eõö]
20560 65 4F BA 18 B4 6B 3B 00 8B A4 3B F0 5E 16 1A 36 | eOº.´k;.‹¤;ð^..6
20570 D9 92 55 52 22 03 2F 00 00 00 FE FF 01 00 08 00 | Ù'UR"./...þÿ....
20580 00 00 10 00 53 79 73 50 61 73 73 77 6F 72 64 53 | ....SysPasswordS
20590 61 6C 74 00 8D 9D 2E 04 45 FE 8E E6 89 8E B0 36 | alt. ..EþŽæ‰Ž°6
205A0 21 E9 E1 D7 03 3B 00 00 00 FE FF 01 00 08 00 00 | !éá×.;...þÿ.....
205B0 00 20 00 53 79 73 50 61 73 73 77 6F 72 64 00 DE | . .SysPassword.Þ
205C0 FE CE 0E EA CE 90 24 7C 5F 3C 62 93 04 E0 96 95 | þÎ.êÎ $|_<b".à–•
205D0 6F D1 E6 6C D3 51 B7 67 E8 9B A4 4E 30 CF 80 03 | oÑælÓQ·gè›¤N0Ï€.
205E0 2F 00 00 00 FF FF 01 00 08 00 00 00 10 00 53 79 | /...ÿÿ........Sy
205F0 73 50 61 73 73 77 6F 72 64 53 61 6C 74 00 D8 37 | sPasswordSalt.Ø7
20600 7B AE 10 54 DB 4C DC 24 E5 9C 74 43 B4 7D 03 3B | {®.TÛLÜ$åœtC´}.;
20610 00 00 00 FF FF 01 00 08 00 00 00 20 00 53 79 73 | ...ÿÿ...... .Sys
20620 50 61 73 73 77 6F 72 64 00 01 0F 72 23 E6 D1 09 | Password...r#æÑ.
20630 EC 72 B4 F7 3E B6 67 2A AC E4 0C 0A F7 99 3C 93 | ìr´÷>¶g*¬ä..÷™<"
20640 8A 70 78 3D EF 03 DA 68 91 FF FF FF FF FF FF FF | Špx=ï.Úh'ÿÿÿÿÿÿÿ
```


Figure 16. Password Sensitive Information. We discovered that this contains salt values, passwords, and previously stored password information.

4.3. Hardware Port Configuration

The UEFI UI contains many settings related to hardware, such as Secure Boot, hard drives, memory, processors, buses, and USB ports. Since there are so many types of hardware ports, we try to analyze how UEFI sets these hardware ports from a reverse engineering perspective. Taking Secure Boot as an example as shown in Figures 17 and 18, we can see that the Secure Boot settings have both selection buttons and drop-down boxes. Through the reverse analysis of the VFR, we can see, as follows, that:

```
One Of: Secure Boot,
        VarStoreInfo(VarOffset/VarName): 0x0,
        VarStore: 0x22, QuestionId: 0x2785,
        Size:1, Min:0
        Default: DefaultId: 0x0,Value(8 bit): 0x0{5B 06 00 00 00 00}
        One of Option: Disabled, Value(8 bit): 0x0{09 07 04 00 00 00 00}
        One of Option: Enabled, Value(8 bit): 0x1{09 07 03 00 00 00 01}
End One Of{29 02}
```

the Secure Boot settings have two options: one is 'Disabled' and the other is 'Enabled'.

Figure 17. Selection Box.

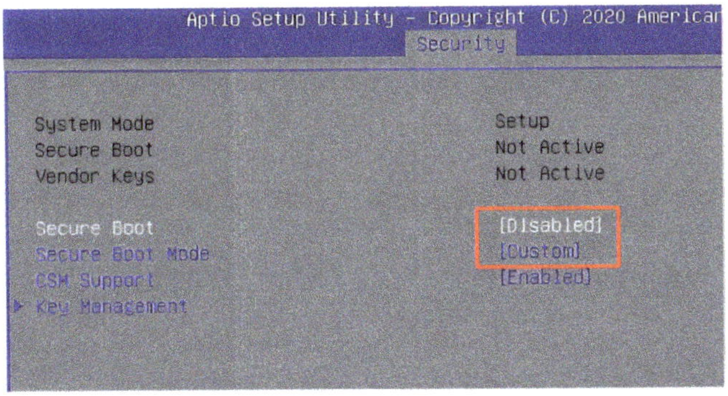

Figure 18. Dropdown Box.

In the previous section, we learned that implementing a drop-down box in UEFI can be achieved by using a combination of EFI FORM BROWSER2 PROTOCOL and EFI HII CONFIG ROUTING PROTOCOL. Therefore, in the decompiled module file, we expect to find the locations where these two protocols are referenced simultaneously. We first arrange the GUID of EFI FORM BROWSER2 PROTOCOL as 60 c3 d4 b9 fb bc 9b 4f 92 98 53 c1 36 98 22 58 as follows:

```
#define EFI_FORM_BROWSER2_PROTOCOL_GUID{0xb9d4c360, 0xbcfb, 0x4f9b, {0x92, 0x98,
    ↪ 0x53, 0xc1, 0x36, 0x98, 0x22, 0x58}}
#define EFI_HII_CONFIG_ROUTING_PROTOCOL_GUID{0x587e72d7, 0xcc50, 0x4f79, {0x82,
    ↪ 0x09, 0xca, 0x29, 0x1f, 0xc1, 0xa1, 0x0f}}
```

and conduct a search. Finally, we located qword A28 as follows:

```
if(qword_140(&qword_A28[2], 0i64, &qword_DCF8) < 0 || qword_140(&qword_9F8[2], 0
    ↪ i64, &qword_DD00) < 0)
    return 0x800000000000000Eui64;
```

and found that this conditional statement called this variable. Then, we arranged the GUID of EFI HII CONFIG ROUTING PROTOCOL as d7 72 7e 58 50 cc 79 4f 82 09 ca 29 1f c1 a1 and searched for it, which was qword 9F8. Therefore, this conditional statement called both protocols. Returning to the original function, we found the relevant strings related to Secure Boot as shown in Figure 19.

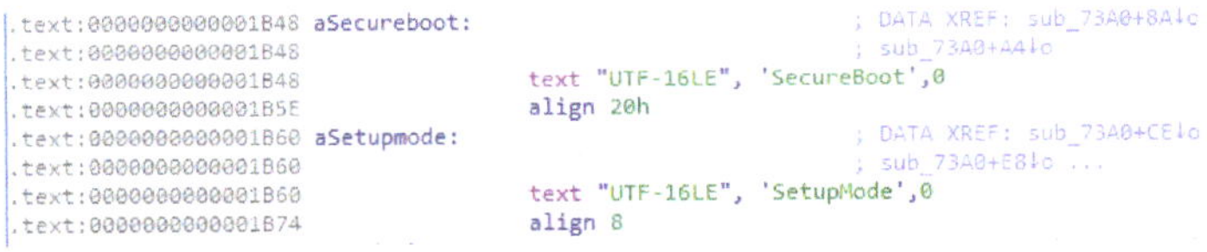

Figure 19. Secure Boot Strings.

5. Discussion

One attack method on UEFI targets its settings. Once we acquire certain sensitive information, like the location of the password in NVRAM, it can be erased via the UEFI shell. Consequently, the UEFI firmware is left unprotected and can be altered at will. Based on HII, it is easy to identify some critical codes, which should be given attention during the UEFI firmware design process.

In the above text, we only analyzed AMI firmware. Even though there are different manufacturers producing UEFI, such as Bysoft and Insyde, since the UEFI UI is developed based on the same HII framework, the UEFI firmware produced by different manufacturers is largely similar at the level of the UEFI UI. Therefore, the analysis of AMI firmware is highly representative. We still provide examples of password failure lockout times for UEFI produced by Bysoft and Insyde manufacturers as shown in Figures 20 and 21. For UEFI firmware produced by Bysoft and Insyde manufacturers, we can see that the password failure lockout times are directly displayed in plaintext without any protective measures. On the contrary, we need to spend a lot of effort to find the password failure lockout times in AMI's firmware.

```
3EB70 74 00 61 00 74 00 75 00 73 00 00 00 14 45 00 6E  t.a.t.u.s....E.n
3EB80 00 74 00 65 00 72 00 20 00 69 00 6E 00 63 00 6F  .t.e.r. .i.n.c.o
3EB90 00 72 00 72 00 65 00 63 00 74 00 20 00 70 00 61  .r.r.e.c.t. .p.a
3EBA0 00 73 00 73 00 77 00 6F 00 72 00 64 00 20 00 33  .s.s.w.o.r.d. .3
3EBB0 00 20 00 74 00 69 00 6D 00 65 00 73 00 00 00 14  . .t.i.m.e.s....
3EBC0 50 00 6C 00 65 00 61 00 73 00 65 00 20 00 72 00  P.l.e.a.s.e. .r.
3EBD0 65 00 73 00 74 00 61 00 72 00 74 00 20 00 73 00  e.s.t.a.r.t. .s.
3EBE0 79 00 73 00 74 00 65 00 6D 00 00 00 14 50 00 72  y.s.t.e.m....P.r
3EBF0 00 65 00 73 00 73 00 20 00 45 00 73 00 63 00 20  .e.s.s. .E.s.c.
3EC00 00 66 00 6F 00 72 00 20 00 62 00 6F 00 6F 00 74  .f.o.r. .b.o.o.t
3EC10 00 20 00 6F 00 70 00 74 00 69 00 6F 00 6E 00 73  . .o.p.t.i.o.n.s
```

Figure 20. Password Attempt Times of Bysoft.

```
1750 00 00 00 00 70 00 61 00 73 00 73 00 77 00 6F 00  ....p.a.s.s.w.o.
1760 72 00 64 00 73 00 20 00 74 00 68 00 72 00 65 00  r.d.s. .t.h.r.e.
1770 65 00 20 00 74 00 69 00 6D 00 65 00 73 00 20 00  e. .t.i.m.e.s. .
1780 75 00 73 00 69 00 6E 00 67 00 20 00 69 00 6E 00  u.s.i.n.g. .i.n.
1790 63 00 6F 00 72 00 72 00 65 00 63 00 74 00 20 00  c.o.r.r.e.c.t. .
17A0 63 00 72 00 65 00 64 00 65 00 6E 00 74 00 69 00  c.r.e.d.e.n.t.i.
17B0 61 00 6C 00 73 00 2E 00 00 00 00 00 00 00 00 00  a.l.s...........
17C0 00 00 00 00 59 00 6F 00 75 00 20 00 6D 00 75 00  ....Y.o.u. .m.u.
17D0 73 00 74 00 20 00 72 00 65 00 73 00 74 00 61 00  s.t. .r.e.s.t.a.
17E0 72 00 74 00 20 00 74 00 68 00 65 00 20 00 63 00  r.t. .t.h.e. .c.
17F0 6F 00 6D 00 70 00 75 00 74 00 65 00 72 00 20 00  o.m.p.u.t.e.r. .
1800 74 00 6F 00 20 00 74 00 72 00 79 00 20 00 61 00  t.o. .t.r.y. .a.
1810 67 00 61 00 69 00 6E 00 2E 00 00 00 00 00 00 00  g.a.i.n.........
```

Figure 21. Password Attempt Times of Insyde.

All UEFI firmware human–machine interaction systems are developed based on HII. Therefore, if an attacker finds a vulnerability related to HII, it could affect all UEFI firmware. Hence, reverse engineering UEFI firmware can help security researchers discover and fix security vulnerabilities, thereby enhancing system protection capabilities.

In the real world, this knowledge will heighten the security awareness of UEFI interaction system developers. Often, developers have a weak sense of security concerning their developments. Understanding the working mechanism of UEFI firmware helps technical support personnel to diagnose and resolve firmware-related issues more effectively.

The potential benefit is the ability to improve the security of UEFI during its use, identifying and fixing potential security vulnerabilities, which can reduce the maintenance costs for UEFI manufacturers. The risk is that it might lead to the exposure of security vulnerabilities, increasing the risk of malicious exploitation.

In terms of Legal Considerations, UEFI firmware may be protected under copyright law and reverse engineering could infringe upon the intellectual property rights of the creators or owners of the firmware. It is crucial to review the licensing agreement of the firmware to understand what activities are permitted under its terms. Regarding Ethical Considerations, even though reverse engineering can benefit security enhancement and education, it is also essential to respect the labor and rights of the original creators.

Researchers should clarify their intentions when conducting reverse engineering to ensure the legitimacy of their actions and take responsibility for the potential consequences.

Therefore, before starting reverse engineering, confirm that the activity does not violate relevant laws, regulations, and licensing agreements. Evaluate the potential security risks that reverse engineering could bring, such as inadvertently creating new security vulnerabilities. Ensure legal compliance and use the acquired knowledge responsibly, but not for illegal or unethical purposes.

This article demonstrates that it is possible to extract critical information from UEFI via the HII framework. In the real world, there have been incidents of UEFI critical information leakage. Following a successful cyber-attack by the Money Message extortion group against MSI (Micro-Star International), some of MSI's internal documents were leaked, including sensitive data such as the BootGuard private key. The BootGuard security mechanism is an important part of Intel's hardware trust architecture, and the leakage of its private key indicates that for certain models of devices, this major security mechanism can be bypassed. Moreover, the leaked materials also included UEFI firmware image signing keys. BootGuard is a crucial integrity protection mechanism in Intel's security system based on the hardware root of trust, which, together with the CPU microcode and CSME, forms the core security mechanisms of the Intel ecosystem. If BootGuard is successfully attacked, or if attackers obtain the BootGuard private key from OEM/ODM manufacturers, they can exploit UEFI implementation flaws, underlying configuration errors, and other vulnerabilities to bypass or counter nearly all known security mechanisms. These mechanisms include system defenses such as BWE/BLE, PRx hardware security mechanisms, SecureBoot, HCVI, PatchGuard, kASLR, KDEP, SMEP, SMAP, and other kernel security protection technologies, as well as various mainstream antivirus software and EDR/XDR systems, achieving persistent control over the device.

UEFI is essentially a loader used to boot operating systems. An open ecosystem and more comprehensive functionality have allowed UEFI to replace the traditional BIOS. After nearly 20 years of development, UEFI has a vast amount of code, making it very difficult to understand. According to statistics, UEFI's share of the BIOS market started to decline annually after reaching 94%. CoreBoot has emerged from the Chromebook laptop market and has occupied a portion of the IoT market, always eyeing the server BIOS. Meanwhile, LinuxBoot has taken a different path, aggressively poaching from the server BIOS, and hopes to secure a foothold in the server market before descending to attack the PC, laptop, and IoT markets. Therefore, in addition to UEFI, there are many free, open-source loaders available such as coreboot, libreboot, linuxboot, and u-boot. When producing computers or servers, companies can choose the appropriate loader based on their needs to ensure that the product is sufficiently secure.

Subsequent research will focus on how to use these open-source loaders to ensure system security and that passwords saved within these open-source loaders are stored inside a secure hardware enclave, if available, or by using state-of-the-art cryptography to prevent cracking.

6. Related Work

6.1. Security Research on UEFI

Researchers Zimmer and Vincent first proposed that before executing the UEFI firmware executable file, its digital signature should be verified to ensure the integrity and legitimacy of the UEFI firmware executable file [32]. This method is based on digital authentication technology and provides a set of signing, authentication, and key management service interfaces to assist users, firmware systems, and operating systems in executing trustworthy operations. However, implementing this method relies on a large amount of authentication information and key information, which burdens the UEFI firmware memory; verifying the integrity of the file before execution affects the boot efficiency of the UEFI firmware [33]. Building upon Zimmer and Vincent's work, the literature [34] proposed a method based on trusted computing. Using the TPM chip as a trusted root node, it establishes a trusted chain for computer system startup to ensure the legitimacy of the executing nodes, thereby securing the UEFI firmware boot process. This method establishes a trusted node on the hardware, starting from the platform power-on to the application execution, authenticating each level and trusting each level, building a complete trust chain, prohibiting the execution of unauthenticated programs, and identifying "self" and "non-self" components in a timely manner, thus constructing a secure computer operating environment. The challenge of this method is how to distinguish between the "self" and "non-self" components. Flexible distinction rules facilitate UEFI firmware applications, but they reduce the security of UEFI firmware. Strict rules ensure UEFI firmware security, but restrict its application, reducing firmware extensibility.

Attacks targeting UEFI are also frequently researched now. SMM (System Management Mode) is a CPU execution mode with the highest privileges, and attackers can modify the UEFI configuration and hardware chip using SMM vulnerabilities [32]. Moreover, attackers may exploit the S3 Resume Boot Script [35], Secure Boot [36,37], UEFI updates, and tamper with UEFI variables, among other tactics. In the face of increasingly severe firmware attacks, analyzing the vulnerability security of UEFI is of significant importance [38]. The paper first introduces the commonly used trusted authentication mechanisms of UEFI. Subsequently, targeting the vulnerabilities in the trust verification process of UEFI during the startup phase, and by integrating the state transition diagrams, the PageRank algorithm, and the Bayesian network theory, an analysis model for the UEFI trust verification startup vulnerability is constructed. The paper also conducts validation and analysis based on specific instances. Through the verification and analysis of the acquired data, vulnerable attack paths and critical vulnerability nodes are identified. Finally, based on the analysis results, security reinforcement measures for UEFI are proposed.

In addition to UEFI firmware for PCs and servers, the firmware of other platforms is also worthy of study. As a critical part in mobile cloud computing, the vulnerability of Android devices can directly affect the security of the mobile cloud. The unsecured Android can be potentially exploited by malwares to obtain the root privilege. Root privilege misuse is the critical issue for Android security, which breaks the integrity of Android security and rises the risk of permission escalation from malwares. The existing solutions still fail to balance the trade-off between the users desires on using root privilege and the Android security, which lays risks in leading to the root privilege misuse. To address this issue, Ref. [39] proposes a root privilege management scheme named Root Privilege Manager (RPM), which adopts root privilege access control to guarantee the exclusive root access opportunity of authenticated apps. RPM verifies the authorization and integrity of root-requesting apps based on the authorization files extracted during app installation and then controls the granting of root privilege based on these authenticated results. In this manner, end users are relieved of the burden of making appropriate decisions when confronted with root access management.

6.2. Reverse Analysis of UEFI

UEFI Image Reverse Engineering is extremely challenging. Some manufacturers use obfuscation or encryption techniques within the UEFI image to protect their code from being easily understood and modified. Additionally, UEFI images usually contain a large amount of complexly structured code. They might encompass numerous different modules, each implementing specific functions. Understanding how each module interacts with others, as well as the overall execution flow, demands an in-depth understanding and considerable effort. In addition, UEFI firmware is designed for specific hardware platforms and likely includes dependencies on specific hardware characteristics. Without knowledge relevant to the specific hardware platform, it may be difficult to comprehend the purpose and behavior of some code. UEFI applications are stored in the PE/COFF (Portable Executable/Common Object File Format), a complex binary format. Understanding the details of this format is crucial for analyzing UEFI firmware. While some tools can assist in the reverse engineering of UEFI firmware, they are often imperfect and require a deep understanding of the UEFI architecture for effective usage. Furthermore, regarding some detailed implementation details and features of UEFI, relevant documentation may not be sufficient. In the article [40], the author proposed tracing the use of the LocateProtocol function. By analyzing the function's parameters and call relationships, it simplifies reverse analysis of UEFI firmware by understanding how the program interacts with various UEFI services. However, we still need an in-depth understanding and experience of UEFI, the PE/COFF format, and fundamental reverse engineering skills. Starting from 2014, the CHIPSEC framework [41] provides a set of modules, including hardware protection and the correct configuration test, which tests for vulnerabilities in firmware and platform components, fuzzing tools for various platform devices, and many more.

7. Conclusions

In this paper, we study the implementation details of the UEFI UI by reverse analyzing UEFI binary images, including UEFI password policy, sensitive information storage locations, and hardware port settings. We are the first to systematically apply reverse analysis techniques to study UEFI via the HII framework.

In terms of UEFI password policy, we found that the implementation methods vary among different manufacturers. By proposing a password policy analysis method based on the standard interface of AMI firmware, we provide a new approach for analyzing UEFI password policies. Moreover, we have identified storage locations for sensitive information related to the UEFI UI, offering a deeper understanding of the security of UEFI firmware. Regarding hardware port configurations, we analyzed how UEFI firmware utilizes the services provided by the HII framework to configure hardware ports.

Our research fills a gap in the study of the HII. Despite the achievements of our research, there are still many areas that need further exploration. In future research, we will continue to focus on the security and performance optimization of UEFI firmware to help manufacturers and users achieve safer and more efficient computing platforms. At the same time, we will also study more reverse engineering techniques and tools to gain a deeper understanding of the implementation mechanisms of UEFI firmware. In summary, this research provides a beneficial starting point for the field of UEFI firmware security research.

Author Contributions: Conceptualization, S.C., Y.-A.T., Z.Z. and Y.L.; Methodology, S.C., Y.L. and Q.Z.; Software, Y.-A.T.; Validation, S.C.; Formal analysis, S.C. and Q.Z.; Investigation, S.C., K.Q., Z.Z. and Y.L.; Resources, S.C. and K.Q.; Data curation, S.C.; Writing—original draft, S.C.; Writing—review & editing, S.C., Y.-A.T., K.Q., Y.L. and Q.Z.; Supervision, Y.-A.T., K.Q., Z.Z., Y.L. and Q.Z.; Project administration, Y.-A.T., Kefan Qiu, Y.L. and Q.Z.; Funding acquisition, Y.-A.T., Y.L. and Q.Z. All authors have read and agreed to the published version of the manuscript.

Funding: This research was supported by the National Natural Science Foundation of China (no. U1936218, no. 62072037) and the China National Key Research and Development Program (no. 2022YFB2701501).

Data Availability Statement: No new data were created or analyzed in this study. Data sharing is not applicable to this article.

Conflicts of Interest: The authors declare no conflict of interest.

References

1. UEFI Specification. Available online: https://uefi.org/specifications (accessed on 8 October 2023).
2. Zimmer, V.; Rothman, M.; Marisetty, S. *Beyond BIOS: Developing with the Unified Extensible Firmware Interface*; Walter de Gruyter GmbH & Co KG: Berlin, Germany, 2017.
3. Jeong, D.; Lee, S. Forensic signature for tracking storage devices: Analysis of UEFI firmware image, disk signature and windows artifacts. *Digit. Investig.* **2019**, *29*, 21–27. [CrossRef]
4. Butterworth, J.; Kallenberg, C.; Kovah, X.; Herzog, A. Bios chronomancy: Fixing the core root of trust for measurement. In Proceedings of the 2013 ACM SIGSAC Conference on Computer & Communications Security, Berlin, Germany, 4–8 November 2013; pp. 25–36.
5. Sutherland, J.A. On Improving Cybersecurity Through Memory Isolation Using Systems Management Mode. Ph.D. Thesis, Abertay University, Dundee, Scotland, 2019.

6. Banik, S.; Zimmer, V. Understanding the BIOS and Minimalistic Design. In *System Firmware: An Essential Guide to Open Source and Embedded Solutions*; Apress: Berkeley, CA, USA, 2022; pp. 145–211.
7. Skalsky, N.; Kirch, T.; Rickey, A.; Rothman, M.A. UEFI and the OEM and IHV Community. *Intel Technol. J.* **2011**, *15*, 40–67.
8. Leara, W.D. Language Applications for UEFI BIOS. Ph.D. Thesis, The University of Texas at Austin, Austin, TX, USA, 2014.
9. Wilkins, R.; Richardson, B. UEFI secure boot in modern computer security solutions. In Proceedings of the UEFI Forum, Nancy, France, 26 September 2013 ; pp. 1–10.
10. UEFITool. Available online: https://github.com/LongSoft/UEFITool (accessed on 20 July 2023).
11. IDA Pro. Available online: https://www.hex-rays.com/products/ida/ (accessed on 20 July 2023).
12. Universal-IFR-Extractor. Available online: https://github.com/donovan6000/Universal-IFR-Extractor (accessed on 20 July 2023).
13. Chess, B.; McGraw, G. Static analysis for security. *IEEE Secur. Priv.* **2004**, *2*, 76–79. [CrossRef]
14. Humphrey, W.S. *The Personal Software Process (sm)(PSP (sm))*; Carnegie Mellon University: Pittsburgh, PA, USA, 2000.
15. Vu, K.P.L.; Proctor, R.W.; Bhargav-Spantzel, A.; Tai, B.L.B.; Cook, J.; Schultz, E.E. Improving password security and memorability to protect personal and organizational information. *Int. J. Hum.-Comput. Stud.* **2007**, *65*, 744–757. [CrossRef]
16. Yan, J.J. A note on proactive password checking. In Proceedings of the 2001 Workshop on New Security Paradigms, Cloudcroft, NM, USA, 11–13 September 2001; pp. 127–135.
17. Summers, W.C.; Bosworth, E. Password policy: The good, the bad, and the ugly. In Proceedings of the Winter International Symposium on Information and Communication Technologies, Cancun, Mexico, 5–8 January 2004; pp. 1–6.
18. Polstra III, R.M. A case study on how to manage the theft of information. In Proceedings of the 2nd Annual Conference on Information Security Curriculum Development, New York, NY, USA, 23–24 September 2005; pp. 135–138.
19. Kuo, C.; Romanosky, S.; Cranor, L.F. Human selection of mnemonic phrase-based passwords. In Proceedings of the Second Symposium on Usable Privacy and Security, Pittsburgh, PA, USA, 12–14 July 2006; pp. 67–78.
20. Schwalb, D.; Berning, T.; Faust, M.; Dreseler, M.; Plattner, H. nvm malloc: Memory Allocation for NVRAM. *Adms@ VLDB* **2015**, *15*, 61–72.
21. Kiltz, S.; Altschaffel, R.; Dittmann, J. Hidden in Plain Sight-Persistent Alternative Mass Storage Data Streams as a Means for Data Hiding With the Help of UEFI NVRAM and Implications for IT Forensics. In Proceedings of the 2022 ACM Workshop on Information Hiding and Multimedia Security, Santa Barbara, CA, USA, 27–28 June 2022; pp. 107–112.
22. Lin, K.J.; Wang, C.Y. Using TPM to improve boot security at BIOS layer. In Proceedings of the 2012 IEEE International Conference on Consumer Electronics (ICCE), Las Vegas, NV, USA, 13–16 January 2012; pp. 376–377.
23. Zhu, R.; Tan, Y.-A.; Zhang, Q.; Li, Y.; Zheng, J. Determining image base of firmware for ARM devices by matching literal pools. *Digit. Investig.* **2016**, *16*, 19–28. [CrossRef]
24. Zhu, R.; Zhang, B.; Mao, J.; Zhang, Q.; Tan, Y.-A. A methodology for determining the image base of ARM-based industrial control system firmware. *Int. J. Crit. Infrastruct. Prot.* **2017**, *16*, 26–35. [CrossRef]
25. Redini, N.; Machiry, A.; Wang, R.; Spensky, C.; Continella, A.; Shoshitaishvili, Y.; Kruegel, C.; Vigna, G. Karonte: Detecting insecure multi-binary interactions in embedded firmware. In Proceedings of the 2020 IEEE Symposium on Security and Privacy (SP), San Francisco, CA, USA, 18–21 May 2020; pp. 1544–1561.
26. Davidson, D.; Moench, B.; Ristenpart, T.; Jha, S. FIE on firmware: Finding vulnerabilities in embedded systems using symbolic execution. In Proceedings of the 22nd USENIX Security Symposium (USENIX Security 13), Washington, DC, USA, 14–16 August 2013; pp. 463–478.
27. Feng, B.; Mera, A.; Lu, L. P2IM: Scalable and hardware-independent firmware testing via automatic peripheral interface modeling. In Proceedings of the 29th USENIX Security Symposium (USENIX Security 20), Berkeley, CA, USA, 12–14 August 2020; pp. 1237–1254.
28. Elsabagh, M.; Johnson, R.; Stavrou, A.; Zuo, C.; Zhao, Q.; Lin, Z. FIRMSCOPE: Automatic uncovering of Privilege-Escalation vulnerabilities in Pre-Installed apps in android firmware. In Proceedings of the 29th USENIX Security Symposium (USENIX Security 20), Berkeley, CA, USA, 12–14 August 2020; pp. 2379–2396.
29. Yin, J.; Li, M.; Wu, W.; Sun, D.; Zhou, J.; Huo, W.; Xue, J. Finding SMM Privilege-Escalation Vulnerabilities in UEFI Firmware with Protocol-Centric Static Analysis. In Proceedings of the 2022 IEEE Symposium on Security and Privacy (SP), San Francisco, CA, USA, 22–26 May 2022; pp. 1623–1637.
30. Haładyn, K.M. An Extension for Ghidra That Adds Support for Reverse Engineering of UEFI Modules. Master's Thesis, Instytut Telekomunikacji, Wroclaw, Poland, 2021.
31. Rohleder, R. Hands-on ghidra—A tutorial about the software reverse engineering framework. In Proceedings of the 3rd ACM Workshop on Software Protection, London, UK, 15 November 2019; pp. 77–78.
32. Embleton, S.; Sparks, S.; Zou, C. SMM rootkits: A new breed of OS-independent malware. In Proceedings of the 4th International Conference on Security and Privacy in Communication Networks, Istanbul, Turkey, 22–25 September 2008; pp. 1–12.
33. Zimmer, V. Platform Trust Beyond BIOS Using the Unified Extensible Firmware Interface. In Proceedings of the Security and Management, Las Vegas, NV, USA, 25–28 June 2007; pp. 400–405.
34. Zhou, Z.L.; Xu, R.S. BIOS security analysis and a kind of trusted BIOS. In *Information and Communications Security, Proceedings of the 9th International Conference, ICICS 2007, Zhengzhou, China, 12–15 December 2007*; Springer: Berlin/Heidelberg, Germany, 2007; pp. 427–437.

35. Bazhaniuk, O.; Bulygin, Y.; Furtak, A.; Gorobets, M.; Loucaides, J.; Matrosov, A.; Shkatov, M. Attacking and Defending BIOS in 2015. In Proceedings of the ReCon Conference, Montreal, QC, Canada, 19–21 June 2015. Available online: http://www.intelsecurity.com/advanced-threat-research/content/AttackingAndDefendingBIOS-RECon2015.pdf (accessed on 8 October 2023).
36. Bulygin, Y.; Furtak, A.; Bazhaniuk, O. *A Tale of One Software Bypass of Windows 8 Secure Boot*; Black Hat: Las Vegas, NV, USA, 2013.
37. Jacob, N.; Heyszl, J.; Zankl, A.; Rolfes, C.; Sigl, G. How to break secure boot on fpga socs through malicious hardware. In *Cryptographic Hardware and Embedded Systems–CHES 2017, Proceedings of the 19th International Conference, Taipei, Taiwan, 25–28 September 2017*; Springer: Cham, Switzerland, 2017; pp. 425–442.
38. Gu, Y.; Zhang, P.; Chen, Z.; Cao, F. UEFI Trusted Computing Vulnerability Analysis Based on State Transition Graph. In Proceedings of the 2020 IEEE 6th International Conference on Computer and Communications (ICCC), Chengdu, China, 11–14 December 2020; pp. 1043–1052.
39. Tan, Y.-A.; Xue, Y.; Liang, C.; Zheng, J.; Zhang, Q.; Zheng, J.; Li, Y. A root privilege management scheme with revocable authorization for Android devices. *J. Netw. Comput. Appl.* **2018**, *107*, 69–82. [CrossRef]
40. Lebedev, P.; Kogos, K.; Vasilenko, E. On Way to Simplify the Reverse Engineering of UEFI Firmwares. In *Advances in Cyber Security, Proceedings of the First International Conference, ACeS 2019, Penang, Malaysia, 30 July–1 August 2019*; Springer: Singapore, 2020; pp. 220–231.
41. Chipsec. Available online: https://github.com/chipsec/chipsec (accessed on 8 October 2023).

MDPI AG
Grosspeteranlage 5
4052 Basel
Switzerland
Tel.: +41 61 683 77 34

Electronics Editorial Office
E-mail: electronics@mdpi.com
www.mdpi.com/journal/electronics

www.ingramcontent.com/pod-product-compliance
Lightning Source LLC
LaVergne TN
LVHW070455061126
851858LV00011B/243